W9-AHJ-836

The RVer's Bible

G·K
Hall
&Co.

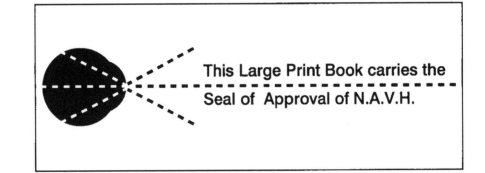

This Large Print Book carries the
Seal of Approval of N.A.V.H.

The RVer's Bible

Everything You Need to Know About Choosing, Using, and Enjoying Your RV

Kim Baker and Sunny Baker

G.K. Hall & Co.
Thorndike, Maine

CHESTERFIELD COUNTY LIBRARY
VIRGINIA

Copyright © 1997 by Kim Baker and Sunny Baker

All rights reserved.

Published in 1997 by arrangement with Simon & Schuster, Inc.

G.K. Hall Large Print Reference Collection.

The text of this Large Print edition is unabridged.
Other aspects of the book may vary from the original edition.

Set in 16 pt. Plantin by Juanita Macdonald.

Printed in the United States on permanent paper.

Library of Congress Cataloging in Publication Data
Baker, Kim. 1955–
    The RVer's bible : everything you need to know about choosing, using, and enjoying your RV / by Kim Baker and Sunny Baker.
        p.   cm.
    Large Print ed.
    Includes index.
    ISBN 0-7838-8286-6 (lg. print : hc : alk. paper)
    1. Recreational vehicles.   2. Recreational vehicle living.   I. Baker, Sunny.
    II. Title.
    [TL298.B26   1997]
    796.7´9´0973—dc21   97-27759

Contents

Part III. RV Lifestyles and Activities

To the Reader

This book was inspired by *On the Road*, the novel by Jack Kerouac. For Kerouac, the vitality of the human spirit was explored from the back of an open-bed produce truck or chewing the fat in an overnight stop in a one-horse town in which anything or absolutely nothing would happen. Each day was a quest for meaning. The characters found at otherwise mundane Edward Hopper–style truck stops inspired novels. There was allegory everywhere.

If this sounds exciting, we suggest a little homework. Read *On the Road*. The story has nothing in the way of how-to information for the modern RVer, but instead paints the richness of a lifestyle that goes where the road takes you. The travels are the story: long, smooth belts of blacktop and strangers with tales to tell; the sweet smell of the pines and the sparkling stars; crowded cities and dingy gas stations.

As an RVer you can create your own stories on the road, as we have. For a week or two, *or for the rest of your life,* your RV can take you where you want to go. Today, instead of bouncing in the back of a truck or hopping a train, you can discover the soul of America (or Canada) from comfortable motorhomes, fifth-wheels, and camping trailers.

In Kerouac spirit, this book is dedicated to the growing legions of RVers who pursue their dreams and search for the real meaning of life. We're on the road again.

Introduction

Across North America and beyond people live, camp, retire, play, and adventure in motorhomes and travel trailers. In our RV we are freed from the nine-to-five shackles. We don't squander Saturdays at the mall or spend Sundays mowing the lawn. Instead, we venture where the road takes us. If we want to stay, we stay. If we want to leave, we just drive to the next place that catches our attention. The road suggests romance. Freedom emanates from each horizon.

As writers, our work can be done anywhere. Our laptop computers provide all the support of a corporate office. We stay in touch with the world with our cellular phone and pagers. No matter where we are, we sleep in our own bed each night — cats purring at our feet. Our RV is home.

Like us, you can pilot your own rig — be it a road-worn forest-green Volkswagen van or a $450,000 shiny silver Newell coach complete with glove leather seats and an Italian marble bathroom. An RV of any sort provides opportunity to explore the beach, the city, or the wilderness — the choice is yours.

You waken to a breathtaking sunrise and, over a cup of steaming coffee, ask your companions, "Should we drive two hundred miles to the Grand Canyon, bicycle the back routes, explore a museum, or try out that cute little taco bar down the street? Or, should we lie back in the sun, take it easy, catch up on reading and painting, commune with nature, and leave the adventures until tomorrow?" If your rig, your enthusiasm, and your budget allow, you can make these liberating decisions on a whim, taking only the changing weather into account.

Home is the highway for millions of active RVers who pilot their vehicles across the continent. To add substance to this claim, consider the Good Sam Club, a widely promoted RVer's camping organization, which boasts more than one million member families.

Since many RVers and most casual campers are not members of the Good Sam Club, the actual number of RVers on the road is difficult to determine. Of course, there are also the millions of people who own minicamper vans and small self-contained trailers. More than thirty million campers visit national and state parks each year. The number of people enjoying (and cooking in) their RVs, campers, and trailers boggles the mind.

The number of RVers swells each year. People sell their traditional homes to take up where Bob and Bing left off in *Road to Utopia*. Others search for what's left of the mythical Route 66 where Jack Kerouac found the diversity of spirit that defines America. Many long for the great outdoors. Some simply seek an easier, less expensive way to live. A few just want to try their luck fishing in hidden streams. For whatever reason, more people are living, exploring, and vacationing in RVs than ever before.

No Stereotypes, Please

Forget all the stereotypes about RVers. People of all ages, political persuasions, and activity levels enjoy life and travel in RVs. No matter what your income or interest, if you've ever thought of getting away or seeing the country, then you are a prime candidate for RV life.

Come. We'll help you take those first steps to freedom and adventure. With a fully equipped RV and a little bit of "I need a change in attitude" you're ready for the best time of your life. This book can help you make a decision on the right road and RVing lifestyle for you.

Why You Need This Book

As you peruse these pages, you'll find no cheerleading on the wonders of living in RVs. Instead, we've put together a practical guide to help you first decide if you even want to be an RVer. Once you make that decision, this book can then assist you in choosing the right options for your personal life on the road.

In spite of the flexibility and freedom of RVing, the lifestyle entails idiosyncrasies. As RVers, you should know the whole story about the advantages and the anomalies of living on the road. For those with this knowledge, the problems in RVing are few and the rewards are many.

It's Not All Romance and Adventure

We obviously enjoy RVing or we wouldn't continue to spend our time on the road, but not everything in RVing comes out easy, inexpensive, or romantic. We learned this lesson and the ins and outs of RVing the hard way — through trial and error.

Ten years ago, with fingers crossed, we bought a used thirty-one-foot Class A motorhome that seemed well appointed. We longed for freedom from the stresses of our previous corporate existence as managers in software companies. After stocking the fridge with too many perishables, we hit the road.

Luckily, our choice of RVs proved reasonable. The selection was entirely subjective, as we didn't know a good value from a lemon. It turned out that we had paid only 15 percent too much for the motorhome (not bad considering the rip-offs we've seen since then). Most important, the rig was in reasonably good mechanical shape. Even so, it wasn't love at first drive.

The stresses didn't fall away — they changed. On the highway, the coach seemed less stable than expected. Driving something the size of a bus took its toll on our nerves until we got the hang of maneuvering around the city. Later, we learned that a fifth-wheel trailer would have better met our traveling style, but when we started we had no idea of the tradeoffs or options available to us.

Knowing nothing about RV camping, on our first night on the road we almost made the dangerous decision to camp at a remote rest stop in central California. This was a bigger mistake than you might think, as armed robbery is not unheard of at rest areas. Luckily, before we stopped for the night, we stumbled on a tiny campground in the hills, also by accident, with inexpensive rates and great people. It was one of those great semiprimitive camps that aren't in any of the guidebooks. We naively anticipated that all the RV parks in our life would be like that one. Friendly. Inexpensive. Full of interesting people. We learned otherwise.

"People could not believe their eyes"

writes Seattle couple, who Dynaflowed this mammoth 4-ton trailer over 3,000 rugged miles to Alaska — behind the family Buick

PICTURED above is the largest trailer ever to travel the Alcan Highway. Yet look what's pulling it — a Buick SPECIAL with Dynaflow Drive.

Small wonder "people could not believe their eyes." No wonder customs inspectors were skeptical that any stock car with a load like that — 35 feet long and 8,800 pounds heavy — could make it.

The 3,000-mile route from Seattle to Fairbanks, Alaska, is rough and rugged. Its mud, slush, ice, snow and steep mountain grades are frequently too much for passenger cars — even without trailers in tow.

But Mr. and Mrs. James Post of Seattle were

confident that in their new Buick with Dynaflow they had a power team able to best the worst — record-size trailer and all!

"Would have been impossible without Dynaflow"

In excerpt form their letter reads, "We hit 80 miles of the sticky mud and we had heard so much about. It was rough — but at least if we had to stop, we felt certain of getting started again. We had endless inquiries on how the car managed to pull the trailer. People could not believe their eyes."

Later, their narrative states, "We were told we could not pull the trailer over Mile 595. Trucks had had trouble getting over that one. Starting up that grade, we stopped breathing. The speedometer hardly registered, but we got over the top . . . and everyone was speechless. . . . If it had not been for Dynaflow Drive, our trip would have been impossible with such a large trailer."

Of course, you may never be Alaska bound — or ever tow a trailer, even over the best of highways.

But the Posts' 3,000-mile run is pretty good proof of Dynaflow's staying power and pulling power in any driving you may do.

Add this to the smoothness and ease you enjoy from every Dynaflow mile, and you can see why it's a "must" on a modern car.

All of which makes it mighty important to see your Buick dealer pronto and let him give you all the other reasons why "better buy Buick" is sound advice.

BUICK *Division of* GENERAL MOTORS

WHATEVER YOUR PRICE RANGE

"Better buy Buick"

Many parks were expensive. Others were crowded and noisy. The park managers often seemed crabby instead of accommodating.

The ensuing weeks brought other discouraging surprises — mostly associated with handling, cleaning, maintaining, and fixing the motorhome. Our adventures encompassed leaking valves at a noxious dump station, stinky LP gas tanks, and a transmission overheating in the middle of the desert. In between, we had fun and met people who showed us the ropes. Eventually we figured out what we should have known before we started and began to confidently enjoy the freedom and entertainment of RVing.

The Book We Wish We Had Had

Now we consider ourselves relatively "old hands" on the road (well, not that old). Based on our experience and the advice of full-timers and campers we've met through the years, we wrote *The RVer's Bible* to be the book we wish we had had when we first started RVing. We lay it on the line, so you can decide whether the RV lifestyle suits you. Before you plunk down a chunk of change and pack up a relatively comfortable conventional lifestyle, read this book. With the information herein, we could have saved money and spent more time enjoying life on the road instead of worrying about the motorhome. We present the good, the bad, and the ugly facts about RVing that can help you make informed decisions about the best rig, camps, and traveling style for your RVing adventures.

We want people to be safe and happy in their homes on wheels. No matter what your preference for travel in your RV, this book can help you avoid the (often expensive and sometimes dangerous) mistakes we made when we started out. Our goal is simply to help you get more enjoyment from your own RV lifestyle.

We've tried to cover the most important aspects of purchasing, maintaining, driving, exploring, and living in a recreational vehicle. We provide the experience-based information that simply isn't available from dealers and camping guidebooks. This book also provides answers and ideas for experienced RVers who may be considering a change of rigs or looking for money-saving tips. As in RVing, there is something for everyone in this volume.

Whether you are considering full-timing in a highliner or week-end trips in a rented van conversion, we think this book will make your foray into RVing more satisfying. We hope you enjoy the trip through these pages.

Things Change

Throughout this book we mention products and contact numbers as examples. Do not construe this as an endorsement of a best buy or a superior brand. We've enjoyed positive personal experience with many of the products we mention, but there is no way we could have tried all the products on the market. By the time you read this book, new products will have developed. Thus, we keep much of our advice generic for all RVing generations. You should look at our advice as a place to start, not as the final word.

Although we have tried to be comprehensive about basic options and considerations for RVing, we may not have identified the best of the current models or products because things are constantly changing in the RVing world. Something new on the market may supersede our suggestion or mention. Our advice: Shop 'til ya drop! Pay attention to the RVing magazines. Getting the right rig, accessory, element, component, gadget, subsystem modification, or service at the right price takes work on your part, but in the long run, the research will save you money and make RVing that much more entertaining.

We spend mornings on the phone looking for the best price on something we've had our eye on for a long time. You should too. Saving money is only part of the equation. It's the fun of getting the best deal, buying the best brand, or getting truly expert advice and subsequent proficient installation that are part of RVing. And, while we would like to think of ourselves as camping experts, maybe there's something you know, or something that, with a little research, you will learn that we don't know. If you want to share these insights with us, feel free. You can almost always reach us by sending e-mail to kimbaker@aol.com.

Part I

Choosing the Best RV for You

Chapter 1

The RV Lifestyle

People have always been wanderers. The human need to explore stems from prehistory, when our nomadic relatives roamed the savanna. Wanderlust abides deep in our souls, as does our need to return to the forest, the mountains, and the open air — or the open highway, for that matter. The way we explore the environment simply changed over the years: from traversing the African deserts in bands, to adventuring across the American plains in wooden wagons, to roaming the continent in Winnebagos, Bounders, Airstreams, and Marathons.

Even if just for a weekend, the need to "get back to nature" drives us all. Exploration characterizes our heritage. Freedom and independence are central tenets of our culture. And fantasies of escape beckon us when we are stuck in rush hour or working overtime in the gray cubicles of Fortune 500 towers.

What better way to flee the doldrums of everyday life and get back to our roots than taking to the road in an RV — a home on wheels that can go (almost) anywhere without leaving behind the creature comforts of civilization? RVs serve as well for quick weekend getaways as they do for alternatives to a home on Mulberry Street. (Yes, Kim once lived on a street of that name.) In RVs the compromises prove minimal — we can see it all and have it all. In RVs we carry our technology with us on our return to a simpler life.

The Early RVers

RVing history parallels America's love affair with the automobile. As early as 1905, during the heyday of the Model T, folks considered car camping a standard form of recreation in America. By 1910, Abercrombie and Fitch featured pages of car-camping supplies in their catalog. Canvas tents and telescoping apartments were adapted to the early autos and trucks. By the 1920s and 1930s campgrounds included facilities that would rival the best modern RV parks, including movie theaters and dance halls. In the 1920s, RV manufacturers started building fully enclosed, self-contained vehicles with beds, kitchens, and bathrooms. Wiedman, a major builder of the period, had models with Pullman-style interiors, complete with wicker chairs and wood trim. They even offered options of refrigerators, cookstoves, chemical toilets, and showers. All this could be had for about $1,000.

The Tin Can Tourists, the first RVing club in America, was founded in 1919. By the 1930s it had more than two hundred thousand members. Until the 1950s the association published guides and ratings of campgrounds and facilities.

RVers Today

Modern RVers follow the traditions of freedom, leisure, and independence that characterized the Tin Can Tourists. The stereotypes depicting modern RVers as retired tightwads are largely incorrect. The people who take to the road in RVs are as diverse as the melting pot of personalities called Americans (and Canadians).

Yes, retirees compose a major segment of today's RVing population, but the RVing population also includes traveling businesspeople, entertainers, families, baby boomers, professionals, pet lovers, entrepreneurs, nature seekers, and weekend vacationers.

According to Go Camping America, a national club that promotes the outdoor lifestyle, more than twenty-five million Americans use recreation vehicles each year — and the numbers continue to swell. We took our first extended trip in a large motorhome while we were in our early thirties. Typical of the new breed of RVing couples, we joined the professional couples and families on the road that compose the fastest-growing segment of the RVing world.

In recent years, we've enjoyed meeting more RVers like the

family from South Africa that rented an RV in San Francisco and set out to see the United States in a summer. This RVing family of four explained their love of the road and lamented the impossibility of such a lifestyle in their native land due to varying road quality and security concerns. The children spent hours choosing routes, looking for campgrounds from the *Trailer Life* and *Woodall's* camping guides. They wanted to go everywhere and see everything. The RV park at Disneyland was next on their itinerary. They asked us which rides to head for first. They assumed that as native Southern Californians we would certainly be fully versed in such information. Since then, we have traveled to the RV park where they stayed and learned that walking through Disneyland in the summer is a lot more difficult than maneuvering our thirty-five-footer through downtown Los Angeles.

RVers are people of all ages and interests. Tired of crowded airports and anonymous hotels, the new RVers want to see the country between their destinations. Many enjoy the advantages of taking their children (and pets) along for the adventure. The baby boom generation that once sneered at RVing has traded status-seeking in their BMWs for the fun, comfort, and adventure of an RV life on wheels. As one optimistic RV tour director described it, "This is a growth industry that hasn't even begun to grow. These [baby boomer] kids are going to love RVing even more than their parents!"

The myth of the typical RVer has been dispelled in our travels over and over again. Yet, in spite of their differences, RVers identify with one another. This camaraderie is one of the "typical" things among RVers. Another involves RVers' shared satisfaction in being able to be home wherever they go. At every camp new friends meet. People often offer to barbecue an extra steak while sharing a story of adventure. Each tiny town reveals a fresh vignette of life to ponder, to cherish, to remember. In each town "typical" RVers pause to tell you about their favorite stops.

Our Lifestyle on the Road

Like the typical RVer, the RV lifestyle is a myth. As with most RVers, our RV lifestyle belongs to us. We use our RV to escape the drudgery of city life and the stress of deadlines. We write our books and our magazine columns with the laptop computer in our rig. Samantha, Kingsley, and Onyx (our cats) go everywhere with us. Sunny occasionally teaches seminars at local colleges (she has a Ph.D. in education and computers). Kim (he has an M.A. in art) sells his paintings at regional art galleries. Snug in the captain's chairs of our truck, with our thirty-two-foot fifth-wheel securely in tow, we search for gold at the end of the rainbow. We haven't found it yet, but we know we're close.

When we're RVing, anxiety and ambiguity evaporate, except when the fuel gauge reads "low" and the road sign warns, "Next Services 85 miles." Our RV offers a ticket with no particular destination. We just go when our hearts tell us to move or the weather indicates imminent snow that might bind us to South Dakota until a spring beginning next July. (Should this happen to you, make sure you're ensconced in an RV with thick insulation and a powerful heating system.)

We favor a part-time, middle ground for our RVing lifestyle. We typically live in the RV for a few months each year. When our wanderlust wears thin, we return to our house-based routine. Then, when we feel the growing dormancy in an unchanging domestic environment, we get extra cash by selling off the unnecessary goods that seem to accumulate in house-based life and pack up our rig for the next outing.

Sometimes we travel great distances just to see the country. We stay a night or two at each spot. Occasionally, we strike gold at a small, inexpensive rural campground with majestic trees, great fishing, and the friendly folks who are the treasures of our RV lifestyle. We tend to forget the schedule when we find one of these havens. Instead, we inquire about the monthly rates on the space. Other times, we spend a large sum to stay a week in an elegant urban campground with complete facilities and enjoy all the restaurants, attractions, and culture a city has to offer.

Build a Life of Your Own

Our on-again, off-again RV lifestyle may not be what you imagine as heaven. Each RVer boasts about different advantages and satisfactions — that's what makes the lifestyle interesting. RVers embrace disparate goals for RVing. That's the whole point: to be who you want to be and to go where you want to go. While some RVers stay put for months or maybe even years, others move from town to town, never staying in a place two nights in a row. Some, like us, work on the road, others only play. Some seek companionship in dense parks, others covet solitude in open air.

Maintaining the rig, setting up camp, and stocking supplies are the commonalities of RV existence. Beyond that, every RVer innovates a personal approach to life on the road.

RVs Have Everything, Including the Kitchen Sink

The diversity of people on the road thrives because of the range of RV options. Modern RVs come equipped with just about everything necessary to live comfortably — for a weekend or forever. RVs are completely furnished, some tastefully. Most units include all the major appliances you'd find in a middle-class home, including the microwave. You can even find rigs with washers, dryers, dishwashers, and trash compactors. The level of luxury is limited only by your budget.

Of course, we can't imagine that Jack Kerouac ever thought of traveling in modern RV style — with washer, dryer, trash compactor, ice-maker, microwave, and dishwasher. Whether Jack would have done it this way or not, you need to decide for yourself the level of RVing that fits your needs and your lifestyle. Do you prefer a unit with a lower payload rating but the ability to carry more consumables for a longer drive? Do you long for the back roads where others dare not go — or is the esprit de corps of an RV caravan with hundreds of rigs traveling the interstates your idea of heaven? Do you want a small rig that travels well on weekends or do you want a coach that will become your home for months at a time? Before you fantasize about clean air and freedom, let us tell you what you can expect when traveling or living in an RV.

Tip: The Places to Go for RV Supplies

When looking for RV supplies, the first place people send you is Camping World, the large RV/camping superstore chain that offers everything from RV engine rebuilds to insect balm (seven kinds). We mention the stores not because they paid us off (they didn't), but because they are the most logical place to go when in need of almost any camping or RV equipment. Camping World is a convenient national chain for RVers. Its stores are located adjacent to freeway offramps in most large cities, which makes the stores easy to find. They typically have plenty of parking spaces for big rigs too. Inside, you'll find everything for the modern RVer, from obscure battery isolators to RV-compatible toilet paper. Camping World's catalog even provides maps to its outlets. And, if you can't get to a store, you can order most of the items by mail. Call 1-800-626-5944 for a free catalog. It's a must have.

Another good source of RV supplies is the Camper's Choice catalog. Just call 1-800-833-6713 for your free copy. We also use RV Direct. Call 1-800-438-5480 for a catalog. Other suppliers advertise in *Motorhome* magazine and *Trailer Life*. We provide information for contacting these magazines in the resources section at the back of the book.

Of course, there are RV supply stores around the country that compete with Camping World, and these are often equally well stocked and may have lower prices on some items. If you need to find the RV supply stores and repair shops near your camp, look under Recreational Vehicles in the *Yellow Pages*. Remember, many products for RVers are available for lower prices at the supermarket or discount stores — so don't just assume that Camping World or one of its competitors is always the easiest and cheapest place to go, even though these stores usually offer the most comprehensive range of supplies.

Dollars, Direction, and Desire:
The Three Lifestyle Factors in RVing

In an RV you can enjoy a country club lifestyle complete with full electric and water hookups, heated pools, hot tubs, sports courses, ballrooms, activity directors, and world-class restaurants. The prices parallel the range of amenities. When you long for nature, try one of the thousands of public parks throughout the continent. Scenery and sunsets. Wildlife and wildflowers. Wind rustling through the trees. And if this sounds too tranquil, there's always the adventure of boondocking — camping free in "primitive" sites at rest areas, beaches, parking lots, deserts, or fairgrounds.

Although your options are unlimited, three factors influence your lifestyle on the road: dollars, direction, and desire. Of these, the dollars in your bank account dominate your choice of rigs, the length of your trips, and your range of campground and travel options.

If you want to live on a limited budget, you'll probably also limit your driving. Budgeting RVers learn to find free parking areas, such as grocery store parking lots (when this is legal) or side roads off the main highways. If living inexpensively is one of your RVing goals, Chapter 22 presents many options for saving money, making money, and budgeting on the road.

Although the ability to live cheap in beautiful (or not so beautiful) surroundings tops the list of advantages commonly associated with RVing, the RV lifestyle also offers the option of taking any and all luxuries with you wherever you go. For a price, you can park next to world-class golf courses with views of the ocean and the facilities of the best resort spas.

Luxury RVing is called *highlining* in road lingo. The highlining set cruises the interstates in bus-sized RVs. Typical luxury coaches cost over $200,000 and feature glove leather upholstery, floor lighting, and Italian marble floors, not to mention powerful diesel engines, bus-chassis construction, and stop-on-a-dime airbrakes. The highlining set stakes out memberships in the most expensive campground chains. The parks feature every amenity — from spas to Spagos. If highlining fits your budget, unlimited options emerge.

You can explore all the places the budgeting RVers cherish — and also indulge in the places they can't afford. Highlining options appear throughout the book.

Beyond considering the budget for your lifestyle, you'll need to choose a lifestyle that fits your desire to socialize, work, relax, or hibernate. We experimented with everything from luxury RV living to a macaroni-and-cheese lifestyle and found each to be enjoyable for different reasons. You'll also need to decide on the directions you want to go on your trips. What places do you want to see? What comforts do you demand? How often should you move? What surroundings soothe your soul? The answers are all in the type of RVer you want to become.

Vacationer, Part-Timer, or Full-Timer?

There are three general types of RVers on the road: vacationers, part-timers, and full-timers. Vacationers take to the road for weekends and weeklong trips. Part-timers and full-timers spend more extended time living in their rigs.

Vacationers typically take to the road for two or three weeks once or twice a year to relax and see the sights. They also make weekend trips as the urge hits them. Vacationers are the most likely RVing group to have family and friends piled in the rig. Sleeping arrangements may be cramped, but fun tops the list of objectives — not comfort. Many vacationers rent their RVs. (Chapter 5 covers all the ins and outs of RV renting.)

Many vacation-oriented RVers prefer self-contained camper shells or small pop-up travel trailers pulled behind four-wheel-drive sports utility vehicles, trucks, or vans. These small rigs provide the flexibility to go anywhere and the comforts of a bed while offering the "open-air" feeling of more primitive camping in tents and sleeping bags. Other vacationing RVers (and even some full-timers) choose self-contained van conversions and small footprint motorhomes (under twenty-four feet in length). These small self-contained units provide most of the amenities found in larger motorhomes, although in cramped quarters. Further, these rigs can park in the many national, state, and regional parks that don't allow larger motorhomes and fifth-wheel trailers.

The Advantages of RV Vacations

People gravitate toward RVing as a vacation option because they want to get the full advantage of their few weeks away from the grind. Vacations that depend on planes, trains, and motels often regress into the endless repetition of packing, unpacking, checkins and checkouts, long lines, and mediocre food in high-priced restaurants. The search for clean restrooms dominates the quest for solace. At the end of the day, nerves frazzle as the search for comfortable, affordable accommodations eclipses all other struggles. Once lodging materializes, all you have to do is unload the car. Tomorrow, the sequence repeats itself.

RVing, on the other hand, offers the possibility of a vacation with freedom of movement and travel at a relaxed pace. On an RV vacation, you roam only where you please, without rigid schedules. Eat when and what you want. Sleep each night in your own bed.

The exponential growth in the number of RVing vacationers proves the popularity and appeal of such vacations. However, if you think an RV vacation means economy, think again. If you don't already own your rig, RV vacations can be quite pricey. Renting and supplying a self-contained vehicle may cost as much as (or more than) a vacation in a swanky resort. Still, the convenience, flexibility, and relaxation can far outweigh the lack of economy.

Part-Timers and Full-Timers

If you take to the road in an RV, you'll meet many part-timers and full-timers who "live" in their RVs for extended periods. The difference between part-timer and full-timer is only the length of time these groups spend in their rigs and coaches. Part-timers include people like us who live on the road a few months a year and then return to a house-based lifestyle when the traveling urge is satisfied. Other part-timers enjoy extended vacations in their RVs a few times a year. Some of these RVers rent their rigs to vacationers when they're not in use. The rental fees may even pay the mortgage on some rigs, although as with anything else, the tax man cometh for the profit.

Some part-time RVers, known as "snowbirds," maintain traditional homes in colder climes in the northern and central United States and Canada. When the snow falls, these flocks head south and spend the winter months in the sun. Some snowbirds bring motorhomes or trailers. Others simply rent, borrow, or reoccupy units that are semipermanently parked in warmer territory. Many RV parks in snowbird regions stand empty all summer. By November the no vacancy signs forbid those without reservations. In Apache Junction, for example, only a few miles to the east of Phoenix, more than two hundred thousand RV-based snowbirds show up every winter — more than quadrupling the population of this desert burg almost overnight. Countless other cities like this in Florida, California, and Arizona cater to the folks in their homes on wheels.

Full-timers are the most committed RVers — many have given up home-based living altogether and spend most (or all) of their time in their homes on wheels. In 1988, the television news show *20/20* estimated that two hundred thousand families, mostly over the age of fifty, considered themselves full-timers. Today, there are likely many times more. Full-timers may follow the snowbirds or park all year in one spot. Full-timers consider themselves a separate breed and their lifestyles bespeak their individuality. Fully dedicated to life on the road, many full-timers enjoy retirement and travel, but others work on the road and prefer the freedom and comfort provided in an RV.

Full-time RVing is not a way of life for everyone. Even avid RV vacationers and part-timers find that more than a few weeks in a rig breeds discontent. Some people feel cooped up, even in the largest motorhomes, and especially when inclement weather abides. The goal for full-time RVing should be a different lifestyle, not a harder one.

Try It Before You Decide

How do you know if you are a vacationer, part-timer, or full-timer — or if RVing fits your needs at all? Well, if your idea of fun involves staying in a nearby resort, checking into a hotel once, and spending all of your time at poolside, then an RV may not be for you. If, on the other hand, your idea of travel includes seeing people and places, spending some time in quiet, rural settings and some time in bustling cities, an RV may be just your ticket for a carefree vacation. Also, if you need to travel with small children or pets, RVing offers decided advantages. Of course, your feelings about travel also depend on whether you hit the road for a few weeks a year or live on the road. If you're considering part-timing or full-timing, you need to start with an extended vacation before you decide whether the RV lifestyle meets your needs.

Before you buy an RV for any purpose, rent or borrow one to learn about the lifestyle and the features you want. Choose a model that matches your desires. Use the rig for two weeks or more. Drive it. Camp in diverse parks. Learn the ins and outs of packing, cooking, fueling, and maintaining the rig. Get comfortable with plugging in to park electricity and running the rig in the wilderness on its own power. Until you've tried an RV, there's no way to tell if you'll be awe-inspired with the freedom or fettered with claustrophobia.

Full-timing or extended stays in an RV may sound intriguing to you. Before you "move in," however, try a month on the road. Don't take your friends, unless they'll be part of your permanent entourage. Try driving on diverse highways. Try getting into various types of parks. Make all your meals on the road for a couple of weeks. Take the RV into the city. After three or four solid weeks you should be able to tell if full-time RVing is a lifestyle you want to pursue. Then look into buying the rig to fit your lifestyle. Not before. Of course, before you move into your RV, you'll have to make many decisions. You'll need to give up furniture, house, and other "large" possessions — and the proximity of your housebound friends and family.

Tip: Homeless?

For those low on resources, RVing may offer an alternative to homelessness. And no, we won't bring this topic up again, but even an old, broken-down RV beats sleeping in a car, shelter, or doorway.

Realizing Your RVing Dreams

Although the romance of the road beckons to many, commanding an RV enfolds negatives as well as positives, just like life in a house or apartment. Unpredictable breakdowns happen. So do undeniable pleasures. The mixture of driving, camping, relaxing, and adventure that makes RV life a wonder for us may be too routine, too adventurous, or incompatible with your ambitions. If you don't take time to understand what you really want from RVing, your RV dream may never be realized.

We want *everyone* who reads *The RVer's Bible* to come away with an objective understanding of the lifestyle, its freedoms, options, risks, and responsibilities, be they owners of a two-month-old, $500,000 bus-style rig or a banged-up trailer that's a literal "hovel on wheels." As you read on, consider how the advantages apply to you, your lifestyle, and your companions — be they family, friends, pets, or the next-door neighbors. Then, after matching rig and traveling style to your needs and dreams, get on the road — and let your own RV lifestyle emerge.

Have You Heard the One About the Traveling Salesman?

David is a dyed-in-the-wool, blue-pin-stripe-suited businessman. He's a top performer who represents exclusive lines of golf clubs around the country. But you'll never find David on an airplane. Instead, he drives a thirty-two-foot Pace Arrow motorhome from city to city to sell his wares. When we asked why he preferred traveling in his coach instead of using a first-class airline ticket, David recounted the crowded airports, stressful schedules, greasy food, and uncomfortable hotel beds. Before he discovered RVing, David laments, he never saw the country or the people. Now, rather than waste days at a tired motel, he enjoys sleeping in the familiar surroundings of his RV and cooking his own food. And David is not alone on the road. Many businesspeople are giving up the lure of Frequent Flyer Miles in order to take their home (and families) with them on their treks to clients and customers.

Chapter 2

So Many Choices:
The Many Kinds of RVs

RVs are not created equal. Manufactured by such companies as Fleetwood, Newell, Bluebird, Winnebago, Airstream, and Teton, RVs come with a variety of options and floor plans that may astound those who have never shopped for a rig. The largest rigs are literally the size of a bus. The smallest rig we know of is the Guppy, a fold-out sleeping trailer the size of an oversized Volkswagen bug.

RVs can be divided into two general categories: those with an integrated powertrain (engine and transmission) and those without an engine, which must be towed by a vehicle that provides the driving power. The ones with integrated powertrains are called *motorhomes*. RVs that must be towed are called *trailers* because they trail a tow vehicle (which can be a car, truck, van, or sports utility vehicle, depending on the size and type of trailer).

Within the categories of trailer and motorhome, RVs come in many flavors: Motorhome categories include Class A, Class C, van conversions, pickup-based campers, and custom vehicles. Among trailers you'll encounter travel models, park models, pop-ups, and fifth-wheels. Within these categories there are even further options. Travel trailers and motorhomes may expand and contract with slide-out rooms. Trailers that travel in half-height format (great for reducing wind resistance) can be raised to full height at camp. Small vans come equipped with all the comforts of home, but in very cramped quarters. At the large end you'll find forty-five-foot motorhomes with the square footage and amenities of upscale apartments.

Short and long RVs serve different masters. Shorter RVs are more useful for wilderness sites and national parks (many of which have restrictions on RVs over twenty-four or twenty-eight feet). Shorter rigs may or may not be more economical in terms of fuel and maintenance, depending on their construction and where you take them, but usually a smaller rig is easier to drive and tow than one of the big rigs. Alternatively, although you may not be able to camp in the wilderness because you can't get there, if you command a long rig — maybe with a slide-out or two — you can delight in the life and luxury of an apartment on wheels. You may even enjoy a full-sized bathtub, if that's important to you.

In addition to a variety of lengths to suit all traveling preferences, RVs also come in all price ranges. What you're paying for in an RV is not always apparent on the surface. In general, you pay more for larger, longer RVs. You also pay more for solid construction. Thus, a smaller, well-built RV may cost more than a larger, low-end unit. We cover some of these differences in this chapter.

For the uninitiated, learning of the wide range of RVing options often expels any preconceived notions about RVing. Sometimes the options breed confusion. In the next pages, we'll introduce you to these options to help you clarify your own priorities. If there is any RVing blood in your veins, you'll likely be able to match one or more of these RVs to your budget and desires.

Tip: Trailers Versus Mobile Homes

What's the difference between a *mobile home* and a *travel trailer?* Mobile homes, also called manufactured homes, usually remain stationary after their initial placement. Dismantling and moving an assembled unit is about as easy as transporting a two-story brick house. Travel trailers, on the other hand, can be carted around the country with abandon and are built to stand up to the stress of rough travel on unimproved roads. Mobile homes are not RVs, but RVs are mobile. Mobile homes are not.

Trailers for Sale or Rent . . .

Many of the first recreational vehicles were trailers. Developed soon after cars became common, trailers provided a vacation option to replace the rented cabin or motel stay. A stay in camp was still much less expensive than a motel or hotel. Since the first generation of trailers had no sewage systems, camps provided showers and toilets (they still do).

Essentially a trailer is a box on wheels. Manufacturers add the basic ingredients of an apartment — cooking facilities, a bathroom, storage space, a bed, and a living area for sitting and dining. Because trailers are passive vehicles without an engine, they require a tow vehicle. The trailer's braking system is controlled by a connection to the tow vehicle's braking system. If you already own a car or truck with the muscle and design to work as a tow vehicle, you're all set once you add the right hitch and a few wires and check out the mechanical safety of the car/trailer combination. RV trailers come in a variety of formats, including pop-ups, travel trailers, and fifth-wheels.

Pop-Up Trailers

Pop-up travel trailers, some of them self-contained, are the smallest, lightest trailers. The smallest pop-ups, such as those by Coleman, are a compromise between tent and RV camping and offer an easy way to get started on RVs. They are cheaper than standard RVs and because of their light weight can also be towed by the average family car. They often have canvas sides and resemble a tent on a small flatbed trailer. Many RVing families prefer pop-ups as sleeping quarters when visiting state and national parks and recreation areas. Most large automobiles can serve as tow vehicles for these units with only a few modifications.

In seasonable weather, the best pop-ups provide many of the comforts of a "real" trailer or motorhome but have the open-air feel of a tent. Pop-ups take up only as much space as a car and can be stored in an extra parking space or a garage. Coleman, which makes about a third of the pop-up campers, first introduced its line in the late sixties, but sold the entire business to Fleetwood

31

Evaluate your needs. What kind of rig is right for you — trailer, fifth-wheel, or motorhome? (You can change your mind later.)

Tip: Visit a large RV lot and inspect the models to get a better understanding of the options and each kind of rig.

Analyze your budget. What kind of rig can you afford? Which do you find the most livable?

Tip: The freedom of the road is in part being free of debt. Should you finance a rig or cut back your expectations?

Shop aggressively to see what's available in your price range. Compare new versus used. Consider features, age, and equipment.

Tip: You may find that a new rig is double the price of a comparable used one. We always buy used, but it's up to you . . .

Zero in on at least three rigs and then use the *Kelley Blue Book* to evaluate their market values versus what the dealer or seller is asking.

Tip: By having more than one rig in mind, you can avoid being trapped by the "perfect rig" and manipulated into paying a higher price by a seller that knows he has a "pigeon" on his hands.

Financing? Get it now as explained in Chaper 4 before making a firm commitment.

When financing is already in hand, you have as much leverage as a cash buyer, assuming your lender appraises the rig at a price similar to what you think it's worth.

Perform a more thorough inspection of the rig, without invasive techniques (save those for later). Study everything from leaks to the mattress wear.

Tip: As you narrow your selection of rigs, you want to inspect them carefully. In used rigs, you want to be assured that $5,000 repair isn't just around the corner.

Rig for You

Discuss price with the seller. With used rigs, pull out your *Kelley Blue Book* in order to unnerve the seller if the asking price is unreasonable.

Tip: The purpose of this exercise is to gauge seller flexibility in price and how they face up to real-world market conditions. A seller who proves uncooperative at this point should be dropped from your list of finalists.

Consider other rigs after the basic evaluation. Narrow your list to two.

Tip: Choose the rig with the best price. If you're buying new, shop price out of state, minding sales tax laws and which state you plan to register the rig. Follow all laws!

If financing, get a firm commitment from the lender. If there's a major spread between what they'll lend and what seems like a fair price, something is wrong.

Depending on your credit, the age and condition of the rig, and your lender's lending practices, major discrepancies point to a problem in the rig's price or your lender's policies.

On a new rig, inspect all systems, construction, and options ordered. On a used rig, use Chapters 3, 6, and 8 to check the vehicle's overall integrity.

You and your mechanic should check every inch of the vehicle. If problems crop up, ask the seller to financially assist in fixing them. If evidence of major body work or a need for expensive repairs becomes evident, pass and keep looking.

Pay and take title. If there are problems transferring title, hang on to your cash. The problems may range from minor paperwork glitches to a rig that's stolen.

Closing on an RV is like closing on a house: you want to hold clear title with the only lien holder, the lender, if you used one.

Follow the steps listed in this book to get ready for the road.

several years ago. Fleetwood and other manufacturers have been steadily upgrading and expanding the Coleman concept.

The typical pop-up trailer has a cable-operated mechanism for lifting a hard (aluminum or plastic) roof. Double or queen-sized beds slide out from both ends and are usually supported with metal rods placed between the floor of the bed and the trailer frame. The walls and the roof over the beds are made out of canvas, although some manufacturers coat it with vinyl. There are also hard-sided pop-ups that cost more and are heavier. Some of these are hard to distinguish from small travel trailers.

The newer pop-ups have a steel frame with an aluminum skin. The floor is made of a single sheet of oriented strand board, a manufactured wood, and is covered with vinyl. Equipment can include indoor and outdoor lighting, gas stoves, sinks, propane furnaces, air-conditioners, water heaters, showers, and toilets.

Maneuverability of the smaller trailers is very good, and in many cases there is full viewing over and around the trailers while towing. Interior size while set up is remarkably large, especially compared to the towed size.

Pop-Up Trailer Prices

Pop-ups range in price from a few thousand dollars for a serviceable canvas-sided unit for family camping to over $20,000 for one of the self-contained, solid-wall units with galley and bath facilities.

The least expensive pop-up and folding trailers offer minimal (or no) livability features. They are literally folding tents. The mid-priced units may offer manual water pumps, portable toilets, a propane stove, and maybe an optional heater. Some offer power converters as an option. The high-priced pop-ups may provide amenities similar to those of travel trailers — but without as much storage. Some of the more expensive pop-up designs are actually travel trailers that collapse for easier towing.

Pop-up trailers are the least expensive RV's. They are often preferred by families that want the feeling of camping and the comfort of a real bed.

Travel Trailers

Travel trailers, as opposed to the smaller, more portable pop-ups, come in a variety of sizes from a small bedroom on wheels to the equivalent of a large apartment with all the amenities and multiple slide-out rooms. Large travel trailers (and fifth-wheels, discussed later) fare as well in their role as a vacation home on wheels as they do as a permanent "camp" on a rural piece of property.

Travel trailers are built close to the ground, so the overall height is lower than that of a Class A motorhome, even though the interior height is similar. Ranging in length from ten to thirty-five feet, travel trailers must be pulled by a properly rated tow vehicle (truck, heavy-duty car, or other appropriate vehicle). Length figures for trailers include the length of the toeing tongue. For that reason, knock off about three or four feet from the manufacturer's length to determine the interior length.

Unless towing the smallest units, the tow vehicle must have a special load-distributing hitch and other special devices designed to control the sway of the trailer, because the load is all behind the tow vehicle. Trucks are the most common tow vehicles for large travel trailers, although utility sports vehicles, including Jeeps, Broncos, and Rangers, many with four-wheel-drive options, have recently emerged as popular tow vehicles for mid-size travel trailers. The combination of sports utility vehicle and travel trailer provides the flexible living options of a motorhome with a wilderness access capability not available in most other RV rigs. Some full-size cars equipped with towing packages are able to tow small and mid-size travel trailers.

The range of trailer construction and amenities runs from simple to opulent. Most travel trailers under fifteen to eighteen feet accommodate one couple comfortably and can sleep a family of four, sometimes six, on a vacation. A small trailer is a little too cozy for full-timing, although we've met happy couples at campgrounds or boondocking doing just that! Walkable space is determined by the amount of interior square footage that can be, well, walked. This negates space temporarily employed for appliances, but the "footprint" for convertible beds (when put away) is included in the equation.

Tip: List Price

Unless otherwise mentioned, all prices are approximate list prices at the time of writing. You may be able to negotiate substantial discounts or package deals, purchase a demo, or buy used for a substantially lower price tag. Then again, inflation may take its toll — so use the information as a rough guide only.

Most larger trailers handle two couples or more people with aplomb, depending on the kind of sleeping quarters incorporated in the floor plan. Some floor plans even provide multiple bedrooms. There are still a few manufacturers that produce "bunk-house"-style trailers that feature sleeping quarters for an extended family or gang of construction workers. In most modern trailers, which come fully furnished, the living area couch converts to yet another bed.

Travel Trailer Price Ranges

You can probably pick up an older, very well worn, but functional trailer for a grand or two. (You can get one for less, but probably wouldn't want it.) New trailers are priced from the very low five figures and up. The Airstream, Teton, and Fleetwood's Avion trailers are among the most luxurious and expensive.

The Low-Cost Travel Trailer (Less than $15,000)

Generally, the least expensive travel trailers are small rigs with Spartan interiors, low-quality fabrics, and basic appliances. You'll get a propane stove but no microwave. A basic bathroom, maybe with a shower, and a convertible couch/bed for additional campers or company visiting. Compact trailers are perfect for a weekend's fishing in a remote location, assuming you have a four-wheel drive

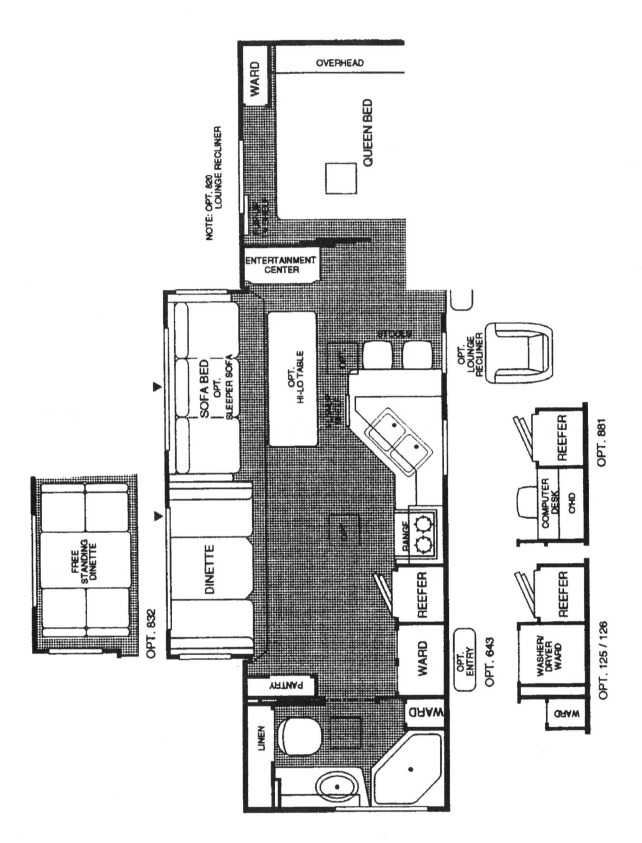

A travel trailer is separate and separable from the towing vehicle. You park a travel trailer, detach the car, truck, or van, and have convenient transportation for errands, seeing the sights, or side trips. Modern travel trailers have floor plans that resemble small apartments.

suitable for the task. There are expensive, small trailers decked out for extended wilderness stays, but among less expensive rigs, you'll be limited to a simple electrical system and basic plumbing. If a bathroom is included it will be nearly child-sized. If such a rig has separate rooms, you may wish to check the soundproofing by tapping on walls; check also the rig's equipment and built-in insulation to be assured of its ability to keep you warm or cool as needed. (Read Chapter 6 to learn how to further inspect the vehicle.)

Low-end travel trailers typically have wood frames and "stick and staple" construction. Insulation will be minimal, if present at all. Aluminum siding is the norm. Expect some rough edges on the cabinetry on a low-end trailer and expect artificial wood and paneling. Appliances may be manually operated, as opposed to automatic. For example, you might have to light the water heaters or pump the water on your own.

The Mid-Priced Travel Trailer ($15,000 to $30,000)

In mid-priced trailers, the tradeoff is among construction, living space, and amenities. Shorter rigs in the upper price bracket include more amenities and better construction. Longer models are more basic, but large enough for families to live in for extended periods. Many trailers in this price range are perfect for a full-timing couple or a family's summer vacation exploring Colorado and the Rockies. Full-timers will find these rigs comfortable for reaching remote state parks and for day-to-day domestic existence.

Most mid-priced trailers offer wood and aluminum framing. The walls are typically laminated and insulated with fiberglass or polystyrene. Exteriors may be aluminum or fiberglass. The fabrics will be higher quality and more durable than those of lower-priced trailers. Some genuine wood may be used in the interiors, although most of the paneling will be artificial. Some mid-price trailers offer attractive windows and brass hardware in the galley and bathroom areas. The appliances will also be better quality.

The flat top. A new kind of trailer has appeared on the market. (At least it's new as far as we know.) To avoid wind problems and make the rig more compatible with ordinary garages and carports, the top collapses onto the bottom, making for a significantly shorter profile.

The Highliner Trailer ($30,000 and Up)

The most expensive trailers tend to include (as you'd expect) the most amenities and quality appliances. They also offer larger storage capacities for camping without power and water hookups. But more important than the larger microwave and extensive sound and video system, the construction is completely different. Instead of corrugated sheet metal exteriors, you'll see shiny stainless metals (à la Airstream) and fiberglass. You'll see laminated walls in some units and real wood cabinets throughout. The upgrades to all interior elements are extensive. For example, instead of a foam mattress, you'll get real bedsprings. Thoughtful storage arrangements are de rigeur. Insulation of these units sets them apart from their lower-priced cousins — making it possible to camp in the tropics as well as the Arctic. Expect quality finishing, attractive interior design, tight construction joints, and better bundling and routing of electrical wires and plumbing. Some models offer leather upholstery as an option. Expect composite countertops (such as Corian) as opposed to laminates.

Such a trailer is completely suitable for full-timing and will have a longer life span than less expensive models, even if you haul it around the globe a couple of times. Note: The upgraded construction increases weight and thus a powerful tow vehicle is a must for handling the longer versions of such RVs.

Trailer Advantages

- Trailers are generally the least expensive RVs, assuming that you don't go out and spend $40,000 on a tow vehicle to pull your "money-saving" trailer.
- Trailers have a long life span, assuming you buy a quality unit. With some new carpet and interior refinishing, a 1970s-era Airstream is as viable an RV as a modern unit.
- Once it is parked and set up, you can leave the trailer and head off to the supermarket for supplies or to see the sights.
- Floor plans are highly flexible, as the floor plan is not dictated by the driver's cab as in a motorhome or by the "upstairs bedroom" as with fifth-wheels.

■ A trailer can be towed with almost any vehicle, unlike a fifth-wheel, which requires a correctly configured pickup truck.

Trailer Disadvantages

✖ As trailers' length and height increase they become increasingly difficult to manage on windy roads and on grades.

✖ Large trailers are difficult to tow, as everything from a cross-breeze to the passing of a tractor-trailer can affect the stability of the trailer. This shift in velocity and control will affect the tow vehicle as well. (Chapters 10 and 15 describe several mechanical options for avoiding the instability.)

Issues to Consider

- Towing a vehicle, especially a large, heavy trailer, takes practice. Try driving such a rig before purchase and, with expert help, match the tow vehicle's abilities to handling such a load. Optional stabilization and gearing equipment may be required, as mentioned in Chapter 10.
- Trailers hold their value better than do motorhomes because there's no drivetrain to wear out.
- With other kinds of RVs, you can access 115VAC house current through a generator (which may be optional), but no trailer we know of is internally equipped for such a unit. A standalone generator is an option, albeit a noisy one.
- Add $200 to $600 for equipping your tow vehicle with an appropriate hitch. (The $600 figure is for vehicles that require suspension modifications in order to mate with your trailer; $250 is more typical.)

Tip: Tax Deductions

At this writing, interest on an RV can be written off as you would the mortgage on a second home! Check with the IRS for current details and restrictions.

Tip: What's a "Park" Model Trailer?

When looking at ads, going through price lists, and hitting the classifieds, you may encounter a trailer described as a *park model*. Sounding like something worthy of hauling through Yellowstone (and cheap when acquired used), a park model is really closer to a mobile home. Yes, you can tow it, but it's really designed to stay in one place most of the time.

A park model is more durable than a mobile home, as the manufacturer assumes owners may move it occasionally. It differs from a travel trailer in that it provides as much interior space as possible without regard to lane width and turning radii — key concerns to those hauling travel trailers. Full-timers who perch for extended stays often choose a durable park model for the space and amenities, generally available at a lower cost than a comparably equipped travel trailer. They drive carefully (and infrequently) to a new town, city, or burg.

Fifth-Wheel Trailers

Unlike travel trailers and pop-ups, which are hitched to the back of a car, van, or truck, a fifth-wheel mounts to a special device in the bed of a pickup truck. Fifth-wheels have an extension on the front of the trailer box that extends over the tow vehicle and a horizontal plate that looks like a wheel that rests on the tow vehicle for support. This plate is where the fifth-wheel unit gets its name. This hitch arrangement requires a compatible tow vehicle, usually a specially equipped, full-size truck or a custom tow vehicle. The hitch places the load in the center of the tow vehicle instead of behind. The broad mount is similar to that of a tractor-trailer rig and is considered more stable by some people, resulting in less trailer-driving-the-car effect (also known as the tail-wagging-the-dog effect). Because the fifth-wheel's hitch resides on the top of a truck bed, the front of the trailer portion can be used as living space. In fact, on most fifth-wheels the area above the towing hitch is the "upstairs master bedroom."

Fifth-wheel trailers (measured from front extension to rear bumper) range in length from twenty-one feet to over forty feet and are similar in range of features to the larger travel trailers. Fifth-wheels offer a wide range of floor plans, including multiple slide-out rooms as options. The units are generally spacious. In terms of functionalism, like trailers (and motorhomes), fifth-wheels range in construction and features from plain and functional to truly luxurious.

Because a fifth-wheel is pulled by a full-size pickup truck, larger units can be safely towed and a roomy fifth-wheel with a slide-out or two is much like an apartment in terms of interior footage and livability. We saw one at an RV show with an option for a second bathroom! A fifth-wheel is usually easier to drive than a car/trailer arrangement because of the strength of the fifth-wheel's hitch. A small fifth-wheel accommodates two couples. A long model with convertible sleeping quarters can accommodate a large family or group of buddies.

Fifth-Wheel Price Ranges

Excluding the separate tow vehicle, new fifth-wheels are priced from $20,000 and up. You can break the $100,000 barrier with a large, richly appointed unit. The construction and features of fifth-wheels are similar to those of travel trailers in the same cost categories.

The Low-Cost Fifth-Wheel (Less than $20,000)

Really more like an inexpensive trailer that uses a hitch to a pickup instead of a trailer-type hitch, these rigs are easier to handle than a similar trailer. They may offer more interior square footage as well. Construction will likely be a combination of steel and wood framing with aluminum siding. Expect interior construction similar to that of the low-cost travel trailers. Some use of fiberglass and insulation may be found in the best of the low-priced fifth-wheels.

Fifth-wheel RVs are often considered more stable to tow than similarly equipped travel trailers. A fifth-wheel mounts on the towing pickup truck much as a semi-trailer connects to a tractor unit.

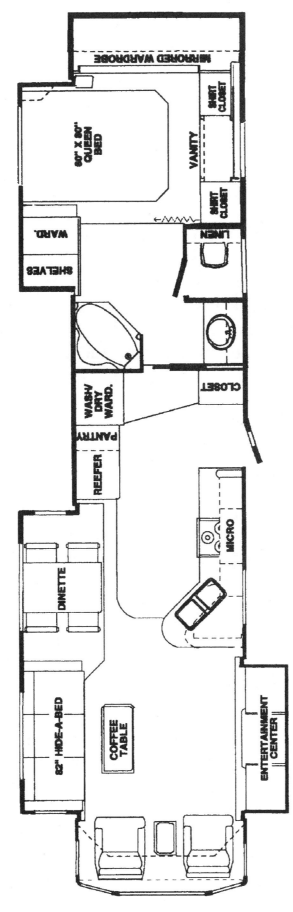

MIRRORED WARDROBE

60" X 80" QUEEN BED

VANITY

SHIRT CLOSET

SHIRT CLOSET

WARD.

SHELVES

LINEN

WASH/ DRY WARD.

PANTRY

REEFER

CLOSET

MICRO

DINETTE

82" HIDE-A-BED

COFFEE TABLE

ENTERTAINMENT CENTER

The Medium-Priced Fifth-Wheel ($20,000 to $45,000)

If you're looking for a fifth-wheel shorter than thirty feet a number of options are available in this price range. As with trailers, longer length at a lower price means fewer amenities and lower-quality construction. Well-constructed, insulated rigs are available within this price range.

The Highliner Fifth-Wheel ($45,000 and Up)

Built more strongly than most houses to take the stress of the road, the finest fifth-wheels are long affairs with slide-out rooms. Most include the amenities of a well-equipped apartment (including washer, dryer, and trash compactor) as well as such self-containment features as a generator with its own fuel supply (separate from that of the tow vehicle) and ample storage. The construction of these quality rigs parallels that of expensive travel trailers and motorhomes.

Fifth-Wheel Advantages

■ Floor plans are spacious in large rigs, since there is a lot of square footage, even without a slide-out section.
■ Like trailers, fifth-wheels have long life spans, since there's no engine or transmission to wear out as with a motorhome.
■ Unhitching the pickup provides transportation to stores and for sightseeing.

Fifth-Wheel Disadvantages

✖ Requires a pickup truck with a powerful engine, if you don't already own one. Some modern pickups with high and narrow beds may not be compatible. We haul our monster with a truck equipped with a turbodiesel engine. You must add the cost of the tow vehicle to the total price of the rig. This often makes fifth-wheels more expensive than comparably equipped motorhomes.

✖ Easier to handle than most travel trailers (at least that's the popular point of view), but still subject to the effect of high winds.

Issues to Consider

- It takes a powerful pickup truck to successfully haul a heavy fifth-wheel unit. It's easier to match the truck to the rig than the other way around.
- Like trailers, fifth-wheels hold their value better than do motorhomes.
- A quality hitch adds about $850 to the purchase price including installation. You may also want to replace the pickup truck's fold-down tailgate with a mesh-type unit that provides less wind resistance. This improves gas mileage and handling in high winds. (Save the original tailgate, in case you should want to sell the truck later.)

Tip: Artistic License

Safety advocates have long worked toward demanding a special license for drivers of RVs. They feel that drivers of such rigs require training and testing similar to operators of large tractor-trailer rigs. Whether such training and licensing is a good idea is up in the air, but at this time no bills have been successfully put in place in any state or at the federal level.

Motorhomes:
The One-Piece Home on Wheels

Ranging in size from modest units less than eighteen feet in length to the units reminiscent of the *Graf Zeppelin,* motorhomes include a drivetrain and living quarters. Available in a broad range of lengths, floor plans, and options, a motorhome is a complete living and traveling environment on wheels. Unlike trailers and fifth-wheels, a motorhome is set up so that the driver shares the same space with passengers in the living space of the coach (all wearing seat belts, please). Together, all members of the party can converse, snack, and otherwise amuse themselves with videos, games, or watching the scenery as the miles tick off.

Complete with drivetrain (engine, transmission, steering, and so forth), motorhomes are considered easier to drive than most trailer rigs. Motorhome prices start in the low five figures and can nearly breach the $1-million mark if built on a full-size bus chassis. Motorhomes range from the short and Spartan to the long and elaborate. They are the quintessential RV — everything from engine to icemaker in one gorgeous box.

Obviously, a drivetrain-equipped unit has significantly more components than a trailer, but owning a trailer doesn't free you of potential mechanical maintenance troubles. Tow vehicles have maintenance requirements similar to those of the drivetrain of a motorhome.

Motorhome Prices

The motorhome price range is much broader than that of towable units. At the low end are units built on a light truck chassis with modest livability features. At the high end, the sky's the limit.

The Low-Priced Motorhome (Less than $50,000)

The least expensive new motorhomes come in two flavors, utilitarian and fancy, but small (short). On such rigs, a generator compartment may be provided, but the generator is optional. You may find well-equipped rigs in this price range, but since length equals room, they may be restricted in interior space, as the operating cabin (the driver's seat) eats into the living area.

Low-end motorhomes offer livability features comparable to those of low-priced travel trailers. The construction varies. On low-end units you may find some wood reinforcing the frame, although unlike trailers, all modern motorhomes have some steel or metal framing. All low-end motorhomes are gas-powered. Expect the units to be built on a basic frame and chassis. Cabinetry will feature plywood and paneling construction, with the occasional laminate for a "real wood" feel.

The Mid-Priced Motorhome ($50,000 to $150,000)

This price range nets you a long, fully equipped, roomy motorhome with fewer compromises as the price moves upward. Personally, we'd recommend a well-constructed and adequately equipped twenty-eight-footer with all metal cage construction and antisway bars over a forty-foot rig that handles badly in the wind because the suspension's design was compromised with the additional length.

Some mid-priced motorhomes are diesel-powered. Some offer rear cameras and monitors as an option. Expect increased use of laminates and real wood and higher-quality appliances, as on better-quality travel trailers.

The Highline Motorhome ($150,000 and Up)

Luxurious: That's the only way to describe the highline motorhomes. These are the rigs of the rich and famous and those lucky enough to have the money. Built to the standards of a bus, they incorporate airbrakes, superior suspension systems, extensive insulation, electronic readouts for every system on the rig (some even offer satellite navigation systems as an option), and a quality diesel engine, usually mounted aft, as on the buses used by the city transit system. Expect such options as rear cameras and monitors for driving safety, leather upholstery and the best fabrics, marble or Corian counters, gold-plated bathroom fixtures, Jacuzzi tubs, security systems, crystal light fixtures, and raised ceilings, as well as slide-out rooms, quality fabrics, and home-style appliances. These rigs can go without hookups for weeks on end. These are houses on wheels and cost as much as if not more than many traditional homes. Naturally, to make an appropriate impression, if you tow a car behind one of these rigs, it should be a Mercedes or a Jaguar.

Motorhome Advantages

■ With proper loading and a quality coach, a motorhome is the easiest rig to drive. Plus, you can access all systems while on the road and even sleep while in motion, although we don't recommend it in case of a panic stop or traffic accident.

■ Upper-line models offer more amenities and luxury than any trailer or fifth-wheel we've encountered so far.

■ This is an all-in-one purchase. There's no worry about incompatibilities between tow vehicle and rig. The generator — if included or added — even shares the rig's on-board fuel.

Motorhome Disadvantages

✖ The "helm" takes up at least eight feet of space that becomes essentially useless when in port. (We kept the cat's litter box in the well of the passenger's compartment when docked.)

✖ Because of the height of the rigs, storage is often a problem with the larger units, especially if your home-based community doesn't allow motorhomes in the street and you live in a home with a standard garage. (This problem plagues the largest travel trailers and fifth-wheels as well.)

✖ Motorhomes can be expensive, depending on the configuration selected. State sales tax and registration fees can be stunning on a highline rig. You may choose to buy in a state where the fees and taxes are low.

✖ There is fast erosion of resale value, as potential buyers consider the condition and wear on the drivetrain of a used unit. A "high-miler" motorhome is a tough sell unless the price is right.

✖ A motorhome requires that you bring a tow vehicle for easy grocery runs, or the complete unhooking of the rig for a trip into town or to see the sights. Alternatives include bicycles and motorbikes.

Issues to Consider

• If the motorhome breaks down, you may be forced to camp

at Motel 6 while the rig is repaired.

- Motorhomes longer than twenty-two feet may be unable to camp in some national parks, and private parks may have limitations on the longest rigs as well. Or there may be a limited number of spaces for long rigs and all of them rented.
- Roomy, extra-wide models (more than ninety-six inches wide) are officially banned in some states, although so far we've never noticed the local highway patrol, tape measure in hand, scrutinizing an extra-wide vehicle. If your plans include extensive in-state camping, check with the highway patrol for local regulations and then choose to abide by or ignore them.

The Classes of Motorhomes

Besides the general issues to consider regarding motorhomes, there are several classes of motorhomes to be aware of during your review of RVing options. After reading this section and visiting an RV lot or two, you'll be able to name these rigs with no more than a glance!

The Class "A" Motorhome

Like the biggest and best-equipped trailers and fifth-wheels, Class A motorhomes are a home away from home for the adventurous weekender and the dedicated full-timer bent on intimate exploration of the continent without seriously compromising the comforts of home.

Class A motorhomes are generally the largest and most expensive type of motorhome (except for bus conversions). The models range in size from about thirteen thousand to thirty thousand pounds gross vehicle weight, from twenty-eight to forty-five feet in overall length, and average from nine to ten feet high. The units come in various widths and some include slide-out rooms. Motorhomes are generally a box on wheels with all the comforts of home inside. They are frequently constructed on custom undercarriages or on a three- to ten-ton truck chassis. It is easy for the passenger to

The best Class A motorhomes, like the one shown here, provide spacious livability and superior stability on the road.

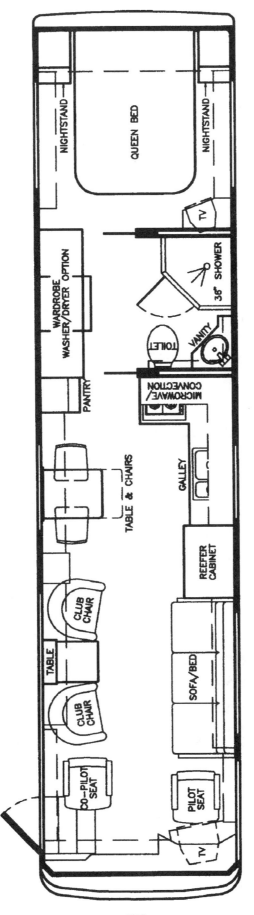

NIGHTSTAND

QUEEN BED

NIGHTSTAND

TV

WARDROBE
WASHER/DRYER OPTION

36" SHOWER

TOILET

VANITY

PANTRY

MICROWAVE/
CONVECTION

TABLE & CHAIRS

GALLEY

CLUB CHAIR

REEFER CABINET

TABLE

SOFA/BED

CLUB CHAIR

CO-PILOT SEAT

PILOT SEAT

TV

55

move from the passenger seat to the back of the coach. The most expensive motorhomes are shaped like buses. In fact, some are actually converted bus designs.

Larger Class A rigs come equipped with a spacious (for an RV) shower/bath, queen-size bed, and a galley that rivals that of a land-based apartment. Dual air-conditioners keep you cool while massive fuel tanks provide a flexible five-hundred-mile range between filling stations. Some big rigs even feature washer and dryer, basement storage, and built-in television monitors with room for a roof-mounted satellite dish. No in-park cable hookup? Look to the stars for entertainment!

Class A Advantages

- A Class A is a true mobile home on wheels. Larger units offer every amenity possible in an RV, including a true queen-sized bed and a bathtub of sorts.
- A quality Class A — one with adequate suspension systems for its size — is the easiest full-size rig to drive as no towing is involved.

Class A Disadvantages

- Because Class A is the most expensive RV format, many buyers will opt for a short model or forgo Class A completely and buy a fifth-wheel or trailer arrangement.
- "Extended" Class As are difficult to drive over bumpy roads and in the mountains. They can be especially problematic on Mexico's back roads as the rear of the coach grinds on the pavement of uneven thoroughfares.
- If you just want to drive around after reaching your destination, you'll need to tow a car or take a bike along for general transportation. Driving and parking the large rigs in town is problematic.

Buses and Bus Conversions —
the Ultimate Class A Motorhome

Some technically Class A motorhomes are called buses or bus conversions. While there are old Greyhounds made over into coaches (and best avoided for the most part), the bus models we're talking about are built as luxurious RVs on a bus chassis (or something similar) and were never intended for public transit. The bus models are the most stable and long-lived RVs on the road. They are also the most expensive.

Should you need a new engine or drivetrain component, better have your pennies saved. But if you want the biggest, most stable, and most custom rig possible, you can buy a bus unit with everything from a center-island cooktop and gas range to a round king-size bed and full-size Jacuzzi spa.

These motorhomes are literally mansions on wheels — although a bit smaller than Tara. Makers include Monaco, Newell, Bluebird, and Marathon. Aside from the price tag, the upside includes more room inside than most couples will know what to do with and an awesome stability that allows safe travel in windy and wet conditions. The tall profile also allows for true "basement storage," since the storage area was built into the chassis to carry luggage.

Bus Advantages

■ These are the best rigs for highway travel and safety. Even though they are either a full-sized bus or close to it, the high-quality suspension and drivetrain make them reasonably easy to handle.

■ There is adequate engine power for towing almost anything while fully loaded.

■ They have beautifully rich interiors with every amenity possible.

■ They have superior security with better locks, window braces, built-in alarms, and even floor-mounted safes for stowing valuables. An anti-intrusion alarm system may be standard.

Bus-style RVs are mansions on wheels (above). The interiors of high-end motorhomes offer opulence as well as functionalism (below).

Bus Disadvantages

✖ The price of the rig is a problem if you aren't ready to invest the mid to high six figures in your rig. Some advice before you buy a used bus to save money: If your state allows it, check the vehicle's history. Some buses have been around the world multiple times. Is that 101,765 on the odometer real or does it reflect turnover at 999,999 miles plus 101,765 miles?

✖ A really big, loaded-down bus eats fuel. While its huge tanks hold enough to creep across a continent, when it's time to tank up, the bill can be scary.

✖ Repair bills for major drivetrain components will knock your socks off! (Imagine a bill for transmission replacement in the five figures!)

✖ Older bus and bus conversion rigs (avoid those with Grateful Dead stickers) may be had for reasonable prices, but when the bill is tallied for neglected maintenance, a promising bargain may become a mechanic's dream and an owner's nightmare.

The Class "C" Motorhome

Class C motorhomes are generally smaller and less expensive than Class A motorhomes. The size typically ranges from ten thousand to eighteen thousand pounds gross vehicle weight, from twenty to thirty-one feet long, and from about nine to ten feet high. Basically, a Class C is any motorhome that has a custom motorhome body mounted on a conventional vehicle chassis. Typically, Class C motorhomes are built on a van-fronted commercial truck chassis. Class C motorhomes can also have pickup truck front ends, or even a Cadillac front end. We once saw a Class C based on a diesel tractor!

In general, Class C motorhomes look like an extended van or truck from the front with a big box for the living quarters extended to the back. The driver compartment is similar to that of a van, with an overhead sleeping or storage area above the driving compartment. The passenger can move from the passenger seat to the back of the unit with slight difficulty getting around the engine hump.

The Class C is intended mainly for weekend warriors making forays to the nearest rural fishing hole, although some people manage to turn well-built units into full-timing rigs. Class C rigs often feature sleeping accommodations in a compartment above the driving cab. They offer larger living accommodations and bathroom dimensions than the micro motorhomes, but nothing on the scale of the largest Class A rigs.

Most Class C floor plans offer ample sleeping accommodations for vacation adventures with a small family or two couples. The rigs accommodate four full-size people easily. Two additional children (for a total of six persons) can be accommodated in convertible facilities on most units. Class C full-timing is limited by storage and weight capacities. However, if you travel light, you can live in a large Class C as easily as a mid-sized Class A. Compare Class C rigs to small Class A rigs before you decide on the best value for your needs. A Class C is often a better overall value — especially if storage and walking space are not priorities for your RVing travels. If a Class C makes more sense pricewise, compare each rig's weight capacity to make sure you're comparing vehicles of equal capacity and strength.

Class Cs are usually easy to drive, although the largest models, when heavily loaded (four adults, provisions, and liquids), are sluggish as the added weight pushes the drivetrain to its limits. (The largest Class Cs may reach thirty-one feet in length and are, in our opinion, grossly overweight and typically unstable when loaded.)

Class C Advantages

■ The Class C is generally easy to drive.
■ The Class C generally costs less than its Class A cousins.
■ Unlike a thirty-two-foot Class A, a small Class C can be parked almost anywhere you want to camp without attracting attention.

Class C Disadvantages

✖ The Class C is easy to overload, as these rigs are built on

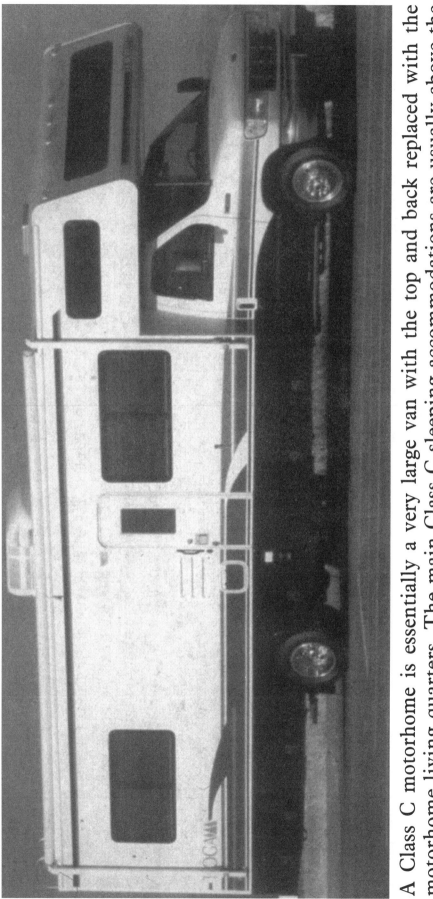

A Class C motorhome is essentially a very large van with the top and back replaced with the motorhome living quarters. The main Class C sleeping accommodations are usually above the driving cab area and in the rear. Some floor plans feature convertible sleeping areas in the dining/sitting area.

modified van or truck chassis.

✖ The longer units often prove unstable on highways.

✖ One of the main sleeping compartments is over the cab. This area can get warm without air-conditioning in the summer. Those with physical disabilities may find climbing into this niche awkward — and thus should look into a longer, rear-bed configuration. A second convertible couch-to-bed is usually available without the climb but must be made up routinely for nighttime/daytime use.

Micro Motorhomes

The original micros, built on a small truck chassis, are a thing of the past. We mention them not because we recommend them (we don't), but because you may encounter micros on the used RV lots. They are tempting for the budget-minded as they're priced very reasonably because they are slow movers. Manufacturers stopped making them because the small truck chassis used for these rigs couldn't handle the weight. These compact RVs are similar to Class C motorhomes but are built on a lightweight truck chassis and are generally smaller (eight to nine feet high and around six thousand to ten thousand pounds gross vehicle weight). The units drive a lot like a passenger van with an extra eight hundred pounds tied down to the roof. Micros offer many of the amenities of their larger cousins, the Class A and Class C motorhomes, but on a much smaller scale.

Some micros feature sleeping arrangements similar to those of the Class C motorhome. Their light weight and reasonable fuel economy make them economical to take on long trips. Further, most micros fit into standard, full-size parking spaces at carports and garages. As with van conversions, their diminutive size brings easy handling and maneuverability as these units lack the height profile of larger rigs. But a small engine weighed down with living quarters means slow acceleration. Micros are especially easy to overload and some, when completely empty of people, provisions, and liquids, are already at or above their rated maximum weights. The federal government has been threatening to clamp down on this problem, and it looks as if most manufacturers have taken notice by moving to Class C configurations on a heavier chassis and van conversions.

Micros are best for two adults who don't mind the intimacy of such a living arrangement. (It helps if you're under five and a half feet tall.) Convertible beds may be assembled in the vehicle to sleep one more than one couple, although this is a very chummy arrangement.

Micro Advantage

■ Small footprint allows the micro to be parked in a space about the size of a van.

Micro Disadvantages

✖ Built on a small pickup truck chassis, these units may be overweight with two adults and a six-pack of Pepsi. Micros are potentially dangerous, with an overloaded suspension and a tall vertical profile for such a small footprint chassis, seriously compromising handling.

✖ Micros are very cramped inside. Cooking in the midget-sized galley may be more work than fun. The bathroom, storage, and living facilities are all on a Lilliputian scale.

✖ For boondock camping, the small tanks and fuel supplies limit the number of days you can survive in the wild without hookups.

✖ Taking showers in those rigs that offer them involves contortions coupled with water conservation.

Van Conversions

To replace the less stable micro models of the past, a growing number of manufacturers offer self-contained motorhomes that begin life as conventional vans. (These are different from Class C and mini motorhomes built on van chassis or truck chassis, as the finished product still looks like a van rather than an RV from the exterior.) Van conversions are the smallest of the fully

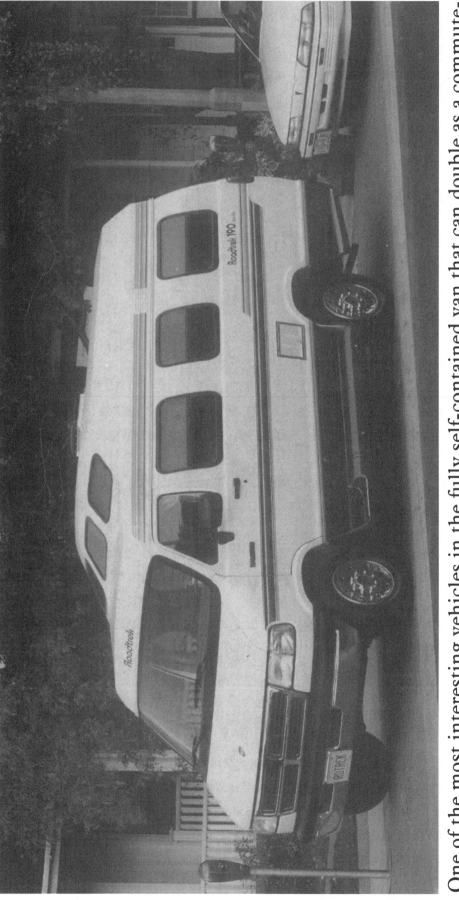

One of the most interesting vehicles in the fully self-contained van that can double as a commute-to-work vehicle or as a weekend abode for the "we're-going-away-for-the-weekend" set. Avoid vans that have been converted by individuals or small companies that do this sort of thing as a side business.

66

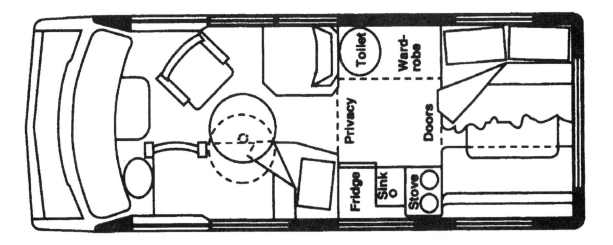

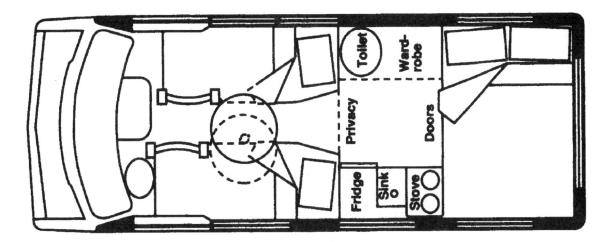

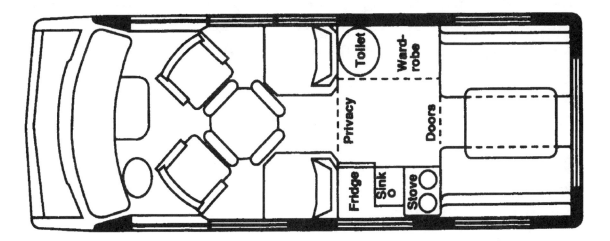

Movies for RVers

RVing is often depicted in the movies as a romantic alternative to real life. Remember the hordes of ragtag RVers who escaped the alien warships in *Independence Day* or the motley group of nuclear survivors in *Mad Max*? Then there are films that feature struggling families residing in travel trailers or custom travel vehicles, including *The Client* and *The Last Starfighter*. Consider these other RV features on your next trip to the video store:

Lost in America: 1985, Albert Brooks, Julie Hagerty. Two burnt-out executives quit their jobs, raid their substantial savings account, and jump in an RV in search of America (or something like that). This parody ends on a downbeat note, but then it *is* a comedy and Julie Hagerty's character's little gaming problem is what ends this on-the-road epic. The RV scenes look like fun, and making that "freedom sandwich" (orange cheese on white bread, naturally) while driving is Albert Brooks's character's idea of *the freedom of the road.*

The Blues Brothers: 1980, John Belushi, Dan Aykroyd. Hardly a zenith in moviemaking, seeing the enraged country-western band pompously sink their RV into the swamp is almost worth the rental price, plus you get to see an orange Ford Pinto station wagon meet its demise on the same ticket!

Harmony Cats: 1980, Kim Coates, Jim Byrnes. A country-western band tours in an RV with "Harmony Cats" prominently painted on both sides. The encapsulated listing pretty much sums up the plot: "A concert violinist sheds his classical training for down-home fiddling with an unlikely country music group." Need we say more? Does have some good interior views of a 1970s Class C motorhome with poorly maintained walnut interior.

Spaceballs: 1987, John Candy, Rick Moranis. Possibly the first real challenge to *Plan Nine from Outer Space* as the worst film of all time. Much of the action takes place in a warp-speed Winnebago. (We assume they keep the O_2 tanks in the much-vaunted basement storage.) It's Mel Brooks's worst effort. On second thought, forget we even mentioned it — even though the Winnebago as a starship was a cute idea.

enclosed, self-contained motorhomes. They are typically constructed on a standard van chassis and offer elevated roof lines. Most have no modifications or only minor modifications to the length or width of the original chassis. Gross vehicle weights are typically in the six thousand to eight thousand range. The typical height of these units ranges from seven to nine feet, with typical lengths of seventeen to twenty-one feet.

The vehicles drive like heavily loaded vans, which is what they are. Although the units may be self-contained, the living areas serve multiple purposes. For example, the dinette area or couch will convert to the bedroom. There has been considerable advancement in van conversion campers since the Volkswagen Westphalia and the Vanigan.

More compact than anything but the smallest micros, a van can serve as both vacation quarters and basic, albeit expensive day-to-day transportation. A robust van-style RV is a home away from home that can be readied for the next trip in the time it takes to fill the gas tank and stock the (small) larder. A van forces you to travel light, as there's nowhere to store anything but a little food and a change of clothes or two.

Van Price Ranges

Comprehensively equipped RV conversions are pricey — mostly in the $35,000-and-up range — as the interior must provide convertible facilities for sleeping, sitting, cooking, dining, and lockdown capability for traveling. The magic of packing a home into such a space requires considerable engineering and manufacturing effort, and the van itself must be modified to withstand the substantial weight of the living quarters and storage tanks.

Van Advantages

■ With such a go-anywhere RV, you can camp on Main Street as well as in a national forest in the Rockies — visit friends and live in their driveway even.

■ This van is more fuel-efficient than its larger cousin, the Class A.

Van Disadvantages

✖ They are expensive for the square footage provided, as makers must ingeniously miniaturize everything while not overloading the vehicle.

✖ They require a fair amount of work on your part, as you must convert the van's interior from sleeping to living/dining quarters and back each day.

✖ Like micros, these rigs are easy to overload. Fortunately, there's little storage, so unless you travel with many bars of gold, this won't be a problem.

✖ All the other disadvantages of the mini motorhomes apply to van conversions.

Issues to Consider

• A van may, in theory, sleep four, but one couple who enjoys each other's company is the normal occupancy limit of such a rig. Even Bob and Carol and Ted and Alice might find the sleeping arrangements too intimate.

• Many models are not self-contained, and they may lack a shower.

• Van depreciation may be significant. Further, you could find a much larger rig for less money, so be sure the van conversion is what you really want and need.

Truck Campers

Truck campers are not really trailers or motorhomes. They have some of the advantages and disadvantages of each. Camper shells installed on pickup truck beds are generally the smallest of the RVs. Campers are attached to the bed of an unmodified pickup truck. Usually the tailgate is removed and the camper unit is clamped to the truck. It is possible to remove the camper from the truck, but this is usually a long task, not something to do in a campground.

Construction of truck campers parallels that of trailers. Low-end

The best modern truck campers offer livability features that rival those of small travel trailers.

campers may have stick-and-staple construction and inexpensive aluminum siding. High-end camper shells may still have wood construction, although some models feature laminates and fiberglass exteriors. The least expensive units lack any self-containment features, such as toilets and showers. The most expensive units offer adequate restroom facilities and quality interiors with good appliances. Some upscale camper shells are fully self-contained, although the living quarters are cramped and the water and fuel capacities are often more limited than those in motorhomes or trailers. As with van conversions, the living area may convert to sleeping area to maximize the space. Obviously, there is no way to get from the driving area to the living area while in transit.

Camper shells offer most of the advantages and disadvantages of van conversions. With the price of the truck included, the total cost of the rig is often similar to that of van conversions with comparable facilities. If you already own the truck, however, a well-designed truck camper unit might be a good option for vacationing couples or very small families who prefer the easy maneuverability and stability of truck campers. If self-containment, live-aboard amenities, and space are your priorities, then a truck camper is probably not an option.

The Custom Rig

Custom rigs are different from customized rigs. Most RV manufacturers allow you to choose floor plans, colors, interior treatments, and options. Some manufacturers will build customized units on standard frames to your specifications. Reputable customizers provide warranties and adhere to industry standards for safety and construction.

There is, however, a unique class of custom rigs that you may encounter in your RV explorations. Legions of do-it-yourself RVers build vehicles of all shapes and sizes. We do not recommend that you consider purchasing a homemade RV, be it a hand-built self-contained van conversion or the Oscar Mayer Weinermobile with a year's worth of free hot dogs. There's almost no way to ensure that you aren't buying someone else's headache or a potential death trap because of inadequate or inappropriate construction.

Almost any vehicle larger than a passenger car can be made into an RV of sorts, and certainly someone, somewhere, has tried it. Custom RVs range from traveling pigsties built in ancient school-buses with cardboard taped over the windows and a wood-burning stove bolted to the floor to million-dollar projects capable of transformation from highway RV to yacht. (We saw the latter in a newspaper clipping posted on the wall of a Las Vegas RV park. We hope the "yacht" portion is more seaworthy than it looks.)

"Yup . . . I Built Her Myself"

Some of these do-it-yourself vehicles are safe and durably constructed by engineers or RV design professionals. Others are built by weekend adventurers or the poorer members of our culture and are full of odd and potentially dangerous mechanical surprises. The truly unique RVs are built by hobbyists, not manufacturers. If you plan to purchase such a beast, we recommend that you and a skilled RV mechanic go over it inch by inch to see exactly what you're getting yourself into. If it means removing panels to check things, with the seller's permission, by all means do it.

Almost anything, mostly bad, can be found in homemade RVs. This may include propane coupling built from garden hose fittings (and yes, unbelievably, we've seen one like this) to fundamental structural flaws that manifest themselves disastrously at 65 mph on the interstates. Be especially careful of any home-brew rig that uses lighter-than-air construction to effect liftoff, especially if it's named *Hindenburg* or the *Akron*.

More Safety in Numbers

Part of the reason for the safety of manufactured RVs is that a number of people are involved in the design, construction, and testing process. Problems can be isolated in prototypes or unmasked during test drives, so you don't have to find them the hard way. Much as flaws are discovered in automotive designs or production techniques, problems inherent in a rig will appear among a number of production units, saving you the trouble of being the sole discoverer. On a commercially built rig such safety problems

73

are remedied through a recall, costing you nothing. But with a backyard-built unit, you have little or no recourse, especially if the seller has hit the road leaving no forwarding address.

Custom Rig Pricing

Anything goes. A converted city bus with a completely hand-crafted/hand-carved wood interior may be priced in the $100,000-plus range even though its mechanical soundness is questionable. A large, brand-new van modified for living might have an asking price of its list plus the seller's "improvements." Pricing is at the discretion of the seller, and you can't fall back onto the values established for like rigs in the *Kelley Blue Book* (explained on page 107) as no comparable vehicle exists.

Custom Rig Advantage

■ Unique vehicles are available for (sometimes) reasonable prices. We saw one that contained a complete jewelry-making facility for a couple who traveled the circuit and sold their wares. Complete with stained-glass windows, casting equipment, and a centrifuge, it wasn't for sale.

Custom Rig Disadvantages

✖ The construction, durability, reliability, and roadworthiness are always suspect in a custom vehicle, even if it started life as a conventional RV. Plan on spending $200 to $500 for a thorough inspection of all aspects of such a rig before purchase.

✖ The rig may require frequent repairs as the ol' schoolbus engine ages or when the driveshaft falls out on Interstate 69 in the snow.

✖ Title and registration may be a problem, especially if the vehicle was reconstructed after an accident. A *really* odd or disheveled rig may not pass muster at borders or with state inspectors and the highway patrol.

✖ Insurance may be equally problematic. What kind of rig is

it? How much is it worth? Is it safe? These simple questions may force even an RV insurance specialist to turn you down. And it's illegal to drive in many states without proof of existing insurance coverage.

Issues to Consider

- Even if it is priced cheap, you may be purchasing a can of worms. Be especially suspicious of a rig that's changed owners numerous times, as there may be a good reason each party has dumped it.
- Such vehicles are difficult to sell unless the construction is slick and elegant. As mentioned, establishing value is impossible. Getting a loan on such a vehicle is equally difficult.
- Look for consistency. An oddball rig with fiberglass so new you can still smell the catalyst, combined with half-bald tires, may be bad news. It's an indicator of someone who works on the rig when feeling "up to it," ignores normal maintenance, and builds things in, shall we say, nontraditional ways. Steer clear.

Other Possibilities

RVers may be confronted with specific RVs not mentioned here, including expandable truck-based rigs, new pop-up designs from which a mighty motorhome grows, and full-sized trailers with slide-outs that compress in height to be parked in the garage. We can't advise you on all of these units, as there are so many. When considering one of them, examine the following:

- Durability: How many summers will this unit survive? How much does new canvas and tenting cost, and will a supplier exist in 2003 that can supply me?
- Quiet: Can I sleep in this rig when it's ninety-five degrees Fahrenheit outside and the drunken neighbors are having a rumba party in the camp nearby? (This could be a problem in any rig!) When setting up the pop-up camper next to a

new Coachman, will I fall asleep listening to the quiet growl of their AC, content in knowing that I don't have their monthly payments?

- Comfort: Is this a sardine can I'm willing to live in for weeks with my family and fellow travelers?
- Mobility: Will the unit safely take me where I want to go if I plan on exploring the wilderness?

Floor Plans and Slide-Out Rooms

If you look at RVs from a few years back, you'll only find a limited range of floor plans and interior views. For example, the standard Class A floor plan put bed in the back, head toward the center, galley amidship, and seating toward the front. Trailers offered more options, but even these layouts were uninspired. Today, however, with the use of new materials, better storage designs, and interior designers with a sense of fabrics and space, a wider range of seating, floor plans, and sleeping arrangements are available.

Even with the new floor plans, however, RVers always long for more interior space. That's why, in nice weather, RVers spread out under the rig's awning (a must-have in our opinion, on any RV). Some newer full-size motorhomes are built on extra-wide chassis (104 inches wide, as opposed to the 96-inch standard). This provides additional room (at an extra cost, of course), but be aware that some states don't allow these extra-wide rigs on the highway. As a further way to add living space to motorhomes, trailers, and fifth-wheels, slide-out rooms (one or many, depending on the size and structure of the rig) have become a popular option in the designs of many RV manufacturers. Slide-out rooms also increase the number of floor-plan options that can be provided in rigs of the same length.

Once in the external position, the slide-out provides additional square footage that makes navigating the interior of the RV more natural. And, unlike an awning, the space created by the slide-out can be used in any weather. If you intend to travel in public parks or set up in urban parks with small parking spaces, the slide-out design may not be for you. Further, the slide-out takes up weight

A slide-out adds significant square footage to the interior of an RV. Not all parks allow them, since the slide-out may extend into the neighbor's outdoor space. You can avoid this problem by not staying in parks that pack you in like sardines.

that you may prefer to use for other amenities.

Other than these limitations, the downside of rigs with slide-out designs is the increased cost and the stability of the rigs when the rooms are out. Leaks are standard problems in inexpensive slide-out designs. There's also the little matter of power draw. Most slide-out rooms are powered to go in and out by batteries. Frequent moves without enough time to charge the batteries may mean a dead vehicle — and a stuck room. In this case, the slide-out must be reeled in with a hand crank or a generator run to recharge the coach batteries or operate the slides.

In this chapter we've presented the various kinds of RVs and the basic advantages and disadvantages of each. There are more things to consider, but you get the idea. Before choosing any RV, make sure it fits your needs, budget, and travel desires. As you've learned in this chapter, the variety of rigs available is both comforting and daunting: Which is right for you? To answer this, you need to decide if you're king of the wilderness or a lord of the flatbush or something in between.

No RV is right for everyone. Your traveling and living plans should dictate the form and format of your RV. No one else's needs are exactly like yours, so consider recommendations with that in mind. But before you make your decision, you should know more about evaluating the rigs and the camping options available to you. After all, it's your ticket to freedom, but you must choose the road to take and the way to get there. Read on. We'll try to help you decide.

Chapter 3

Buying and Selling
Your Dream Rig

RVs are sophisticated machines. In many ways buying an RV is akin to purchasing a home. In fact, your RV purchase will likely be the second-largest personal investment you make, next to the purchase of your home. (Actually, some people spend more on their rigs than they spend on their houses.) Just as you must fully evaluate how the "house" fits your day-to-day living requirements, you must match your RV to your personal needs and lifestyle.

Take the purchase seriously. Do your homework. Consider construction quality, amenities, and market value. Analyze drivability and livability features. Sit in the seats, study the fabric quality, snoop in the cupboards and closets, and look under the bed. Check out the subtleties of construction, such as the finishing of nails, screws, and edges.

If you're considering trailers and fifth-wheels, bring your tow vehicle if you have one. Hook up and test the two pieces running together as a single entity. Is the match made in heaven? Alternatively, ask the dealer to set up the unit with an in-stock tow vehicle. (Never settle on a towed rig without towing it first!) If a motorhome suits your fancy, admire the vista from the captain's "command" chair and study the controls. Drive the beast. Analyze the visibility options (windshield, mirrors, and rear camera/monitor).

Make notes so you remember everything you observe. On test drives, one of us drives while the other takes dictation on the handling, noises, and vibrations. On one motorhome test, a panic stop almost put the unbuckled salesperson through the windshield. (Bet he wore his belt on test drives after ours!)

After the road test, go home and compare notes from other tested rigs. Make your selection carefully. Let the "deal of a lifetime" proposed by a high-pressure salesperson slip through your fingers if necessary. Use patience and persistence to locate the right rig at the right price.

Even after all the checking, research, and driving, part of your RV decision will be emotional — based on the lines of the vehicle, the color of the carpet, and the feel of the rig. But defer the emotion until you've taken all the practical steps we recommend here. The steps will lead you to a good choice, even if the decision is ultimately based on the gut feeling about one unit as opposed to another.

Note

All but the oldest RVs have numerous internal systems such as the water heater, pump, and the mysterious black box that converts campground electricity to charge your rig's twelve-volt batteries. Throughout the book, we call these systems subsystems. They are significant in their importance to day-to-day RV living, but the failure of the water heater is less tactically threatening than the automatic transmission chewing up a couple of gears.

Do Your Homework First

Before considering any RV purchase, arm yourself with information. Good information is better than a good deal when buying an RV. We suggest that you follow these steps when gathering information on RVs and RVing lifestyles:

- **Read the RVing magazines.** Before we buy a unit, we spread a year of back issues of *Motorhome* and *Trailer Life* and lustrous RV brochures all over a table and drool over each new model. We dream of driving a shiny new forty-foot Monaco and contrast it with life in an upscale camper van. There are so many models, options, and floor plans that a visit to a large dealer's lot is a weekend's free entertainment.

(We've provided a list of magazines that review RVs in the General Resources section at the back of this book.) Read the vehicle reviews as well as the features checklists for new rigs. Although the reviewers have their subjective preferences, especially regarding floor plans, you'll have some general guidelines about the things to look at when you're testing rigs for your own needs.

- **Ask the RVIA for information.** The Recreational Vehicle Industry Association (RVIA) has established standards for safety and construction. RVIA members must meet or exceed these standards. The RVIA can provide a list of manufacturer members. Although the RVIA won't recommend specific models, it is a useful clearinghouse. You can also contact the dealers' associations and consumer RV groups listed in the references section of this book to compare their standards and RV reviews.

- **Check out the buyer's guides.** *Trailer Life* and *Woodall's*, among others, produce annual guides that list specifications, floor plans, and accessories for most RV manufacturers. If these aren't available at your local bookstore or RV supplier, we've provided addresses to order a copy direct from the publishers.

- **Visit RV shows.** The RV magazines and RVIA provide lists of RV shows around the country. Go to as many big RV shows as you possibly can. Even if you aren't planning to buy a new rig, you will see many different layouts and design styles in a brief period of time. You'll also see new products and get ideas for different ways to equip your RV. Visit the shows during the slow periods, so you have time to talk to the dealers. You can buy RVs at a show, but we recommend that you wait, at least until the end of the show. Besides, you can't test-drive the RVs at most shows. Some people get caught up in the excitement of RV shows and end up with bad deals on RVs that don't really meet their needs. Don't let this happen to you. If you do buy at a show, make sure you have already done all the homework and inspections we suggest here.

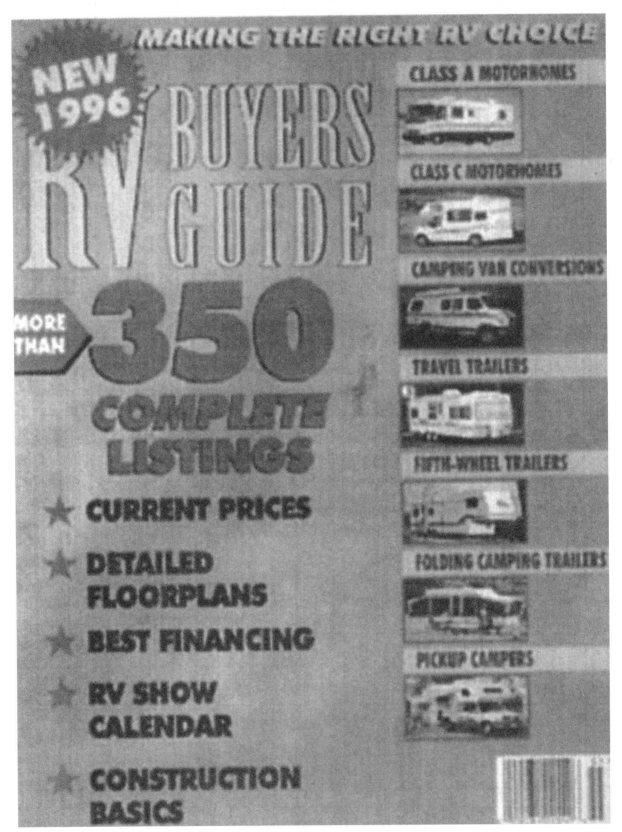

RV buyer's guide. Guides like this one are found in the magazine sections of large bookstores.

- **Talk to experienced RVers.** RV owners are the best source of RVing reviews. Go to some parks and talk to people who own various kinds of rigs. Full-timers will have the most insight into the durability and reliability of various models. Most RVers are obliging about sharing information regarding their experience with models, layouts, and dealers. Some RVers may even let you go inside and look at their rigs. RVers generally love to tell stories, so anticipate having your ear talked off. Occasionally, you'll find someone who knows about a good RV for sale at a reasonable price at the same time.

- **Start the search and review each unit in detail.** Take a few weekends to look at RVs on various lots. Use a checklist like the one provided in this chapter for each RV you consider. Make many copies of the checklist and go through the list thoroughly with each rig you might consider owning. Don't worry about what the salesperson thinks. Just take your time and go through the list. Include comments and impressions about the vehicle and the dealership. When you look at many RVs, you start to forget which one had the nice upholstery, the big awning, the larger generator, the extra storage shelves, and other features. The questionnaire allows you to compare all the rigs based on the same features and helps jog your memory long after you've seen the unit. If you have a camcorder or Polaroid camera, take it along. After you have looked at two or three dozen rigs over a few weekends, the Polaroid pictures or videotape can refresh your memory.

- **Drive the units you are most interested in owning.** Many people buy RVs on the basis of interior livability alone. Don't do it. You'll have to drive your unit as well as live in it. Check out the handling, visibility, brakes, and other items. Drive it through some city streets and on the highway. If you don't feel comfortable driving a large unit, have the dealer give you some lessons in a parking lot before you hit the road (and read Chapter 12 of this book).

Getting Ready to Buy

Motorhome, fifth-wheel, or trailer? Slide-out, extra-wide, twenty-footer, or forty-footer? Washer and dryer, icemaker, and trash compactor? Decisions, decisions. What about the floor plan and the color scheme? After doing your homework, you should be armed with answers to these questions. At this point, you're getting ready to buy and you can start the purchase cycle. Here are the general steps we recommend before you start talking about the purchase of specific vehicles:

- **Know your budget.** After reviewing all the possibilities, match two or three types of units to your budget. You should know what you can afford and what you want before you narrow your RV choices. Consider not only the cost of the unit, but the operating expenses, insurance, annual registration fees, and maintenance costs.

- **Know how you intend to use the RV.** If you plan on extended trips into extreme environments, you want a unit that has high road clearance so it doesn't drag its tail on rocky roads. It should also firmly store supplies, food, and lock-down cooking ware in cabinets designed for rough travel. If extreme temperatures are involved, the unit must be insulated. A shorter rig works best in the wilderness as it's easier to drive on mountain roads. The rig's interior should be ready for the dirt from the woods too. Look for easy-to-clean surfaces and dirt-resistant fabrics. If your adventures feature resorts and paved RV parks, a longer and more luxurious RV will better suit your lifestyle. You'll have more interior space, additional amenities, and room for extra passengers. More space makes RV living easier, especially when several people travel together for extended periods.

- **Know your personal priorities for livability.** Be able to answer questions like: Do you need more living space or more sleeping quarters? Do you prefer livability over handling? Do you want a front, eat-in kitchen floor plan or a midrig galley with a fold-out table? Know exactly what you want and why.

Then, go back and see the units you think you like again. You want the most solid, well-designed, well-built structure that fits your budget and your needs. If you're planning on full-timing, you want a rig that you can really live in, not just exist in. If you're a weekender or want a rig for yearly vacations, your needs for self-containment are different and you may get by with a smaller and less expensive rig.

- **Consider the long-term value of the rig.** In general, "towables" hold more of their original value than motorhomes because drivetrain wear and mileage are not a concern. Aside from the internal systems, about all that can fail on a towed vehicle is related to its wheels, brakes, and hitching system. Structural weakness can also be a problem, but that's true of all homes on wheels, not just trailers. Look at the track record of the manufacturer and the resale record for similar models from the past. This will give you a pretty good idea of the life span and value you can expect to maintain over the life of your rig.

- **Identify sellers of your favorite models.** Follow the guidelines for choosing a dealer that we provide later in this chapter. However, don't compromise on what you want if there isn't a local dealer. Go out of state if you must, even though we generally advise using a local dealer if you can. If you're looking for used, peruse the RV magazines and the *RV Trader* if it is distributed in your area, or get on the World Wide Web and search the classified sections in the RVing sites.

- **Line up financing and unload your existing rig first.** With financing in place, you'll enjoy better negotiating leverage with the dealers. (Check out Chapter 4 for more information on financing.)

- **Choose the right seller and make your purchase at the right price.** With knowledge in hand and persistence, you can visit the most usurious lot and come away with a good deal or at least avoid those "specials" that aren't so special.

- **Follow the additional guidelines in this book.** In the

following pages and in subsequent chapters we provide information on selecting dealers, negotiating the sale, checking out the mechanical condition of the rig, and evaluating the features of an RV. Read the book and following guidelines before you start the negotiations for purchase.

New or Used?

One of the first things you'll have to decide is whether you want a new or a used unit. Should you spend more to get exactly what you want or purchase a used rig and get more for your money? And if used seems okay, then how used? A one-year-old motorhome or a tired but cheap fifth-wheel with ten years of full-timing on it? The new versus used decision is a tough one. Look at both new and used rigs before making a decision to go either way. That will help you decide whether pristine is more important than price.

Going new *is* expensive. Because some people have the funds to buy and sell a new rig every few years there is a steady stream of almost-new vehicles placed into the used RV channels. A well-maintained used unit may be almost as good as a new one, especially as your first rig. Used motorhomes are often a better deal than a new coach. A two-year-old motorhome may cost 40 percent less than new. A similar fifth-wheel may be 25 to 35 percent less. On the downside, buying used forces you into the previous owner's decisions in regard to the floor plan, colors, and accommodations. But, with enough shopping — out of state if necessary — you may still find the perfect rig for significantly less money than a new unit with comparable features.

Still, there are decided advantages to buying new. As the RV industry enters the twenty-first century, manufacturers have learned how to build better, safer products overall. If you own an older rig, you'll be amazed at the improvements in construction, amenities, and fabrics. Colors are lighter and brighter. Appliances are more functional. And most units incorporate entertainment technology into the base design. (No more television/VCR on the floor or table.) Here are some other advantages of new rigs:

Tip: Pass on These Used Rigs

When buying used, avoid purchasing a rig that hasn't been used for a long period of time. When an RV is parked, especially if the RV is unprotected against the elements, rubber seals dry out, sun bleaches paint and interiors, and rust may occur in any and all systems, including the engine.

Avoid former rental rigs unless the warranty is extensive. RVs rented out frequently may receive consummate care from the rental agency, but once out of sight, rough treatment by inexperienced or even abusive users is not uncommon. Thus, you don't really know how the RV has been maintained.

- Improvements to the suspension, braking systems, and cooling systems.
- Better fuel economy on most units.
- Improved construction making for a lighter but sturdier vehicle.
- Energy efficient appliances.
- Improved safety features, such as better wiring, smoke detectors, security systems, and air bags.

For these reasons, the choice between new and used is not always easy. In most cases it's the pocketbook that drives the desire for one over the other.

Tip: It Looks So Big Inside!

When studying print ads and brochures, you may be impressed with rigs that look bigger than a house. Consider the way ads showing automobile interiors transform a Geo Metro into something resembling a Mercedes-Benz. RV makers use the same kind of ploys. While some rigs with slide-outs are quite roomy, no RV interior photo is realistic unless shot by a seller who is an amateur photographer equipped with a Polaroid. Instead, a wide-angle lens is used that artificially inflates the interior shots. The actual rig won't look that big when you're inside.

Choosing a Dealer

Most RVers purchase their rigs, new and used, from RV dealers. Obviously, Rocket Ronald's Recreational Rigs, or any RV dealer you find in the phone book, can sell you a new or used RV in the blink of an eye. They may even have a great selection and free hot dogs on Sundays. However, before choosing an RV from a dealer, here are some questions to ask:

- How long has the dealer been in business? You want to avoid the companies that go in and out of business with the RVing seasons. Choose a dealer with adequate inventory on the lot and a track record.
- Is the dealer a member of the Recreational Vehicle Dealers Association (RVDA) and Chamber of Commerce? These associations will provide information about the length of time the dealer has been in business.
- What do other RVers say about the dealer? You can get information on dealers from members of local RV clubs and manufacturers' RV clubs. Almost every manufacturer has RV clubs; the members should be able to tell you about the dealers they have used successfully (and not so).
- Are there any Better Business Bureau complaints filed against the dealer? A lack of complaints is no guarantee that the dealer is good, but a large number of complaints is pretty good evidence that something may be awry.
- Are the service department and maintenance facilities comprehensive? Meet the service manager. Make sure the company has expertise in all aspects of RV maintenance and repair, including not only the mechanics, but the plumbing, electrical, and HVAC systems. Check that the parts department maintains adequate inventory for your particular model.
- How does the dealer prepare the rigs before delivery? Good dealers should be willing to tell you exactly how they check and prepare every item in the rig. They should be willing to walk you through the inspections and operations of all items. In addition, they should provide instruction on driving, towing, hitching, and any other technical requirements to safely operate your rig. Some dealers also offer seminars and training

sessions to improve your skills and enhance your enjoyment of the RV.

Beyond the Dealers

Not all the best deals on RVs are to be found at dealers' lots or RV shows, even if you do your homework to find a good company. If you're willing to bargain and spend some time looking around for a rig, here are some alternatives to dealers to consider for your RV quest:

- **Buy factory-direct.** Not all manufacturers will sell directly to the public, because they don't want to alienate their dealers, but some do and provide a substantial discount. With a full warranty, which will be honored at any dealer that handles the brand and its subsystems, this shaves thousands off the price of an expensive rig.

- **Purchase from the bankruptcy court or the bank.** RV lots open like mushrooms after rain and close almost as quickly, especially in the South and Southwest. Existing inventory is auctioned off. Be careful, as in frenzied bidding you may pay more for a unit than it's worth. Such inventory may be physically damaged, and the maker won't cover an engine run without oil and ruined. Check the odometer too. In some states it's possible to fudge the paperwork and sell a low-mileage used rig as new, depending on the title transfer process, if there ever was one. The people handling the auction may not have correct information. That puts the burden on you to carefully evaluate what you're purchasing.

- **Consider private sellers when looking for used RVs.** When shopping "used," don't limit yourself to RV lots. Hit the newspaper and RV magazine classified ads (and the World Wide Web sites for RVers). Look for a copy of the *RV Trader*, available at most convenience stores. Without the dealer's markup, a sensible seller can save you thousands over the same rig on a sales lot. We found nearly $9,000 difference on a fifth-wheel priced on a lot compared to a nearly identical unit being sold privately. Guess which one we bought?

- **Look into estate auctions and repossessions.** Many good deals can be had if you're willing to search the auction announcements. You can also contact banks and financing firms and let them know you're interested in buying a quality repossessed RV.

We have bought rigs from both private parties and dealers. This gives us the largest number of options and we see rigs and brands we never knew existed, even if we ultimately don't buy them. As you would expect, you'll find more used Winnebago and Fleetwood products — both very popular manufacturers — than those built by smaller (but equally reputable) companies. If you're not sure about a manufacturer, contact the RVing associations listed in the General Resources at the back of the book for information.

An Amazing RV . . .

The Advanced Vehicle Design Lab (or something like that) built the unique GMC motorhome. These units are decades old, but their stunning design and strong construction make them one of the most popular used vehicles, even though with, by now, well-worn fixtures they can be very expensive to keep up. Look for them on the used lot. Then step back and think about how such a contemporary vehicle was designed in the 1960s and still looks more modern than today's best motorhomes.

Check Out Everything Before You Buy

Before you pay for any RV, new or used, be it motorhome, trailer, or camper, check it out from front to back. Modern recreational vehicles are generally better constructed than older units as manufacturing has embraced new technologies. Manufacturers have learned from the multitude of mistakes in the past. Really old hulks — we jokingly call them *toaster ovens* because of their "fabulous sixties" designs — may be literally falling apart at the seams, especially those that have traveled the distance from the Earth to the Moon and back.

We take you step by step through the evaluation of the mechanical operations of a rig in Chapter 6 and the drivetrain options in Chapter 7. We then describe the subsystems of RVs, including power, water, cooling, and heating, in Chapter 8. Check out the operation and status of all these systems. Have an RV mechanic perform the evaluation for you if you don't feel confident enough to do it on your own. Better yet, do both to assure that nothing gets missed. Most RV shops will check out a used rig free or for a very reasonable price, especially if they think they'll be getting your maintenance business after the purchase

New Rigs, New Bugs

Problems are not limited to used rigs. It's just as important to inspect a new rig before delivery as a used one. Even that shiny new fifth-wheel or highline motorhome just off the lot may have problems that need ironing out before taking a long trip. Follow our steps for the wet test in Chapter 12 before embarking on your first trip. Anything from uncooperative blinds to a water heater that won't heat to a slide-out room that doesn't slide may need to be addressed under warranty. Yes, the new rig will be under warranty — but it's still no fun to find out about the plumbing that backs up into the rig, even if the repair will be covered by the manufacturer.

The Inspection

Every RV, be it self-propelled (motorhome) or towable (trailer or fifth-wheel), has a number of internal and external systems that you must check. Inspect your new rig just as you would a used one before closing the sale. It helps to have a knowledgeable and cooperative seller. In fact, a dealer or seller who won't allow you to check these systems may have something to hide. Pass and let him see you getting ready to go on to the next classified ad or dealer. This may effect a sudden change of heart.

A physical inspection should always precede the test drive. Who knows, you might find enough problems to rule out the necessity of a driving test because the unit is so compromised you wouldn't want it anyway. The inspection should be conducted on a cool, bright day, with ground dry enough that squirming under the vehicle doesn't turn into a mud bath. We prefer checking under a vehicle while it's parked on asphalt or concrete, because leaks are easier to see, and there's no risk of its sinking into the mud with you underneath it. Before any physical inspection, the RV should be blocked effectively so there's no way it can roll. Brakes are not enough. If you need to jack it up, this should only be done on solid, level ground.

Tip: Keeping Your Mental Transmission in Overdrive!

We can't tell you *everything* about buying and owning a rig. You, *yes you,* must also use your knowledge and cross-checking of facts to make sure you're buying the right rig at the right price. There are turkey rigs out there, most of which are still a lot of fun, but everyone wants to get his money's worth be it through purchase or a no-strings three-day rental. Be concerned when a salesperson or seller tells you about how a unit incorporates "exciting new technology" or that a rig is $5,000 more expensive because it was "custom built for a little old lady who only went camping on Sundays." (We'll spare you the range of stories you'll hear.)

Chances are you'll meet a fifty-fifty mix of professional salespeople and confidence artists. In many instances a line of bull is totally innocent, other times it is just bull. That's why you need to take time before you buy to check out everything on the unit, period.

Checking Out the New Rig
Before Taking Possession

When taking possession of a new rig, always check it carefully for damage that occurred in transit, missing options, or accidental substitution of interior floor plans, incorrect drivetrain, and even mismatched carpet color. Rarely is there a problem; however, if a mistake is made that can't be easily rectified but is one that you can live with, you can ask for a discount. Don't, however, accept a gas engine when you paid for a Detroit Diesel! *Inspections should be done only in bright daylight — never at night!*

Walk the exterior of the vehicle looking for mismatched paint or panels that don't fit indicating damage in transport.

⇓

Look under the rig for loose wires and drooping components. Chances are, there won't be any.

⇓

Enter the rig, sniffing carefully for mildew. That telltale odor indicates a leak. Do not accept the vehicle until you have proof of repair.

⇓

Verify that all options are installed and working. Checking your list against the sticker is a useful exercise. Verify model number to ensure that upgrades are correct.

⇓

Run each system individually. Ask the dealer to provide adequate fuel, water, and propane. Then test *everything*.

⇓

Drive the vehicle, listening for knocks, rattles, screeches, and other noises. Take it on the freeway for a thorough test while judging handling and noise.

⇓

Check under the vehicle for leaks after the road test.

Getting Ready

Before starting the inspection, you need a partner — *and not the seller* — to help you through the process. It helps greatly if this is someone familiar with RVs and camping. We once paid an RV saleswoman $100 and also bought her lunch to have her assist with the process on a day when Sunny absolutely could not take time away from a teaching assignment.

In retrospect, it was money well spent. She found problems that even as experienced RVers we wouldn't have noticed. Her analysis drove the price down to a reasonable level. Her logical arguments based on years of experience were impossible for the seller to rebuff. So $100 plus a lunch with a fun lady cost us about $145 (with tip), and it saved us more than $2,500 in repairs and must-do upgrades!

Don't Wear the Tux

Dress down for inspection day because you may get greasy or worse. Kim has an old flight mechanic's jumpsuit that looks as if it first saw action in World War II. (It looks old enough to have crossed the Delaware with George Washington, but flight suits were rare before the invention of aircraft. Maybe the ballooning Montgolfier brothers?) On its breast is the name "Kerk" and a partially torn patch from a long-disbanded air squadron. Purchased for change at a garage sale, and hued in an unsightly dark blue-green, it adds an air of formality to the proceedings. For a dirty, greasy inspection under a rig, it's perfect.

Bring at least one bright flashlight with fresh alkaline batteries and a pile of rags for wiping greasy couplings (and hands) following your inspection. Bring also a pair of latex kitchen-cleaning gloves for inspecting the gray (bath and dishwashing) water and black (sewage) water systems.

Show Those Pearly Whites

Try to keep it as friendly as possible during the inspection, although you should check *everything.* While an unscrupulous seller or dealer may have reasons for keeping you away from the more, um, sensitive parts of a vehicle, some may simply take offense that you don't trust them, or complain that your inept "inspection" may cause damage. Try to keep that toothy smile in place even while crawling under the vehicle looking for leaks.

Ask for Maintenance Records

Verify that the mileage and the wear seem plausible. We've seen rigs with eight thousand miles on the odometer that look inside as if a family with six kids lived in them for years. And that may be exactly the situation. People who don't keep up the interior probably don't change the oil frequently enough either. Inspect the exterior for apparent damage and have a mechanic inspect the wheels as well as the braking system.

Check Everything

We provide guidelines in Chapter 6.

Tip: Does It Need Love or Money or Too Much of Each?

When shopping used, you will face an unenviable quandary when scouting multiple rigs. Almost any used rig will need love: cleaning, minor repairs, and interior updating. If the price is right, buy it. But if the unit needs extensive repair, retrofitting, or rebuilding, ask yourself, "Why is this vehicle in such pathetic shape?" Then get a *written* estimate for fixing it and making it safe and suitable for your needs. *Then decide whether it's worth it or not.* Keep in mind that not all problems will manifest themselves during an inspection. Who knows what lurks under that hard-to-start V-8's greasy exterior or in a trailer that constantly smells of leaking propane?

Checking Out the Used Rig

Purchasing a used RV takes time and patience. You need to identify any problems and delicately assist the seller in getting a grip on the market realities of selling the rig.

Walk the perimeter of the vehicle looking for mismatched paint or panels that don't fit, indicating damage. Look for suspiciously new paneling or wallpaper inside too.

⇓

Look under the rig for loose wires and drooping components. Look also for leaks as explained in Chapter 6.

⇓

Enter the rig, sniffing carefully for mildew. That telltale sign indicates a leak. Study all wall panels for stains and warpage for the same reason.

⇓

Test every system from water pump to converter operation. Go over *everything* with fuel and fluids in place. Test that all fold up/down tables and couches work.

⇓

Drive the rig. Look for loose steering, weak brakes, untoward noises, bumpy handling, and inoperative gauges or a non-working cruise control.

⇓

Check for "post-drive" leaks under the coach. Question the seller thoroughly about problems encountered.

⇓

Have the rig inspected mechanically and use Camping World (or similar) inspection of internal functions.

⇓

Finalize the price (work the seller down to cover repairs and meet market realities if necessary). Inspect the title paperwork. Does the mileage match? Is the vehicle reconstructed? (If so, pass!)

⇓

Make the purchase, acquire clear title, and register the vehicle. Get the owner's sign-off on the registration notarized if required in your state.*

---

* Your motorhome purchase is subject to smog control laws in most states. If the gas-powered engine/exhaust systems have been modified, have it "smogged" *before purchase even though you'll have to do it again after purchase.* Smog control system modifications are illegal and can be expensive to rectify.

Tip: Dawn-of-Time Motorhomes

Really old motorhomes may have engines that demand leaded gas. They'll run on unleaded, but ping and struggle up hills. If you're broke enough to buy one, get a fuel additive for older engines at an automotive parts store. When the top half of the engine is finally rebuilt, modern, hardened valves will eliminate this problem.

Around the World Eighty Times

Note that mileage is not necessarily a reason to reject a rig. Many high-mile motorhomes are still a good deal. If the overall condition is good, the interior is livable, and an RV mechanic gives the unit a thumbs-up (after a thorough inspection), a quality coach may last for twenty years or more without major problems. Have a body shop inspect the chassis and construction for sagging while you're at it. Yes, you may have to fix a few things, but many RVers are also scrupulous mechanics who really look after their rigs.

Establish the Livability Index

Rigs that check out mechanically also need to meet lifestyle criteria. You're buying a place to live as well as a vehicle to drive. Thus, you need to understand the space and livability features of each rig. Look at a lot of floor plans on similar-size rigs before you decide what's best for you.

Check out the bathroom on each rig by pretending you're actually using it. Consider cleaning the bathroom — does it seem easy or difficult? Stand at the sink and run the water. Try to see in the mirrors. Sit on the toilet. Stand in the shower. Where will you put toiletries and grooming supplies? Now, consider ventilation. Some rigs offer split baths that offer more flexibility for multiple travelers. Others offer tub and shower units that provide more general space for bathing. Make sure you get a bathroom you'll feel comfortable using. Some prefer smaller bathrooms for easier cleaning. Others prefer larger spaces for more privacy. There's no right or wrong — only individual preferences. Get what you want.

Check the galley area in each rig as well. Pretend, just as you did with the bathroom. How many burners? Is there any counter space? Are the countertop materials durable, lightweight, and easy to clean? What about storage and accessibility? Will the refrigerator actually hold anything useful? Can you reach the microwave? Is there any dining space? Galley arrangements vary considerably. Again, get the features that you want.

While you're at it, check out sleeping arrangements, general storage, fabrics, colors, and general ambiance. Also consider the traffic flow through the rig. For example, some people object to front and rear galley designs because they mean hauling trash and food through the rig to the side door. Others like the arrangement because of the open cooking area and increased counter lengths of a front or rear cooking area. Some don't like the galleys in the rear of trailers because the contents move around more in the rear in some rigs. For every floor plan, you'll find multiple opinions. What's right for us may not be right for you. That's why manufacturers offer options on the living arrangements, and that's why you have to decide for yourself.

Driving Miss Daisy

After the physical inspection, it's time for the drive. Again, we provide lists of things to look for in Chapter 6 and driving instructions in Chapter 12. A unit that won't start, for example, may need as little as a fresh battery, or as much as a new engine. Don't buy such a beast. If a new battery were all that were needed, the owner would have already done it. Assume the worst and move on to the next rig, rather than risking thousands of dollars for a new drivetrain or other expensive repair. Listen for noises on the test drive. Write them down so you don't forget to ask the mechanic about them later.

If it's a towable RV, the test drive is best done with the vehicle that will actually be used to haul the trailer. But, unless you're buying the tow vehicle as part of the package (common) or happen to have a vehicle with a reasonably compatible hitch, such a test is difficult or impossible. We recommend buying the tow vehicle before the trailer (or at the same time). Fortunately, there's far less potential for serious mechanical failure in a trailer than a motorhome. But matching the tow vehicle to the trailer requires expertise and experience. If you don't know how to check the hitch weight and balance, have a mechanic do it for you. Pushing the limits of a tow vehicle by choosing the wrong trailer can cost major repair money. Don't expect that the average car or truck salesperson knows anything about towing. Go to an RV shop or RV dealer to get the real scoop on towing capacities, hitches, and performance of the tow vehicle in tandem with the trailer. Bring someone with experience to check out the handling.

Accidents Will Happen

Never opt for a "fixer-upper" when choosing an RV. RVs cannot be rebuilt like houses. A unit that has been poorly maintained is not worth your time or money. If the vehicle has obviously been in a collision, stay away. Even small accidents can cause fuel tank ruptures. We've seen more than one rig burned to the ground after only a minor accident. (Alarmed? Don't be. Just be careful.)

If there's any evidence that an RV has had anything but a "fender-bender" well documented with photos, insurance records, and body shop estimates, pass on it automatically. Otherwise, there's no way of knowing whether the unit was lightly sideswiped by a little old lady on her way to church on Sunday or the top edge was sheered away by a low-lying bridge.

Yes, it's true that almost any vehicle can be made roadworthy with quality repairs, but you have no way of fully grasping the complete nature of the damage or whether the repair crew cosmetically covered the wrecked portions, kludged the rebuild of the damaged area, or compromised significant structural members. The current seller or owner may not tell you the truth or may not know anything about a fix handled one, two, or three owners ago. For this reason, tap for Bondo, the filler used in damaged bodies, under which *anything* could be (it sounds *very* solid), study structural angles, and rely on the expert opinion of a professional body shop before you buy the rig.

Rule of the Road

The longer you plan to live in or use the vehicle, the more consideration must be put into its selection. Just as in choosing an apartment or house, little things you may overlook during a quick inspection may drive you nuts in the long run. For example, we once borrowed an elderly trailer with a main "dining table" that folded down between two permanently mounted benches. The problem? Not enough clearance to fit two adults comfortably in the chairs with the table in place. Good way to stay on a diet, though.

The Art of The Deal

Now that you think you've found the right rig and have inspected it thoroughly, you want to buy the unit *at the right price*. We don't want you to be turned off by what we have to say in this chapter on sellers. The game is the same as that played when buying a new or used car — only the numbers have more zeros after them. Out in Phoenix, Arizona — RV central — there's a dealer who proclaims "No bull!" in its ads. And there's the more realistic competitor's ad that maintains, "Well — just a little bull."

Yes, it's true. We aren't fully trusting of people selling recreational vehicles, just as we aren't trusting of all car dealers. Our advice? Avoid dealers who bad-mouth other dealers, offer absurd trade-in allowances, ask you to fill out credit applications before you drive a rig, or fail to produce title on used units.

We regret to report mixed results with RV sellers of all types — be it the brazen salesperson with a plaid sports coat and white patent leather shoes or a private party who meets you with the rig in a parking lot so you don't know where he lives (if he actually lives anywhere). While some salespeople are highly ethical and knowledgeable, some simply aren't. You must be careful, just as you would be when shopping for a car. Many RV salespeople actually get started on used car lots, and sometimes you can uncover their origins by the glad-handing approach and that toothy crocodile smile. You must establish the credibility of your salesperson, the dealership, and the deal to avoid getting, well, taken for a ride. For that reason, unless you have your heart set on one model or line of new RVs, you may find yourself spending more time shopping for a reliable dealer than for the actual vehicle.

Private sellers aren't necessarily honest either. You must read the tea leaves carefully to ensure that you are paying the right price for the rig that's right for you. Again, take your time and don't be pushed into a sale, even when the seller gives you the infamous "I've got another party who wants it" line. You have almost no recourse against a private seller who puts fifty-weight oil in the engine to keep it from blowing blue smoke on a test drive. At least with a dealer you can use the Better Business Bureau's Autoline program if the rig turns out to be lemon yellow.

Big-Ticket Sales

RVs are expensive purchases that usually take a long time to get from "Can I help you" to "Enjoy your new rig!" The process between is called the *sales cycle,* and it takes a special kind of salesperson to stick with the process and ultimately "close" you. That's why you'll get reminder cards from the dealership, phone calls on hot deals, and even birthday cards from dealers you talk to. We even had an owner's wife phone and literally beg us to take on an expensive rig that we had previewed but had no interest in. That was after seven or eight calls from the salesperson and his sales manager. You may even be encouraged to try a unit for a weekend — after all, a few more miles on the odometer won't hurt, assuming your insurance is up to date and the dealer has every indication that you're a qualified buyer. Look for sales-people who are attentive, but not cloying. Too many calls may mean too little business — a bad sign. Of course, Sunny once received a bouquet of roses *after* purchasing a rig — that was a nice touch, and since the gift was after the sale, we simply enjoyed the flowers and appreciated the gesture of goodwill.

Tip: Same Company, Different Brand

Visiting a large RV dealership may impress you with the number of choices of what appear to be several different brands. They may indeed be made by several manufacturers, or you may be seeing a single company's various product lines sold under different names. Many manufacturers make not only a number of models, but also several "brands." Fleetwood — one of the largest American makers of motorhomes, trailers, and fifth-wheels — sells its products under several names. Each brand represents a price range, but they all come from the same company. Fleetwood's popular Bounder line of motorhomes is list-priced from $55,600 for the large twenty-eight-foot, nine-inch model to $71,500 for a thirty-eight-foot, ten-inch veritable "road whale." Bounders include more options than we have room to list here.

Fleetwood also builds the Southwind, Pace Arrow, Flair, American Dream, and several other lines of motorhomes in addition to trailers. Each line has its own pricing, and you would expect to pay more for a thirty-foot Pace Arrow with few options than a Bounder of the same length fully equipped. Of course, the variation between these two lines of coaches is deeper than whether there's a rear television cam for backing and monitoring a towed vehicle. Differences in the quality of fabric, carpet, cabinets, fixtures, and, most important, construction and mechanics are factored into the price. Yes, it's all very confusing.

"Such a Deal!"

Novice or expert RVers can be taken advantage of when purchasing a rig. Without comparison shopping you could pay 25 percent too much or pick yourself a fresh lemon. Could you afford to pay 25 percent too much for a house? Then you shouldn't pay too much for an RV either. That's why we've included a real-life experience of our own from which you can judge or at least forgive the flavor of other comments made in this section. Read on.

Tip: Not Sure Whom You're Dealing With?

You can learn a lot about your salesperson on an RV lot by casually asking what he used to do before joining Dipstick Dick's Deep Discount Drive-Off Deals. Your salesperson may be fully credible, highly experienced, and, most important, own and enjoy an RV of his own. Or he may be a weekend seller moonlighting to pay the rent, with little experience (or ethics). A salesperson with an inexperienced or inappropriate background or one who is vague about what would appear on his resume should be avoided. Chances are the person won't be working at the dealer the next time you visit. If you have a problem and need a helping hand inside the company, you'll have to go elsewhere.

Getting Taken for a Ride

Our initial inexperience in RVing almost cost us $15,000 of our modest nest egg gained from selling everything we owned, worked for, and cashed out. When we decided to try full-timing for the first time, an RV dealer, based in the San Diego area (and still in business, unfortunately), almost talked us into a used Class C. It was one of the first ones we'd seen. We had no experience evaluating RVs. The rig, a well-used, ten-year-old, twenty-foot Winnebago with tacky plastic slipcovers over the seats, was priced at $30,000, *"but only if we bought today."*

"Special sale, good deal, perfect shape." The works were thrown at us by the salesperson and his boss. They skipped the "smell that air of newness" line. But, if we'd given them more time, such a claim would certainly have been forthcoming. Barely escaping alive "to think about it over lunch," we learned the retail book value of that run-down rig was (barely) $14,500. We could have bought two of the same model with change left over for what this dealer demanded as a supposed special price. In this unit's condition, $10,000 would have been more realistic. We could have bought three of the things!

Tip: Add-Ons

Most ludicrous charges, such as dealer prep and extra mark-ups, can be negated when buying new, but what about an add-on you need to finance that the dealer doesn't sell or charges in excess of market pricing for? Get the dealer to add the amount to the cost of the rig, with the understanding that he will cut you a check upon purchase. You then buy the option from whomever you choose after shopping for the best price.

That's why we urge caution at the dealership, no matter how highly recommended the dealer is or how large a discount is available. Be especially wary if you hear the ludicrous line, "That price is good only if you buy now."

Choose the Salesperson Too

RV dealerships function much like automobile dealers. In fact, some are auto sellers with a side lot for their recreational vehicle concern. Most sell new and used rigs and may handle RVs owned by private parties on a consignment arrangement (explained later). Even good dealerships may have a few sales pigeons to steer clear of — so choose your salesperson as carefully as you choose the company. As we've already mentioned, knowledge is the most important aspect of choosing both coach and seller.

You may be inclined to choose a salesperson based on his ability to handle your transaction because of its complexity rather than because of the dealer's selection of rigs and reputation for service. Don't do it. If you do require financing or want to trade in the ol' 1972 trailer that made it to Alaska and back thirty-five times, you give the salesperson an opportunity to control you and structure the transaction as he hides some of the cost and builds it into the purchase price or financing scheme. (Note the use of the word *scheme.*) This arrangement costs you money.

Working with Private Sellers

While the best deals in rigs are often found with private parties, this is not always so. The main problem is that private sellers, possibly suffering from extreme anxiety, may overvalue their rigs based on what they paid for the unit. This is not to say that deals aren't out there, but you can pay a private seller too much for his used rig, just as you can at a dealer's lot.

A seller with a really overpriced rig is a tough negotiation. Unless you must have that particular unit, look for someone who has the rig priced in the ballpark of reality. At least at an RV lot, you can work through some of the pricing structure and reach a compromise figure. With some owners, your lowball offer may insult them.

Even *Blue Book* values (explained next) won't always help. We had one joker who, when we cited retail "book" value for his rig as about 20 percent less than his bottom line, snarled that the rig was worth more to him than that. We heartily agreed, got in our car, locked the doors, and left before Dr. Jekyll completed the transition into Mr. Hyde.

Establishing Book Value

The most reputable dealers will display the manufacturer's suggested retail price in the window of new rigs. This becomes the starting point for any negotiations. For used rigs, barring a few incidents in which the seller is offering what can only be described as an overpriced wreck, the *Kelley Blue Book*, available in separate iterations for motorhomes and towed vehicles such as trailers and fifth-wheels, can help establish the value of a used rig. If you're looking at a tow vehicle, get a copy of *Edmund's Car Prices Buyer's Guide* (available at bookstores and newsstands) or get information from Consumer Reports (P.O. Box 8005, Novi, MI 48050) on the vehicle you're considering.

There's nothing more amusing than listening to an RV salesperson, complete with obviously contrived folksy accent, go through a complex spiel on a used RV and then watch his (or her) jaw drop when you calmly pull out your *Blue Book* from pocket or purse and look up the published worth of the used unit and its options. Like a giant vacuum, the book sucks the hot air out of the corniest sales gimmick.

How Much Would You Pay for It?

Beyond looking at the books and shopping prices at multiple dealers, a wondrously simple technique for evaluating the "street value" of a rig is to look at the rig and its price, and then take a step back and ask how much you would sell it for if you were already the owner. Does the worn artificial woodgrain wallboard of the interior make the price appear high? How much to replace the eight balding tires? Is the unit in prime condition or seriously shopworn?

When taking into account all the flaws, wear, and mandated mechanical repairs, how much would you ask if you had to sell the rig in its present shape? Now . . . would you pay that much today, taking into account the cost of repairs, upgrades, and modification? If the answer is an enthusiastic *"No!"* keep looking.

Tip: Where to Get a *Kelley Blue Book*

Q: Where Can You Get a *Kelley Blue Book*?

A: From the Kelley people.

Alternative 1 (recommended): Kelley publishes two separate guides on used RV prices. One covers motorhomes; the other, trailers and fifth-wheels. You can order the books (prepaid) by calling 714-770-7704 and ordering the book relevant to your purchase. While $47 may sound expensive, the investment could save you thousands on the purchase of a used RV.

Alternative 2 (recommended less highly): You can usually telephone an RV dealer with whom you are not working and ask the value of a rig. In his earnestness to talk you into one of their rigs, he will look up the one you're eyeing and give you its actual value according to his book. If possible, look at the book yourself to ensure you aren't being fed a line. Also ensure that options are included where appropriate. Banks that handle RV loans can also do this, but you may need to call several before you find one with a current RV book.

Tip: Investigating a Used RV

When buying an RV from a private party, make sure to ask the questions we list here. If the answers don't sound reasonable, pass on the deal.

Why are you selling the rig?

How long have you owned it? (Ask for proof.)

How do you maintain the rig?

Were there any other owners?

Do you have any warranty or service contracts on the rig?

What do you like best about this rig?

What don't you like about the rig?

Ways to Save Money on New RVs

It is very hard to haggle on the price of a new RV after a certain point. The dealer markup can be high (20 percent or more), but good dealers invest significant labor in preparing the RV for delivery. If you are willing to do the prep work and install the accessories yourself, you might be able to get a rock-bottom deal. We don't recommend this unless you are experienced and confident in your mechanical aptitude. Good dealers test the pressure of the water system and propane system, lubricate the lift system, adjust and test the electric brakes, and complete other basic preparations before delivering the RV to you.

However, there are some general ways to save money on new RVs. Here are some workable suggestions:

- **Buy last year's model.** Because the "carrying cost" — the amount a dealer pays to keep an expensive inventory on his lot without purchasing it outright — is high, dealers "lend" last year's models to smaller dealers to sell. Depending on the arrangement, it may be significantly less expensive than this year's model because the dealer wants to dump it. Warning: A unit sold thus may not be covered by the maker's warranty if an "unauthorized dealer" handles the transaction. Get the unit's serial number and model name and call the maker for information on its policies toward *gray-market* rigs.

Subsystems will still be covered even if the rig isn't.

- **Price shop around the country.** Since there are thousands of used RVs of all kinds on the market, keep looking until you find the right one that's priced right. Even if you find the perfect dealer in terms of service and convenience, investigate the prices at two or three other lots or at RV shows before you make your final offer. Compare sticker prices as well as "asking" prices. Manufacturers are not required to post sticker prices, but most good dealers display them as they would on a car. The sticker price is a useful starting place in the negotiations. Ask for the dealer's best, fair price first. This eliminates a lot of the game playing. Now, ask other dealers for their best, fair price for the same rig.

- **Have financing in place in advance of the negotiations.** The best way to negotiate with RV sellers is to be preapproved by a lender not affiliated with the sales transaction (read the next chapter for more information on getting financed). With financing in place, when you approach the seller, be it dealer or private party, you have the leverage of a cash buyer. This lets you control the transaction. You aren't just another time-wasting "tire-kicker" or someone impossible to finance — you're a real buyer. If the dealer can ultimately provide a better financing arrangement, great. Meanwhile, if you come into the negotiations with money in hand, you'll be able to negotiate price from the outset, without financing getting into the picture.

Making the Deal

After establishing what you really should be paying for the vehicle, you're ready to negotiate. Some people consider this the fun part. Negotiate down from the best price quotation you received. Never deal in terms of monthly payments. Monthly payments are a financing arrangement — not the sales price. Negotiate price only. Avoid getting sucked in by tactic and pressure. Don't fall for the "today only" lines. After giving the salesperson your best offer, and allowing the dealer a fair profit, you'll have a good deal and a new rig to take on the road.

Selling Your Rig

There comes a time when all good things must come to an end. It's a sad day when you must part with that fifth-wheel, trailer, or motorhome with which you've explored the length and breadth of North America or even the Western Hemisphere. Of course the tears fade as the old rig drives away and the shiny new rig pulls up and the smiling dealer hands you the keys!

We put advice about selling your rig in this chapter because you will probably want to sell your old rig before you buy a new one. Occasionally, a dealer will really want your rig because of its condition, but most of the time trading in your RV actually costs you money, as the dealer adjusts the price of your new rig to keep the deal equitable from his point of view. Thus, more times than not you'll get the best return on your investment by selling your rig yourself as opposed to trading it in at the dealer's lot.

What's It Really Worth?

Selling an RV successfully demands more than just horse trading (interesting choice of words, huh?). Selling an RV in good shape is easy, but getting top dollar takes more work. First you must appraise your rig's current market value with the *Kelley Blue Book*. Book in hand, calculate your rig's worth, adding options and variations on the model you own. (Most rigs range from what car dealers call a "strippy" with no options to "loaded" with nearly everything.) You must also account for the wear on the unit. Has it spent a few bucolic Junes in the cool Appalachians or have you driven it the length and breadth of Mexico, bouncing pothole to pothole on side roads in search of the perfect camping spot?

Maintenance is another point of value. Are you selling a meticulously maintained rig with a like-new interior and carefully waxed exterior skin? Or is it something that appears to have participated in cliff diving in Acapulco with a few weeks' soaking in the ocean's brine? (In the latter case, move the pricing from the "mint" column down to the "average wear" and "worn" categories.)

Advertising the Rig

There are many (some inexpensive, some free) channels for advertising your used rig. These include the classified sections in RV magazines (*Motorhome* and *Trailer Life* have the widest circulation), newspapers, and the newsletters of RV clubs. You should also consider an ad in the *RV Trader* (for only $25 you get national exposure and a picture of your rig). In addition, you can place announcements on the bulletin boards at most RV parks and in the RVing sites on the World Wide Web.

We've had the best luck with short ads in newspapers or trade magazines that hit the highlights without spelling out every feature. Buyers call for the missing information, and we *do* put the price in, as many prospective buyers won't call without a price. Of course, you can always put signs in the windows. (Beware that it is illegal to park in many city streets and some RV parks with the signs displayed.)

Showing the Rig

Before people start calling to look at your rig, do the following:

- Wash the rig thoroughly, inside and out. Clean the carpets with a professional extraction system (or have them done at an auto detailer). Let the RV dry for at least forty-eight hours before showing the unit.
- Clean out all the cabinets and drawers.
- Put clean sheets and comforter on the bed. Clean the curtains if necessary.
- Deodorize the refrigerator and put chemicals in the toilet.
- Inspect for loose parts and hinges. Tighten them as necessary.
- Partially fill the tanks for the test drive.
- Perform any basic maintenance required, such as caulking,

oil change, or radiator flushing. However, don't make major repairs until the buyer makes them part of the negotiation. Chances are you'll be able to negotiate the repairs as part of the sales price, often saving money over the actual cost of paying for the repairs yourself.

On Consignment

If you don't want to hassle with showing your rig and negotiating the sale, you can sell your rig on consignment through dealers and consignment specialists. You can find these dealers in the trade magazines. Most large dealers take RVs on consignment. You must negotiate the commission and your bottom-line sales price in advance. In order to avoid potentially nasty, although unlikely, legal complications, you should do several things when putting your rig up for sale on consignment:

- Do not give the dealer title, agreement, or power of attorney to sell your RV. Otherwise, should the dealer leave town or file for bankruptcy, it is not likely that you would be paid in a sale arrangement or ever see your rig again. In the unlikely event that you are selling a $100,000 RV, the dealer might collect the cash, pay off the mob, and file for bankruptcy or head to the Isle of Man the same day. It's not likely but that leads us to . . .
- Insist on a consignment agreement. This can be as simple as a few lines of text on paper or, more likely, the dealer already has a standard agreement to review. Such an agreement should specify that you, not the dealer, own the RV. It also lays out terms of sale, commissions to be paid when the dealer unloads it, and other factors. Should you face a particularly convoluted agreement, don't sign it. Sell elsewhere or do it yourself. (You can take the agreement to an attorney, but the cost of his or her analysis, negotiation, and possible court time may negate the advantages.) It's not likely but before you sign the agreement . . .
- Check that the agreement doesn't authorize the dealer to do any required repairs or maintenance without your approval.

Otherwise you may find out that the dealer decided to replace the refrigerator and took twenty hours to do it. The cost is deducted from your payoff. We were dinged with this clause once and it cost us $2,500 that the dealer's service department was entirely entitled to keep. We had failed to see the clause in the ten-million-word agreement printed in type so small we needed a magnifying glass to read it.

- Visit the rig regularly. Drive by the dealer's lot at least twice a week. See if the RV has even moved. It should be washed. When the dealer is closed, your rig should be secure. Make sure the company doesn't look as if it's packing up for better pickings.

- Keep your rig insured. Most dealers' insurance explicitly excludes any vehicle that is not the legal property of the dealership.

Avoid Selling Abroad

Don't try to sell (or buy) your rig outside your home country. If you live in Canada, sell the rig in Canada. Big trouble awaits you in terms of title, vehicle inspections, and taxes for vehicles outside your country of residence. There's no upside in buying out of your country — unless you work with a dealer who is prepared and equipped to handle all the legalities for you in advance.

Making Trades

You'll read many ads like this in the trade magazines and RV newsletters: "Will trade 1990 Monaco with all options for house. Prefer Northwest, but other areas considered." Translation: "I [we] have an expensive motorhome and don't like the RV lifestyle [or one of us, sadly, has become too ill to travel]. We will trade our paid-off equity in a top-of-the-line coach for a ground-based house."

A sad situation, yes. However, trades can sometimes be a good deal. Not all trades are morose. Some people simply get tired of their lifestyle and trade land-based home for rig and vice-versa as they move through the years. Others are horse traders and change rigs like they change shirts. Before trading any unit, study the local papers and talk to multiple dealers.

Closing the Deal

When sellers come to look at your rig, treat them as you would like to be treated. Let them inspect the rig. Have the paperwork and maintenance records available for review. Know your state's selling procedures in advance. Have the title ready. Know what is required for registration, insurance, and bill of sale by the department of motor vehicles.

Let the prospects drive the unit — but make sure you go along in the passenger's seat. Before letting people get behind the wheel of your rig, make sure they have experience driving such a unit. Try driving around an empty parking lot if you're not sure about their driving prowess.

When the negotiation starts, be fair about the value and the condition of the rig. Have a rock-bottom price in mind, and don't go below this. Tell the buyer to shop around if he or she is not willing to pay your bottom-line price. If you've done your homework about resale value, you'll be able to get a fair price for the rig.

When it comes down to exchanging money for the rig, make sure you get cash or a cashier's check. As soon as you sign the papers, send a letter to the motor vehicle department with information on the transfer of title to remove yourself from liability for use of the rig, as required by your state or province — and don't forget to contact your insurance agent to make sure you change the policy.

This about covers the ins and outs of buying (and selling) a rig. However, there are still things you need to know about financing and insuring your rig before you buy. The next chapter covers these further financial considerations.

Chapter 4

Financing, Insurance, and Warranties

With sales prices in the five and six figures for most new units, financing is a necessary evil for most RV buyers. You should shop for financing as carefully as you shop for your rig. Remember — it costs money to borrow money. You should weigh whether financing is right for you, if you can get it at all. What fun is the open road if you spend $12 a night on a budget campground, $1,200 a year on camper registration, and $1,200 a month for your loan? That's not freedom, it's indentured servitude to an RV master. And, while some manufacturers, especially during slow economic periods (or gas shortages), offer low rates for carrying RV "mortgages," rates tend to be in the 10 to 18 percent range, depending on your credit history and the finance company. Those with shaky credit will find the percentage shifting toward the high side.

Of course, even if you do have cash for your rig, cash is not always the cheapest way to go when buying an RV. When you give up your cash, you lose the earning power of your money and the opportunity potential that cash provides. However, if you have plenty of cash on hand, you can likely get the best financing deals. After figuring in the opportunity costs of using cash and comparing the financing costs, you'll be able to determine the best deal for you.

Most of us don't have this option. We must shop for financing for all but the least expensive rigs. The good news is that almost anyone can get financed somewhere, regardless of flaky credit, an "iffy" salary, or time spent behind bars in Attica in the 1960s. But if the interest rate and terms nearly bankrupt you, what kind of fun is that? One dealer in the Denver area who financed almost anybody offered finance charges from 14 to 17.5 percent, and the vehicles on the lot were priced at least 20 percent above what they were worth. Buying one of his tired rigs meant both a large monthly payment and a vehicle that was impossible to sell for the payoff, if that became necessary.

If You Must Finance . . .

Credit has more potential repercussions than you may realize if you are new to the finance game. We don't like phrases such as "selling your soul," but at some level that's what you are doing regardless of your financier. Freedom *is* an essential part of the RV lifestyle, and owing large monthly payments isn't exactly our idea of a carefree lifestyle. But if you must finance your rig, as most of us must, here are some tips for reducing the pain:

- **Compare dealer financing to other sources.** The dealer's financing scheme may actually cost more, as the finance company rebates some of the money you pay to the dealer as a "thanks for the transaction" transaction. Since this *gratis* roll of dough has to come from somewhere, it's collected from a "loan origination fee" or from higher interest rates on the financing package. Either or both come directly out of your pocket.

- **Watch for prepayment clauses.** If you pay the loan off early, you may be assessed a fee. Strike this clause or finance elsewhere if it consists of anything more than $100 for paper processing. Such a clause limits your ability to trade up, trade in, or go permanently land-based.

- **Refuse any clause that restricts movement of the vehicle.** Oddly, some contracts for RVs restrict your ability to travel. You may be restricted to a city, county, state, country, or radius from a city center. Heavens! You're buying the thing *to provide the freedom to travel.* Don't sign such an agreement. Go elsewhere or don't buy at all.

- **Watch for the common financing tricks.** The last step in the sales cycle is the title and financing paperwork. The person handling this procedure is usually a commissioned salesperson. He or she will attempt to coerce you into an extended warranty or special insurance. Pass. You can likely get superior coverage at a lower price elsewhere. You may be heavily pressured. Ask politely to complete the paperwork with a firm "no" to each pressure tactic. (We once had the "loan officer" at a car dealer actually hissing at us with rage when we repeatedly turned her down, as she had lost the $100 spiff on the sale of the contract.)

- **Get a simple interest loan and pay it off as quickly as you can.** Make payments larger than the minimum required by the loan. Make these payments as high as you can afford. In this way you can save thousands of dollars of interest over the life of the loan. You'll also increase your equity in the rig should you need to sell the unit.

- **Shop for financing.** You can shop for pre-approved financing (which will always be contingent on the appraisal of the RV you buy) from these sources:

Banks and credit unions.

Collateral loans based on stocks or a second loan on your house.

Life insurance policies, if you have a large policy or are looking for a little rig.

RV loan specialists, such as the Good Sam Club (SamCash, 1-800-444-1476, Ext. 525), and RV financing companies, such as Essex Credit (1-800-431-5626). Many of these firms advertise in the trade magazines and RV club newsletters.

Laughing All the Way to the Bank

While it's normally not at all funny, getting financed is relatively easy, assuming that you have a reliable source of income and reasonably good credit. (It helps to have $50,000 on deposit with the bank making the loan, but it's not necessary.) If you meet these requirements, and if the unit's appraisal passes the bank or credit union's critical eye, then you've got yourself an RV loan.

Even for loans on new units, most banks will demand to see the vehicle or pictures of it. A few may send a representative or appraiser physically into the field to check out the vehicle's condition, unless you are working through the dealer and they have an established lending relationship with the bank or finance company. The appraisal is more of a problem for older units no longer listed in the famous and infamous *Blue Book*, but it may also be a godsend should a seller demand a price not in accordance with the market. A loan representative looks at the brand and age of the RV and then adds any meaningful options (from a *Blue Book*'s point of view) to derive a net value of the vehicle. The loan offered is based on a percentage of this figure, less your down payment and service fees. Of course, approval of the appraisal is required in addition to your three-page application, title statement, firstborn, left thumb, and lifetime of payments.

Financing Alternatives

If your banker seems squeamish at financing the rig of your dreams, try one of the lenders that advertise in *Motorhome*, *Trailer Life*, and other RV magazines. These operations understand the collateral value of RVs better than does the junior loan officer at the First Bank of West Yarmouth. Don't apply to all of them, but talk to the companies about their programs, briefly explain your situation, and ask if they can help.

Financing Used RVs

Like financing a used car, getting someone to carry the paper on a used rig is a little more difficult than getting someone to put up for new. Older models are especially difficult, unless you put up a savings account as collateral or have an especially comfortable relationship with your lender. An inspection is usually a must for a used unit as the lender will want to ensure that the unit doesn't look as if it was previously owned by a pig farmer who used it to take his charges to market on Tuesdays.

Weak Credit

If you have an unsteady job doing seasonal labor, are self-employed (like us), or the loan officer doesn't like the way you wear your hair or tie your tie, your application for an RV loan may be rejected. Most financial institutions have a thousand reasons at their disposal to refuse a loan, and this refusal may not be even vaguely related to the real reason. It may be that the loan officer doesn't like your overall credentials, but in the rejection letter, a claim states that your debt-to-income ratio is inadequate, even though you make $100,000 a year and have no outstanding debt. Other old standards for turndown excuses include: "The rig's too old," "You're too old," "The down payment is too small," and "You paid your Sears bill late once back in 1992." The list of available excuses is longer than a fifth-wheel with its tow vehicle. Complicating the problem is that the bank knows nothing about recreational vehicles. If you're a full-timer, imagine for a moment just how nervous a lack of permanent address would make a stuffy loan officer. That's why RV specialists often are the better option for RV financing.

Try This if You Get Turned Down

Increasing your down payment is one tactic for improving your chances of getting a loan. A bank or finance company that might turn you down with 10 percent down may happily approve you with 50 percent. With more of your own money invested, they're convinced that you're less likely to default on the loan. In fact, should you get turned down on any sort of loan-against-collateral — for a house, a car, an RV, or that new fridge with water and ice in the door — asking the lender "How much down to carry this paper?" will almost always net an agreement, assuming you have the cash on hand to meet the lender's (usually negotiable) requirements. Even a recent bankruptcy can be worked around (with steady income and enough down payment) if you've received your final discharge from the court.

Tip: Get Financed Only Once

During one of our short-lived land-based living arrangements, we decided to replace an ancient Mercedes we'd bought well used with a new car, as the venerable machine was dying of old age and costing a fortune in parts each month. On a breezy Saturday, we hit auto row and looked at everything from Lexus to Lincoln. At each dealership, financing paperwork was filled in by the salesperson since we planned to lease instead of purchase. Unbeknownst to us, each dealership quietly ran credit checks on us while we were on the test drive. This multitude of queries stayed on our credit report for years.

Wasting Your Time

There is a law against discouraging borrowers, which requires that a bank process your application before it can issue a "thumbs-down" response. This allows a bank to waste your and their time assembling an application and the required paperwork and still turn you down flat. Originally aimed at alleviating discriminatory lending tactics and "redlining," this law has been a dismal failure in both regards.

We get around this by simply asking something along the lines of "Do you think it's worth applying, or is my situation too complicated?" Any response less than "Yes, you should apply right now!" means that the lender probably won't give you the loan, but can't tell you that until the paper has gone through the two-week mill of the application process.

If you *are* denied credit for financing an RV, you have the right to know what is in your credit file. You are also entitled to know why the creditor has turned down your application. This information must be provided free of charge by the lender. You cannot be (legally) discriminated against because of sex, marital status, age, race, religion, or national origin.

Tip: Misrepresentation to the Lender

The dealer may still cheat the finance company/bank/whatever by substantially overvaluing a trade-in. In one incident we saw at a Porsche dealership, the dealer simply claimed in writing, with the buyer's signature, a substantially larger down payment than was actually made. Both these activities are, at least in theory, criminal, and you should avoid either approach unless you don't mind a stretch of free camping in San Quentin RV park. (Try to think of it as an RV camping space with an "all-concrete look.")

Lending Arrangements that Aren't Right for You

If you have an adequate down payment, know your rights, and shop around, you'll probably find legitimate financing for your dream rig. But, before you sign on the dotted line, make sure you haven't been taken in by one of these financing no-nos:

- **Usurious rates: Those who charge more than 15 percent on an RV loan when you can get the same loan (with good credit) for 10 percent or less.** No one should charge usurious rates, but lenders do try to get what the market will bear. If rates are too high or you have bad credit, buy less than your dream motorhome with cash and enjoy it. When you get your credit back in shape, then shop for the ultimate rig.

- **Pay-for-life plans.** There are ten-, fifteen-, and twenty-year loans available for RVs. Such lengthy payments tie you down for longer than you may want the rig. The interest charges may actually exceed the purchase price of the rig over the life of the loan. If it takes more than ten years to get the payment small enough for your budget you're probably buying something beyond your means. Consider a less expensive rig instead of the longer loan.

- **Add-on interest.** Avoid RV financing that employs the *rule* *of 78s* or add-on interest rather than *simple interest*. A complicated financing principle fully understood by bankers and loan sharks, the rule of 78s means that for the first two-thirds of the loan's life, you're paying mostly interest rather than principal. Should you decide to sell or trade at month thirty on a five-year rule-of-78s–based loan, you'll find that little of the principal has been paid. In this same period the RV (assuming it was purchased new) will have depreciated significantly.

- **A second mortgage on your home.** Avoid lenders who not only hold title to the RV (legitimate), but also demand a second mortgage on your land-based home, should you own one. Should you default, the lender can not only "repo" your rig but take away your house as well.

- **Complex contracts.** Complex lender contracts that require an attorney to understand, negotiate, and explain should be avoided. Find another lender.

- **"Oh, we have lots of rigs, but let's talk about financing first. Your last name first, with middle initial. And we need your Social Security number too . . ."** A dealer that seems more concerned about your loan application than helping you choose the right rig is trouble for a number of reasons. Such a dealer is looking to first ensure your creditworthiness. Your needs are a distant second because the dealer's concern is a sale, no matter how inappropriate to your lifestyle. Such a company may run your paper through five lenders in five minutes, each loan office querying your credit. The focus on credit indicates that the dealership receives a sizable percentage in the form of a commission or rebate from the lender. In the long term, guess who ends up paying for the privilege?

- **The *Titanic* revisited.** Beware of dealers that "self-finance" elderly rigs that other houses won't touch and lenders won't handle, regardless of down payment. Chances are that for the "convenience," you're paying double the worth of a creaky RV and a punitive interest rate. Found mostly on the sec-

122

ond-string auto rows (look for dealers selling used Pintos, Vegas, and diesel Oldsmobiles, among other wrecks), this is where novice RVers get taken to the cleaners. Avoid these lots unless you are looking for something really cheap. Pay cash to avoid the dealer's usurious financing scheme. As a cash buyer, ignore the sticker price and offer no more than the rig's worth.

Tip: Carry Proof of Insurance

At a traffic stop, many states demand that you produce not only a valid license and proof of registration, but also proof that you are insured. Routinely issued by insurance companies, your proof document should be kept in reach of the driver's seat in case you get pulled over. We even carry proof of insurance when renting a rig.

Insuring the Beast

The best insurance for RVers includes regular maintenance, careful driving habits, and running a tight ship. But since the loss through theft or mishap of an RV can be catastrophically expensive, conventional insurance should be part of your RVing budget. Insurance is mandatory in most states for *all* motor vehicles unless yours is parked for keeps on private property. You should buy coverage, not from the agent who covers your car (if you own one), but from an insurer that specializes in RV packages.

Why buy from an RV insurance specialist? Because few conventional insurers know anything about RVs. A regular insurance broker may provide a policy that's inadequate or inappropriate. It may specifically exclude living in the vehicle, as does the car insurance on our old Mercedes. And what constitutes living? A two-year trip full-timing around the nation? A two-week vacation in Yosemite? Or a two-hour nap by the side of the road?

With conventional auto coverage, should your vehicle be damaged or destroyed in a car accident or the engine burst into flames, you're covered. But if insurance company investigators find that you live in the vehicle — however they define *living* — you may receive no reimbursement. Or (and don't laugh) you may receive a check for $532.93 for "glass breakage" covered under the terms of the policy even though all that's salvageable from your $50,000 rig is a steering wheel cooked medium-rare.

Full-Timers

Full-timers should freely admit their intended use of the vehicle. An old trick is to say you only drive it for a two-week vacation, when in fact you really live in the rig. Such a lie saves money, as rates are higher for a vehicle that's used as a home on wheels. But should you full-time and claim otherwise, your insurer may have the right to reduce or dismiss your claim.

Shop for Rates

We don't need to tell you to do this. If a previously unheard-of company offers a low price, check it out before signing up. Most states have an insurance commissioner who tracks complaints. Make sure the company has been in business for many years and offers references.

RV insurance is surprisingly reasonable, given the high price of the rigs. This is because RVers in general are safe drivers. The insurance rate structures for RVs are based on conservative drivers, most over the age of fifty-five. The age factor is figured into the rate for RV insurance, so drivers under the age of fifty-five get to take advantage of the low rates. RV insurance rates are also based on rigs' being idle for most of the year. Of course, the rate for a $100,000 motorhome will be more than the rate for a $30,000 van conversion — but not as much more as you'd expect. Even so, it's still worth the effort to shop around for the best deal.

Besides shopping for price, you should look for RV insurers that process claims efficiently (*Consumer Reports* often reports on insurance companies), provide toll-free numbers for assistance on the road, and use understandable forms and policies. If you want to save money on your insurance and are willing to accept some limited financial risk on the road, buy only the amount of liability insurance you really need and increase the deductibles on your policies. Drop any coverage that is duplicated by other policies. For example, you may not need to insure your trailer for liability because the insurance on the first vehicle may already provide this coverage. If you already have life and health insurance, drop the medical coverage on your vehicle insurance.

Always ask about discounts and make sure you get all you're entitled to receive — discounts for multiple cars, nonsmokers, good driving, seniors, and the installation of antitheft devices, among others. If you're a full-timer, you can reduce your insurance rates by carefully selecting your state of declared residence. Rural areas offer cheaper insurance than urban areas. Check it out.

The Coverage to Carry

Your RV insurance should provide liability coverage for bodily injury and property damage and vacation liability (for injury to people around your rig when it's parked in the campground). The amounts you carry should depend on state law, your own net worth, and the value of your rig.

You'll also need medical payment, collision, and comprehensive coverage. Of course, while collision and comprehensive insurance from most companies may reimburse you for the cash value of your unit, you may want to consider a company like Alexander & Alexander that provides replacement cost coverage as an option.

Warning: Limited Coverage

If you're in an accident in Mexico, your tow vehicle or motorhome will be repaired. But if someone steals the 454 Chevy engine, fancy wheels, or personal effects from a rig, *this is not covered*. Only complete removal (theft) of the RV is insured on most Mexican policies. Claims for vandalism are equally invalid.

Tip: You're Right, It's All Fixed!

Mexican insurance issued by Mexican companies is based on the value of your vehicle and is set at rates determined by the Mexican government. The agent simply studies a series of tables to ascertain vehicle value based on purchase price and the length of your stay in Oaxaca (or anywhere in Mexico) and provides you with a fixed price. Take it or leave it. Those choosing to "leave it" should leave their rig safely stored in El Norte and take the train instead.

Canadian and Mexican Insurance

You must prove that your rig is insured once you reach the checkpoints inside Mexico (80 to 120 kilometers from the border) and at the border in Canada. Most U.S. policies will cover your rig while you are vacationing in Canada. However, only a few U.S. policies cover you when you head south to Mexico.

In Mexico, you'll need to provide paperwork verifying coverage. In the event of an accident, these documents are your "get-out-of-jail-free" card, even if the collision or other maelstrom was precipitated by a Mexican driver. Get a written report before leaving Mexico (if your rig is capable of operation) and file your claim before leaving the country. If the rig is completely destroyed, this report will provide you with the mechanism for collecting your claim and free you of ownership of the vehicle from the Mexican government's point of view.

You can buy insurance near the border, but consider Sanborn's, which has a lengthy (good) record insuring Americans traveling to Mexico. We spoke to Gary Pottinger at Sanborn's in Nogales (520-281-1873), and he explained that it provides a free guide/logbook, covers fender benders once you're back in the States, and even provides bail money for auto accidents that mysteriously happen after an overdose of tequila. (Avoid this problem by staying off the road when trying the local *bebidas!*) The coverage limit is $100,000, so don't drive the Marathon down there without special arrangements. Coverage can also be arranged by fax at 520-761-1215. You can also join Sanborn's club, which brings rates down and nets a free and informative newsletter.

Other Insurance Options

You could probably insure your gold teeth if you wanted to, but here are some valid insurance options you should consider for your rig and traveling needs. As always, some insurers provide better policies and rates than others on these optional insurance programs. Investigate your insurance policy and addenda thoroughly. Read every word before you sign on the dotted line.

Roadside Assistance and Towing

Should your rig die amidst the tumbleweeds of Texas, it's reassuring to see a smiling mechanic driving the large tow truck your way. Roadside assistance and towing programs are offered by Good Sam, AAA, and other companies. These insurance policies will get you to a garage or on your way if you run out of gas. A gallant mechanic may be able to fix your rig and get you back on the yellow brick road in minutes. Otherwise the truck will tow you to the nearest service center that can handle your rig. Note: Roadside assistance and towing programs provided by conventional insurance providers may charge significantly extra for towing an RV. They may even send a truck incapable of hauling a large, heavy rig. Make sure your policy covers what you need covered.

Mechanical Breakdown Coverage

Sorry we can't give you better advice here: Different from roadside assistance, mechanical breakdown policies — if you can find one — cost more than simple towing and emergency roadside service. They also cover the cost of repairs outside simple wear. Look for a complete policy with rental car and hotel stay coverage included. Consider how you'll reach the emergency line when you are out of cellular range and no pay phone is within hiking distance. You also need a guarantee of response time, unless baking in the Georgia heat or cringing under the glare of a Manitoba polar bear is your idea of fun.

When querying major insurance agencies with "Do you offer mechanical breakdown insurance for RVs?" we were met with the universal response of "Huh?" Prudential once offered this service, but a company spokesperson explained that they do cover locomotives but no longer RVs. Odd — you can get your fifty-ton locomotive insured against breakdowns, but not a basic Pace Arrow motorhome. Chances are you'll need to look to the RV insurance firms for such coverage.

Personal Effects Insurance

Many policies cover your rig and its built-in stereo, but are somewhat looser in their interpretation of loss of personal effects. The agent may want to know why you're traveling with a $10,000 Silicon Graphics computer workstation, as this sounds like a work-related item that must be handled with a separate business policy. Here's what we did to ensure that our personal effects were covered: We listed all items worth more than ten bucks, and we submitted a copy of this list (with serial numbers where appropriate) with our policy. The company agreed to cover all goods listed, and if someone steals the plastic plates and cups, we won't bother filing a claim.

If you have personal effects coverage on your home, the personal effects you carry in your RV are probably covered to a certain amount — typically 10 percent of your home policy limits. Check with your agent *and* study the policy's fine print. Keep in mind that your insurance agent may not be fully versed in the parent company's current coverage. (Your agent doesn't like reading lengthy policies any more than you do.) If the coverage isn't adequate, have the amount increased by your agent. If you don't have a homeowner's policy, you can buy personal effects insurance from RV insurers and other companies.

Warranties and Guarantees

How many of you have purchased an appliance with a twelve-month warranty only to see it fail just out of warranty? Hmmmm . . . we see a lot of raised hands here. It looks as if most of you have had this experience. At one time or another, the same goes for RV components, although the best-constructed models have few problems if you follow the prescribed maintenance regime. The good news is that consumers are protected better than ever, even though disputes remain commonplace.

On a new RV, all systems are warranted, but the drivetrain warranty will be very different from that of the microwave. The chassis and drivetrain may have separate warranties from the living quarters and appliances. We suggest you go through the large plastic bag of owners manuals and warranty cards to see exactly what *is* covered. Look to see what coverage is afforded, for how long, and what you must provide for service. You may need to produce your rig's bill of sale to repair a faulty water heater, but a defective fuel injector is repaired based on the maker's or seller's guaranty without any paperwork.

Dealers are required to provide written copies of all warranties provided on the unit and its contents before purchase. The warranties must be easy to read and understand. All terms and conditions must be spelled out. Besides the written warranties provided by manufacturers, almost all products have implied warranties even if they don't have written warranties. Implied warranty laws vary from state to state, but generally manufacturers are legally obligated to promise that a product will do what the product is supposed to do, unless the item is sold "as is." Be aware that some states don't allow "as is" sales. Forget about verbal warranties and promises from a dealer or seller — most of these are not binding.

To maintain the warranty on the components in your rig, you must use the products according to the manufacturer's guidelines, perform the required maintenance as documented in the manuals (and make sure you document this in some way), and follow the manufacturer's procedures for submitting a warranty claim. In particular, you should be aware of the length of the warranty, the problems and parts that are covered, and whether labor charges for repair and consequential damages (such as loss-of-use damages) are included under the warranty before you make a claim.

Pointing Fingers

An RV of any sort is a compendium of products, from the sheet metal made by Aaa Co. to the refrigerator made by Zzz Co. Responsible RV makers will help you get any of their subsystems repaired under warranty and with appropriate compensation or recourse for shoddy work or uncooperative or bad faith response to stated (written) warranties. You should poll other RV owners to see how they were treated after purchase. The consumer-oriented columns in both *Motorhome* and *Trailer Life* are useful, not only for filing complaints but also for observing how companies deal with problems.

Who Fixes What?

The length of warranty coverage is important, but you must also ensure that the terms of repair are workable when you do submit a claim. Warranty disputes are often rooted in repairs that take too long. A faulty and dangerous driver's door that only the manufacturer can fix is a major inconvenience and should be repaired quickly. Likewise, should seals fail on the sewage system, you want a local shop to send a serviceperson out or at least be able to repair the unit without a two-hundred-mile trip to Joe's Authorized Service Center. The locations of authorized service providers are critical to your warranty support.

Avoid any warranty program that requires shipping the offending item back to the factory. Unless it's something small and easy to remove and reinstall, this could result in physical risk to you. The best fix for most difficult-to-find equipment problems, assuming you have a helpful RV dealer or repair shop nearby, is to replace the offending unit and see if the problem goes away. If it does, then you can go up against the maker for a permanent fix or replacement.

One important aspect of warranty service is the service network for the rig. Does your brand of rig have a number of dealers and service sites nationwide that are authorized to perform warranty service? If there are no dealers in the areas you plan to frequent, try another rig. Also be aware that manufacturers who have been in business for a long time will have a warranty service track record. New manufacturers may build a good unit but lack the dealer network and warranty service of more established manufacturers. The warranty and service network should be considered in your purchase decision. If there is only one dealer in the state or province that services your brand of rig, choose another brand.

Extended Warranties

Beyond the manufacturer's initial warranties, a variety of extended warranties or service contracts can be purchased on new and used rigs. Some of these are provided by the original manufacturer, but most are through third-party companies that may or may not be reputable. Before paying for an extended warranty of any kind, know the answers to these questions:

> What exactly is covered? Read every word. Sometimes so few items are covered that the warranty is virtually worthless.

> Who is behind the coverage and how long have they been in business?

> Where can you get service on the warranty?

> What are your obligations for maintaining the unit and documenting the service in order to keep the warranty in effect?

The Warranty on Used Rigs

Most used rigs are sold "as is" within the limits allowed by law. However, depending on who sells you your rig, you may be offered an optional insurance policy (extended warranty) as part of the sales transaction. Sometimes these warranties are a good value. Many times they're just false security. We're still waiting for a $100 refund for a repair to a Volvo engine made back in 1976. The insurance company went bust before our claim was paid. Before you pay for the policy, make sure it has value.

Tip: The Red VW Jetta

Yes, this is another car story. (We've had better luck with RVs than tow vehicles and cars.) We leased a screaming-red Jetta to tow around the country behind a motorhome. But at stop lights, the car with just fourteen miles on the odometer would almost shake out our fillings with steering wheel vibration. The service manager agreed after a brief stint driving the vehicle that something was wrong. After we had driven it for one day, it spent five days in the shop with no progress on diagnosing the problem. Angry, after repeat phone calls, we threatened (in writing) to invoke Arizona's version of the lemon law. Within minutes of our fax, a honey-voiced customer service manager offered us the choice of any Jetta on the lot. He even threw in free window tinting (remember, this was Arizona with its attendant heat and sun). With maximum efficiency, title was transferred and a black Jetta, instead of a red one, followed our motorhome of that period.

Is It Bright Yellow?

While it's true that RV construction of everything from power plants (the engine) to frames to subsystems has improved, you may still encounter a lemon in your travels. While the horror stories of the early years told by 1970s motorhome owners are rare, you must take action if your new rig turns out to be a turkey. You can use lemon laws in place in many states, but dealers and manufacturers are adept at getting around them. A hot water heater that won't heat should be addressed at the local level, but a rig that shudders and shakes on the freeway or stalls constantly is a candidate for lemon law or Better Business Bureau action. Repeated and demonstrable problems are the easiest to resolve. The rule for staying out of trouble with a problem rig is to document everything. Document each manifestation of the problem with a thorough description. Multiple problems? Document each separately with mileage, dates, and time. We hope you'll never have to act on this advice, but here are the steps we recommend to resolve serious problems:

132

Tip: Autoline Works!

As the owners of a lemon Infiniti Q-45, we were stonewalled by the dealer and the manufacturer. Autoline got involved and made Infiniti cancel the lease. Our superior documentation convinced the arbitration panel that the car was indeed a lemon when it repeatedly lost power in traffic and on the freeway. It performed fine in their test drive, but our records convinced them that everything was not right. Document everything. If you present an overwhelming case, it will run roughshod over the feeble argument put forth by most dealers and manufacturers!

First, if a serious problem manifests itself soon after you take delivery, demand (politely) that the dealer fix it. If repairs fail, demand, via certified letter, a new rig or a refund of your money. Send a certified copy to the manufacturer. Typically a rig that's been in the shop more than a set number of days within the first thirty days of ownership is deemed a lemon by law and you can be released from ownership. You must file paperwork and aggressively invoke governmental enforcement to make this work. That doesn't mean that the dealer won't make it as difficult as possible, because it doesn't want the rig back either.

If you're out of the lemon law period but still in warranty, insist on getting the problem fixed in person, even if this means returning to the dealer you bought the rig from. If the problem is safety related, such as brakes that fade quickly, stop the rig immediately even if it means pulling onto an empty sidewalk. Let the dealership tow it rather than risking your life. If this doesn't work:

Second, write a "commanding letter" to the dealer and maker demanding a replacement rig or full refund. Write down each problem in a logbook, with the time and date of each occurrence. (If you drive a bus RV, you are required by law to keep such a trip log anyway — so you might as well get in practice for the day you buy that new bus-size rig.) Demand that if they can't fix it, they replace or refund your money. Send this letter certified and send a copy to the state (or provincial) agency that regulates dealerships. If this doesn't work:

Third, call the Better Business Bureau. This agency runs an arbitration program called Autoline that attempts to resolve differences between buyer and seller. A formal panel of volunteers studies the dealer/manufacturer's case and your documentation. Both parties "testify" before the panel, and the panel will require a demonstration of the problem, including a test drive if appropriate. In thirty days, it rules. You may get anything from a full refund to a determination that the dealer deserves at least one more chance to address the problem. The process is binding on the dealer/maker, but you can elect not to follow the panel's advice. If this doesn't work:

Fourth, if you are unhappy with Autoline's arbitration decision and the coach is expensive, consider filing suit through formal legal channels. This is a weighty decision, because legal fees mount quickly and a large RV maker may have a small army of attorneys on staff with time on their hands. Alternatively, park your vehicle prominently in front of the dealer's lots with a large lemon banner painted on it with words to the effect, "XXX Dealership sold us this lemon. They may sell you one too." Such a banner should be large and easily readable by potential suckers, er, customers driving by or entering the lot. Do not park on the dealer's property, because after one warning they can have you arrested for trespassing. Don't break any laws. Good luck.

In this chapter we've looked at the fiscal responsibilities of RV purchases. We advise you to carefully study the multiple warranties and insurance policies involved with any RV. Careful analysis of these items frees you from worrying about your rig and keeps you protected from a major calamity.

In the next chapter we'll look at the basics of renting an RV. Renting is a great way to try out the RV lifestyle. Renting also proves cost effective for the RVer who doesn't have time to use a rig more than a week or two a year.

Chapter 5

Renting an RV for Fun or Commerce

We've mentioned the option of renting an RV in earlier chapters. Renting avoids the pitfalls of ownership: big payments, major repairs, storage, and the towing bill from Port Mansfiel to San Antonio, Texas, should you experience a major breakdown. Most rental units are motorhomes, although a few companies rent truck and trailer rigs. You can rent a rig and head off into the sunset toward your place of vacation, or you can park a rig on site and never leave the campground.

RVs are commonly used for family vacations. Some people rent RVs as extra housing during the holidays. Businesspeople and companies also rent RVs as trade show headquarters, meeting rooms, and alternatives to hotels on a variety of business trips. In general, there are four reasons for you to consider renting a rig:

1. If you're unsure of the RV lifestyle or want to try a particular kind of rig, renting offers the opportunity to try the lifestyle without making a commitment. Take the rig out for a few days and sample the open road. Do you love it? Do you dislike it? What do the other members of your entourage think? Pro or con, the rental price will be less than the initial purchase price of any rig.

2. If you know you love RVing, but can only find a week or two each year to go camping, consider renting instead of buying. For most intermittent RVers, ownership of anything but the smallest pop-up rig is not cost-effective.

3. If you want to set up a camp for a few weeks, but don't want to drive there, consider renting a rig near your destination. If you're planning on a two-week vacation with Mom and

Pop, who live in a veritable cottage, for example, rent an RV and park out front (assuming local ordinances don't forbid it). Then plug in and camp out. You get the advantages of staying with Mom and Pop and the advantages of staying in your own hotel room, all in the same spot.

4. If you need an extra room for guests or visitors, but don't want to build another house, consider renting an RV to park near the house. The rig can also be used for tailgate parties and family picnics while the guests are in town.

Where to Find Rental Rigs

RVs can be rented through a number of local firms. Most cities will have local numbers for RV rentals. Look under "Recreational Vehicles — Renting and Leasing" in the *Yellow Pages*. You can also rent from private parties. Contact the RV Rental Association at 703-591-7130 for a list of private rentals in your area. For $5 to $10, you'll receive a catalog of RVs for rent by companies and private parties. Another resource that's nationwide is Cruise America. Call them in the United States at 800-327-7799. AAA and CAA also provide lists of RV rentals to members.

Some companies (and people) offer ancient rigs for rent or rigs that deserve more maintenance than they receive. A really ratty rig rented sight unseen may be uncomfortable for living or suffer serious mechanical failures, most likely when the closest repair shop is one hundred miles distant. For this reason, we prefer a local "landlord" so we can physically inspect the coach before committing to three weeks in a drafty wreck.

An alternative to renting from an agency is to rent or borrow your neighbor's unused rig, assuming you return it in pristine condition with fuel tanks topped up and the holding tanks drained and flushed (more on this later).

Renting Through the Net

As if you haven't heard enough about it already, the World Wide Web on the Internet is an RVer's paradise for renting (and most other) information. Most rental companies have Web pages. Use any search engine, such as Yahoo or WebCrawler, to search for recreational vehicle rentals. You can request more information from most companies through the Internet. Or, if you're in a rush, most listers provide conventional phone numbers and "snail mail" addresses.

Grind 'Em Down

Don't accept the "list" price for rig rentals, especially in off-season. Talk to the owner or manager — not the clerks — and get the per diem rate down. You can also reduce or eliminate the deposit (see the next section). In the quiet times of the year, most camper rental agencies would just as soon rent at a discount as have a yard full of rigs sitting empty and unreserved.

The Deposit

Most RV rental agencies will accept your credit card as a guarantee against damage. If you lack a credit card, you'll find renting an RV as difficult as renting a car without one. Cash can be used as a deposit at some agencies, but the amount will be substantial. After all, you are driving off a rig that may be worth $50,000 or more. When you leave a deposit, get (in writing) the terms for returning your deposit and how long the process takes.

Insurance

When shopping for a rental RV, find out if insurance is included. We once rented a rig over the phone by presenting a Visa card. Ready to roll, we were informed of the $29.95 mandatory insurance charge that wasn't already included in the rental price. When we walked out, the angry rip-off artist, er, owner tried to charge our card for two days' rental, but Visa sided with us and refused the charges.

Before renting, call your insurance agent, assuming you have one, and ask if two weeks in an RV are covered under your existing policy. This assumes that you have comprehensive coverage (insurance talk for covering everything) and a clean driving record, and the policy covers you when you drive vehicles not owned by you (common). After settling on a rental unit, ask, if necessary, that your agent fax your coverage to the rental agency. Do it Monday through Friday or your agent won't be there to help.

Mexico and Canada

As mentioned in Chapter 4, American insurance is not valid in Mexico. Some policies don't cover Canada either. You must also have a letter from the rental agency authorizing you to take the rig out of the country. Many rental companies will refuse you this privilege, and the rental contract may specifically state that Mexico and Canada are off-limits. If you're renting a rig for Canadian adventures, we recommend renting the rig in Canada or renting from a company that specifically endorses use outside the United States. Note that Canadian companies may not allow the rig out of Canada either — so read the fine print on the contract, and make sure your insurance covers the extent of your travels.

Without Reservations

Should you want to rent a rig for a vacation, especially during holiday seasons, reserve early. If you're too late to get exactly the rig you desire, get your name on as many waiting lists as possible and wait for the phone to ring. We've done this and have almost always been called about an available rig to meet our vacation needs.

More RVing 101

We'll never forget the couple who parked next to us and couldn't start their rented trailer's stove. In a panic they pleaded with us for help. They were nearly ready to call a tow truck and give up on the trip. Box of self-striking matches in hand, we demonstrated the operation of propane tank valves and how to locate and light the stove's tiny pilot light. We got a free and quite tasty dinner out of the deal.

You may not be lucky enough to have us parked next door, but most renting agencies will spend time training you in driving the rig and operating the subsystems. If you're an old hand, you won't need this handholding. But if you are new to life on the road, this training is key to enjoying your trip. Make sure the service is provided for free.

Keeping It Up and Running

For most rentals you are responsible for fuel and oil used on your trip. (It's hard to believe, but at one time rental companies provided fuel and oil as part of the daily rental rate!) In addition to keeping the gasoline or diesel tanked up, you are also responsible for everything from brake fluid to coolant. Before leaving the lot, ask the attendant who trained you about each fluid requirement. Of course, if the radiator springs a slow leak between Safford and Phoenix, Arizona, technically, it's the responsibility of the renting company to address the mechanical deficiency. Still, you and your family will have to contend with the Arizona sun while you wait for a tow vehicle. For this reason we suggest checking out the rig for leaks and operation (see Chapter 6) before you sign the rental papers.

The Breakdown

RVs sometimes fail, especially motorhomes with a lot of miles and the kind of care renters afford them. Before renting, ask what kind of emergency road service is included, how you reach the emergency providers, and how long they take to respond. You must also have in writing the company's emergency provisions for you, your family, and traveling companions. Do they put you up in a nice hotel (with meals) while service is under way or abandon you on the shoulder of the freeway where the breakdown occurred? Know in advance. The terms are (or should be) in the rental contract.

Renting an RV Checklist

COMPARISON SHOPPING (By rental company)			
Confirm the rental rates (how much?)	$		
Any extra charges? (how much?)	$		
Sanitation charges (how much?)	$		
Cleaning deposits/charges (how much?)	$		
Preparation fees (how much?)	$		
Generator fees (how much?)	$		
Chemical fees (how much?)	$		
Mileage fees (how much?)	$		
Pet charges (how much?)	$		
Security deposit (how much?)	$		
Fuel charges (how much?)	$		
Drop-off charges (how much?)	$		
Extended rental discount (how much?)	$		
Insurance (how much?)	$		
TOTALS BY COMPANY:			

The Rules

Most renting organizations have rules that go along with the vehicle. To enforce them, a sizable deposit may be required or your credit card will be charged. Your entire deposit might be applied to cleaning the rig, as spelled out in the contract. We recommend a thorough scrutiny of the contract before reserving the vehicle. You might even be charged for a cancellation, even if you notify the agency weeks before your trip. Questionable clauses should be crossed out and initialed by you and the renting agency. Too many rules and complex terms in the contract? Head for the phone book and call around until you find an agency that doesn't demand the unreasonable. Unfortunately, most rental companies cannot allow towing a boat or extra car. It's not because the RVs can't handle a towed vehicle, but because the insurance companies have determined that it is too risky.

Extras

When scrutinizing the contract, look for extra charges for cleaning, generator use (why include one if you can't use it?), and oddball fees such as a roll of 49-cent toilet paper priced at $2 per roll. (Hey, we aren't kidding!) A sensible RV renter will negotiate all such obligations. An unreasonable renter (rare) may include a clause that charges you for an oil change even if you rent the rig for three days and increment the odometer by a mere 149 miles. If you don't notice it in advance and strike it out, you're stuck for the fee.

One-Way Rentals

One-way rentals are possible if you pay extra, and the amount depends upon which company you rent from, the type of vehicle, and the rental location. Cruise America, for instance, charges different rates according to the state. Obviously, a circular route is not ideal for some travelers, but you do save money.

Checkout Time

All but the most casual renting companies will check you out and then help you check out the rig. That ding in the left front wheel well — it gets marked down on a schematic of the rig so you won't be charged for it when you return from your voyage. Mark down all damage, stains, and smells before you drive away.

Okay — How Much?

Motorhome rates range from $50 a day for a small, basic rig to $250 or more per day for a really plush unit. There's also a per-mile charge on most rentals. For extended stays you can often negotiate lower weekly or even monthly rates. When budgeting your vacation, remember that you'll still have to pay the park fees, fuel charges, and entrance fees, just like those who own their RVs. Truck campers and travel trailers average $50 to $120 per day. Not as many agencies rent them as rent motorhomes. If you are new to camping, go for the motorhome, because it's easier to handle than a five-thousand-pound trailer hooked up to your ancient Oldsmobile Cutlass. Not all cars — especially small ones — take a towing hitch, and there's usually an extra rental charge for this as well.

Upon Return

When returning the rig, fill up the fuel tanks to the level specified in the contract and dump and flush the holding tanks. Otherwise the rental agency may charge a premium for fuel and a service fee for handling the tanks. Unless some other arrangement was negotiated as part of the rental, if you want your cleaning deposit back, return the rig in the same condition you received it. Throw out the trash. Vacuum the interior. Wipe counters, drawers, refrigerator, and windows. You get the idea.

Saving Money on Your Rental Rig

You can save money on RV rentals if you act wisely. The following summarizes our recommendations for getting the best rental deal on your vacation home on wheels:

- **Shop prices.** RV rentals vary considerably. And don't be afraid to negotiate with the agent. Many firms will negotiate prices, but not many advertise this fact.

- **Rent from a friend or private party.** If someone has an RV doing nothing in the parking lot, he or she will likely be happy to consider renting the rig to you for a couple of weeks. Make sure you and the private party have adequate insurance on the rig, however, and draw up an agreement which states that you will be responsible for returning the rig in good, clean condition and without damage. Also, if you are renting from a private party, make sure you have specified who will be responsible for mechanical repairs should they occur. (The risks of private-party rentals often lead people to the more expensive RV rental firms. If you are uncomfortable with the people renting the rig or the agreement, go elsewhere.)

- **Avoid holiday rentals.** Try to schedule your RV outings at less popular times, or toward the end of the vacation season. The discounts in off-season are substantial at most firms.

- **Ask about discounts for seniors and club memberships, as appropriate.** If you don't ask about discounts, the companies won't automatically give them to you.

- **Follow the terms in the rental agreement — exactly.** You'll save money if you fill up the fuel tank and dump the holding tanks before returning the rig. You must also make sure you abide by any maintenance terms in the contract, such as changing the oil and filter. You could be liable for engine damage as well as a penalty fee for failing to do so.

Renting is really not different from owning an RV from the standpoint of possibilities and travel requirements. Everything we recommend for loading, stocking, and entertaining in RVs applies to renters as well as owners. After you rent rigs a few times and try out the lifestyle, if you decide you love the freedom that RVing provides, consider buying your own RV. However, remember that owning an RV requires maintenance and storage that rental units don't demand. The true economy (and joy) of owning your own RV is only realized when you regularly use the rig.

Part II

The Mechanical
Side of RVing

Chapter 6

The Mechanical Inspection

We include this chapter on the mechanical inspection of your rig for three reasons: first, to make you aware of the components that are important to the mobility of your rig; second, to provide you with a list of systems to review when buying an RV; and third, to give you a framework for inspecting the performance of your RV on a regular basis while on the road.

Structural Integrity

If you're a *Star Trek* fan, you know about the ramifications of hull failure when conditions are less than, shall we say, "user friendly." While you don't need to worry about loss of oxygen pressure, you do need to be aware of the structural limitations of your rig. You don't want to end up like Wile E. Coyote in a Road Runner cartoon with your motorhome slowing down because the rear end fell out a mile back near Cucamonga. You need to be aware of the construction basics of recreational vehicles to evaluate the quality and structural integrity of your vehicle.

The structural strength of an RV is the key to the rig's life span and your safety while traveling. Well-built RVs must exhibit an appropriate amount of rigidity coupled with some flexibility when under stress. If this idea of flex is new to you, keep in mind that all large buildings, especially those located in earthquake country, have a little bit of flexibility built in to accommodate earth movement without breaking down. Older RVs of all kinds may have lost structural integrity, and if you go after the least expensive but largest new RV, you may find that walls creak when winds are high and sides buckle as the sun warms the exterior — definite signs of less-than-perfect construction.

The Chassis — The Underlying Strength of Your Rig

Motorhomes are either built from scratch by the manufacturer, including the custom-made chassis/frame, or built on a standard chassis/frame manufactured by someone else (typically GM or Ford). Motorhomes, at least the less expensive units, are built on the chassis of small pickup trucks (micros), vans (Class C), and trucks (Class A). Custom chassis and frames are typically built for the more expensive units. Trailers and fifth-wheels tend to be built from the bottom up by the manufacturers — and the quality varies significantly among manufacturers, so you do need to consider the chassis construction of towed vehicles as well. Be aware that you may have separate warranties for the chassis and drivetrain (if there is one) and the rest of the rig, depending on who built what.

Many large motorhomes are built on a chassis smaller than that of the completed vehicle, with the least expensive vehicles completed with the smallest (and least expensive) chassis. That means that a twenty-eight-foot coach might rest on a truck frame meant for a twenty-foot truck intended to deliver vegetables. This is called an *extension,* and although there's nothing inherently wrong with the concept, some manufacturers' ideas of how to extend a chassis and how far to extend it are better than others.

Rigged Construction

Most rigs incorporate one or more materials in combination with steel for strength and wood for its (relatively) low price. Here are the most common structural formats you'll find when looking for RVs:

- All-wood construction (termites optional, but available). This kind of rig is largely history unless you plan on renting a 1950s unit for ice fishing in northern Manitoba or collecting antique units for restoration (yes, there are clubs for people who do this).

148

Tip: Buy the Book!

RVing from A to Z, by Bill Farlow, is a great introduction to RV mechanics, should you want to learn about things like gear ratios and vapor separator valves (some of *our* favorite topics). Pick up a copy at supply stores such as Camping World.

- All-steel frame and exterior construction, with custom interiors built with various materials. The steel bodies are found on only the most expensive units, such as buses.
- A steel frame underneath, combined with wood vertical members, and fiberglass exterior panels. Fiberglass and other synthetics are most often employed as part of the exterior "sheeting." This material is light and has plenty of flexibility, but it lacks the strength mandatory for structural stability without reinforcement of the wood-and-steel frame. The use of fiberglass and synthetics with steel or wood is the most common type of modern construction.

In the future, new glass/polymer materials that make steel look as weak as a wet paper towel may be seen in RV construction, especially as these new materials become cost-effective compared to wood, fiberglass, and steel. Until these new materials are proven, we suggest caution in the purchase of a vehicle using new materials. The first fiberglass pleasure boats, for example, had more than their share of problems because manufacturers lacked experience working with the substance. Your new glass/polymer rig — if and when there is one — might have similar troubles when material starts disintegrating after five years of use, three years out of warranty.

While steel can rust and suffer from corrosion, wood suffers from a greater range of damage and deterioration problems. A wood-only frame lacks the structural resilience needed for long-term life, and you might find its endurance failing at a very bad time on a busy freeway. Everything from bacteria to bugs can weaken it, and water damage from roof leaks can be near fatal. Dry rot and waterlogging dog older units of mostly wood construction, especially in units that have spent a lot of time in the warmer, wetter climes of the country.

Strange but True

When driving to Toronto, Canada, we encountered a serious thunderstorm about seventy miles south of civilization. Driving in nearly blinding rain, we observed a family of five in an ancient station wagon pulling an inexpensive but relatively new trailer.

Right in front of us, an unexpectedly severe gust of wind blew the trailer off the road. The unit wasn't simply blown onto the shoulder or into a ditch, but shredded into near toothpicks. The remains ended up in a farmer's field adjacent to the highway. The good news? The family was shaken up but no one was injured. Thank heavens the kids were in the station wagon and not in the trailer.

In units that show evidence of roof corrosion, chances are water has entered the unit through the roof and damaged the frame. You can look for internal stains from leaks, but they may not be evident, and there are some parts of any RV that you can't get at to look at without a costly tear-down. Paint and wallpaper can also disguise this kind of evidence, at least until the first heavy rain.

To be fair, there's no reason quality vehicles can't be built with wood, as the ships in which Europeans discovered America were constructed using the same material. It's just that all but the most expensive units are built on an assembly line of sorts, and you know about that leak in your 1977 Buick that was assembled on a Monday morning . . .

A major advantage of steel support cages and strong, thin shell materials is not only their strength over wood, but their (usually) lighter weight. A rig built with plywood and particleboard is very heavy, decreasing fuel efficiency while at the same time reducing the margin of safety and longevity. And should fuel prices skyrocket, such a rig is expensive to run.

During gas shortages, especially that of the early 1970s, RVs became as popular as rats in the basement. This could happen again and the price of fuel does go up and down like a seesaw. Those RVers simply interested in traveling (and that's the idea, isn't it?) didn't worry about gas prices. They simply scaled the

Chassis construction. The best RVs employ custom steel chassis and frames. These provide strength that offers stability and extends the carrying capacity of the rig.

length of their trips back (still fun) and ignored the situation. Besides, while you may hear constantly in the RV books and mags that sticking to 50 mph improves gas economy, in our experience it does little but frustrate the motorists behind you who want to go for the 65- or 70-mph limit rather than drive like snails. New RVs with fuel injection, or at least well-maintained engines, won't experience much fuel economy improvement at 50 over 65 mph, unless they're significantly overloaded. Could this be you? (Read Chapter 9 to learn all about weight limits for your RV.)

Establishing Integrity

Whether buying or maintaining your vehicle, you want to locate problems, especially those that might require costly solutions. You probably won't want to break down the engine to see if the camshaft is a few too many thousandths worn from driving lifter number seven. But you can look for a number of other things before running up a bill for a shop's complete analysis. Regular inspections may save you the heartache of dreaming about new gingham curtains and a trip to the Tetons only to find that your vehicle has, at best, weak long-term prospects.

Test It Wet!

To check RV subsystems and look for leaks, you must have water, fuel, and propane in all tanks. There's no way to locate leaks, check appliances, and run subsystems such as the water heater and pump unless the tanks are full. To perform these checks, you'll need access to a hose (and water) that the owner doesn't put down the toilet. (Bring your own hose, if necessary. For $10 you can get a fifty-footer at most discount hardware outlets.) The vehicle should also have reasonably charged batteries. You'll want to have shore power available too, to check electrical operation. For a 50-amp, 240-volt unit, this may mean a trip to an adequately equipped campground, to jack in. In a house equipped with an electric dryer, and the right kind of plug, you may be able to hook in, but don't count on the plug's being compatible.

Tip: Autoshop 101

You should fully inspect the mechanical operations of engine, transmission, axles, and brakes, but detailed advice is beyond the scope of this book. Hire an RV mechanic with references and reasonable rates to do the detailed inspections that can't be covered here.

The Inspection — from Bottom to Top

Normally a vehicle inspection starts from within the engine compartment, heads underneath, and then works through the exterior and living quarters. When checking out an RV, you follow the opposite order, to keep the grease and dirt you would otherwise acquire from contaminating the (one hopes) pristine interior. Here's how to go about it, and keep in mind that we haven't included everything about all brands and varieties of vehicles, as that would take a book or two in itself.

Check Out the Underlying Construction First

The manufacturers of quality rigs almost always have detailed diagrams of chassis, interior, and shell construction. If these aren't available for your rig, the best way to understand and analyze construction is to look under cupboards and, if possible, under floors and the roof. A masterly rig will have a mostly steel frame at least at the floor levels. Evidence of cheap wood construction is usually bad news, especially if you find stapled two-by-four (or similar) supports sheeted over with exterior and interior finishing materials such as vinyl-coated "wood" paneling. If you're a bargain hunter — let's say you want a sleeping trailer for less than a grand or two — you would have to expect and accept this kind of build. But full-timers and those looking for a lasting investment will want a more sophisticated mix of materials and higher-quality construction.

If the rig has been lengthened, check that it is still stable. Some manufacturers add length to their vehicles without adequate structural support for the rear part of the vehicle. Check for clearances on a long vehicle with an extended chassis. On some extended units, clearances are diminished, even though the manufacturers claim a variety of modifications to accommodate the additional and unexpected weight. You can partially fix this problem by adding extra rollers, similar to those added to mobile office furniture, such as file cabinets, and you'll see these on some RVs. These keep the rear end from dragging, but the best solution is to choose a rig with an appropriately long chassis that doesn't need this kind of kludge, er, fix.

Determine the type of insulation provided in the construction of the rig. Gauging insulation effectiveness is difficult unless you happen to have a wind tunnel on hand as well as a team of engineers armed with a broad range of environmental testing instruments. But you can study the rig's construction, use the hose test explained below, and consider the price. It usually, although not always, comes down to "You get what you pay for." An inexpensive trailer may have Styrofoam or fiberglass as insulation (they actually work), but then have skimpy protection in the roof against sun and lack anything but a thin layer of underbody coating to keep out the cold. An expensive rig will have a carefully designed insulation scheme.

Check the Interior for Wear and Damage

After assessing basic construction of the vehicle, examine the condition of flooring, fabrics, carpeting, curtains, cabinets, drawers, and paneling. Inspect for damage. Look for interior wear in the form of worn furniture and carpets. Unless the interior has been overhauled, you can get a good idea of use and maintenance levels with a simple inspection of the rig. Look for water damage under everything. Inspect and operate all the appliances, including burners, pilot flames, oven, refrigerator, heating, cooling, electrical systems, and propane fittings. Sniff for leaks around propane and gas devices. Inspect for leaks with soapy water. (Preferably, have a professional check the entire LP system before purchase.) Run the generator. Check for noises. Make sure the appliances work with the generator running. A professional can assess whether the generator output meets specifications.

Feel the padding and stuffing of chairs, couches, and beds. Sit in them. Do they feel freshly stuffed, worn as though Attila the Hun's army had used them for twenty years, or just mildly worn in accordance with the age of the vehicle? Upholstery and carpet can be replaced in any rig, but it does cost money.

Check the Exterior Structure

Now go outside the rig and check for corrosion, leaks, and structural problems. Look for dents, gouges, and dings that may indicate accidents or inappropriate storage. Check for loose moldings, warps, and damaged siding. Check all the vents for cracks and damage. Make sure all vent and window cranks operate smoothly. Check all mounted devices, such as the air-conditioner and television antenna, for proper mounting and operation. Check the lights all around. Check that the caulking is in good shape around all seams, windows, vents, and juncture points. If the caulk looks too new, look for evidence of recent leaks. Too much caulking may indicate a problem with leaks. Bulges indicate leaks or structural damage — investigate these thoroughly. Check out all glass windows and windshields. Inspect the tires for wear and sidewall cracking.

Check out the roof. Study the seams of the roof in which panels meet or those that make up the siding. Newer RVs will be coated with a material that protects against corrosion, and this material should be even and without subtle cracks (get out the magnifying glass) called "crazing." If the roof is especially dirty, as will happen if the rig is parked for long periods under trees, you may have to hose it off. Ensure all windows and roof vents are securely closed before taking this step.

Now look for plastic damage. Most RVs, except those in the expensive range, employ a fair amount of plastic and fiberglass-type compounds for exterior storage doors, engine access, and so forth. Paint damage to these panels is common, but if one is badly cracked it should be replaced, and this isn't cheap (if you can get a replacement panel at all).

Tip: Replacement Parts

Unless you're rebuilding an old schoolbus-type RV, many of the parts used, such as locks, roof vents, bathroom fixtures, and latches, are standard and are used on many coaches in many price ranges. Did you forget to close a ceiling vent and shear it off entering a garage? Head to the local RV supply store with what's left of it. Chances are they can replace it with one exactly the same.

This kind of damage is especially significant if it will allow water into storage, engine, or passenger compartments.

- Corrosion of roof seams often indicates a serious and expensive problem. You should pass on this unit or insist the owner have the problem corrected at his or her expense. You may find that such damage has allowed water into the walls as well as the ceiling and that the damage is significant and structural.
- A leaking roof can lead to rust of structural elements. Wooden structural members may rot or warp if the leak is left long enough. Newly applied sealant may indicate a cover-up job on the part of the seller, or it may mean simple timely maintenance — check to determine which.
- Check that doors and windows operate smoothly. If doors and windows are stiff it may indicate accident damage that was ineptly repaired. You may even see rigs with appendages such as inoperative vents placed to hide the malfeasance beneath, be it rust or evidence of more catastrophic incidents.
- Rusty RVs are best avoided because you have no way of knowing how much actual damage exists between walls and flooring. Loose moldings or panels may indicate the failing of the interior frame. Gently move moldings from side to side and don't be afraid to get up on the roof and do the same. We once had a camper van, bought in Florida, in which, when you lifted the large rubber mat in the passenger compartment, you could actually watch the road below. We bought it cheap, obviously.

156

Tip: Looking for Bubbles in the Finish

One of the most expensive repairs you can make to an out-of-warranty RV is for delamination of the exterior, which is indicated by the presence of (initially) tiny bubbles. Study all sides of a rig in search of them. Do this in bright sunlight, not in the dark with a flashlight. Estimate about $2,000 to $4,000 per side to fully repair this problem. Better still, pass on the rig, because if you fix one side, there's no guarantee that the problem won't appear elsewhere.

Exhausting One's Options

In motorhomes, one of the first places to show evidence of deterioration, aside from the roof, is the exhaust pipes. There, heat, noxious gases, and weather blend to quickly rot the metal. Very new exhausts are as suspect as rusty ones. And for a large and decrepit exhaust system, complete replacement is expensive, even if it's the sole mechanical flaw.

Oh-Oh, New Paint

Other points are worthy of study if recent repairs are in evidence. Did the rig really need a paint job to make it look nicer (unlikely, as such work is expensive). Or is this a quick cover-up of rust or poorly repaired damage from an accident?

A major problem for older units is the failure of the window seals. Possibly not that robust even when new, these seals are a major source of environmental leakage, in which outside air affects inside temperatures. We test this in our coach by hosing each window down from the outside (naturally) and looking for leaks internally. After ensuring that all roof vents are tightly closed, shoot each closed window and door from outside for about ten seconds, hosing the edges and the middle if it's a sliding window. It helps to have a partner (not the seller) watch inside to see if water leaks in. A seller that won't allow this procedure probably has a good reason for refusal, and you should pass on that coach.

Tip: Rusty Belts

Rust, corrosion, and chemical damage can be found almost anywhere on a coach. In the "rust belt" of the Northeast, it's usually worst under the coach and in and around wheel wells — anywhere that salty road spray may hit during driving. In RVs that have spent substantial time in the tropics — Florida, for example — you may find rust in the strangest of places, as salt air and high humidity combine to spark it in any nook or cranny — behind the bathroom's medicine cabinet, for example.

Crawl Under the Vehicle for a Good Look

Look for dings and pits on the chassis that may indicate off-road use. Verify that supports are solid for all the tanks, including those that hold water and fuel. Inspect the underbelly and wheel wells for rust. Look for obvious repainting to hide such problems.

Check the tires, wheels, and brakes thoroughly. The rig should have quality radial tires, as these ride and handle better, although they cost more than the basic truck tires encountered on many RVs. (We provide more information on choosing tires and tire safety in Chapter 16.) Look for excessive tire wear and, God forbid, retreads. (A new set of Michelins will set you back about $1,200 for six tires.) Bad brakes, defective connecting cables, and trashed wheel bearings require the diagnosis of a mechanic.

Some units have "airbag suspensions" that provide a smoother ride, or they may have been retrofitted to an RV to handle more weight or smooth the cobblestone ride effect on rough roads. These units use air for cushioning and should be tested at the same time as the tires.

We once took a rig — a rented motorhome — on the road that was impossible to control without laborious steering and keeping the speed to less than a snail's pace. At the first RV shop we could find, the mechanic found no serious defects but found that the tire pressure and the air-cushion pressures were low and severely unbalanced. The shop added air to match all systems, and off we went with the rig receiving a new lease on life. Best of all, no charge! The shop manager said "air is free," so he wouldn't charge us! But it makes you wonder what the last renters of this rig did to control it! You should follow the weigh-in instructions in Chapter 9 to determine the rig's true carrying capacity.

Check Under the Hood

On motorhomes, after evaluating the interior and exterior structures and the tires, open the hood and check out the engine compartment before starting the rig. Pull or lift the cover off the engine, being careful not to get grease on the interior. This may be a heavy operation and, if the weather is warm, not any fun at all. Suggestion: Let the seller do it. Here's what to look for, and if any of these procedures make you the least bit uncomfortable, pony up and have a professional RV mechanic perform them.

Look the Engine Over Thoroughly

Check the radiator cap and fluid levels. Check for rust. Look for leaks. Check hoses and belts for wear and cracks. Does the engine look well maintained? Are there leaks, a thick layer of grime, or evidence of serious overheating, such as melted plastic parts? Look also for cracked spark plug wires (indicating old age) and general lack of attention. Open the air cleaner. Is the paper filter a nice bright white or pale yellow, or does it appear to be factory equipment from 1985?

Excessive grime may mean benign neglect or it may hide a leak that collects road dust. For an especially dirty engine, insist the seller shell out the $10 and have it cleaned. Many dealers steam-clean the engines of their used RVs. This makes for a pretty-looking engine but also hides serious leaks because the cleaning removes the evidence. Insist on a twenty-mile test drive and then reinspect the engine. Evidence of leaks may remanifest itself in this period.

Check the fluid levels. Did the owner allow the oil level to reach near the bottom of the stick? Check the transmission fluid too, and don't forget the brake fluid reservoir. You should also inspect the oil, radiator, and coolant reservoirs after driving to make sure the levels haven't changed.

Tip: A Dead Battery or Just Corrosion?

A dead battery? It could be invisible corrosion from a loose connector supplying approximately zero volts of electricity. Here's an example: A friend's classic Porsche ($$$) wouldn't start. There wasn't even enough power for a dim glow of the interior lights with the doors open.

With the vehicle stone dead, he called the tow truck, while we — having been through this scenario on other vehicles — tightened the bolts on the odd dual six-volt batteries using an inexpensive crescent wrench. On returning our friend was stunned, because we had the car happily idling and even the headlights shone brightly in that night's heavy fog. You could face a similar situation with your tow vehicle or motorhome engine batteries or those that provide power to other systems. Make all connections tight, top up battery water, and replace the heavy cables that feed the RV's starter and coach systems every year or two.

Check Out the Batteries, but Plan on Immediate Replacement

Check the batteries for undue corrosion. Check the water levels. Even so-called sealed batteries need distilled water added every now and then during the summer or in especially dry parts of the country. If the rig does anything but start immediately, have the existing batteries replaced right away unless the seller can document their age as less than six months. You'll save yourself a lot of trouble, even though it costs a little money. Use only deep-cycle marine batteries because the heavy use of camping is too much for standard automotive batteries. Shop price too, because you may save $100 or more on batteries by buying at Price Club/Costco rather than at the RV dealer.

Tip: Mileage on Motorhomes

Older motorhomes are worth far less than newer ones, especially if the mileage is high. Sometimes, crafty sellers, with a little touch-up paint and a bad attitude, will "fix" the apparent age of their unit. Two points will reveal an older unit: Look at the rubber on the foot pedals. Does their apparent age match the mileage? Are they brand new? Does the mileage on the odometer match their condition, and does the speedometer look much newer than the other gauges or does it show years under the sun? Another check for self-powered vehicles (motorhomes): Look at the fuel entry port, open the flap, and unscrew the cover. Does it look as if ten thousand nozzles have been inserted in a vehicle with a supposed seventeen thousand miles on it? Note that none of these "tests" are infallible, as some owners park or live in a rig for a year between trips, but they should be a part of your overall evaluation.

Start the Engine and Listen

Start the engine. Did it start smoothly? Don't drive yet. Listen for untoward noises — knocking, hissing, grinding, and clicking. We're not going to get into engine noises in great depth as that would take another book. Mechanical information is already available in countless do-it-yourself books, and you probably don't have the tools or nerve to tear down an engine and transmission anyway. Even a compression test of the cylinders is difficult on some units, and you might not recognize oil in the coolant, which indicates an expensive problem. However, you can identify some major problems just by listening. After running the engine for a few minutes, check for overheating, then check under the rig for leaks. If leaks are red or brown and slippery, expect problems. Now, after listening to the engine, do you feel confident enough to go for a drive?

Go for a Test Drive

Before you back away from your parking spot, check out the brake lights and backup lights. Work the signals. If all is in order, start the driving test. Expect to drive for at least thirty minutes. Drive the rig in a variety of conditions: freeway, city street, and country road (if possible). Constantly check for overheating of engine and transmission.

We go into more detail on driving the rig in Chapter 12, but for now, check the power of the rig and engine responsiveness, transmission noises, brake operation (test the brakes before you get on the highway), balance, and stability. Trailer brakes should operate in tandem with those of the tow vehicle, as well as independently with the emergency or manual control lever.

Stability is a key factor of your driving enjoyment and safety in an RV. Stability should be tested on hills, while braking, and on turns. While you're at it, look for:

- Spongy brakes or brakes that pull the vehicle to one side.
- Responsive steering that does not pull to either side on a straight, level road.
- Grinding noise from the transmission or excessive pinging or odd engine noises. On pushers with the engine in the rear, have your coconspirator go back there and listen, while holding on in case of an emergency braking episode.
- Excessive sway or bounce, indicating bad shocks or springs.
- Inoperative controls such as the turn signals, dash heater, dash AC, and gauges and readouts. (You might as well assume the cruise control will be broken and budget for getting it fixed.)

Inspecting Used Trailers and Fifth-Wheels

Buying a used trailer or fifth-wheel is less risky than buying a used motorhome, because trailers don't have an engine and transmission to worry about. If all of the internal and external systems work and seem well maintained, the wheels and braking systems are sound, the hitch is secure, and the frame and walls seem solid and free from water damage, then the trailer is probably okay. But before taking off for the wilderness, take time to look for two serious problems: vehicle damage from a road accident and structural weakness (common in older trailers).

Accident damage is often hard to identify. Unlike damage to a car, where most surfaces can be studied, with a trailer or fifth-wheel, new siding and a touchup may effectively hide an incompetent or inadequate repair job. Asking the seller rarely helps because he or she may not know of damage before purchase or may simply not tell you. Instead, study the exterior for repainted areas, doors and windows that stick or fit badly, and lines of the body that appear crooked or out of alignment with mating surfaces. Severe damage may also appear in the interior as warped walls, doors, and cupboards that stick or are difficult to close, and fresh wood and ceiling work in an otherwise older unit.

The basic mechanical inspection of trailers and fifth-wheels includes the obvious body and interior inspection, but the most significant items — brakes, axles, and the hitch — require an expert's experienced eye. That's why you want someone with serious trailer repair experience to take the wheels off and check what lurks underneath. You also want to pull the rig, if possible, to see whether there are problems with the unit fishtailing or pulling to one side with your tow vehicle or the one included in the purchase. Your expert can discover most of these problems without a "run," but we would still advise pulling it if a suitable tow vehicle or hitch is at hand.

After the Test Drive

Upon returning from the test drive, get under the vehicle again. Use wheel blocks to ensure the unit doesn't roll over you and be careful of hot surfaces such as the exhaust manifold pipes. Look for leaks. Slow ones may exist as spots of greasy dirt, as this tends to stick to the leaking substance. While most seals don't cost that much to replace, their repair isn't cheap either. While you're in the neighborhood, visually inspect the exhaust system. While there's no easy way to gauge the internal integrity of a muffler, you can look for holes and serious rust.

Fluid leaks near wheels indicate serious braking system leaks or (less likely) grease leaking from a bearing or joint. Lastly, look at the rear end (if this is a vehicle with rear drive). The presence of new oil could indicate that an expensive rebuild or replacement is in order.

Get the Lowdown

If you're just doing a regular checkup on a rig you already own, any indications of problems should be brought to the attention of a mechanic before they become bigger problems. If you're inspecting a possible purchase and you are still comfortable with the vehicle after the drive, have the unit evaluated at a credible RV repair shop. The mechanic can check out the systems, tell you whether that big greasy spot amounts to anything, and present you with an estimate that you, in turn, can use to negotiate the sale. You will likely have to pay for this inspection, but chances are that the cost will be less than $150, and it could save you far more than that. You don't want to buy and then find yourself saddled with a serious problem that went undetected. If the problems are numerous and serious, pass on the rig.

If drivetrain problems are found that require tearing down the engine, transmission, rear-end systems, or steering, look for another rig, even if you like the body and interior. Who knows what else lurks under the "hood."

If your rig checks out after all these inspections, you're probably in good shape to hit the road.

In the next chapter we look at propulsion — the use of energy and Mr. Isaac Newton's principles to assist and resist your rig's movement in space (or along Route 66). Actually, the chapter is on engines employed in drivetrains — in both gas and diesel and in both tow vehicles and motorhomes. Hang on to your hats!

RVer's <u>Basic</u> Mechanical Checklist

DATE	(7/23/97) →			
Engine compartment fluid levels				
Air cleaner — how clean?				
Change fuel filter when fuel changes ★				
Belts and hoses, bulges or cracks?				
Change oil 2,000 miles or 3 months				
AC topped up or converted to R12?				
Check for hidden bubble in radiator				
Study fuel line for leaks or aging				
Frayed tubes, lines, or wires?				

★ In many regions of the U.S., gas composition changes with the seasons as mandated by law. This sudden change can unleash a lacquer-like substance that can clog your fuel filter.

ROAD READY?

Check tire pressure			
Have brakes and bearings checked by pros			
Check the pressure of the spare tire			
Check generator maintenance schedule			
Test generator starting and power			
Test water pump operation			
Test hot water heater			
Test refrigerator			
Fill and evacuate drainage systems			
Check all exterior lights with helper			
Test/check smoke/gas detectors			
Examine fire extinguisher condition			
Emergency cones/flares/reflectors aboard			

TESTING IT

Basic drive test			

Copy and use this form, dating each use.

Chapter 7

Push Me–Pull You:
All About Drivetrains
and Transmissions

Unless you plan on a horse-drawn RV (reportedly popular in Third World domains), you'll need to buy a tow vehicle or settle on an appropriate power plant configuration in a motorhome. Drivetrains vary in terms of power, gas/diesel mileage, and reliability in starting in different weather conditions. Your drivetrain should remain cool when climbing long hills. Most important, you need an engine to produce sufficient torque for the weight rating of the towed trailer or motorhome. The engine and transmission combination must also provide adequate acceleration for the rig to keep up with other road traffic. (Yes, we've done 6 mph up a hill and felt like fools as the fleet of cars tailing us grew ever longer and the turnout was still miles away.)

Go Gas or Diesel?

If you choose a mid-priced rig, you'll likely get a gas engine. But if you have the budget, you'll probably have the option of choosing a diesel-powered rig. There are significant differences between engines powered by these fuels that you should consider before you decide which is best for you.

Gasoline is far more flammable than diesel. That makes diesel safer in most collisions. Diesel fumes don't precipitate explosions anywhere near as easily as gasoline fumes. This advantage is also a negative, because with its slower burning properties, diesel doesn't provide as much raw power as does gasoline. That's why turbines (turbodiesels) are often used to boost a diesel engine's otherwise sluggish behavior. (We tow our fifth-wheel with a turbodiesel pickup and it's worked out well.)

Diesel fuel also thickens faster than gasoline at low temperatures, which slows fuel delivery, detonation in the cylinders, and starting in cold months. Expensive diesel systems include warming equipment in the engine for alleviating these problems. That's also why you see big tractor-trailer rigs with complete or partial vinyl covers on their radiators during the winter — too much cooling through the radiator thickens the fuel, and it fails to burn efficiently.

Big Fish/Little Fish

Choose a gas engine on a rig if you need fast acceleration, as in a van-based RV that you plan to use to commute to work in congested New York or Los Angeles. It must accelerate from a freeway ramp metering light to 65 mph in seconds in order to merge with the flow. Go diesel if you have a heavy rig and you intend to travel long distances. The exact point when a diesel engine makes more sense than gas is dictated by the actual weight of a loaded motorhome or towed vehicle and your budget. (Large, quality diesel engines cost substantially more than their gasoline compatriots.)

Diesel engines are almost always the choice on big rigs (if you can afford them) because gasoline engines can't efficiently haul a heavy load. In essence, while gasoline can provide rapid propulsion, diesel can provide more torque (strength). Diesel also provides better mileage than gas. But in a heavy rig, this difference may be noticeable only on long trips. The reason tractor-trailers use diesel engines instead of gasoline is that beyond a certain weight range, all but pricey gas-turbine engines lack the power for the task.

Tip: Got a Gas Engine with a Turbo?

Turbo-driven gas engines demand that after you park, you let the engine run for about a minute with the shifter in park. This gives it time to replace the super-heated oil in the turbine case with cooler oil and increases the turbo's life.

Onboard
Travel
Information
System
the RV Navigator
OTIS
the RV Navigator
FOOD
FUEL
TOWN
SHOP
AREA
HOSPITAL
SERVICES
CHOICES
DIRECTIONS
CAMPS
FACILITIES
ACTIVITIES
SITES
ENTER
EXIT
NEXT
ON
STATE

Don't Go for the Diesel Blue-Light Special

As you can imagine, not all diesels are created equal. An inexpensive diesel may be highly troublesome, as many Oldsmobile owners discovered in the late 1970s. Look for Cummins, Detroit Diesel, or similar quality engine. And, yes, these cost more than a Brand X engine, but they're tough boys. Our ancient (1979) diesel Mercedes had nearly a quarter of a million miles on it when we sold it to help purchase a new rig. Large diesel bus engines can go five hundred thousand miles or more without major retrofit.

A Snipe Hunt

You can buy gas on almost any corner where two thoroughfares meet or at any freeway exit with a gas station (though the price may be high). Diesel can be found mostly where truckers are likely to look for it, such as at freeway offramps or inconsistently on major boulevards. Big tanks are the best solution to avoiding low fuel situations. Depending on your destinations, fuel availability may be a factor in choosing gasoline or diesel power.

Keeping Engine and Transmission Cool

We were thinking about calling this section *Cool Runnings* after the Disney movie in which the Jamaican team enters the Olympic bobsled event. The importance of running your RV transmission and engine cool cannot be overemphasized. In the next pages we cover some of the ways to keep your engine and transmission running cool.

Maintain a Less-Than-Warm Relationship with Your Transmission

It's easy to forget the transmission. It's normally a quiet little guy consisting of a bunch of precision gears that transmits power from the engine to the driving wheels. When it acts up, however, you become aware of it very quickly with anything from refusal to shift to vibrations that feel as if they'll shake out your fillings (or at least knock the stuffed Garfield off the side window). With a heavy load like that of an RV, transmission cooling must be addressed. Whether you drive a self-contained motorhome or an independent tow vehicle, boiling transmission fluid can result in a loss of control and power. It may also stop you in your tracks as quarts of liquid pour from emergency relief valves onto the highway. Suddenly you find your engine racing but going no-where.

Most pickup truck and motorhome (really truck) transmissions do not assume that you will be carrying living quarters instead of a payload of Dr. Pepper. Unless you're buying a well-chosen top-of-the line unit, you must depend on an auxiliary transmission cooler to keep things cool. You should have one added to your motorhome or tow vehicle. Mount it in front of the radiator. You should definitely get a transmission cooler if you have an automatic transmission and are upgrading a vehicle from standard use to ready it to tow an RV.

Cooling system manufacturers claim that 90 percent of transmission failures are due to overheating. There are many options for upgrading the engine cooling and transmission cooling systems to accommodate towing requirements. Some are reasonably priced and can be easily installed by the backyard mechanic. Coolers are made with either finned pipes (like a radiator) or "stacked plates." The stacked-plate designs are smaller (for the same rating) and are considered better. Make sure you get one big enough. You really can't overcool a transmission unless the weather is incredibly cold. Even then, all you will notice is sluggish shifting until the weight of the rig heats the transmission fluid.

Tip: Extra Fluid

While this may sound obvious, whoever changes your transmission fluid must take into account the extra capacity that the transmission cooler and its feed lines take and bleed and add extra fluid to accommodate it.

Most motorhomes come equipped with a transmission cooler, but at the advice of an impartial RV mechanic, you may choose to replace it with a larger one for more effective cooling. Our mechanic laughed when he saw the factory-installed transmission cooler in our long-replaced 1983 motorhome. Since he had a larger used unit in good condition, he replaced ours for the cost of an hour's labor. We aren't exactly sure what changes this made, but in hot weather on grades, shifts seemed more positive and the transmission spent less time "hunting" — that is, trying to choose the right gear. A transmission fluid temperature sensor might have further clarified the results.

Cooling Old Man Engine

Keeping the engine cool is the key to giving your rig a long life. It's been said that the exhaust manifold on 454 Chevy motorhome engines glows a dull red when climbing a long hill. We can't verify this since we prefer to keep the lid on the engine at all times, but such heat buildup gives you an idea of how much temperature can be produced by a large engine working under a heavy load. Your best defense against overheating is keeping the oil topped up and the water-based cooling system in perfect condition. That means the following:

- A radiator that's unobstructed and in good condition. If yours leaks, *never* try radiator leak sealants. They may fix the leak, but they'll also reduce cooling efficiency.
- Replace all hoses and belts annually, whether they need it or not.
- Drips from the water pump are a deliberate indication of impending failure. Replace the pump at once. This is not a failed seal, but an engineered safety indicator.

Replacing a radiator is expensive, and is therefore not advisable unless yours is worn out. There are other tricks for increasing radiator cooling that are less expensive. The first of these is increasing air flow through the radiator. The air-conditioning condenser and add-on coolers will reduce this air flow. If you've added such equipment, consider an electric fan on the front side of the "stack" of coolers. A fan for pushing air through the radiator can significantly improve cooling and can be wired to a switch on the dashboard or to a factory-installed electric fan (using a relay). Fans start at about $65. There are also add-on systems for spraying water on demand in front of the radiator. This is a solution only when climbing hills (otherwise you'd run out of water). These spray systems are most effective in dry climates.

Transmission Regearing, Replacement, and Add-Ons

If your tow vehicle is pulling a heavy trailer or fifth-wheel, you may want to have the transmission modified before purchase with gears better suited for handling a heavy tow load or add an auxiliary transmission unit. Some auxiliary units are designed for motorhome users as well as tow vehicles. Correctly matched to your vehicle and the tow load, such modifications or add-ons provide better fuel mileage, which justifies their cost. More important, they improve your ability to handle both the upside and downside of hills and mountains. A big rig climbing a steep grade may have trouble maintaining a speed above the single digits. With a parade of cars trailing behind, the situation is hopeless, as stepping on the accelerator fails to add any apparent power to the drivetrain.

Tip: Transmission Troubles

When buying a used tow vehicle or motorhome, the first item to have a professional RV mechanic check is the "tranny." These wear out first on cars and trucks not equipped for RVing or prematurely aged hauling trailers. Inexpensive or older motorhomes may have a similar problem if the maker didn't include an adequate transmission cooler or the weight of the coach exceeds what the transmission can bear. A new or rebuilt transmission isn't cheap, although, if the RV price is right, replacing this unit may make economic sense. Again, beware of older tow vehicles that may have hauled the Space Shuttle from Edwards Air Force Base in California back to Florida. Note that a worn transmission may point to heavy wear elsewhere.

174

The Auxiliary Transmission

One option for keeping the trans cool involves the addition of an auxiliary transmission gearing unit. The auxiliary systems are designed with gear ratios (the output of the engine versus the speed of the wheels) for those living on wheels. The units may offer switchable settings for fuel economy versus power. Priced (with installation) between a few hundred dollars and a few thousand, these units can save you substantial amounts of fuel and make a large, heavy rig much easier to handle on the up- or downside of hills. The concept here is not to save fuel but to allow you to operate a tow vehicle or motorhome in the engine power range prescribed for various road grades. You may use the most fuel-efficient setting for level roads, then change gears to climb that 7 percent grade — a tradeoff of fuel economy versus power versus vehicle control, as more power improves maneuverability in an emergency.

Attached behind the standard transmission, with a shortened driveshaft, in the normal setting the auxiliary trans is nearly unnoticeable. But, when it is kicked on, the engine revs higher to produce more power and the secondary transmission translates the higher engine speed into more torque rather than more speed. These "underdrives" allow you to climb grades at reasonable speeds in the Rockies *and* get the best fuel economy and keep the engine cool on the flats of Kansas.

Several vendors offer auxiliary transmissions, but one company, Gear Vendors Under/Overdrive, offers a videotape that succinctly explains why such a unit may or may not be appropriate for your rig. Yes, it's $15, but certainly more entertaining for RVers than *Leave It to Beaver*. Call 800-999-9555 to order a copy. Even if you buy an auxiliary transmission from another company or pass on the idea, this tape is highly informative.

Regearing

Many pickup trucks can be regeared at the factory or by an after-market shop with a transmission arrangement that makes them more suitable for hauling trailers and fifth-wheels. We advise caution. Before ordering such modifications, get expert advice on what works best for the load you plan to tow. Tow-style gearing may also make for a vehicle that runs at high revs whether you are actually pulling a trailer or heading for the grocery store. In hot climes, this contributes to overheating, premature engine wear (in extreme cases), and a hot and noisy ride. You should try to work with an expert to fashion a workable compromise between towing vehicle and trailer.

Add One at a Time

Choose the add-ons that save money, add enjoyment, or increase the safety of your rig. We recommend adding one major subsystem at a time if you wish to add any at all. For example, simultaneously adding a turbocharger and an auxiliary transmission will make a difference in performance — possibly an unpredictable one — but you'll find it impossible to decide which is doing what. If your rig begins behaving oddly or soaks up fuel like an oil boom, you won't be able to determine the source of the problem, because a rig is a unique system in which changes may produce unexpected results. Unless purchasing options as a package that legitimately makes sense, take it one step at a time.

Beyond engines and transmissions, there are unique aspects to operating RVs that aren't covered in the auto and truck handbooks. The next chapter covers the living subsystems (water, heating, cooling, and electrical power) that make your RV a home.

Chapter 8

Water, Heat, and Power: The RV Subsystems

Subsystems on RVs once consisted of two-burner Coleman stoves and a can of water. Today's RVs include complex subsystems that duplicate the power and water operations of a suburban home. Everything from a built-in washer and dryer to satellite TV are commonplace on modern rigs.

In this chapter we explain the most common subsystems necessary for living in your RV. When weighing the purchase of a new or used rig, use this chapter to locate and evaluate each system. Naturally, not all rigs include all systems, and on a new rig, ordered from the factory, you can choose to add or ignore options you can't afford or have no use for. As explained in Chapter 9, each of these components adds weight to your rig. Too many options and you'll be overweight before so much as stepping inside.

Tip: A Lot of Scenic Windows?

To reduce fuel and power consumption, consider where you park. Want to keep cool without the AC? Park under a broad-branched tree. Want winter warmth without a heater? Park in the sun, if there's any available. The number and size of the windows and whether they're tinted influence the effect of these passive temperature control options. GMC's classic motorhome has enough big windows to fry occupants on a sunny day in the Wyoming winter. Windows score high for sightseeing — but make sure the window covering and shades are adequate to keep the heat in and cold out when you don't want to enjoy the vistas.

Tip: Insulation

Another factor is the insulation unit and the construction of the environmental control system. Forced-air heating and cooling are superior to roof-mounted air-conditioners, as temperatures are even throughout the RV. Tinted windows help too. Effectively insulated walls are also important, as otherwise you get what we call the car-in-the-sun effect in which the sun heats the interior ten to thirty degrees extra, or more. With windows sealed in the southwestern sun, interior temperatures will quickly exceed the 150 degrees Fahrenheit mark. Even dual air-conditioners can barely keep up with the outside heat.

Heating and Cooling

Human creatures demand creature comforts. A well-equipped, properly constructed RV accommodates a comfortable variety of heating and cooling options for warm winters and cool summers. Still, rigs vary substantially in maintaining comfy indoor climate conditions. Investigate these abilities *before* you buy, as some rigs won't keep their cool in Phoenix in July or produce adequate heat for that must-do ski trip to Aspen in February.

Your goal should be a rig design capable of keeping all interior areas approximately the same temperature all year round, without breaking the bank for fuel or electricity. Heating and cooling the small interior of an RV is relatively easy compared to heating and cooling a two-thousand-square-foot house, but it requires energy management taken for granted at home. Too hot? Too cold? At home, you probably just adjust the thermostat and forget about it until the power bill arrives next month. In an RV, you must manage temperature control to conserve resources or follow the seasons. Then you can take advantage of what we call "360-degree climate control" — all windows open for flow-through ventilation provided by nature's breezes.

Hot Stuff

Assuming you aren't camping in Alaska in a drafty old rig, your heating system should be easily able to maintain an even sixty-five degrees Fahrenheit interior temperature when old man winter does his damnedest to freeze you. You also want a system that uses energy resources modestly. Monitoring of these resources is equally important, because you don't want the propane tank to run dry in the midst of a snowy night.

Forced Air

The most common heating system in modern RVs is the propane-powered forced-air heater that, with a fan, delivers a noisy but workable flow of warm air through vents around the rig. These systems produce enough racket in some coaches to preclude sleep until you get used to the jet engine sound effects in the sleeping area as the system switches on in response to the thermostat. Forced air requires both propane and electricity to operate. Its downside is that in a large rig, battery-powered fans will drain your energy resources quickly when not hooked up to park power. However, if you keep an eye on the propane gauge (should you have one) and plug in, forced air will keep your rig as warm as toast through all but the coldest mountain nights (assuming your rig is insulated, that is).

Hydronic Heat

Superior to standard forced-air systems is the hydronic heating system found in highline motorhomes. Sounding like something for growing plants, it's the most effective (and most expensive) heating system for RVs. Unlike forced-air heat or simple wall-mounted heaters that produce spotty heat in some rigs, hydronic systems provide even temperature in any weather. The hydronic system channels warm water through the walls and evenly heats the coach. In some hydronically heated coaches, you can separately regulate the temperature in two or three "zones" of the motorhome. This same system heats the water for that marble-lined shower or extra-large (by RV standards) bathtub that can be found in highline rigs. Rigs with hydronic heat are recommended for those with large balances in their checking accounts.

Heat Pumps

Some RVs come with heat pumps. These are air-conditioners that can run in reverse to produce hot as well as cold air. One unit and thermostat handle both chores. Heat pumps work well but only when you have access to the AC power required to run the coach air-conditioning. Note: We have never used a heat pump in an RV, but they are commonly used in the homes of the southwestern deserts. Once the temperature drops below freezing, they become less effective. You should check a heat pump's capabilities before heading for polar bear country.

Engine Heat

Engines have been used to heat vehicles since the invention of the automobile. Your rig will have dashboard heat for use while traveling. Like your car, it only works while the engine runs, not while parked in camp.

Heat from Other Sources

When hooked up in the cold, you may find your toes turning blue even when your rig's heater is doing its best. Consider adding supplemental heating. Here are a few options:

- **Electric heat.** Use an electric heat strip to warm the coach. Get one that shuts off instantly when tipped over. Never use it while in motion!

- **Ceramic heaters.** Essentially a variation on a simple strip heater, these units are safer, but take longer to heat.

Warning: Engine Operation in Camp

There may come a time that, due to a breakdown of some sort or rig limitations, you consider using engine heat or AC to control cabin temperature while camped. Never do this, because carbon monoxide may build inside your vehicle, putting you to sleep for good. This is especially deadly during snowstorms when snow building up around your rig forces traces of exhaust inside.

- **Hot water heaters.** Essentially a poor man's hydronic heating device, these sealed, water-based systems are safe, but take a long time to heat. We put a fan on one to distribute the heat faster. It helped! (Never put a fan on any flame-based system!)

- **Gas or catalytic heaters.** Dangerous, perhaps deadly, in an RV. Never run any kind of heater that burns gas or chemicals. Never use the stove or oven for heat. Ventilation is required. Opening a window may be inadequate, and it lets in the chill you are attempting to negate. Your propane furnace is properly vented by the RV's maker, and that's why, assuming no squirrels have stored their nuts in the vent, it's safe to run with windows sealed.

Keeping Your Cool

If you're a summer camper, you'll want to use air-conditioning to cool your rig, unless you plan on spending July and August at seven thousand feet in the Rockies. Most RV air-conditioners are roof-mounted units or, in highline coaches, central air-based systems similar to those used on a city bus. On most RVs, pod-style units perch on the roof and deliver air to the interior space directly beneath them. Extra-long rigs may have as many as three AC pods up top. Highline coaches use forced-air duct systems to deliver the unit's cool breath to passengers.

Tip: Emergency Cool-Down

When the engine threatens to overheat while climbing a steep grade, rather than blowing a gasket, both literally and figuratively, turn on the heater for a few minutes, even if it's ninety-five degrees outside. The cool water in the heating coils inside your vehicle will drop the engine heat into the safe zone long enough for you to get to the side of the road.

Engine-Driven AC

In addition to the systems designed for camping, most motorhomes also have engine air-conditioning. Identical to a car's air-conditioning, they are powered by the motor and produce cool air only when the engine is running. Designed to keep the cockpit cool when driving, this system has no relationship to cooling systems used in camp. In really hot weather in the deserts and Florida, we've been forced to kick on the generator to run a rooftop unit to keep the cats sleeping (or hiding) in the back adequately cool.

Is That Cool or What?

Bring a thermometer to test the AC system. It's difficult to tell whether an AC unit is producing cold air or simply evaporating moisture from your skin when you put your hand over the vent. The AC outlets should measure in the forty-five-degree range after they've had time to come up to speed. Place the thermometer right in the AC outlet. Note: This procedure assumes that you're evaluating the rig on a hot day, not when it's twenty degrees Fahrenheit outside and the thermostat ignores you because it's too cold in the rig.

Upon activating the AC, listen to ensure the compressors are coming online in each AC unit. You will immediately hear the fans, but you're looking for a buzzing noise that indicates compressor operation. If they're already running, shut them down for at least five minutes and start them again to confirm the compressor activity. (The five-minute wait allows pressure to escape from the compressor. Otherwise, you could accidentally freeze the unit.)

Made in the Shade

Options for cooling reach beyond mechanical solutions. Proper use of ventilation is one alternative. Another is the installation of awnings down one side and on all exposed windows of the rig. Electric fans work well too, although a twelve-volt model designed for use from battery power may make more noise than cool air. If you opt for the ventilation solution, you'll want screens on all open windows to keep the local fauna out of your coach. For best flow-through cooling, simply head for the hills — with or without a can of Folger's coffee — and take advantage of the cool mountain breezes.

Awnings: Shade You Carry with You

Parking under a big oak tree works great. But you can bring your shade with you (although the oak works better). Most RVs are equipped with at least one large awning, always located on the right (passenger) side of the RV to match the arrangement standard in North American campgrounds. Upper-line RVs may have awnings over each window as standard features. You can add awnings to almost any rig.

Tip: Get a Thermometer

A heating or air-conditioning shop can sell you the correct kind of thermometer for measuring AC output. (Made of stainless steel, it looks like a cooking thermometer.) Too cheap to buy one? Use a swimming pool thermometer instead. Its temperature range is right for RV air-conditioners as long as its range extends below the fifty-degree mark. Give it a few minutes before taking a reading.

Note: Thin Air at High Altitudes

High altitudes are cool but devoid of adequate oxygen for those with heart or lung problems. When in doubt, check with the doc before the drive if you plan to sleep over at an altitude higher than Denver (approximately five thousand feet).

The main awning extends your living space, adding an outdoor "living room" that may have more walkable square footage than the interior of your rig. Pulling out and stowing an awning is like using a roll-up blind. The awning allows you to enjoy the great outdoors from a lawn chair without getting a sunburn. The best arrangement is an awning on the same side as the exterior ventilation for the refrigerator as this keeps the sun off both you and the "refer" for maximum cooling efficiency. Trailers also allow you to prop up their rock shield over the front window and use it as an awning. Some shade rooms come with netting to keep mosquitoes and other pesky critters out of your living area. For small rigs, special lightweight awnings offer some sun protection, although the gossamer material won't block sun and rain as effectively as their weightier cousins for the big rigs.

Maid in the Shade

Most awnings are durable, but for maximum life they require occasional cleaning with special cleaners. Available at RV stores, these cleaners are important for removing contaminants that eat awning material. Cleaning also removes the acid particles precipitated by smog, tree resins, and pollen, and the general buildup of crud. This should be done at a park with a good water supply. Ask the manager first. In most camps you get free water for drinking, laundry, and showering, but washing your rig and awning is hardly ecologically sound in areas prone to drought. We've been politely turned down more than once for awning and RV washing days when local water was scarce. Go to a truck-washing depot (these usually recycle water) if the park doesn't have facilities for washing down your rig.

Wear protective lenses when washing the bottom of the awning because the chemicals are strong. One of Kim's eyes became cloudy after an unprotected wash. It cleared up by the next day, but why take the chance? Even a pair of cheap sunglasses will help.

Tip: As Seen on TV

The perfect cleaning tool for RVers is a brush connected to a hose. RV shops sell brushes with four- or six-foot handles. Connect the handle to a long hose, get a bucket of mildly soapy water (use dish soap), and go to town. The same technique works great on awnings also. You may want to use an awning cleaner instead of dish soap. You can wax your rig too, but even with the rub-on-dust-off polishes, it takes time to wax a massive fifth-wheel or motorhome. We know, having done it more times than we can count. Don't forget that RV washing may be frowned upon in environmentally sensitive regions in which storm sewers (if any) drain into natural waterways.

Tip: The Weather Report

Awnings should be stowed when a storm approaches. As strong as a quality awning and support structure are, they behave like a sail in windy conditions. We stow ours even when walking to a nearby restaurant, since weather has a habit of unexpectedly taking a turn for the worse.

Underfoot

To get the utmost utility from an awning, most RVers put a large mat made of plastic grass of about the same footprint size as the awning underneath. This is cool to walk on and keeps sand and soil at bay. (We use a Japanese straw [tatami] mat for this purpose; it weighs nearly nothing and sand just falls through it.)

You can use almost anything that's durable, is lightweight, can be cleaned with a hose, and rolls compactly for storage. Don't try to substitute household carpet, because it's too heavy and impossible to keep clean in sandy or wet conditions. Trapped gunk adds weight and makes for a soggy, mildew-prone outdoor perch.

At the Gasworks: The Propane System

In RVs the main source of heat, refrigeration, and cooking power is liquid propane gas. Naturally, the amount of propane you carry and how you use it are directly related to how long it lasts, although energy conservation plays a major role. (At night, set the thermostat for sixty degrees Fahrenheit.) Propane in its liquid form is inexpensive, comparatively easy to store, clean-burning, and available at gas stations and RV and camping outlets. Some parks may offer to deliver propane directly to your rig for a small additional charge. In a trailer, propane storage is usually in two tanks on the tongue. The tank's outputs are tied together. Removable, they can be carted to the gas station independent of the trailer or fifth-wheel. In motorhomes, a variety of propane storage configurations can be found underneath the rig. Typically, you'll find the tanks near the wheel wells or axles.

At the top of a tank, propane reverts to gaseous form. That's what feeds your rig. Never turn a propane tank upside down in respect to the gas outlet. This could force liquid propane into your rig's lines with dire results.

Propane: Treat It with Respect

Propane, especially in liquid form, should be treated with the same respect you should have for gasoline. It's incredibly flammable, prone to leak, and, unlike gasoline, under extreme pressure; it's one of the reasons we don't recommend homemade RVs. We once saw one with a propane system partially built with garden hose fittings sealed with thick coatings of silicone rubber (if you can imagine).

Warning: Fire/Explosion Hazard!

Propane is highly flammable — that's why it makes a good fuel. Propane tanks always leak slowly or may intermittently bleed off excess pressure in the same manner. That's why they're mounted *outside* RVs of all kinds. Never store removable tanks inside an RV, house, or garage. Do not leave containers in any enclosed environment such as the trunk of a car for any longer than a trip to the refueling station. Dismount them when parking a trailer in a garage. We hope we don't need to warn you against smoking around propane, but you may not know that you must turn off pilot lights and propane flow to refrigerator, heater, and stove before filling the tanks. Follow the instructions on the tank's exterior and any supplemental instruction guides. Always tell attendants if a tank has been open to the air so they can use a tiny amount of LPG to flush out atmospheric contents and associated moisture.

In all propane setups, a regulator is affixed to the tank connector that feeds the actual RV's propane lines. All fittings should be tightened as directed, and since a motorhome's tanks are fixed, you usually must take the unit to a garage, though some parks have service people who will come around on a truck and refuel you on the spot, so to speak. We leave the vehicle during this process after checking that *all* pilot lights are extinguished. (We have a checklist for propane refilling as well as for breaking camp.)

Warning: Kids, Don't Try This at Home!

Kim, then in sixth grade, watched a maintenance man for the elementary school try to track a leak with the odor of natural gas strong in a classroom of about twenty students. His technique? Moving a lit match around all of the fittings of the gas furnace while a room full of kids and an obviously uncomfortable teacher looked on. As unbelievable as it seems, we've heard of people using this technique to locate LPG leaks in RVs. If you try this technique *and locate a leak,* you may find yourself towing that great trailer in the sky.

We'll never forget the time in Vegas when the guy refueled the tank and, with the nasty aroma of the gas everywhere (the odor is actually a chemical added to normally odorless propane to make you aware of its deadly presence), went off a few yards to light up an Old Gold . . .

Sir . . . I Have Your Connection Now . . .

Whether working with your trailer's tanks, motorhome systems, or the backyard barbecue, you should check that all connections are intact. In a modern trailer, fifth-wheel, or motorhome, this may require unscrewing a few panels or getting underneath the unit, scraping off caked dirt, and checking the connections. (If there's a substantial buildup of mud, grease, and debris, don't "dig" to reach the lines, as this may in itself cause damage, especially in units that use fragile materials such as flexible tubing or rubber hoses.) In older trailers, the lines are probably in plain sight, and may have been added in homebrew fashion (not a good omen). Have any even marginally questionable line replaced *before* use.

A Bubble Bath for Leaks

To check connections or even a suspected leak in a propane line, follow this standard procedure. Mix one part liquid dish soap with five parts water. Then, propane valves open, use a small paintbrush to "paint" the mixture around all fittings, including suspicious-looking parts of the lines and hose. (Keep in mind that you don't want to overtighten connectors, because this can damage the propane plumbing and precipitate a leak as well.)

Leaks coated with the solution will manifest themselves as bubbles. Should you see any bubbles, immediately shut down the propane tank valves or disconnect them, if the leak is at the tank outlet, and get it fixed. If the connections are tight, you need professional service. (If the mechanic has a nervous twitch when working with the gas, then maybe you should get service elsewhere.) Regularly replace any rubber hoses directly exposed to the sun, such as those affixed to a trailer tank system that lead to an internal connection.

Powering Up: RV Electrical Systems

The magic of the home on the road is its ability to use energy from multiple sources. When one source is unavailable or expended, another can sometimes be used to replace it. The three standard sources of power on RVs are gasoline/diesel, LPG, and electricity. (Yes, some older stoves use other fuel sources, but you get the idea.) Electricity is the most versatile energy source in RVs. Hooked up, any appliance or convenience available for the home can be instantly powered. On the road, or roughing it, twelve-volt power runs everything from lighting to portable computers and telephones. Amazing.

House Versus Coach Versus Shore Power

When reading this book or other RV magazines and publications, it's important to know what the power terminology means. Here's a brief glossary of power terms you should know when talking to RV service people:

- **Engine power.** In a tow vehicle or motorhome, engine power is used to drive an electricity-producing alternator, which runs fans, headlights, gauges, and the CD player and charges the batteries at the same time. (While we describe 12-volt power, the actual power in most rigs is between 13 and 14.5 volts.)

- **Coach or house power.** A separate set of batteries provides power to the RV. The "house power" runs lights and any other twelve-volt appliances.

- **Shore power.** Shore power is that provided by an AC outlet, be it in a campground hookup, your garage, or Sandy's house. (When discussing shore power, explain it as 115 volts. It can range from 112 to 120. An old campground with wiring problems or full of energy-guzzling rigs running AC may knock this down to an inadequate 105 volts or even less.)

The underlying concept of a recreational vehicle's electrical system is that a single system can be used by both batteries and "shore power" (plugged in or hooked up to the electrical grid). This lets you roam the country on just twelve volts, taking advantage of campground power only when it's convenient or you need it to run big-draw appliances such as air-conditioners and microwaves.

The electrical systems of a modern RV provide enormous flexibility, but it helps if you understand the basics of the systems, so that you know where to look when the inevitable problem occurs. Electricity is a critical element for all but the most out-in-the-woods camping. (Even then, you'll need at least some power to restart your rig, unless it's equipped with a hand-cranked starter like a Model T Ford.) Electricity powers everything from the interior lighting to starting the engine to reruns of *The Dukes of Hazard* on your rig's TV. Even your refrigerator when in propane mode uses a small amount of electricity to run controls, though gas does most of the work.

Tip: Saving Power

This one comes from "Bud" — a camper since the Great Depression, who runs an RV campground. In his eighties (we think), when a major campground waterpipe sprung a leak, did Bud call a plumber? No. He got a well-worn shovel, dug the pipe up, and fixed it himself!

Bud has modified his motorhome, a 1970s-era Apollo, in many ways. One modification makes a lot of sense for those who want to avoid reliance on shore power or a noisy generator to recharge the batteries. With the simple addition of light socket adapters, Bud replaced the internal incandescent light bulbs, like those used for automobile taillights, with fluorescent and other low-current units. That way, when out in the sticks, Bud and his wife can light their camper as brightly as a baseball stadium and don't have to think twice about the power drain on the batteries.

A Heavy Load

The basic tenet of RV power is not unlike that of a house. You have a certain amount of electricity available. In a home, unless you live in a fifteenth-century Bavarian castle (too drafty for us), it's unlikely that you'll exceed the limit provided to you. But in an RV running two air-conditioners, a television, multiple incandescent lights, and a microwave while simultaneously charging the unit's batteries, you can overload the circuits pretty quickly. Pulling too much current can not only damage your RV's equipment and wiring, but may cook the campground's power outlet and meter at the same time. This won't win you any popularity contests with the camp's operator or your blacked-out neighbors.

How Much Is Too Much?

You need to study each subsystem's owner's manual, or ratings stamped on plates affixed to the device, to match what the camp claims to provide to what your RV is actually drawing. Normally, this is a simple procedure. Make a list of how much each unit draws and add another two or three amps for power loss in wiring or the converter. (We talk about converters later in the chapter.) If you're over the limit, devices will run erratically or cords will get hot. Shut down everything and let it cool for thirty minutes. Then restart using only essential systems. Run heavy-draw appliances separately. Don't run the air-conditioner while using the microwave and watching TV.

Hot Links

When plugging into an ordinary outlet, wait fifteen minutes after turning on appliances and feel the cord, the hookup box or circuit breaker inside the building you're sucking power from, and the outlet where the plug meets your rig's plug. Lukewarm is probably okay, but if they're hot, shut down all electrical appliances immediately! Too much current is being "culled" from the lines or there may be other problems. You could precipitate a fire in your rig or your host's camp, house, or wherever you're plugged in. If everything works as it should, the circuit breakers will pop and turn everything off for you.

A Warming Trend

One way to check electrical fittings for loose or damaged wiring, or excessive current draw, is to gently touch the outside of plastic plugs and connections with your hand. (Don't do this in pouring rain and never touch bare metal wires or plug connections!) If a plug, switch, or outlet is physically hot, it indicates a dangerous condition in which electricity is not being conducted correctly. Corrosion, loose screws, or bad wires are present making electrical transmission more difficult and producing the heat as a byproduct.

This is a cycle, with more heat building more resistance until something gives. The circuit breaker or fuse blows — either in the campground or your rig — a fire starts, or the connections of the operating device melt down and fail. A simple touch of the hand once in a while can reveal electrical problems before they become disasters.

Tip: A Power Play

When setting up in a campground, especially if it's summer and you'll be running the AC much of the time, inquire if and how electricity is billed. Some camps build it into the cost of an overnight stay. Some charge extra for units with 50-amp service. At the end of your stay, the campground operator comes out and reads the meter and charges you to the penny for the power you've used. Save money by running the AC as little as possible and supplement open windows with electric fans.

Hooked Up

When your rig is plugged in at a campground, the power is being used two ways — to charge batteries and to power other devices on the RV — be they 12-volt (interior lights) or 115VAC (air-conditioners). You need to understand how electricity is being used in comparison with the quantity available and its price for delivery by the hookup. We use the example of the draw of a single air-conditioner and a microwave to explain current throughout this section because this combination is an example of a heavy electrical load. It's one issue that summer campers will face frequently if they want to cook while staying cool. And a jammed summer campground has some campers using more than their share of power.

Current Affairs

For about $40 to $50, you can buy an ammeter, simple and safe to use, that measures your rig's power draw in amps. You can get one at Radio Shack or almost any electronics store that sells electrical parts (not just toasters and washers and dryers). You lightly clamp the meter onto your rig's plug wire while it's connected to the hookup with appliances running and you get an instant reading. In a camp that charges excessively for electricity, the meter is inexpensive insurance against a surprise bill at the end of your stay.

It is also an important component in monitoring your rig's load to ensure you aren't exceeding the hookup's rating. If you know that a campground's power limit is 15 amps and appliances are behaving oddly, pull out the meter. If it shows you're drawing 19 amps, better shut off the air-conditioner while microwaving those delicious Kraft Macaroni & Cheese dinners. This meter can also be used to look for "ghost power" use — that's power drain when everything in the rig is apparently shut down or disconnected.

There are four kinds of current you will encounter when camping: 15-amp, 20-amp, 30-amp, and 50-amp service. Progressive campgrounds provide more than one level of current (amperage). In older campgrounds or those in public parks, you'll most likely

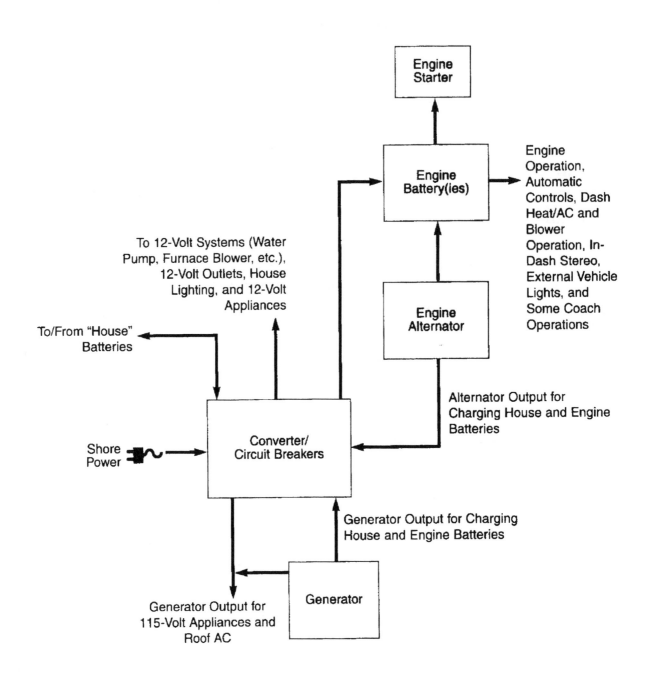

**15 or 20 Amp
115 Volt Service**

**20 Amp
115 Volt Service**
You may encounter
this plug at a house or
business. Use the
same plug you use for
15/20 at an RV park

**30 Amp
115 Volt Service**

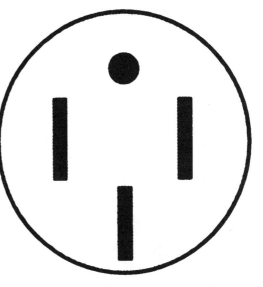

**50 Amp
240 Volt Service**

meet with 15 amps. In rundown parks, don't count on even this level of current. If appliances won't run or behave strangely — for example, shutting down or failing to start — and the park looks as if it was last remodeled in the Nixon years, then assume that campground current is limited to less than 15 amps. You'll usually run across low power in parks not listed in the campground guides because they don't meet guide standards. These ragtag parks may at the same time be located amidst beautiful, natural settings and a lot of fun if you can live without every electrical convenience while camped.

Note that each kind of service (15/20, 30, and 50 amps) requires a unique plug (see diagram). You will need an adapter to connect a 50-amp-capable RV to 15-amp service. Don't assume that because the adapter fits you can treat a 15-amp service as 50 amps! You only have 15 amps to play with, even though your system is rated for 50 amps and you were able to establish a working connection to the electrical service. Surge protectors are also available that convert the plug configuration while guarding against power surges and brownouts.

Tip: One More Time!

We've tapped (maybe a bad choice of words) into the concept that if you plan to use an extension cord or adapter, it must be adequate for the electrical load. Too thin a wire, such as a drugstore household extension cord, fries the 30-amp circuits common in modern RVs. Why? The wires can't carry enough current. It's like hooking a garden hose to a fireplug. Yes, water will come through, but at a pressure that will destroy the hose.

Electrical pressure works in even nastier ways. Rather than a small geyser, it may cause a fire or shut power down for an entire campground. Damage may be severe to your pocketbook as well as to trip plans when you receive the repair bill for the RV's electrical systems and the campground's expensive underground wiring and power metering systems. To avoid such problems, head for Home Depot or Home Base and get an extension cord that's rated 5 amps higher than you plan to draw.

15-Amp Service

The most basic campground current is 15 amps. You'll it find in older campgrounds and public parks. It's adequate to run one air-conditioner or the microwave, but not at the same time. The AC unit should be shut down while the food is cooking. There's also enough electricity to slowly recharge your rig's batteries, although this goes faster when you aren't using "heavy-draw" appliances or electric space heaters. (Recharging ability is also determined by the amount of power the converter provides.) Fifteen-amp power takes a standard three-wire plug like standard home appliances (see diagram).

20-Amp Service

Twenty-amp service is standard at new but basic campgrounds. The extra 5 amps of power adds enough "overhead" to protect against brownouts and make the initial heavy power draw of an air-conditioner starting up easier on the unit. The service may use the 15-amp plug or a 20-amp plug (see diagram).

30-Amp Service

Common in newer campgrounds is 115-volt power with 30 amps of current. Most new rigs are equipped for this service because they also have an air-conditioner and microwave to run. Even with 30-amp service, running too many devices will set circuit breakers and fuses a-poppin'. For the power-hungry, you can get away with running the microwave and the AC simultaneously and maybe a small TV. Thirty-amp service is the minimal standard for campgrounds built after the mid-1980s.

50-Amp Service

The most power-hungry arrangement is 50-amp service — nearly enough to light a (very) small town. Found in expensive rigs, this is enough electricity to run multiple air-conditioners, microwave, the refrigerator, and a computer with a twenty-one-inch monitor — all at the same time.

Unfortunately, 50-amp power is mostly found at expensive RV parks built in the last decade or two. Older RVs and inexpensive rigs can't take advantage of it anyway. If the park bills for power separately from overnight charges, the power bill for a 50-amp setup may approach (or exceed) campground rental charges if you run two air-conditioners full-time.

Low Overhead

There's usually a little amp room to spare in campgrounds built in the last fifteen years, assuming that the hookup you're using hasn't been damaged by water or the oxidation of the wiring. Most campground electricians build in some overhead so that a 15- or 30-amp load can run safely even if peak demand briefly pulls an amp or two extra when an air-conditioner starts up. Even so, don't count on it! If a surge while starting the microwave actually draws 30 amps, even for a second, you could pop circuit breakers and blow fuses in your rig *and* the campground.

Hot Tip:
Where There's Smoke There's Fire . . .

Never smoke near or subject RV-style/automobile batteries to open flame. A byproduct of charging and use is hydrogen — that fun element that's the most flammable atom known to man. Nonbelievers should watch the infamous landing of the hydrogen-floated blimp *Hindenburg* — a classic sequence in black and white found on CD-ROM encyclopedias as standard fare. Seeing it once will convince even diehards not to smoke near lead-acid batteries.

Batteries: An Important Resource

We've mentioned batteries frequently throughout this section, and for good reason. If they're dead you will have a rig without power, unless you're hooked up to shore power. The batteries are a key component in everything from starting the engine to keeping the refrigerator running even if it's in propane mode.

Modern motorhomes usually keep their batteries near the engine to provide the shortest electrical path for the heavy current demands of the starter. Trailers and fifth-wheels often have batteries near the propane tanks on the tongue, but we've seen them lots of places. Automobile-style batteries, a type of lead-acid battery, are simple and reliable (well, most of the time). You use one to start the engine and a second set to run the "house" functions of the coach. Shore power, the engine's alternator, and the previously mentioned self-powered generator are used to recharge the batteries.

RVers use marine-style batteries, another type of lead-acid battery, like those used in boats. These have a longer life, take and hold a deep (heavy) charge, supply more current when necessary, and handle abuse of all kinds better than those from Pep Boys. These are called deep-cycle batteries, because you can discharge them to near zero output and then slightly overcharge them without significant damage. They also take a "deeper" charge, which means they hold more electricity than a conventional battery, although you must allow adequate charging time to take advantage of this added capacity. Marine batteries cost more initially, but they'll save you headaches and their longer life pays for their higher initial price.

Top up batteries with distilled water only and don't overflow them. Otherwise, you'll have something akin to sulfuric acid running down the paint of your rig, and it's an excellent paint remover. (We found this out in a recently purchased classic BMW 635CSI whose battery cracked and dumped its liquid down the paint, making a real mess. The offending battery turned out to be made by England's Lucas, insultingly known in automotive circles as the *Prince of Darkness*. Oh, well.)

Sealed batteries can also be a problem if you spend your travel in the dry Southwest. The water may still evaporate, albeit slowly, but you'll have to pry the top off the unit and top up the water. We know, because we've lost several "sealed" batteries in the summer heat of the desert.

Eight Is Enough

A big Newell coach/bus has eight (yes, eight) batteries. Of these, two start and run the unit's big diesel and the other six run, as Newell puts it, "the home." With these batteries properly charged, you could probably drive one unhooked to Africa, camping in the Azores, if you could figure a way over the Atlantic Ocean. (At this writing, no pontoon options are available, but some highliner RV makers' R&D department is probably hard at work on it.) Now if we could just afford one with Corian countertops and those white glove leather seats . . .

Converters

RVs contain a mysterious unit with flickering light-emitting diodes (LEDs) called a converter. Depending on the layout of the rig, it may be under the bed, in a sub-basement storage well, or somewhere near the main electrical panel in a trailer (which can be anywhere). The purpose of a converter is simple and, to this date, we've never had a problem with one, although the potential is certainly there for a blackout if the unit is mistreated.

This unassailable box, usually full of fuses or circuit breakers, converts shore power (plug-in power) to twelve volts of DC current for replenishing, albeit slowly, your unit's batteries and running twelve-volt systems on your rig. In motorhomes, it can recharge both coach and engine batteries, while keeping them electrically separated. Most converters can also convert the generator output to twelve volts for charging the engine and house (coach) batteries.

Fortunately, all but the oldest units recognize when your batteries are charged and shut down to avoid overcharging or "boiling the batteries." Note: Converter technology has improved significantly. An old or add-on unit may be severely limited in the power it can deliver and its options. Relics found in late 1960s trailers may be capable of little more than charging the house battery and running a light or two. Their operation will be totally manual, with you throwing switches to activate the unit.

More on Converters

Should you have a power failure in the coach, check not only the normal fuses and/or circuit breakers, but also the converter's fuses and breakers, as there may be a separate panel for each. The converter's fuses may be located behind a panel mounted on the unit. If you have separate fuses/breakers for the coach, they can be anywhere. Look in your owner's manual. Some converters require removal of their cover to get to these items — the designer's idea was that they would never need replacement. *Never remove this cover panel when hooked up to shore power or when the generator is running. Deadly voltage may be present! Follow manufacturer's instructions to the letter.*

More About Fuses

As if you hadn't had enough about fuses already, your tow vehicle or the engine of your motorhome may have a separate set that has nothing to do with the camper. The tow car/truck/van manual will point out its location. If your motorhome is built on a separate premanufactured chassis, this booklet will show you where to look.

Smart Chargers

Not all converters recharge the batteries, and some take their time in doing so. "Smart chargers," now available and included in some rigs, charge the batteries faster and monitor their status regularly should the current level fall while the rig is in storage.

More Power, Mr. Scott!

Besides the campground hookup, there are several other sources of electricity at your command, depending on the kind of rig you drive and how it's configured.

Engine Power

Just as in cars and trucks, in a tow vehicle or motorhome an alternator charges the batteries as you run the engine. RV systems have two batteries: one for starting and operating the engine and a separate one (or more) for providing power to the coach. They are electrically isolated from each other. Thus, if you drain the "living-area" batteries watching World Wide Wrestling with Hulk Hogan, you can still start the vehicle the next morning. The running engine will charge both the coach and engine batteries in motorhomes. In fifth-wheels and trailers, charging both sets of batteries requires an adapter kit and a larger alternator for the tow vehicle.

The Generator

Newer motorhomes over twenty feet have a generator included, as this is becoming a standard item on coaches. Optional on large fifth-wheels, and even a few trailers, it functions much like "shore power," charging the batteries while simultaneously running internal devices such as the microwave. (Trailers may use a portable unit or rely strictly on battery and shore power.) Generators produce 115 volts of electricity with all but the least expensive units capable of running heavy-load appliances such as air-conditioners. They can recharge your coach batteries after a long camp without shore power, run an air-conditioner or two while on the road, and provide shore power regardless of where you are or what you're doing. (To avoid running the motorhome's tanks dry, once the fuel level reaches a certain point, delivery ceases and the generator coughs to a stop. You still need to ensure that even at this cutoff point you still have enough fuel to reach a gas or diesel station.)

Tip: Deadly Power

The generator produces enough energy to electrocute you. If it didn't, it wouldn't produce enough electricity to run appliances. Never touch the generator's output wiring when it's running or if you're attempting to repair it.

Starting a generator consists of pushing a button a few times inside the RV or in the generator compartment. Older ones with pull cords (yes, like lawnmowers) are not unknown, although we've never encountered one. Essentially a lawnmower engine driving a tiny electrical generating plant, this system can be used to run the main air-conditioner while not hooked up or to recharge weakened batteries.

Your generator may annoy neighboring campers as these units are *loud*. (Newer units are somewhat quieter.) Both gas and diesel units are available. Your diesel-powered motorhome shouldn't need diesel for the engine, propane for the stove, *and* gasoline for the generator. Choose a diesel generator instead (but keep in mind that it's harder to start in the cold). Imagine pulling up to the local gas station and asking for three separate fill-ups!

Generating Discontent

The generator is probably the most problematic major system in any RV. But, as far as we can tell, trouble starts when owners or users fail to follow the maker's essential operation and maintenance instructions and prematurely wear out "the little engine that *formerly* could." After all, an RV generator works hard to please but must be taken care of. Sometimes called an *Onan* after the principal brand, they need regular maintenance. Otherwise the motor will freeze or the unit will fail to start. Follow the maker's instructions to the letter, especially those on oil and sparkplug changes. That way the device will always be ready should you need it. Unlike an automobile engine, these units fail quickly when not taken care of.

Kim once helped an angry motorhome owner rebuild a unit. Things stored in the vented compartment near the generator were damaged, most likely because of heat buildup. Luckily, the owner didn't keep anything but nonflammable tools and a large collection of spare parts in the compartment. This model motorhome located the generator directly under the master stateroom's bed. Imagine if, instead of steel tools and bolts, the owner stored winter clothing down there. Better still, try *not* to imagine it.

Noisy Neighbors

On expensive motorhomes, the generator is very quiet, both inside the camper and to surrounding neighbors. On less expensive units, the generator sounds to neighboring campers as if you're mowing the lawn at 5:00 A.M. Unless the generator is a really quiet unit, sleepless campers may assemble a torchlight procession and head for your vilified rig at 3:00 A.M. to shut you down. Avoid having them tie you to a Zip Dee lawn chair coupled to the generator's output with jumper cables. (Besides, this probably voids Zip Dee's otherwise unassailable warranty.) Run the unit as little as possible, especially in the warm months, when other campers have their windows open for cooling and to enjoy the sound of the crickets and bullfrogs.

Watt's Up, Doc?

Most generators are rated in wattage output. Your appliances also have a wattage rating. (The wattage is the total amount of power required to run an appliance.) Add up the appliance wattages for all units that may operate simultaneously. Then add 15 percent for error or the surge of a unit's electric motor starting up. If this figure exceeds the generator's wattage rating, run fewer appliances simultaneously to avoid overloading the generator, overheating wires, or possibly damaging electrical systems.

Tip: You Wouldn't Like It Either

When starting a generator, give it a few minutes to warm up before turning on the appliances it will power. Just like you, waking and rising, it's hard for your generator to go from sleep to producing large amounts of current until it's ready. (The more current drawn, the harder the engine that powers the generator has to work to turn the generating mechanism.) Turn appliances on one at a time. Generator coughing and sputtering are evidence of a "genset" in need of repair, or you are demanding too much power with too many appliances.

Shutdown time? Turn each appliance off and give the generator a few moments to cool without load before shutting it down.

Stalled Out

You can stall a generator by applying an excessive electrical load on the system. Think of the electricity produced by a generator in terms of a lawnmower engine. A lawnmower may cut the grass weekly with no problem, but should you let it grow for a couple of months (the grass, not the lawnmower), the mower may stall, since it lacks the initiative to handle four- and five-inch grass strands when it's made for lopping off an inch of growth.

The same is true of your generator. Running too many appliances and electricity-based subsystems will overheat or stall it. Avoid such abuse with sensible management of electricity as this kind of overheating may necessitate a replacement generator rather than an inexpensive overhaul.

Solar Power

You can add a solar system that feeds the batteries with the power of the sun to any RV. Obviously, these work better in sun-drenched states such as Nevada or Florida than they do in New Hampshire or Washington. Since many RVers follow the movement of the sun, the growing popularity of solar power makes sense. Until a few years ago, the systems were expensive, unreliable, fragile, and unproductive. Modern solar cells produce significant recharge current and don't break down like the old ones did.

If you use solar power, you want to be sure that a one-way regulator is in place and functional. This ensures that the solar cell charges the batteries rather than the battery power working in reverse to melt the solar cell. Incorrect current flow can also drain and damage the batteries in the process.

Modern solar power should be considered by every RVer in any size rig. We'd like to see this as a standard option on more units, since the sun costs nothing — well, so far anyway. Solar power units should be removed, covered, or insulated during long-term storage. (We unscrew our unit and store it indoors.)

If you're interested in solar, here are some providers that offer more information on solar power systems suitable for RVers:

RV Solar Electric
14495 N. 73rd St.
Scottsdale, AZ 85260
800-999-8520

This company sells solar panels, inverters, and other systems to the RV market. It offers a newsletter and solar planning booklet, and publishes the book *RVers Guide to Solar and Inverters*.

Backwoods Solar Electric Systems
8530 Rapid Lightning Creek Rd.
Sandpoint, ID 83864
208-263-4290

This company offers a good catalog of solar and power options.

Real Goods
966 Mazzoni St.
Ukiah, CA 95428
707-468-9292

The company publishes the *Solar Living Sourcebook*, a useful guide on everything you ever wanted to know about building and running off-the-grid power systems. The company also sells solar electrical supplies.

Inverters

The opposite of a *converter* is an *inverter*. Inverters produce 115VAC when no shore power is available. Found in camping shops that cater to RVers and mail-order magazine ads in RV publications, inverters do the opposite of a converter: They convert battery power (12VDC) into household current (115VAC) from the batteries. You can, in theory, run any household device from one of these units. In practice, they can drain your coach batteries, because unlike a generator, an inverter drains your batteries rather than your fuel tanks. (Quality inverters sound an alarm or close down when battery power gets low.) It helps to have a rig with multiple batteries that are freshly charged before running an inverter with a heavy load such as a full-size television/VCR for a session watching *Lawrence of Arabia*.

Inverters do have advantages that you should consider. For one thing, unlike a chugging generator, they're silent except for a faint hum, and most units shut down to a trickle of battery draw when you aren't drawing power from them. In a small rig where there's no room for a generator, the inverter is the only option for 115-volt power when not hooked up to shore power. This may be a plus or minus, depending on the nature of your RV's electrical system and how much battery charge you have at hand.

Tip: Watt's Up, Doc?

When looking at an inverter to gauge its compatibility with your needs, you may find your appliances rated in amps and the generator's output capabilities rated in watts. Here are the simple conversion formulas:

Watts = Volts × Amps
Amps = Watts ÷ Volts

```
┌─────────────────────────────────────────────────────┐
│                      Hot Tip                         │
│                                                       │
│  When running any kind of device off inverted power,  │
│  such as                                              │
```

Hot Tip

When running any kind of device off inverted power, such as a handheld power tool, if you notice the unit becoming excessively hot, shut down the load (the device you're running) immediately. Too much heat indicates "dirty power" because the inverter is either of low quality or overloaded, or your twelve-volt batteries are reaching near-death status.

Power Struggle

You must match an inverter's power delivery capability with your planned employment of the unit. Consider the inverter's amperage and wattage output in comparison with the demands of the device you plan to operate from it. The inverter's rating should exceed that of the device by at least 25 percent in case there's a surge as you hit the trigger on an electric drill or turn on the big-screen TV you borrowed to watch the Super Bowl.

Down in the Dirt

Almost any inverter can be used to run something like a small heater, which isn't that particular about electrical quality. Still, solid state inverters with voltage "smoothing" are the best. You want quality, clean power for running devices such as electronics. Such a unit is mandatory for running "intelligent" electronics (TVs, computers, lava lamps, and so forth.) Devices with simple heating elements, fan motors (usually), and incandescent lights don't care about dirty power. Units with transformers or solid state circuitry will be damaged by electricity that's not adequately filtered. Inverters that produce contaminated power tend to use your battery's energy more efficiently, because less power is wasted in the "cleanup" process.

Take the call-around-the-RV-stores approach to get a consensus about which unit to buy and carefully match it to your planned wattage requirements. We like the units that also feature extensive overload protection. Too heavy a load, an alarm goes off and the unit shuts down in ten seconds if you don't turn something off. This protects you, the inverter, and the electrical devices. Of course, if you're in the middle of writing something on a computer, this shutdown could be bad news, as you've lost the work done since the last time you saved it. Most of the time it isn't a problem.

Keeping a Weather Eye

There are new technologies for monitoring the increasing complex power requirements of RVs. Unlike the simple amperage meters in the dash of a tow vehicle or motorhome, these intelligently show the status of the total charging system and help you better evaluate when it's time to crank up the generator or engine, replace the alternator, head for shore power, or buy a new battery. Not inexpensive at $249 to $349, these require professional installation. Consider the Link 100 unit (phone 1-800-446-6180). These may also include a low-battery alarm to warn you when the power is getting low. Some power inverters include these abilities as well, but only when they're online (in use).

The Water Systems

Self-contained RVs sport three water systems. First, there's the fresh water system that supplies the rig with everything from drinking water to the medium for flushing the toilet (in most rigs). Second, there's a gray water tank that collects water from the sinks and shower. Third, there's a black water tank for sewage containment.

Fresh water is delivered from a large storage tank hidden somewhere on the rig (and powered by a pump) or, if you're hooked up to a public water supply with a hose, the water flows to your rig directly as it would in a home.

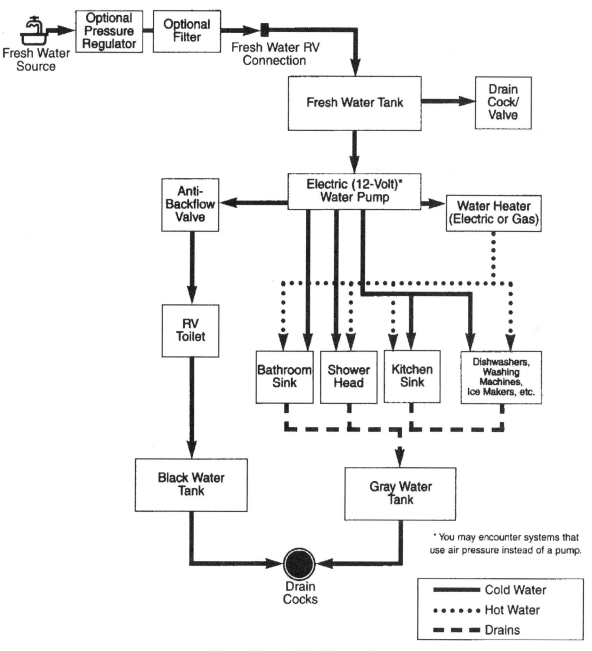

Simplified RV Water System

Tip: Mexico on Five Toilets a Day

No, we didn't think up this insultingly cute title (we're not that smart), but we've certainly experienced the Aztec Two-Step in Mexico. Don't even brush your teeth with dubious tap water. Should you get it, go to the local *pharmacia* or general *tienda* (store) and buy Lomatil. It will make you sleepy, so keep the RV, of whatever nature, parked and take a nap even if it means a couple of days' stay. Avoid alcohol, but drink lots of purified water. If this is not available (and even if the campground claims that the water is "purified," it may have made you sick), drink bottled water, soda, or anything that's canned or bottled, or purchase purified water from ice-making factories. (Get directions to *fabrica de hielo*.) Still sick after forty-eight hours? Find a pharmacist who speaks English and ask for the next step or find a doctor. You may have dysentery, which requires medical attention. Mexico has excellent medical resources, especially in cities and large towns. Don't rush off to the local Mayan ruins until you are fully recovered!

Water: The Elixir of Life

When you were a child, did you ever drink water from a garden hose in the summer? If so, you know how H_2O modified with plasticizers from the warm hose tastes (ugh!). Avoid drinking these toxins by bringing your own hose and *never* use one provided at an RV campground or rest stop. (We don't even want to think what it may have been used for.) Use only hoses made for handling drinking water. An ordinary garden hose adds unhealthy chemicals to the water, especially on hot, sunny days. Instead, use a hose (from an RV store) that states on the label that it's specifically designed for RV drinking water. Replace the hose as soon as it begins to discolor or after a year's worth of sun if you're a frequent or full-time RVer. Buy a second well-built hose for flushing the black water system and *never* substitute one hose for the other.

It's the Water and a Lot More . . .

Do not assume that water is pure, even from a mountain stream or so-called bubbling brook. There are bacteria living in natural water environments that can make you seriously ill. It's true, as far as we know, that natural water sources are self-cleaning, but Farmer Joe might have a few cattle "on the range" a couple of miles upstream. We hope we don't need to tell you what that means.

Municipal water systems in the United States and Canada are for the most part safe. Mexican tap water can make you sick, even in campgrounds where it is supposedly "purified." When in Mexico, buy water from the local ice company or stick to sodas or an occasional beer (more on previous page).

Checking Out the Water System

When appraising the water system, you first want to ensure that the system doesn't leak. Then make sure that with water in the fresh water tank, the pump works. (Test this *without* fresh water connected.) You should hear a thump-thump-thump when you turn on the faucet in the kitchen, showing that the pump is active. Then check that the toilet performs reasonably well in the flushing department. The next investigation involves the vehicle's sewage system. Remember, the kitchen sink, shower/bath, bathroom sink, washer/dryer, and dishwasher water goes into the gray water tank. (In really small van conversions where room is at a premium, all waste water heads for a single black water tank.)

Filter Systems

The best filtration system is probably reverse osmosis, but these systems are expensive and waste a lot of water. There is a miniaturized reverse osmosis system available for RVs at Camping World, but in addition to the price tag, it takes up significant space and few rigs can spare that much room.

A more workable, less expensive, and less effective alternative is an inline filter connected between the water source and the rig.

We use one that combines "activated charcoal" with traditional purification through gauzelike filter membranes. In changing the filter element every two months as recommended by the maker, it surprises us how much crud comes through the water lines at some campgrounds. Note that inline filters reduce water pressure from campground sources. For drinking water only, there are also cartridge filter systems (like the one made by Brita) that filter water into a pitcher.

What a Filter Can't Do

Even an expensive water filtration system can't remove bacteria from drinking water. In a rural setting there may also be farm pesticides and chemicals polluting the life-giving fluid. If bacteria are a problem, boil the water on a propane stove for at least twenty minutes before drinking it. Inexpensive water purification tablets are also available in most camping supply stores. Chemical contamination may force you to another location for water or demand that you buy bottled water for drinking and cooking. The only way to remove all chemical toxins is through a condenser water purification system like those used on sailboats — an unlikely option on RVs.

For shower use in areas with questionable water, keep your mouth closed while bathing. When refilling your water tanks, it's best not to introduce questionable water into your RV's fresh water tanks, because unless you have easy access to the tank, there's no way to get every drop out to make the tanks clean, sanitary, and pollution-free.

More About Water

One last thing that too many RVers don't know about is that the fresh water tank in an RV, like almost any tank of water, needs regular cleaning and sterilization. This keeps the growth of microscopic critters from building up on the walls of the tanks and attendant plumbing. As you would assume, bacteria and molds become more of a problem during the warmer seasons. Once a month, we fill the tank in a location where water is plentiful, add one cup of ordinary chlorine bleach (not the lemon-scented or no-scent kinds) per ten gallons of capacity, and then drain the tank into a suitable depository, as we would empty the gray water tanks. Before draining, let the mix stand for at least an hour when parked, or (better) twenty minutes of driving and sloshing time. Then run all faucets for five minutes to nail pests lurking there that can resupply the culture you just purged from the tanks. A quick rinse and then refill, and everything's ship-shape.

RV supply stores have chemicals that accomplish the same thing and probably do it better. But when we're out in the sticks, the closest Camping World or RV supply store may be half a state away, so we have become accustomed to relying on our own simple methods. Perform this exercise monthly in the summer and every two or three months in the winter (unless you're in a warm-weather climate, such as Florida, where you should stick to the monthly schedule).

It helps if you can see and reach into your tanks to inspect whether their walls are slippery, indicating a "creature" buildup, but this is difficult in all the RVs we've lived in. It also helps if your tanks can be completely drained. (You should leave the tanks empty when not in use except in winter. See Chapter 14 for advice on winterization.) Some tanks can't be drained dry without opening a hand-sized drain plug, if they can be reached at all. Thus, the bleach procedure must be done each time you bring your rig out of storage — even if the tanks and pipes were "empty."

What? No Water?!

Many campgrounds, especially old, unremodeled ones, lack enough water pressure for today's super rigs. Built at a time when water use was limited to filling a pot to boil spaghetti, the parks can't keep up with showers, dishwashers, toilets, and icemakers on modern RVs.

If water is delivered as a trickle in the morning and there is no sign of anything wrong (such as a crew of sweaty guys digging up pipes with old shovels or a raucous backhoe), try waiting a couple of hours. By that time, everyone will have showered and cooked enough Cream of Wheat to feed an army. Once the water demand is reduced, everything should return to normal. Peak use times are traditional: morning and evening (bathing, cooking, washing dishes) and on Saturdays in urban parks when everyone does the laundry they've put off all week. You will quickly learn the pattern during an extended stay.

Alternatively, rely on your RV's water systems by filling the tanks during periods of water availability. Then you won't be directly dependent on the park's water supply and its ups and downs throughout the day. If we're not staying in campgrounds, we fill our water tanks at roadside rests, service stations, or city parks. (Ask permission, of course.) For filling from nonthreaded water outlets, get a "water thief" from an RV supply store.

Under Pressure?

Campground water pressure varies from a fast trickle to enough to blow your RV's plastic plumbing to pieces. And, if that isn't enough to complicate matters, within a single camp, sites vary, with one area delivering too much pressure and another raising complaints from residents that it takes twenty minutes to fill the coffeemaker. As mentioned in the previous section, pressure may vary according to the time of day and other factors known only to Neptune, god of the seas and apparently of RV water delivery systems as well.

Tip: The Hot Alternative

We've never experimented with one of these, but the IN-CINOLET is promoted as a toilet that incinerates human waste into ash without water (Research Products, 214-358-4238). Now if it could just burn the kitchen trash too. Suggestion: Don't be sitting on it when the incineration takes place. Got that?

The Fourth Amendment:
The Right to a Well-Regulated Water Supply

There's little you can do about inadequate pressure except allow the campground to fill your tanks while you sleep. Then run with your rig's pump from the onboard tanks. On the other hand, too much pressure can be a serious, but avoidable, problem. Buy a water pressure regulator ($8), which, when mounted between your water line (hose) and your RV's input, limits pressure. More expensive units feature pressure gauges and allow you to set the amount of water pressure you desire. Keep it around 40 psi or less for most rigs to be on the safe side. (Unless we're in a hurry to tank up for the boonies, we keep it even lower.) Screw it into the entry side of your external water filter to also protect your filter and minimize setup and camp-breaking time. This way, two units become one.

No regulator? *Come on, it's only eight bucks.* Okay. Barely turn the water on by barely opening the camp's water cock to make a pressure regulator of sorts from the valve and keep an eye on things in case the pressure suddenly increases with a massive surge. Before hooking up your rig, visually inspect the water flow from the outlet to choose a setting faster than a drip but less than a fire hydrant. For filling, a weak stream is safest, even if it takes an hour to fill the tanks. Watch your rig's tank indicators and, better still, visually inspect tank levels if you can see them without unscrewing panels from the rig.

A Little More About Black Water Systems

Essentially, the black water system is a sewer on wheels. It's drained at RV dump sites that exist in campgrounds, parks, and some rest stops, camping stores, and gas stations. Drainage is handled with a flexible hose consisting of a long wire coil covered with plastic, which is more fragile than it looks. Therefore you should take care to clean and store it safely. Replace the hose as soon as it appears brittle or the connectors begin to fit too loosely — otherwise leaks will develop. There are several other things to keep in mind to keep the system functioning in a sanitary manner and get along amicably with other campers.

Cleaning Up for the Next Person

You can probably guess what we're going to advise here. Clean up your mess. All dump stations are equipped with a hose specifically placed there for quick washdown of the dump site. Leave the site sparkling clean for the next campers. *Never use a public hose intended to provide fresh water for cleaning dump sites, drainage hoses, or holding tanks! Use only the hose intended for washing down a dump site for that purpose.* Campers who ignore this rule may find themselves strung up to the nearest tree by other RVers or presented with a fat ticket issued by the local constabulary.

Dumping Procedures

Dumping your tanks is a minor adventure, of sorts. Clean rubber gloves literally on hand, carefully connect the output end of your sewage hose to the rig's outlet and then the dumping inlet. Release the black water first, giving it plenty of time to fully drain. (Check the RV's tank indicators for empty status, but as mentioned, these gauges aren't always accurate.) Then close this valve and open the gray water tank. This water cleans your sewage hose and the RV's valve connection and dilutes the sewage in the dump. Carefully disconnect your hose, first from the RV, holding it in the air to drain any remaining contents into the dump. Stow the hose carefully by locking it down in its storage tube or compartment and close the lid on the dump. Inspect the site and use the washdown hose if necessary. Good for you. An unpleasant job well done.

Tip: Empty When Full

The best time to empty the black water tank is when it's nearly full. That way, there's enough liquid to flush all the solids from the tank. Emptying a partially full tank may leave the undissolved material in the tank. If you must dump before a long voyage, fill the tank with water first and *then* pull the plug.

Tip: Avoid Hose Problems

Hooked up with the sewage hose and not worrying about it? Don't leave the hose connected for months in the sun or it will rot the hose. Hailstorms can punch holes in the plastic. Believe us — you don't want the hose to rupture in the middle of a drainage procedure. We even carry a spare hose. When packed in its shipping box, it weighs next to nothing and takes up less than half a cubic foot of space in a rarely attended storage compartment.

Hooked Up for a Month?

Why not pull the drainage cocks for both the gray and black water and leave them open for convenience? Don't do it. Leaving the gray water exit valve open won't make much difference (except to the environment), but leaving the black water open can cause significant problems as solids accrue. It's the liquid in the black water (flush water and urine) that keep the solid matter from solidifying in a corner of the tank. Solidification is cumulative until the tank has no capacity remaining and your rig gains a hundred pounds of unwanted sludge.

This serious sedimentation problem is caused when the liquid has been allowed to drain from the tank and left the solids behind. For this reason, always ensure that liquids remain in the tanks and don't leak out. Minor buildups of solids can be remedied, major ones take a repair shop or a new tank (not cheap). You can also try our miracle cure explained in the tip on the next page. (Well, maybe we're hyping it a bit at that.)

Holding Tank Chemicals

You must add chemicals to your black water tank to keep ugly, stinky organisms from growing in there and, to put it nicely, making your rig unpleasant to occupy. Look for tabs, liquids, gels, or powders at the RV stores that claim to be biodegradable or check with other RVers to see what they use. Warm weather camping requires more chemicals, as heat promotes growth. Avoid nonbiodegradable products (such as solvent and preservative-based chemicals), as these won't do a better job, but will make your discharged black water difficult to process into ultimately pure groundwater through the Earth's natural processes. You'll recognize these when you open the package. The chemical will smell strongly of paint thinner or unusually sweet-smelling alcohol (formaldehyde).

Miracle Black Water System Cures

Although solids build up in your black water tank, especially if you don't ensure that they drain along with liquid waste each time you dump the tank, you can get all but the worst buildup out of there. First, flush the tank by repeatedly filling it with fresh water (not from a drinking water hose) and then opening the drain cocks while connected to a dumping station. No luck? Buy some additives, from Camping World or a similar store, designed for this purpose. They also sell two systems for forcing water into the tank to remove debris.

One More Movie for RVers

2001: 1968, starring Keir Dullea and Gary Lockwood. No, we aren't recommending this movie because we equate the fictional spacecraft *Discovery* with an RV, but instead because of what maverick director Stanley Kubrick claims is the only intentional bit of humor in the film. The stuffy project director, Dr. Floyd, is in a craft on the way to the moon. When he has to relieve himself he approaches the restroom and is confronted with the very lengthy instructions for operating the "Zero-Gravity Toilet." RVers, especially those in charge of the black water and chemicals, will chuckle.

Tip: Saving a Little Money

Yes, you can go to the RV store and buy the $1.50 roll of special RV toilet tissue, but you can buy RV-suitable paper much cheaper at any supermarket or Price Club/Costco. To see if it's compatible with RV sanitary systems, drop a square into a bowl of water and immediately try to poke your finger through it. If it goes right through, then the material is suitable for RV use. If you succeed only in pushing the paper into the water or seconds pass before penetration, it's not a suitable tissue for an RV septic system.

Try This First

Fill the tank halfway with water and add the chemicals. Then head off down the road. With luck, the additives, combined with the constant splashing around of the partially filled tank, will break things down. Really jammed tanks or those in which the waste has had time to solidify may require repeated "treatments." In theory, a trip on a potholed road will speed the process, but this is rough on the rest of your rig and should be avoided.

Is It Really Blocked?

What you need to find out is whether any of these systems are partially blocked. (At best, a blocked system is a nasty repair job and can also be an expensive one.) Not every mechanic wants to mess with it. Modern RVs have gauges showing the contents of all "wet" tanks, but they may not accurately reflect the actual contents of each tank. You can check the working capacity of each tank by filling and then measuring the output until the tank is fully drained. This works fine for the gray water, but it's not much fun for the black water tank.

Alternatively, holding the valve open in the kind of toilet standard in most RVs, fill it using a one-gallon milk or water bottle until the water level reaches the bottom of the toilet's open valve. If from "empty status" a twenty-five-gallon tank takes only fourteen gallons before water backs up into the toilet, then you have a problem.

This is a potentially messy procedure and you must use a "legal" dumping area since sewage is involved. The purpose is to discover whether the tank is clean or solid sediments have built up in the tank requiring a cleaning or replacement. You should stick this nasty chore on the seller or his agent if you are buying a rig used or on consignment.

Refrigerators

The Modern RV Bi-modal and Tri-modal Refrigerators

Technology has evolved the RV refrigerator into a power-conserving device that requires little maintenance and can pull energy for cooling from four sources: shore power, generator (assuming you have one), propane, and, on some units, batteries. You can choose which mode you want to run in, although where you are and what you're doing usually dictate the most appropriate power source.

Honey, Grab Me a Cool One from the Icebox

Older trailers may have a true icebox that requires you to buy a block of ice before each trip and put it in a container with the food and beer. But, unless you're really looking for something cheap, chances are you'll have a unit that actually keeps things cool with the use of modern technology and power.

Keeping Fresh and Cool

Aside from the drivetrain in a tow vehicle or motorhome, the refrigerator is the single most complex system on the road, but, unlike the aforementioned generator, it is surprisingly trouble-free. Rather than employing a compressor as do home units, most RV refrigerators use ammonia in an amazing design that uses heat to extract heat from the interior and produce cool. There you have it — the basis of RV refrigeration. (Okay, some highline rigs do have regular refrigerators with compressors and large freezing capacities, even Sub Zero models, but these are not standard for most of us.) You can have a refrigerator fully stocked with almost anything, for breakfast, lunch, dinner, or that must-have late-night snack, if you keep the previous advice in mind when loading and operating the unit.

Mode Switching

On most RVs, you manually switch the source of power you plan to use for operating the refrigerator. Unless the trip is unusually long, we usually switch the "reefer" off and run on shore power when we arrive. This naturally means not opening the unit's door. Its heavy insulation suffices to keep things cold. Otherwise we use propane or a brief stint of the generator to maintain adequate temperatures inside the unit. (At one time running on propane on the road was a problem, with air flow blowing out the flame that powers the refrigeration process, but manufacturers have redesigned their units with "flame-out" sensors to prevent this dangerous problem.)

Since the RV refrigerator offers several modes of operation, should one fail, try the others. In a powered camp, run on shore power, but if that fails or the campground has a power outage (not uncommon), switch to propane mode. Out of propane and not hooked up? Switch to battery power if your refrigerator is so equipped. Keep this use to a minimum if you want to be able to drive away the next day.

If It's So Great . . .

Why this impressive technology used in the refrigerator and not the roof air-conditioners? Simple. This system can effectively cool an eight-cubic-foot sealed interior space (the refrigerator's storage area) and even make ice and store frozen food, but to cool the interior of an RV, shore or generator power is required, as several hundred cubic feet of space are involved. The advantage of the RV refrigerator system is that you can keep food cold even in places where there's nada power for AC units.

Keeping Food Cold

Refrigeration is vital to maintaining anything but canned beans for your expedition, unless you want to freeze your food in the snow. Using an RV refrigerator/freezer takes some practice. For one thing, on many models you can't stick refrigerator magnets to the front. You need to learn how to manage the refrigerator and freezer in an RV if you want to enjoy really cold drinks and fresh food. Here are some tips.

Get Spaced Out

Instead of jamming as much as you can into the fridge, provide some room around each item for air circulation. This is especially important when items are added that are at room temperature, because an RV fridge cannot cool warm goods as fast or efficiently as that big Kenmore at home. RV units don't circulate air as well, and those foods sensitive to fast bacterial growth, such as milk, won't stay good as long in hot weather in an RV.

Produce Some Blow-By

Buy one of those battery-powered refrigerator fans from a camping store that helps move the air around. Unlike home reefers, there's little air movement in an RV unit. Consequently, without this fan, some areas of the refrigerator and freezer may be warmer than others. Add a thermometer to the interior too, so you can tell when the temperature is too warm.

Sunblock

Park your rig with the refrigerator side under a tree or other source of shade. If this is impossible, park so the refrigerator faces east, to avoid the western sun, which is the hottest during the warmest part of the day. Another easy fix, already mentioned, is a rig in which the awning, if there is one, is located on the refrigerator side. Unfurl it and open a cold can of soda from the refrigerator as a reward for your efforts.

Too Cool for Words

In case you missed junior-high physics, cold is a function of lacking or removing heat — not an energy-light chore, even in the high-tech 1990s. One of the options on many RV refrigerators, especially those from the past two decades, is running on twelve-volt battery power. Sounds neat, huh? You, in the middle of nowhere, without a hookup, can keep that six-pack of Coors as cool as a cucumber using battery power. Well, if your fridge is so equipped, it's true — you can, but the enormous demands placed on the coach batteries for this exercise will drain them, and too much repeat use for such purposes will destroy even the toughest marine battery in short order.

Twelve-volt operation of the fridge uses *enormous* amounts of current in addition to the normal hard-on-the-battery surges common to engine/coach requirements. With twelve-volt power, cooling room-temperature comestibles is nearly impossible, as the power to remove heat is simply not available without a more efficient system than a mere twelve-volt battery can provide. (Forget chilling that hot casserole in the refrigerator, as the heat will cause other food to spoil from the warming of the fridge. Cool items to room temperature before putting them in for storage.)

Dogging It

You can dog the door of the refrigeration unit for travel so it won't pop open, but the contents may still shift while you are in motion. For that reason, we suggest that fragile or heavy items such as bottles of barbecue sauce (buy in plastic if possible) and canned sodas be secured without compressing them together, as this affects cooling efficiency. We do this with plastic trays, like the kind you see in most home refrigerators. Allowing some movement, they restrict the ability of contents to roll from one side of the fridge to the other. If something does break (rare), its contents are contained in its travel tray. You can use anything for a tray, including Tupperware, plastic food storage containers (get big ones), or, if you are desperate, cardboard boxes, cutting them short enough to fit in your refrigerator's shelves.

In this chapter we looked at the subsystems of recreational vehicles. It's these systems that turn camping into living in RVs. You can drive your house on wheels and have most of the amenities you have learned to appreciate as a civilized human being, if you know how to manage the systems. In the next chapter, we'll look at weight capacities and weight management (no, not ours, the rig's), which decide exactly what you can and cannot take with you on the road!

Chapter 9

Weight Management: The Good, the Bad, and the GSBTD

All rigs have two weight ratings: the GCWR and GVWR. The *gross combined weight rating* (GCWR) is the weight of the vehicle when empty — no passengers, provisions, liquids, or fuel. The *gross vehicle wet rating* (GVWR) is the maximum weight the vehicle can handle when fully loaded (wet is another term for loaded in RV lingo). "Fully loaded" includes everything from pets to people to food stocks and all tank contents, including the contents of the sewage reservoir. Anything of weight that you add, upgrade, or load, or that walks into an RV becomes part of a rig's "weight signature." Rigs cannot exceed the maximum "wet rate" without risk of handling problems and premature damage to the suspension, brakes, and tires.

The spread between the GCWR and the GVWR ratings is important. Subtracting the GCWR from the GVWR provides a rig load potential — the amount of weight you can safely add to the payload. Sadly, this may be less than you would expect, even in expensive RVs. More difficult to determine is the RV maker's credibility in assigning these ratings. For example, a motorhome chassis arrives at a maker's factory with a maximum GVWR as determined by the engineering team at the chassis manufacturer. As the RV manufacturer adds modifications to the chassis, such as heavy-duty shocks, air bags, and bigger tires, it may increase GVWR for no justifiable reason. (Manufacturers are allowed to rate their own rigs, and some builders are more honest than others.) That's why we developed our own rating system, the GSBTD — *grossly surprised by the difference* — to evaluate the real-world cargo-carrying abilities of a trailer, fifth-wheel, or motorhome.

The GSBTD — Our Acronym

This is our phrase. It's really a measure of the difference between the BS of the manufacturer/seller and the actual ability of the rig to carry cargo. The ideal rig has a broad range between the GCWR and the GVWR. This gap allows you to add that much weight to the vehicle and still be within the manufacturer's rating for the rig. The more the rig can carry (the gap between the GCWR and the GVWR), the more people and provisions you can safely transport. For a long trip into the boonies, the ability to carry provisions is vital.

The GSBTD: When comparing rigs, you may be GSBTD *(grossly surprised by the difference)* between units of similar size and price. Where a quality rig may allow as much as fourteen hundred pounds of people, cargo, and fuel, a unit that appears very similar may provide for a mere four hundred pounds of extra weight. Two adults, gas/diesel, water, and a week's worth of food exceeds this second rig's maximum by half a ton. Heavily overloading this rig for a month, and driving dirt and gravel roads to reach really rural camps, may precipitate a serious mechanical failure or incident. Even if it rides great now, what are you looking at ten years down the road?

Desperately Seeking Information

The GCWR and the GVWR are stamped on a metal plate inside a door and are also located somewhere else, perhaps in the engine compartment. When buying a rig, politely demand that the seller find the plate and scrape the accumulated mud from it so that you can make a note of its specifications. With the unit's serial number, contact the chassis manufacturer for the original weight specification and compare it to what the seller is claiming if the number differs.

Ideally you want a rig that comfortably handles your entourage, with all tanks full (don't forget water, fuel, and propane weights), along with personal effects, sports equipment, and back issues of *Motorhome* you haven't had time to read yet. Include everything from food to flatware in this calculation. Weigh items on a bathroom scale if you can't estimate the weights. Place loose items in a doubled grocery store paper bag to keep them on the scale. Finding reliable weights for items under ten pounds requires a more precision scale. Or group the items in a paper bag and weigh them together with heavier items.

Checking It Twice

The best way to double-check the manufacturer's estimate of weight (we'll call them "weight guestimates") is to verify the numbers. It's easy in a coach built on top of a plain vanilla truck chassis (just call its maker), but nearly impossible on a custom-built chassis, where anything goes. For rigs built on a custom chassis (highline motorhomes and most towed vehicles), hire a truck mechanic to spend an hour going through the suspension and adding together each element's weight abilities to generate an estimate. Locate a suspension expert for trucks, or an expert at an RV shop with no connection to your seller. Shell out $120 for a written report — it's money well spent. Should deficiencies be found, you can use the report to ask for corrections to the vehicle. If the seller is uncooperative, always remember, there's no shortage of quality RVs for sale.

Your Weight and Fortune

You want a safe, easy-to-control, and predictable-handling RV while on the road, unless you plan to camp somewhere permanently. The only way to tell how much your rig *really* weighs is to weigh it. As much as we hate to say it, some manufacturers misrepresent their units' weight. This isn't done with a rigged scale, but with estimates made before the addition of the supposedly optional air-conditioners, a generator, microwave, and awning.

The way to cross-check weights is to weigh your vehicle before purchase if possible. No, you can't use an ordinary bathroom scale, but you can weigh your rig at a commercial truck stop. These are located throughout the industrial/warehouse districts of every city. Or look under Truck Stops in the *Yellow Pages* and head to the one closest to you. There is a fee, but it rarely exceeds $15, even if you need each axle weighed separately. If you haven't already purchased, this is a great opportunity to check the integrity of the figures supplied by the seller or manufacturer. If you plan on adding roof pods or a generator, these should be included in the calculation of GCWR and GVWR. Their weights can be obtained from the manufacturer's literature.

Getting Ready Because Here I Come

Before weighing in, if the rig is used — even for demo outings — you must ensure that it's truly empty and void and flush out water and holding tanks. Solid sediment accumulation in the black water tank will skew the weight rating even if the RV's gauges indicate that tanks are empty. Since there's no safe way to evacuate the fuel and propane tanks, it helps if you can guess or trust the RV's indicators to establish the approximate contents. Use these figures and your estimates of tank contents to establish weights. A gallon of gas weighs about six pounds; diesel about seven pounds; water/sewage, eight pounds; propane, about four and a half pounds.

The People Under the Stairs

Within the past few years, something called basement storage has become common in motorhomes. Simply described, this is the addition of height to the vehicle to provide large storage bins between the vehicle's bottom and the floor of the living area. There's enough room for an enormous amount of goods — probably more than a nonbasement unit could accommodate in all its cabinets, closets, cupboards, and lockers. The problem with basement storage is simple — just providing the space doesn't mean that the rig has the power, suspension, or structural capability to actually handle this load on the New Jersey Turnpike on a breezy day.

One analyst did a weight scale test of a rig touting substantial basement storage. While, yes, there was lots of room, when the rig was loaded with two people, minimal fuel/water supplies, and food, the "basement" could transport no more than a load of chicken feathers without exceeding its GVWR limits. Even with modest provisions of canned goods in the pantry, the rig was overweight. Of course if you deal in chicken feathers and keep your canned food to a minimum, then this might be the rig for you.

The Discovery of Gravity and Its Effect on RVs

A motorhome with a rear that sags and a front that stands up in the air indicates a serious overload amidships or aft or failed suspension components. In a motorhome, a raised aft section may point to a lightly loaded coach or a failed front suspension in an older unit. The former is acceptable, but the latter must be remedied.

When hitching a trailer or fifth-wheel, does it take ten friends sitting on the front of the trailer to force the tongue onto the ball or fifth-wheel hitch? This is a common, but (usually) easily remedied, problem. But to remedy it, or for general information, you should weigh each axle of your rig individually. To get the total weights, use a scale for tractor-trailers. Weigh the entire rig at one time. You also can add the individual axle weights together, but a number of factors related to leverage may skew the results.

Motorhomes

Treat multiple rear axles, if you have them, as a single weight entity. Once both front and rear axles are weighed, study your owner's manual for the weights each axle should carry. The rear wheels carry the heaviest portion of the load, even on a rig with the engine in the front. Micros may have nearly similar ratings, because there's not much physical distance between them. If the rig is weighed without you and sizable pets, don't forget to add your personal weight, and don't fudge it either.

Front too heavy? Look for unusual loading schemes or, in Class As, the use of a bed that folds down from the ceiling near the cockpit used for storage. Look too under the sofa, which makes for convenient storage. Remove extra weight and weigh the vehicle again. On Class Cs and micros, analyze the contents of the bed or storage area over the cab. Then throw away or reposition the "bricks" as you find them.

Rear too heavy? (You want the rear axle to be heavier than the front axle because this adds stability to the rig, but you don't want more weight than is recommended for it.) Look for weighty items in the basement storage if you have it. Then go through all kitchen cupboards and other storage areas to see what's pushing the weight envelope. Pay special attention to foodstuffs in pantries (more on this later). In many Class As, a large storage area is provided under the bed if there isn't a wheel well there. Clean it out.

Trailers and Fifth-Wheels

To weigh a trailer's axles, it needs to be under tow by the vehicle that will pull it. With a trailer or fifth-wheel, you are looking for two things: the weight of the trailer and its imposition on the tow vehicle. A trailer with too heavy a load up front will push down too hard on the tow vehicle's rear suspension. Too much weight in the trailer or fifth-wheel's rear and the towing hitch will be difficult to mate to the tow vehicle and there will be increased risk of separation on the road. You want the trailer's tongue to bear down slightly on the tow vehicle's hitch so gravity, in addition to the mechanics of the hitch, keeps them together.

Your trailer and tow vehicle will have weight ratings for each axle. (Getting weights for a tow vehicle may take several phone calls to dealers or the manufacturer, particularly if the vehicle is older or built by a defunct company, such as American Motors.) No axle should exceed its maximum weight when the trailer or fifth-wheel is hitched. With some arrangements, the problem is obvious without the weights. Hitching, even with the correct hitch height (see Chapter 10), forms a "V" with front of the trailer and rear of the car pointing toward the ground.

What Weighs Too Much Where

Once you've analyzed the weight along the coach or tow vehicle, stand behind it and look at the perpendicular weight as the trailer leans. Looking at the back of the coach on level ground, such as a mall parking lot, use a tape measure to ensure that reasonable balance has been distributed across the narrow interior of the coach and any storage pods installed up top.

If sag is detected, further rearrangement of goods is required or a suspension problem exists, which must be diagnosed by a mechanic. Use a tape measure to check the distance between respective sides and the ground or mark a stick with each side's height and compare the marks. Again, this may result from overloading on one side, uneven tire pressure, or suspension problems.

Tip: Trouble on Wheels

We were once stopped near a Phoenix, Arizona, intersection for several minutes. A police officer eventually got the traffic, including us in the motorhome we were driving at the time, moving again. Passing the site of the problem — a car accident of sorts — we saw a sizable travel trailer sitting in the roadway attached to a hitch, an automobile bumper, and what looked like the hindquarters of a small car. The rest of an unimpressive Korean import sat thirty feet away, looking somewhat the worse for wear. Fortunately, no one was hurt, but hitching this monster load to a small car was a potentially deadly arrangement. You could follow an RV dealer's overly optimistic advice and unknowingly do the same thing with a trailer.

A Managed Approach to Weight Loss

Whether you drive a motorhome or tow a trailer or fifth-wheel, the drivetrain is always a singular concern. Why? Because, with the exception of pricey bus-chassis-based RVs, you're probably overweight or at least pushing the envelope, even if you carry what you consider the bare essentials of existence. One of the most important aspects of managing weight is the way in which the vehicle is loaded with people, provisions, and paraphernalia. To load an RV, you must think as if you're loading a boat. There have been certified nightmarish incidents of ships capsizing when passengers suddenly went running to one side of the ship because of fire on the other side. You certainly have also read about large trucks rolling or performing theatrical maneuvers on the freeway *as their load shifted.* The same thing can happen in RVs.

When a load shifts in transit, a large amount of weight suddenly moves within the truck's trailer or bed, causing an enormous change in the weight distribution and a sudden and serious change in the physical inertia of the vehicle. It's like loading the trunk of a car with ten bowling balls and taking a curve at 65 mph. The weighty bowling balls all shift, causing an unexpected change in the vehicle's weight and handling characteristics. As the load shifts, you'll look like Cary Grant as a drunken driver in Hitchcock's *North by Northwest.*

The same problems can be created in an RV by overloading one side of the rig or stowing heavy goods, such as cases of canned foods, in the upper storage bins standard in most vehicles. In the past, vehicles were designed with too much integral weight on one side, such as the refrigerator, water, and holding tanks all on the passenger's side. If this side also includes a slide-out pantry loaded with canned goods, the rig will behave oddly at best.

To avoid weight shifting, and to properly balance your rig, follow these general tips:

- Pack items with partitions, boxes, or shelves that prevent movement of weight during transit.
- Store heavy items toward the floor or bottom of the rig, if possible. Store lighter items in upper cabinets. Make sure all latches are secure. Add partitions and storage straps as nec-

essary to confine goods within storage spaces. We often stuff pillows and blankets into open cabinet spaces to prevent shifting (and cut down on rattles) when the rig is in motion.

- When possible, put heavy objects or collections of objects that account for significant weight over an axle. Avoid putting the heaviest objects behind the rear axle.
- If the tongue weight of the trailer is too light, increase the tongue weight by storing heavy items forward of the axle.
- Distribute the weight evenly throughout the rig. The rig should be balanced after loading, with no obvious leanings up, down, or sideways.

Tip: Should You Drive While Half-Tanked?

Assuming you're not heading off to back-country Canada where supply stations may be few and far apart, you can cheat the odds by traveling with as little liquid as possible. Empty all holding tanks before you travel. Fill a few soda bottles with water and leave the water in the tank for toilet use on the road or empty it and use rest stops. Gas station and restaurant facilities can also be used if you are making fuel or food purchases there.

Travel with a minimum of petrol or diesel and as little propane as is required to run the refrigerator, or leave it empty and turned off. Reduction of liquids — one of the heaviest items you can transport unless you also truck in gold bars — cuts weight substantially. This, of course, assumes you can top off once you reach camp, unless you're headed for Death Valley.

To give you an idea of RV liquid weights: 50 gallons of water plus 100 gallons of diesel plus 25 gallons of propane, with *empty* holding tanks, works out to more than 1,500 pounds! (As mentioned, gasoline weighs less than diesel. Note that some Mexican diesel is slightly heavier than the American variety because [we assume] of variations in the refinery specifications.) Hey, an innocuous case of Coca-Cola adds more than 15 pounds!

A Weight Loss Program of Sorts

Liquids, from fresh water to sewage, are weighty to drag around the country. The pantry is a prime source of weight problems. Most pantries are located amidships over the wheels to alleviate balance/weight/control problems, but you still have to pay for the fuel to transport them and liquids take up space you may not have available. "Permission to come aboard, sir?" should be denied to multiple flats of canned goods ranging from sodas to everyone's favorite, Green Giant Waxed Beans and Okra.

The best way to lose weight is through a reduced diet. Sound familiar? Unless you plan to park informally in the middle of the woods (possibly illegal anyway) or at a campground half a continent's distance from a store, you can pick up provisions as you need them using your tow vehicle. Or, in a motorhome, you can unhook and head to town for provisions.

Avoid carrying heavy tanks of liquids, and while your motorhome may hold more than one hundred gallons of fuel, that doesn't mean you need to use the complete capacity, unless you're headed miles into a "No Services" area like Florida's Everglades. Otherwise, you're using fuel to haul fuel. This is not a practical or environmentally suitable solution.

You can also save weight with careful selection of foodstuffs as do backpackers worried about the weight and bulk of their packs. Assuming pure water (or snow) is available at or near camp, dried food allows you to carry the maximum amount of nourishment with the minimum weight, and not always at the cost of allure, flavor, and texture. Such foodstuffs include pastas of all kinds, beans, dehydrated soups and mixes, flour and grains, dried fruits, spices, and even dried meats, fruits, and vegetables. A bag of dried peas tips the scales far less than a can or a bag of frozen ones, and dried peas taste just as good in soups and other dishes.

Long trips mean stocking up, especially if you're heading into the woods without a Piggly-Wiggly superstore around the corner. That inconvenience may make you want to carry far more edibles than you need or than your RV can safely carry. (See GSBTD, in a previous section.)

Other Weight Savings

If you won't use it or don't need it, don't bring it! We could tell you a story about the couple towing *two* cars (before the police got to them), and we'll never forget the road-weary "micro" motorhome with three (yes, *three*) large storage pods atop plus gear crammed to the ceiling, visible through its windows. It was so overloaded that it's hard to believe the tires weren't rubbing, as, in our guess, the geriatric springs barely handled this ancient rig when it was totally empty.

If you watch your RV's weight, you'll manage to have fun. In the next chapter, we talk about towing and tow vehicles. Although not our favorite topics, for those of you who choose trailers or who tow cars behind their motorhomes, the chapter is a must-read. The rest of you can skip the facts on hitches and such and move on to Chapter 11, where you'll learn how to get your rig ready to roll.

Chapter 10

Towing, Tow Vehicles, and Towed Vehicles

In this chapter, we'll look first at mating tow vehicles to trailers and fifth-wheels. Then, for those who drive motorhomes, we'll look at towing a travel vehicle behind the rig. Mating the tow vehicle to that being towed is important. Otherwise sway will affect stability. On improperly matched vehicles, even moderate crosswinds or a passing truck may precipitate a loss of control.

In the past, we've bought a fifth-wheel or trailer first and then matched a tow vehicle to it, based on the unit's weight and the kind of power required to drag it up a hill and control it while going down one. Some long-timers recommend the opposite approach: Get the tow vehicle first and then, based on its capacities, match a trailer or fifth-wheel to it. In the end, the advice is the same: Make sure that tow vehicle and towed vehicle like each other.

Matching the Tow Vehicle and Trailer

Obviously, there are vehicles that can't safely tow trailers. Compact family cars are incapable of towing anything but a snowmobile or two on a basic towing platform. Light trucks with six-cylinder engines are slightly more capable, but not up to pulling a five-thousand-pound trailer up a grade.

Towing a large travel trailer requires the power, cooling, and structural strength of a rear-drive, V8-equipped truck, sports utility vehicle, or full-sized sedan. There are even heavy-duty diesel trucks made particularly for towing fifth-wheels and travel trailers. Some of these look like small semitrucks and cost $40,000 to $100,000 or more. You must match the tow vehicle (whether car, van, truck, sports utility vehicle, or custom towing rig) to the RV you'll be towing.

Where to Get Vehicle Tow Weights

While it may take several long-distance phone calls, you can ask the manufacturer about towed weight limits. Before making your calls, have the size and number of cylinders handy (5.7 liter V-8, for example). Another source is back issues of *Trailer Life*, which prints an annual list of the most tow-worthy vehicles and the weight of the trailer each can handle based on engine size. When considering weight, always take into account the payload.

The Family Car

If you'll be using a standard family vehicle (car, truck, van) to tow a travel trailer, you must ensure the vehicle is roadworthy and equipped to tow another vehicle. That means it should be well maintained, with a strong engine, and it should not be loaded excessively, in addition to the trailer load. (Don't pull a trailer with a station wagon loaded with bricks.) Some car and truck manufacturers offer an optional trailer-towing package that increases the rated load of the vehicle. Owners of existing vehicles will want to add a competent towing package to their tow vehicle.

A towing package typically includes upgrades to the suspension, radiator, alternator, and flashers that must support the trailer's lights in addition to the car's. You'll also need to install cooling systems for maximum engine and transmission life. To ensure that your vehicle engine and transmission are properly cooled, you will also need to add the following systems to the two vehicles if they are not already included as part of the tow package:

- Trailer wiring harness.
- Brake wiring.
- Trailer battery charging system (if your trailer or fifth-wheel is self-contained).

Don't Exceed the Weight and Height Limits

Okay, we harp on this point, but safe towing depends on working within the weight limitations of your tow vehicle–trailer combination. Determine the manufacturer's maximum weight ratings for your tow vehicle and rig combination and always stay within these limits. First, look in the manufacturer's literature for the maximum weight (GVW) the vehicle can tow. Some light truck manufacturers list a different max GVW capacity for fifth-wheel towing than for bumper towing. (The fifth-wheel capacity is often higher.)

Next, you'll need to look in the manual for the gross combined weight rating (GCWR). The GCWR is the maximum combined weight of the tow vehicle and the load you will pull. This is considered the most important towing weight specification.

Anything you put in the trailer adds to the weight. Further, you can't move things from the trailer to the tow vehicle without accounting for the weight. The weight in the tow vehicle adds to the GCWR — and you can't exceed the GCWR any more than you can exceed the GVWR. Confused? We discussed weight capacities in more detail in Chapter 9. You must have missed it, or maybe we simply confused you even more.

Even with an upgraded towing package, because of the height of large fifth-wheel trailers and the expanding storage capabilities of modern travel trailers, it's easy to exceed the towing weight allowances. To calculate GCWR, you must determine the actual weight being towed and the total weight of the trailer and two vehicles combined. Start with the dry weight of the trailer. (Manufacturers often understate this weight, so you may want to take the vehicle to a truck scale.) If you know the true dry weight of your trailer, add in the weight for all fluids, food, clothes, and supplies. Then add a bit more for good measure. This amount should never exceed the GVWR of the trailer. Next add this weight to the weight of the tow vehicle, ready to go (include you, the kids, the food, the dog, everything). If this figure does not exceed the GCWR of the tow vehicle, you're almost ready to roll.

Some vehicles also specify a limit on tow frontal area (GVF) in square feet. Finding the maximum GVF can be difficult. Not every towing guide provides this information. However, calculating the GVF is rather easy. First, measure the width and the height of the trailer. Subtract the distance from the road to the trailer floor from the height. Multiply this number times the width. If the calculated GVF is less than the manufacturer's maximum GVF, you're okay to travel.

The last consideration involves hitch height. First, determine the amount of room above ground that your trailer needs to be in order to be towed level. Then determine the height of the tow point of the vehicle. The heights should be the same. Most likely, you'll find they are not. However, you'll have a more stable combination with less high centering and bumping of the rear end on the ground if the heights are close to the same.

There are hitch drops available for adjusting rear mount hitches. Many fifth-wheel hitches have a height adjustment, as do some trailers. Another solution to the hitch height problem is to have your RV professionally raised or lowered.

Minimizing Wear and Tear on the Tow Vehicle

People are often concerned that towing places a severe strain on the tow vehicle, causing it to wear out faster. It does if you don't select the correct type of tow vehicle. However, if you choose a tow vehicle with appropriate weight capacities, the wear issue is not really that great if you carefully maintain and equip your tow vehicle.

Be sure to change transmission oil and filters regularly. You'll likely see increased wear of the brake pads as well (even though you have brakes on your trailer), so check them regularly and replace them earlier than you would on a vehicle without towing duty. (See Chapter 13 for more on routine maintenance.) Engine oil coolers are another way to keep the tow vehicle operating at lower temperatures, especially on small, high-performance engines. These differ from transmission oil coolers in having bigger passages for higher flow rates. Typically, these attach where the oil filter goes. The (relocated) filter and cooler are connected to the fitting with a flexible hose. Again, consider using a synthetic oil, even though it's more expensive. Avoid oil-thickening treatments like STP. According to Click and Clack of *Car Talk* fame, there's little scientific evidence they benefit engines and there are reports of prop airplane engines using these materials stalling in flight.

Hitching a Trailer

DATE →			
HITCHING BASICS			
Match vehicle "roll" angles			
Block trailer wheels firmly			
Measure from inside of ball socket to ground (write in measurement)			
Measure all four corners of tow vehicle to ground (write in measurement)			
Adjust ball height and couple			
Attach/lock spring bars			
Attach/lock safety chains			
Make electrical connections and test brake lights and turn signals			
Raise tongue jack and visually inspect both vehicles for balance			

Double-checked by:

Checklist for hooking up to a trailer. Have your dealer or seller take you through the hitching steps for a trailer.

Keep the Drivetrain Cool

You should reread the sections on transmission and engine cooling if you plan to tow anything. Keeping the drivetrain systems cool is the key to long-term towing. Cooling systems deteriorate with age unless properly maintained, and you want the maximum cooling efficiency possible for RVing. If your radiator has clogged passages, the cooling capacity will be substantially reduced, even though it may be sufficient for light duty. Have your radiator flow-tested (not pressure-tested) before towing. If the flow is restricted, have the radiator replaced or "rodded out." Also, examine your tow vehicle regularly for collapsing hoses. (The hoses should have a spring in them. Without the spring, they can collapse under negative pressure at higher rpm.) Also check the antifreeze levels regularly. Check also for weak pressure caps, glazed or loose belts for the fan and water pump, thermostat performance, and proper fan clutch operations. If your vehicle has electric fans, check the sensors that switch on the fan and the fan motor.

For maximizing the tow vehicle's performance, you will also have to adjust your driving habits. Slow down. Be aware of traffic. Watch the curves. Watch the engine temperature at all times. If your engine is getting hot, shut off the air-conditioning and slow down. Turning on the heat will also take up some of the load. You can also reduce the load by stopping and placing the transmission in neutral. If your car has an electric fan, don't rev the engine. Opening the hood also improves air flow, which can provide 15 percent of your total cooling capacity. The heat output of a four-speed transmission goes up when the torque converter locks or unlocks. Keep the vehicle in overdrive on level terrain.

About Fifth-Wheel Hitches

Fifth-wheel hitching is a simple affair compared to trailer coupling. Choose a quality hitch and don't overburden an inadequate pickup truck with a big fifth-wheel and you're almost in business. Decisions still must be made about the kind of hitch (there are two basic types), the structural strength needed to manage your rig, and whether you want a quick-release hitch that frees your pickup's bed for other uses.

The Basic Hitch

The standard fifth-wheel hitch is a simple, yet solid affair. Connecting the truck to the fifth-wheel, it allows the trailer to move up and down in parallel with the truck to accommodate uneven roads and hills and valleys. Swivel is allowed so that the rig can take corners with the truck at a different rotational angle than the fifth-wheel as both vehicles slide through the turn.

The Latest and Greatest?

A new kind of hitch provides these basic abilities, but it also allows tilt. Should the truck be on a surface not parallel to that of the trailer, the hitch allows a moderate amount of "twist" independence between one vehicle and the other. Having experimented with both the basic and the newer hitches, we would recommend either, although those pulling large fifth-wheels with plans for travel over unimproved roads should seriously consider the latter. The ability of this hitch to tilt slightly makes coupling a fifth-wheel to its hitch slightly easier by adjusting to the few degrees difference in pitch. As you would expect, these cost more than standard hitches unless you are willing to settle for a tilt model built on simple rubber bushings.

One Last Issue to Consider

Mismatched hitch height can be a problem in getting truck and fifth-wheel to mate. Many models allow you to adjust the hitch height from the bed. Too high and the back of the fifth-wheel may catch on a speed bump or driveway. Too low and, when combined with inertia over bumps, the tow vehicle and even the leading lower edge of the rig may rub on the payment. Have an expert show you how to do it. Every combination of hitch and truck has its own idiosyncrasies.

Hitching a Fifth-Wheel

HITCHING BASICS			
Match vehicle "roll" angle			
Block fifth-wheel wheels firmly and lower tailgate			
Use the fifth-wheel's jacks to raise it over the coupling plate			
Remove the pin and open the coupler lock			
Back the truck **carefully** to couple the two vehicles			
With the brakes set on the truck, inspect the coupling for a firm "lock"			
Replace the safety pin if coupling satisfactory			
Make electrical connections and test brake lights and turn signals			
Lift fifth-wheel jacks and lock			
Unblock fifth-wheel and stow blocks			
Double-checked by:			

Checklist for hooking up to a fifth-wheel. Have your dealer or seller take you through the hitching steps for a fifth-wheel. Practice in his or her presence at least once.

Tip: Breaking It In

As with everything from the tow vehicle's engine to the brakes and tires, your "tilting" hitch must be broken in too. The first week or two of driving may find you dissatisfied as the two vehicles' unequal sideways torque doesn't meet the dealer's promises. Give it time and the hitch materials loosen up. Suddenly a smile will cross your face as a bumpy ride over a crossing seems smooth and easy.

Tip: A Runaway!

Should your hitch fail, you will immediately notice heavy sway from the trailer. Don't slam on the brakes because you could jackknife. Instead, slow gradually as you move to the side of the road. You'll feel and hear the trailer bumping the back of the tow vehicle. That's okay. Your goal is to get off the road safely and out of the way of other drivers.

Braking Systems

When towing the smallest of trailers, often all that is needed is to hook it up and go. Most tow vehicles can safely handle units of one thousand pounds and less. Standard recommended safety equipment includes safety chains, marker lights, turn signals, and brake lights. When towing more than one thousand pounds, the safety requirements depend on the size of the tow vehicle. For trailers fifteen hundred pounds and over, it is recommended (and often required by law) that one have independent wheel braking on the trailer.

Brakes for trailers come in two general types: surge and electric. A surge braking system hydraulically actuates the brakes as the system senses pressure on the tow ball in the trailer tongue when the trailer decelerates against the tow vehicle. The advantages of surge brakes include simplicity in attachment to the tow vehicle and fully automatic braking action. The disadvantages of surge brakes include the complexity of brake adjustments, the amount of "pushing" on the tow vehicle while braking, and uneven braking action when coasting down hills.

With surge braking systems you can't actuate the trailer brakes independently of the tow vehicle. Electric brakes incorporate electromagnets inside the brake drums, which actuate the brake shoes, in proportion to the amount of voltage put across the system. Thus, a brake controller must be installed in the tow vehicle and connected to the tow vehicle's braking system. Some braking controllers are connected directly to the tow vehicle's hydraulic brake lines. These systems provide smooth stopping but are subject to leaks (and thus lost braking power). Many vehicles with antilock brake systems will not operate efficiently with the hydraulic brake controller. For these vehicles, an electric brake controller is necessary.

Electric braking units detect when the brake pedal is pressed and control the trailer braking through the use of pendulums or accelerometers. The advantages of electric brakes are the simplicity of the braking system and the fact that the trailer brakes can be actuated independently. The disadvantages include the fact that the tow vehicle must be wired for the electric brakes. Worn or incorrect wiring can cause brake failure.

Safety Chains Required

With all trailers, you should use safety chains to connect the trailer to the tow vehicle in the event that the trailer becomes uncoupled or the tow ball breaks or comes loose. The chains used should be strong enough to securely connect the trailer to the back of the vehicle, and should be crossed so the tongue of the trailer will fall into the cross if it ever becomes unattached. If the hooks are installed so they are inverted as they are passed through the safety hook loops, the hooks are much less likely to be bounced out in normal use and become disconnected. The slack of the safety chains should allow full movement without binding. Be careful that the chains don't drag on the ground.

In addition to trailer brakes and safety chains, it is common (and often required) to have a system that automatically actuates the brakes if the trailer ever becomes totally disconnected from the tow vehicle. This is called an emergency breakaway braking system. We sincerely hope yours never needs to activate.

Towing Vehicles Behind Your Motorhome

We've seen everything towed behind motorhomes, from a complete woodworking workshop (with lathe), to Jet Skis, to cars as heavy as the micro motorhome attempting to haul them (must have been fun in the mountains). There are no specific limitations to what you can tow, as long as it's not explosive, a corrosive or an oxidizer, oversize, or overweight for the highway. But the towed vehicle or towing platform must have current registration from its native state. You should register all your vehicles in the same state, because the police may have a tough time understanding multistate registrations — especially with a motorhome from Florida, a car registered in California, and a platform licensed in Montana. In addition, vehicles such as motorcycles must be registered separately unless you don't plan to actually use them on the public roads. Boats and snowmobiles must also be registered. Fortunately, while you must register your horse trailer, you won't need plates or a sticker for the horses — at least not so far. (Of course, you'll need veterinarian records when crossing some borders — so know the rules before you go.)

Tip: A Menace to Society

Should you tow an obviously excessive load, lose part on the highway, or tow something in a risky manner, you could be subject to a ticket. Everything must be properly loaded, brake and turn signal lights must work, and mountainous overloading will not go unnoticed by the highway patrol.

Platforms Versus Wheels

There are two ways to tow a transportation vehicle behind your motorhome. The first and easiest connects your car to your motorhome with a flexible bracket. The car rests on its own tires and moves up and down with the lumps and bumps, with the towing rig allowing vertical flexibility. This system is more akin to simply pulling the car. There's no towing platform to register separately, and the simple hitch has less chance of hitting the ground as you go over speed bumps.

The second method is with a towing platform. The towing platform carries the car or other vehicle like a trailer. Towing platforms have weight capacity ratings, just like other trailers. The platforms hitch to your motorhome much as a trailer hitches to a car. Since the hitch must be low on the RV's back bumper, there's an additional possibility of bottoming out on a hill or speed bump. The platform does save wear on the front tires of the towed vehicle and provides a method for towing cars that can't be towed on their own four wheels.

There are towing platforms to tow almost anything, from motorcycles to ultralight aircraft. The platforms consist of a simple two-wheeled trailer that may or may not be custom-built for the application. For example, a platform for carrying two motorcycles may contain wheel wells for the bikes to add stability and lockdown points for security.

Tip: Lighten Up to Go Faster

If you plan on towing a small car behind a motorhome for in-camp transportation, you must ensure that there is enough power for towing the entire rig up grades. Obviously, towing a small pickup truck is less strain than dragging a 1979 Cadillac, but we've seen some very unlikely matches in our travels, slogging up grades at 4 mph. Reduce the weight in the rig if you're having problems, or get a lighter vehicle to bring with you — or, in really bad cases, consider another rig or try using bicycles for transportation instead.

The Hitch

Towing anything behind a motorhome is similar to towing a trailer. You want a slight downward pressure to keep the hitch in place, but not so much that you put significant pressure on the motorhome's suspension and overload it. With the tow vehicle in place, weigh the motorhome's rear axle to ensure that you aren't overloading it. An expert "hitchman" can fix this problem in part with subtle adjustments to the hitch. Another solution is to tow your car with a tongue arrangement built onto the car. These fold back over the hood when you're ready for a spin away from camp. Because this coupling doesn't add weight to the motorhome — it flexes vertically as the rig takes the road — it won't affect the rear axle weight significantly.

What Kind of Vehicle to Tow?

Tow the lightest vehicle you can that meets your needs. If you won't be using a platform, you want to tow a vehicle that turns the wheels without rotating transmission elements or the engine or adding miles to the speedometer. A variety of solutions exist, but some vehicles, especially four-wheel-drive units that might appeal to the rural camper, simply won't work without a platform. There are cars and trucks that can sustain damage in any kind of towing, unless the trip is brief, such as a tow to a gas station if they break down.

When choosing a tow vehicle or considering an existing one in the family, we verify its compatibility with long-distance hauling. Yes, you can disconnect the driveshaft to avoid problems, but this is hardly a convenient or workable method of transport, in our humble opinion. Don't get one opinion. With make, model, year, and serial number in hand, call these three sources for information:

• The senior mechanic at the local dealership for the car involved. It helps to call the dealer that sold the car originally, be it new or used, because it will have a greater sense of obligation for providing the right advice.

253

- The manufacturer. Makers of cars have expert service advisors, the best of whom can take one of their vehicles apart and assemble it, eyes closed. This person or group will know exactly what transmission links are used on your car down to the serial number. Reaching these people is difficult. Ask your local dealership for help or a phone number to try.
- Other RVers. See someone towing a car or light truck that you can afford? Ask him how it's worked out. If he's been dragging it around for more than five thousand miles without problems, it will probably work for you.

In this chapter, we've looked at the basics of towing and hitches. The basics of maintaining a balanced rig have been discussed in the last two chapters. We can't emphasize enough how important an experienced pro is in making the right connections to your vehicles. Get advice. Ask for instruction. You can follow all the rules set out in manuals and RVing books, and your growing body of knowledge, but a real "hitchman" saves you time and money and improves your success in towing (not to mention your safety). These pros can do more in two minutes with a glance, a few measurements, and a certain magic than we can accomplish in books. Who knows, maybe after a few years on the road, you'll be one of these towing wizards too.

Tip: Two Products for Towing Front-Wheel-Drive Cars *Without* a Platform

Remco (1-800-228-2481) builds two units of interest to front-wheel-drive owners. First is their Axle-Lock. Once it is installed between the engine's transaxle and the wheel, you can unlock the wheels so that as they rotate, movement is not transmitted to the transmission. When you arrive at camp, a quick turn of each engages the drivetrain to the wheels.

The second product is their Lube Pump. If you leave the transmission engaged (without Axle-Locks), this system lubricates the transmission when the engine isn't running. Some cooling is also provided.

Chapter 11

Checklists and Procedures: Setting Up and Breaking Camp

Preparing for a road trip is more complex than in a Bing Crosby on-the-road adventure in which everyone jumps into a top-down convertible without so much as opening the doors and roars off into the sunset. As a prudent RVer, you should carefully plan, pack, and load your rig after checking all aspects of its roadworthiness. Since we've done it many times, we'll share our advice with you for getting ready, setting up when you get there, and breaking camp when you're ready to move on. *You,* of course, should take our guidance as suggestions rather than as rules that must be followed to the letter. Depending on the length and nature of your trip, adjustments should be made to accommodate your needs, lifestyle, and destination. For example, forget the down jacket for that July trip to Louisiana. On the other hand, those with uncharted destinations should pack clothing appropriate for everything from a Montana blizzard to a heat wave in Texas.

Making a List and Checking It Twice

We recommended several weeks of putting your thoughts on paper before committing to a long vacation or a full-timing lifestyle. Make lists of "to-do" tasks to cover all the things to pack and prepare before you hit the road. In this chapter we've included basic information and checklists to get you started.

Tip: Prescription Medicines

While on the road, you may have trouble keeping a supply of prescription medications. Most doctors won't prescribe more than a couple of months' supply, and HMOs can be incredibly difficult to deal with. Recently, ours put us through at least twenty phone calls before agreeing to fill a prescription set for an extra thirty days.

HMO users should consider taking the company's prescriptions-by-mail affiliate or plan on visiting an emergency clinic and getting a short-term refill. If you're in Canada, some items can be sold directly by the pharmacist, though you'll have to justify your request. In Mexico, almost anything short of narcotics can be had over the counter. Avoid bringing these items back to the United States, as the customs authority takes a dim view of, for example, Canadian 222s (aspirin with a small quantity of codeine).

Things to Bring

Forget anything? This checklist is just to get you started. You will probably want to make your own with only the items you need and anything we forgot. (Note: this list is a superset — no one in their right mind carries ALL of these supplies.)

Foodstuffs
Check out Chapter 24 for general advice. Don't forget spices, pasta, rice, beans, flour, bottled lemon juice, vinegar, oil, sugar or honey, baking soda, canned tomato sauce and paste, baking powder, dry milk, coffee, and hot chocolate mix. (If you have just these foods, you can always make a good meal.)

Apparel

❏ Bathrobes for modesty when you open the windows in the early A.M.

❏ Bring clothing appropriate to your trip. Bring warm coats/sweaters too in case of an early/late winter storm. You can always take clothes off, but should winter hit, you must be prepared! The layered look works well for RVers since they move through anything from warm deserts to snow-topped mountain passes.

❏ Swimsuits/cover-ups

❏ Sleeping shirts

❏ Rainwear/boots

❏ Umbrella for rain or Sunbelt sun

Cleaning Up Your Act

❏ Cleaning cloths

❏ Sponges

❏ Broom

❏ Handheld vacuum cleaner

❏ Whisk broom

❏ Cleaning brush

❏ Glass cleaner for windshield and windows

❏ Spot remover (try Resolve)

❑ Laundry soap

❑ Dish soap

❑ All-purpose cleaner (Formula 409 or something similar)

Health & Safety

❑ First-aid kit (a good one in a waterproof container)

❑ Prescription medication

❑ Insurance information

❑ Physicians' names and telephone numbers

❑ Fire extinguisher (have one per fifteen feet of rig and one in the galley)

❑ Flashlight with multiple sets of batteries (at least three!)

❑ Medications (Make list and check health plan requirements for travelers! Consider mail-order services.)

❑ Smoke detectors

❑ Sunblock/sunglasses

❑ Water purification tabs

Bathroom

❑ Toothpaste and toothbrushes

❑ Soap

❑ Shampoo/haircare products/implements

❏ Toilet paper (RV compatible)

❏ Towels and washcloths

❏ Shower supply holder to hang over the showerhead

Galley

❏ Aluminum pots and pans with nonstick surface

❏ Microwave-compatible mixing bowls

❏ Measuring cups and spoons

❏ Pot holders

❏ Cookie sheets

❏ Tablecloths (tough plastic) for campground picnic tables

❏ Utensils

❏ Barbeque set

❏ Dishes, cups, mugs, glasses (Microwavable, lightweight ones are best.)

❏ Ziploc bags (very useful even outside the galley!) in various sizes

❏ Plastic containers with lids

❏ Plastic wrap

❏ Aluminum foil

Engine/Mechanical Maintenance

❏ Air cleaner element (bring two for dusty environs)

❏ Brake fluid

❏ Coolant (enough for complete replacement)

❏ Heavy-duty jumper cables (Avoid ones made in Taiwan or China.)

❏ Oil (enough for complete replacement)

❏ Power steering fluid

❏ Transmission fluid (enough for complete replacement)

❏ WD-40 (a lubricant that frees and protects most mechanical assemblies)

Emergency Items

❏ CB radio (Consider an "emergency" model if you're unfamiliar with CB.)

❏ Flares

❏ Tire/rig jacks and spare tire

❏ Coleman or similar lights (no fragile glass, please) for low battery time

❏ Tire inflation sealer/inflation kit (It may not work but it's worth a try.)

❏ Weather radio (Radio Shack)

❏ Collapsible water jugs

❏ Gas can

Entertainment

❏ Camera and film (extra batteries if required)

❏ Camcorder and blank tapes

❏ Audiotapes of music or books or CDs (Consider a mobile CD changer.)

❏ Craft supplies

❏ Paper and drawing pencils or crayons

❏ Fishing poles and gear

❏ Paperback books

❏ Playing cards/games

❏ Satellite or local TV

❏ VCR/video disc/CD-ROM movies and games

❏ Videotapes for rainy days — both commercial movies and home movies

Keeping in Touch

❏ Log book for travel records, addresses of people you meet, and documentation of in-warranty problems with your rig

❏ Address book of family and friends' contact information

❏ Notebook computer for work, communications, games, and even route planning

❏ Cellular phone

❏ Portable computer printer for computer printout of letters, business correspondence, and a daily log if you keep one

❏ Stationery

❏ Stamps

Pets

❏ Bring extra pet supplies — you may be surprised at the cost of pet food and cat litter in rural locations

❏ Leash

❏ Flea/tick spray or powder

❏ Carrier for small pets (This is important in case you must turn a motorhome over to the mechanics for service. Many hotels will allow pets when confined. [That doesn't mean you must keep 'em locked up once you get the room.])

Sleeping Quarters

❏ Blankets, sheets, pillows, and pillowcases for appropriate number of travelers

❏ Earplugs or "wave generator" sound machine to block out noisy neighbors

❏ Down comforter or extra blankets for cold nights (Electric blankets work if your rig can handle the current draw.)

❏ Sleeping bags for the kids or guests

General Supplies

❏ Wooden matches

❏ Votive candles and holders

❏ Box of batteries or use rechargeables (Bring the charger.)

❏ Chemical supplies for the black water

❏ Paper towels

❏ Plastic garbage bags

❏ Plastic trashcan (one for galley, one for bath)

❏ Plastic or cardboard storage boxes in various sizes

❏ Shower curtain (if necessary)

❏ Extension cords and outlet adapters (heavy duty)

❏ Circuit/polarity analyzer

❏ Grounding adapter for 15-amp and 20-amp service

Travel Information

❏ Camping guides

❏ Comprehensive road atlas sets (computer versions can plot the route for you!)

❏ Travel guidebooks

Useful Items

❏ Cigarette lighter power adapter

❏ Electrical adapters for converting rigs to the local power source

❏ Portable 115VAC electric space heater with tilt protection

❏ Self-striking matches

❏ Portable fans (12 volt)

❏ Extra lightbulbs

❏ Binoculars to investigate the landscape as you travel or survey routes through valleys or congested traffic

❏ Collapsible bicycles for local transportation

Outdoor Living Supplies

❏ Hibachi or portable barbeque

❏ Barbeque utensils

❏ Briquettes for barbeques

❏ Doormat for wiping muddy feet

❏ Roll-up mat for under awning area

❏ Portable awning or tent (if not already attached)

❏ Mosquito netting

Tip: Have You Expired?

Plan ahead should your driver's license or vehicle registration expire while you plan to be away from home. Most states will extend your license if your driving record is clean or issue longer-duration license plate stickers should you offer a credible explanation for requiring an extension. Avoid the "you're no longer a resident" hassle by describing your trip as a vacation.

What to Bring

You need to prepare a list that includes what you need on the road. Many items can be purchased or replaced on the road, but if you're camping in the sticks, prices may be high, if the item can be had at all. The list provided here is a good starting point for things you'll need to pack.

If you are going for a long haul, you may also choose to carry personal mementos on your trip. Most RVers personalize their rigs in some way. For example, we hang Kim's small pastel paintings (the frames must be securely screwed to sturdy bulkheads). Full-timers will find the choice of what to bring a difficult one. The rule is always: priorities for living first; gewgaws last.

Leave behind any objects that are irreplaceable or extremely fragile. Grandma's silver gets placed in a large safety deposit box with insurance papers and stock certificates. Selected snapshots of the family come along in a small waterproof box for an occasional runthrough. We leave duplicates or negatives in the safety deposit box, so new prints or copies can be readily created. Computer users can scan hundreds of family photos and look at them on the computer screen any time they want.

Papers

You should carry essential papers with you in a waterproof, fireproof file box (available at all large business supply stores). Here are the basics that should be included:

- Registration and ownership documents for the rig. This includes your current registration or a rental agreement if the rig is rented or borrowed. For the latter, a dated, formal letter that spells out when the rig must be returned is appropriate. It should be signed by the actual owner. A copy of his registration should be attached.

- Proof of insurance. Many states now require that you provide proof that a vehicle is insured and meets their minimum insurance requirements. Should you visit such a state even though your state of residence doesn't have such a requirement, you may be in for a delay until your insurance is verified. Better hope you aren't stopped on a weekend or holiday when your insurance company's offices are closed.

- Current driver's licenses for all drivers. If you plan to cross borders, get a photo ID for those too young or unwilling to drive. Child "theft" is a major concern of border personnel. An appropriate photo ID will prove the child is really yours.

- Proof of citizenship (usually a passport) if you are a foreign national. If you are a citizen of a country other than Canada, Mexico, England, and a handful of others, you may also need a visa. Check for current requirements, as they change constantly.

- Permits for any weapons carried. Note that both Canada and Mexico frown upon weapons possessed by visiting foreigners and even their own citizens sometimes, so we suggest leaving them behind if these destinations are in your plans.

- Valid passports help entering any country, but should you plan to visit countries south of Mexico, such as Guatemala or Belize, a passport may help you across the border that much faster. All group members outside of babies should have passports or be described on parental passports by name. Babies should have some kind of paperwork too, in case customs worries about the child being stolen or crossing a border without permission of the custodial parent. (Nice world we live in, huh?)

- Travelers checks and credit card.

Things to Leave Behind

Goods to leave behind include a variety of precious or weighty items that will simply complicate your travels, waste precious storage space, and add weight. Besides, when the wonders of nature await you, who needs sterling silver dinnerware and cut-crystal glassware to enjoy a simple dinner on a rough-surfaced picnic table?

Furniture

Remember, you're piloting a ship of the desert and rough seas are not unknown. Anything not bolted down can become airborne, as did our coffeemaker. It may hit the driver or passenger in the head in midflight. Fortunately, this decision is often made for you, since most rigs won't have space for the cherrywood end tables, anyway.

Expensive Goods

Leave anything of great worth or sentimental value at home or in secure storage, even if it isn't fragile. Theft is always a possibility, although the floor safe option will discourage the casual thief even if he can find it. Part of the fun of RVing is the freedom not to have to worry about things. Your Fabergé egg may indeed be worth worrying over: If you bring it with you, you may spoil your trip as a result.

Fragile Cookware and Dinnerware

We've had great luck with Corelle. It handles the microwave and propane oven and cleans up easily. Drop it or have it shift in a cabinet in a panic stop, and it's unlikely to break. Too bad, prettier patterns aren't available. You can use the old camper's inexpensive standby — plastic — but it will crack. The cheapest stuff will melt in a microwave.

As for cookware, you will find that seventeen-inch skillet too large for most RV stoves unless you run two burners. It will also have to be stored in a closet designated by the coach designers for use as a wardrobe. The exception is the large highline coach, which may even feature an island in the kitchen. If you're a gourmet chef, have your checkbook appropriately stuffed for the purchase of such a rig or settle for simpler cuisines or smaller portions while camping.

Expensive Jewelry

Leave the diamonds, gowns, and the tux behind. Unless you plan on using your RV as a gateway for social functions, the clothes will get dusty and the Cartier watch may grow legs and walk away while you're off to get a bite to eat. Owners of expensive rigs should be especially careful not to flaunt their wealth in "fleabag" parks and rest stops. Problems are rare, but not unheard of. Besides, you may spend more time worrying about your possessions than enjoying yourself.

Large Electronic Devices

Electronic devices have already boosted RVing from a specialized form of living and vacationing to a lifestyle that almost anyone feels comfortable with. But should you plan a wilderness trip or use poor judgment when loading your rig, you may find that big TV or Pentium PC with a nineteen-inch color monitor more a liability than a pleasure. There's no reason you can't travel with an incredible array of electronics (should you desire to), but bring only those with modest weights and unpretentious power consumption, and of a size that's easily stowable.

Naturally, with these suggestions in mind, compromises can be made. If you must carry that eighty-eight-key synthesizer and you're a touring musician, then a modification to your rig will lock down the instrument while traveling and a pop-up table will provide limited practice space using the rig's built-in speakers for audio feedback. But you should not make the cardinal error: trying to convert an RV into a complete four-bedroom house. It can't be done and you shouldn't attempt it. Instead, bring only what you need and replace that sixty-pound desktop computer and large monitor with a six-pound notebook. All it takes is cash.

For Full-Timers:
Checking the Excess Baggage

Can't carry everything? Reduce goods to the most important items, such as Grandma's silver, important papers, and objects of sentimental value, and store them. The best depository is your parents' house, as storage is free. Otherwise look for self-storage outlets and find one with a good price and a secure location. Study your assigned "locker." Evidence of stains on wood (water leakage), bugs, gnawed wood, or droppings from rodents, or a general lack of credibility and a convoluted contract means moving on. At one extreme is a storage location with a casual approach to criminal security. At the other extreme is self-storage in Bellevue, Washington, that claims a nuclear war wouldn't damage your stored goods. As you can imagine, there's a price spread between the former and the latter. Leaving goods behind or disposing of them is a reality for full-timers and those planning an extended stay. Here are the options, although none of them is without caveats.

- A storage company, such as The Best Little Warehouse in Texas (our favorite name for a storage locker operation). These offer lockers of several sizes, and assuming you aren't storing a houseful of furniture, they work out nicely. Check your unit out before renting. Make your payments on time or they'll auction off your goods.
- Relatives. You may have members in your immediate family with an empty garage, attic, or basement. When storing, explain what will be stored and for how long. Keep in touch, in case the in-laws decide to sell Tara (the mansion in *Gone with the Wind*) or don't know what to do with your large collections of Picasso forgeries.
- Friends. This can be a good option if you have friends you

269

can trust. It can also create problems. An ex-friend of ours has several valuable antiques and some of Kim's sculptures. After a business deal that went south for reasons we had nothing to do with, angry with us for some reason, this ex-friend still has our property and remains incommunicado. We have no recourse, short of legal proceedings, for getting it back.

- Moving and storage companies. Great for packing and moving, storage is very expensive at such facilities and small, valuable items sometimes get lost for reasons unclear. But we could make a few informed guesses.

- Your RV's basement compartments. Forget this option. Extra weight, risk of theft or fire, and other mishaps render this option null and void. The exception is the full-size Marathon bus, which is extremely secure. But it is priced at more than $500,000, and few of us can afford one as a storage bin.

- Home. Do as a college professor we know did. Lock everything you care about in a secure room and then offer the furnished house for rent to someone you trust. Since the lease may be short-lived and you may want to limit potential renters to people you know personally, make the rental rate especially attractive. This works best when you have a fixed return date. This professor took his one-year sabbatical so his renters (our friends actually) knew when they had to search for new digs.

Tip: A Source of Money for Full-Timers

Disposing of a home and goods you forgot you owned, let alone used, adds cash to your endeavor. At one of our asset sell-offs, we participated in a multifamily garage sale and sold junk, er, assets worth about $20 to us for nearly $400! Plus, the organizers asked only that we pay our share of the garage sale costs.

Admittedly, it was strange to come home to a nearly empty 2,400-square-foot house (already sold), but a few months later, we didn't remember most of what we had sold, so it must not have been especially important after all.

Stowage Tips

All but the most basic, older RVs have numerous storage compartments. As explained in Chapter 9, you must exploit these compartments carefully, without overloading your rig, for safety reasons and to increase the longevity of suspension components of your rig. Later in this chapter we discuss balancing your payload for predictable control of inertia. There are some particulars we've learned from other RVers or the hard way, which in this section we'll pass on to you. In a new rig (or new but used rig), before using storage compartments soak them with a garden hose while they are closed and then inspect each one for leaks. While it's true that rain falls mainly on the plain — vertically — wind-whipped rain may actually hit your rig from the side or even in ascendant motion. Basement compartments may also be splashed and sprinklered.

Clothing and Bedding

- Use plastic wrap or plastic bags for protection when storing goods for the off-season or periods of little or no use. Buy the wide plastic wrap if possible from a restaurant supply store or a place such as Price/Costco or Smart & Final.
- Avoid the use of mothballs. They make you sick if you sleep with them long enough. Instead, avoid moths by keeping window screens in place and doors firmly closed. We've wired our porch light to turn off when the door is opened, so that the circling moths go away. Of course, this approach only works when interior lights are low.
- Wash still a bit damp? Use the AC to dry out the air and your clothes. Take hard-to-dry items such as comforters to the dry cleaners. Yes, it costs a few bucks, but you face either mildew, if you dry it in your rig, or moths, if you hang it outside in anything but the hottest sunny weather.

Here are some tips that will put your galley and bathroom in condition for travel and minimize racket and breakage while driving:

271

Preparing the Galley and Bathroom

- Place clean towels between stacks of plates to protect them from each other. In a motorhome, in which galley noise can drive you nuts, take the additional step of securing all such items. We stabilize noisy kitchenware with a heavy blanket wedged into the storage compartment.

- Secure stacks of metal pie plates, cookie sheets, or baking sheets with large rubber bands or bicycle clips. This silences an otherwise less-than-sonorous racket from the galley in a motorhome.

- Transfer boxed supplies, such as instant mashed potatoes and flour, to sealable containers upon purchase or once opened. Otherwise, tape them shut with packing tape or wedge them so they won't shift during travel. Don't assume that crude resealable containers will remain sealed. Some will at home, but on the road, they'll open up and dump their contents on everything. What a mess.

- For refrigerator tips, see Chapter 8. You can use the same simple storage system for RV cupboards in bath and galley.

- Many RVers squeeze the Charmin hard enough to render it oval instead of round so it won't unwind in the rig during travel. We used to do this until one of our cats discovered the arrangement and unrolled it anyway. Now a fat rubber band secures the roll instead.

Tip: Valuable Property

We've already cautioned you against bringing items of value, but even a VCR used nightly may have appeal to a thief. Store such items where they're hard to get to and out of sight of anyone looking in your windows. While nothing will deter a professional thief (most of whom gave up stealing VCRs when they became priced at less than $150 retail), other goods should be locked down if possible. Many computers, for example, offer an accessory locking feature that allows you to attach them to something unlikely to get stolen, such as the steering wheel in a motorhome or a massive eyelet and nut bolted to the frame.

Storage Pods

Seen atop many rigs are cream-colored storage pods. These are permanently mounted to the roof with (one hopes) waterproof screws and hold everything from scuba gear to winter wear during August. Pods are an excellent storage option, but you must account for their weight in your weight guestimates or weigh them loaded on a scale as explained in Chapter 9. On most rigs, the pod is mounted above or slightly forward of the rear axle(s).

One large pod on the roof of a big motorhome can hold a lot of gear. But never mount more than one, unless you plan to use them for extremely lightweight provisions or supplies. On a micro motorhome, forget adding a pod, as the rig likely exceeds its weight limit with you and provisions.

Roof pods are, in theory, waterproof. But extreme rain or windstorms may allow moisture into a pod. For that reason, anything that can be damaged by water should be tightly wrapped in plastic. The contents of the pod should be inspected occasionally for moisture buildup or water in the bottom. Pods are also an easy target for thieves, padlock or no. We keep only lightweight goods such as clothes and other easily replaceable items in ours. You should too.

Overdoing It

One of the easiest mistakes to make is to pack everything so carefully that your storage scheme has one or more of the following negative effects:

- The storage medium, such as a heavy blanket, weighs more than the item being protected.
- Goods are packed so ingeniously and tightly that you can't find what you're looking for without total disruption of your storage scheme.
- Items are packed in drawers, cabinets, and bins the way you might casually toss a pair of balled socks in a drawer. Then, after a bumpy ride to camp, you find serious damage as the item moved at every sharp turn or quick stop. If glassware is involved, these concussions may be fatal.

Easy Access

Goods used frequently should be stored for easy access. You wouldn't store the coffeemaker used for a quick early-morning brew in an outside locker. Instead, find a location close to the kitchen, so that if you're half asleep, it's right there. But, at the same time, fragile items should be stored the most carefully. For example, you wouldn't put an expensive short-wave radio in an otherwise empty drawer, in which it might be damaged as it slides around, as happened to our pricey Sony multiband.

Heavy Loads

Should you plan on trafficking in rock and mineral specimens, rather than overload your rig, do as the woodworker did and use a trailer. Even then, you must still take into account the amount of tongue weight involved and not overdo it. Instead, store shipments with an established mailbox company and keep an inventory of each. Then when it's time, order them to ship Box 11 when you're getting low on geodes.

Get Loaded!

As we mentioned in Chapter 10, correctly loading an RV is important to on-the-road stability. Bringing the right provisions, tools, fluids, and entertainment materials is also part of the equation. We mention the weight management basics here again because weight management is so critical to your safety and your enjoyment of driving.

Maintaining an Even Keel

Again, a poorly loaded RV is difficult to handle. You want to keep the weight toward the bottom and distribute it in accordance with the vehicle's design. Motorhome makers assume that weight will be concentrated over the rear axles. Trailer and fifth-wheel makers assume that weight will be distributed on top of the axles but with enough forward of the axles that the tongue or hitch has downward pressure for proper coupling. All vehicle makers assume that side-to-side weight will be evenly balanced.

Adding heavy items, such as cases of canned goods, to upper storage compartments on one side of a vehicle will make it difficult to control. Instead, store weighty items low in the vehicle and attempt to distribute the weight equally on both sides.

A Balancing Act

As you camp, provisions will be used, shifting weight. After an extended session, we go through the food storage areas and adjust the remaining goods to keep our balance, so to speak. Should you be one of many RVers who make and sell crafts while traveling, pay special attention to your raw materials and inventory. Surprisingly, we do see RVers who sell heavy goods from their rigs — everything from canned tuna to collectibles and antiques. With an impossibly heavy cargo, it's hard to believe that their rigs make it from flea market to flea market.

The Preflight Checks

Chapter 13 explains our basic RV maintenance schedule, but there's more to packing and going than just checking the mechanical systems. After loading all of the food, clothes, and other supplies required for a successful trip, go through the pretrip checklists for the interior and exterior of the rig to make sure your rig is ready to drive off to its next destination. We use such a checklist every time we leave home or break camp. Make photocopies of the lists as appropriate and fill them out religiously so you don't find that you drive away without water for bathing or propane for cooking.

You'll also need to use the checklists for setting up and breaking camp. Again, going through the checklists should be a ritual. The first time you forget the checklist will be the last. It will be the time you tear off the roof of your rig because you forget to bring the TV antennae down or pull out the side of your living room because you left the power cords plugged in. Before we learned about checklists, we almost did both of these things. You've been warned.

The RV in Summer

Summer is RV season, and many RVers follow the summer south as the winter drops the temperature and snow. There's little to think about during the summer months — your RV is built for these climes with its air-conditioners and the prospect of a lazy barbecue under the awning. Significant summer considerations include maintaining the sterility of the black water tank with more additives than you need in winter and the inability to get into RV parks or acquire free camping space along the coasts. Your rig's refrigerator will be slightly less efficient in the summer as less cool air is available to help the unit extract maximum effect from the cooling area. You may also choose to avoid the Sunbelt in the summer, instead heading for the mountains or northern destinations to skip the fiery summer sun of the deserts and tropical heat and humidity of the South. In other words, life's soooo tough. But winter is a little different. Read on . . .

The RV in Winter

There are two possible responses for an RVer in winter: storing and winterizing a vehicle (covered in Chapter 14) or living in it while Jack Frost lurks just a windowpane away. Storing a vehicle is a matter of readying it so that cold air doesn't freeze water pipes or turn engine lubricants into molasses mixed with condensed water. Living in an RV in winter requires a more active approach to keeping Old Man Winter at bay.

When Santa Claus (and Snow) Comes Through the Roof Vent

Living a winter in an RV can be a lot of fun if you have a rig equipped for it or do what we do — migrate south as the leaves fall and the chill increases each night. But you can stay put and brave the cold while enjoying skiing, building snowmen (and -women), and turning off the refrigerator and cooling it with gallon bottles of snow and ice to save propane for other activities such as avoiding freezing to death.

We're not going to tell you that North Dakota is fun in February. No, sir. Wintering in an RV requires settling in a locale where access to food and propane delivery is nearby. Even then, you may dream of Florida or California, but not feel comfortable traveling, especially when high mountain passes with unpredictable weather block your route. Highline coaches are best in frozen weather because their designers assumed that winter travel would be a must and money existed in the design budget to enhance the rig to keep all systems "go" regardless of environmental conditions.

The Gas Engine in Winter

Gasoline has few winter-related problems unless you're camping in Siberia. (Not a lot of fifty-amp hookups there, we understand.) Your engine's first line of defense is the fuel filter. Change it regularly to keep water buildup from condensation turning to ice and blocking fuel delivery.

The Diesel Engine in Winter

Diesel works best in warm weather, although with correct management and plenty of idling upon starting, as specified in the owner's manual, it's a cold-weather fuel as well. (Notice, we didn't say, "Some like it hot.") In those cold months in which even gasoline thickens slightly, the wrong or untreated diesel fuel becomes somewhat waxy in consistency. This means it won't flow from fuel tank to engine without significant warming and no amount of cranking will do it either. (Don't drain your batteries trying!) This can be more than a minor annoyance if you're stuck in Donner Pass in a blizzard. We head for Arizona deserts in winter, so we've never experienced any cold-related problems, but we've met other campers who have. Here's what to do and what not to do:

An Electric Down Jacket

As mentioned, your rig should be equipped with heaters in the manifold to warm the fuel and assist it in becoming liquid before starting the rig. Pickups and motorhomes, barely expensive enough to be fitted with a diesel, lack this mandatory winter support. Don't confuse the glow-plug light with manifold heaters — they are not one and the same, although we once had a pickup truck salesperson claim otherwise.

Avoid Fuel from Those Lazy, Crazy Days of Summer

Use up fuel bought in the summer — diesel number two — and buy in the cold season, when it's blended with diesel number one for winter use. Do this only with approval from the engine's maker. (Yes, this mixture is smellier, as if diesel weren't bad enough already.) This winter mix, which most truck-oriented diesel stations sell, stays liquid in lower temperature than the summer version.

Spike It

There are a number of additives on the market that thin diesel or make it more combustible in the cold. Buy several kinds to experiment with and add one when you "diesel up" on an almost empty tank to test which works best. Follow the maker's directions and add exactly as much as needed for the fuel you've accrued. Skimping, because of cost or because you forgot to buy enough, renders the additive less useful than it should be.

The Best RVs for Severe Weather

If you're going to use your RV in cold weather (or very hot weather, for that matter), look for a motorhome equipped with a winter weather package (which includes extra insulation, expanded heating options, and protected pipes). Most major motorhome makers offer such packages as an option. Beware of poor winter-worthiness on any bargain RV. (Insulation and heating are not the strong suit for most low-priced recreational vehicles.) If you have the resources to buy and maintain a motorcoach on a bus chassis, you might actually find one that's been custom made for severe weather, but our advice is to beware of claims of winterworthiness of any standard motorhome.

The newer rigs with a basement offer additional insulation and warmth for short winter stays. Not only is the basement good for added storage, it also acts as a good barrier from the cold outdoors. Many newer units also offer a second furnace, which comes in handy when the weather gets below zero. We have gone on a few ski trips in Colorado, and after a day of skiing it is nice to know your RV heater systems can keep up with the cold.

If you're a winter camper, when looking at your prospective purchase make sure to look at where the water pipes are routed. Most (if not all) newer motorhomes have the water pipes running along the bottom of the wall inside the living compartment. On some older models the water pipes run under the floor, which is not a good idea for winter travel. When the pipes freeze and burst, that's the end of the trip. Look for RVs that have holding tanks in heated compartments if you intend to do a lot of winter RVing.

One quality RV built for severe temperatures is the Teton fifth-wheel. Teton, one of the most expensive fifth-wheel manufacturers, offers an Arctic package on its fifth-wheels that is climate controlled to minus thirty degrees and has R25 insulation on the floor and roof. In addition to storm windows and insulation, Teton also encloses all tanks in the heated area. The water lines in the floor between bath and kitchen are heat-taped. The Teton homes are also quite luxurious, with Corian countertops, tile and wood plank floors, and superior overall construction. Some units offer slides for additional living area. (Obviously, these heavy units require an equally heavy-duty tow vehicle.) At this writing, winter-capable Teton fifth-wheels are priced in the $75,000 to $95,000 range (or more). The Arctic package adds about $1,000 as an option. Add a $30,000 tow vehicle to the total cost to get a true comparison to similarly equipped motorhomes.

Tip:
Two Things to Avoid and Two Suggestions

Don't buy diesel fuel in a warm winter place such as Tucson, Arizona, and then assume it's mixed right for a trip through the snowy ten-thousand-foot mountain passes of the Rockies.

When the frost is on the pumpkin, try to buy diesel from a busy truck stop. There, you have a better chance of getting a winter mix than at a small station that is still unloading its summer supply. As you can imagine, this is more a problem in the late fall and early winter. (There's less chance of water in the fuel at a truck stop too.)

Stuck with summer diesel? If the tank's only a quarter full, fill it with "winter" diesel and forget it. If you have a nearly full tank, add the maximum amount of additive and cross your fingers (see Spike It, next page).

Going to Mexico? Make sure your rig has a device that filters water from the fuel. Mexican diesel frequently has water in it and this will stall your rig. In fact, a water filter is a good idea anyway.

Snow Tips for RVers

If you plan to stay in snow-laden areas in winter, here are some additional tips that may help to keep you snug in your home on wheels:

- Put some antifreeze in the holding tanks to prevent freezing.
- Keep the roof vents clear. The refrigerator, heating intake, and exhaust vents must remain clear for proper ventilation and operation.

- Add skirting. Put some flexible skirting around the bottom of your rig if you plan to park for more than a few days. This will prevent snow from getting under the rig and helps insulate the undercarriage. Skirting is available for this purpose from most major RV supply stores.
- Look for sheltered campsites. However, beware of staying under trees that may have loose branches that will fall onto the rig when they are weighted with snow.
- Add weatherstripping to all outside compartments if these openings are not already weathertight.
- Add thick, insulated draperies and storm windows if your rig isn't already equipped with them. Keep the drapes drawn to keep the heat in the rig.
- Take along a blow dryer and canned deicer for thawing drains and frozen doors.
- Don't forget your chains or snow tires if your motorhome or tow vehicle can handle them.

Stocking Up for Life with the Bears

The night before heading for "bearsville" (meaning we intend to camp in the wilderness without hookups), we spend the night in an RV park to use shore power to fully charge batteries, stock up at the local supermarket, fill all tanks full, and then take a deep breath and head for the woods, mountains, desert, beach, or whatever. We also gas/diesel up and stock up on propane. Where necessary, we carry extra water for desert life, and the pickup truck used to haul the fifth-wheel has an optional diesel fuel tank mounted in the bed, just behind the cab. This gives us a range of almost four hundred miles between fill-ups, as the truck already has a larger-than-standard fuel tank built in. Keep in mind that provisioning adds weight. You should distribute weight as suggested in Chapter 9.

The Spare Tire

Depending on your destination, you may want to carry spare parts as insurance that you will make it back to civilization on wheels rather than on foot. We carry extra engine and transmission fluids and an extra spare tire, and fit all wheels with innertubes to reduce the risk of a flat. (Check with the tire seller, manufacturer, and RV maker before adding tubes to your tires. They can build up heat, causing premature tire failure when mated to an incompatible tire.) A complete replacement of all belts and hoses may be in order if you're really heading for the boonies. This may set you back about $200, but a radiator hose exploding in Mound City, South Dakota, may cost you a lot more than total replacement. Other items you may want to bring include:

- One or two extra fuel filters and air cleaner elements on an extended trip — especially a dusty one.
- A water purification kit (or deal with the weight of carrying extra water, which is heavy). This is not for use as your primary drinking water, but for employment in an emergency when you can't use melted snow or must rely on creek water for drinking.
- First-aid kit. This is a must for boondock campers. Purchase a comprehensive kit and a book on first aid to go with it.
- Sunscreen and bug repellent.
- Flashlight (get two big ones) and extra alkaline or lithium batteries.
- Foldable shovel to free tires stuck in mud or snow. Ten pounds of sand is also helpful for the latter event.
- Jumper cables in case you kill your batteries somehow. Buy sturdy ones with thick wires and strong bonds to the clamps. The $6.95 specials may not start your engine and will disintegrate quickly.
- An extra month or two of your daily prescription medicines in the unlikely event you are stranded. You may need to explain to your pharmacist, doctor, or HMO why you need additional medication, but the ones we've worked with have been completely understanding once we mentioned traveling. Note that prescriptions for narcotic drugs (tranquilizers, pain-

killers, and sleeping pills) are not honored in states that don't adjoin the one in which they were prescribed, although you may be able to buy them by mail. This is true for both paper-based prescriptions and those phoned in. Canada and Mexico both have less restrictive laws in this regard.

Tip: The Open-Door Policy

In rigs in which the water supply is hidden behind kitchen cabinets or other interior storage, leave the cupboards open to keep the tanks and lines warm. Also leave a small light on so you don't trip over the open doors while on a nighttime expedition to the refrigerator for a snack.

Of course, you'll want to include food, toiletries, toilet paper (and septic tablets), and whatever else you need. If the total weight of this conglomeration grossly exceeds your vehicle's gross weight capabilities, then scale back your trip and plan on less time away from civilization or look for heavy objects to dispose of and lighten the load.

In this chapter we've looked at the basics of getting ready for the road for all kinds of RV trips. Now you're ready to roll and head off into a glorious sunrise. For many readers this means leaving the smoggy city with its congested traffic for cool air and the scent of the pines. Worry about forgetting something? Don't. You can always pick it up along the way if your credit is good.

Interior: Pretrip Checklist

DATE →			
GALLEY			
Arrange fridge contents for travel			
Set refrigerator to propane mode			
Cushion galley cupboard contents			
Remove loose items on counters			
Turn off water heater			
Dog cupboard/refrigerator doors			
BATHROOM			
Rubber band around toilet paper			
Rubber band on hose-style shower			
Stow cosmetics/toiletries			
Close sink drain			
Close/dog doors			

SLEEPING QUARTERS

Convertible sleeping quarters locked down	Bed #1			
	Bed #2			

GENERAL

Begin engine warm-up			
Walk interior for loose items, check doors			
Ensure pets are indoors			
Check all gauges			
Glance in side mirrors for last check			

Copy and use this checklist, dating each use. Each column is good for breaking camp once. Blank spaces are provided for your rig's special requirements.

Exterior: Pretrip Checklist

DATE →			
THE BASICS			
Ensure all BBQ/firepit coals are cold			
Stow exterior items			
Lower antenna/sat dish			
Stow awnings			
Turn off water heater			
Unplug if rig is hooked up			
Read power meter (if appropriate)			
Climb roof and padlock pod			
Unblock/chock wheels **w/ brakes on!**			
Check tire pressures			
Walk around rig for visual inspection			
Check underneath for new leaks			
Lift/stow steps to coach main door			
(Motorhomes — lift electric levelers)			

FLUID LEVELS

Fuel			
Propane/LPG			
Oil			
Transmission fluid			
Brake fluid			
Coolant			
Power steering fluid			
_____			
Fresh water			
_____			
_____			

Chapter 12

Driving Your Rig

Learning to drive an RV — even a big one — is much easier than you'd believe. Because brakes and steering are power-assisted, you don't need the physical strength of the bus driver you've seen with huge biceps cranking that giant steering wheel to round a turn. An RV's steering wheel is much like the one found in any passenger car and equally responsive. The automatic transmission (in most tow vehicles and all motorhomes) saves you from shifting except on major hills — no clutch even. Even so, we'll suggest some practice exercises in this chapter to help get those who are initially uncomfortable with handling what amounts to a truck to feel as easy in the driver's seat of a rig as they would handling an automobile.

Driving small rigs, including micros, vans, most Class Cs, and smaller trailer and fifth-wheel designs, isn't much different from jumping into the Taurus for a quick hop to McDonald's. Larger rigs take a little bit of practice, but most drivers master them in less than an hour following our program of instruction. We recommend that all RVers go through it regardless of rig size to become familiar with the rig's handling characteristics and to learn how to obey hand signals for backing into camping spots. Fortunately, you won't need to learn to parallel park, because all but van and micro-style motorhomes won't fit into demarcated street parking spaces anyway. When at the mall, choose the empty spaces around the perimeter of the lot, since no one is using them anyway.

Note

If more than one driver needs training, bring them all along and perform each exercise by taking turns rather than one completing the program and then another starting it. That way each can observe the others' mistakes and learn how to avoid them.

Driver Ed

You may remember a high-school class called Driver Education. No longer available at most schools, as funding for it has evaporated, it worked. Statistics proved that participants had far fewer accidents, so we put together a basic one for RVers. The following steps provide training in driving and handling any rig. We would advise that those working with extra-wide motorhomes (more than ninety-six inches wide) spend a little more time getting accustomed to the vehicle's width.

A Semester's Credit in a Couple of Days

It will only take you a couple of Sunday mornings to accomplish your complete driving lessons following these steps. (Early Sunday — with the sun already up — is the time of choice. Parking lots are deserted and traffic is light on roads and freeways.) You can skip this tutorial and hit the road without any training, as Kim did. But you'll feel more in control of the rig after parking lot practice sessions and a gradual buildup of skills and time behind the wheel. You owe it to yourself, other drivers on the road, and that "back-in" campground space to spend a few hours behind the wheel before heading from Nantucket to San Diego on a whirlwind trip. And you might learn something that better prepares you for an emergency, should one occur while you're at the helm.

Note

This section assumes that you are already an experienced driver of passenger cars. While many people take their initial driving lessons and subsequent driver's test in a car, truck, or van, a motorhome is not the vehicle for learning basic driving skills.

Step One: Acquiring the Resources for the Lessons

Purpose: To get ready.

a. To get started, purchase six orange traffic cones from an RV store for maneuvering around. (You get double use from the cones. Stow them for use in a roadside emergency.)

b. You need an instructor — preferably someone already familiar with handling an RV or a large truck. The instructor will perform three functions: driving the "training" rig to the lot so that you won't have to, teaching you the ropes, and using hand signals to help you practice backing your rig in for parking. (Some lots that rent RVs will train you as part of the package. Or rope your seller or salesperson into the task as part of the purchase price.)

c. A long measuring tape helps, but it's okay to eyeball the cone setups if the local hardware store wants $49.95 for a fifty-foot tape. You can substitute string, using a one-foot ruler to mark each foot on the string and coloring it with a felt pen.

d. Find a large parking lot such as that of a megamall to conduct beginning practice early Sunday morning. The lot should be striped so that you can use the lines and rows as pretend road striping. A large factory or school lot will also do as long as no one is about (especially children) and you aren't violating any No Trespassing ordinances (these should be posted at the entrance). Ask for permission if such signs are posted at a mall. The security people will usually have no problem with your request, although they may watch as you practice, and they'll want you gone by the time the first shoppers arrive.

Tip: Starting Your Diesel Engine

As mentioned, a diesel engine employs much greater compression than its gasoline equivalents. For that reason, the starter needs to be more powerful and the batteries to crank such a device must deliver more current for longer periods than a gas engine requires. While you should never use cheap batteries in any RV, buy exactly what the manufacturer recommends to give that stiff diesel the crank it deserves from the starter. This proves triply true in cold months when diesel fuel is thick and batteries are not working at maximum efficiency. Long cranking in winter weather may drain old or inexpensive batteries stone dead. We allow gas and especially diesels some warm-up time, especially in cold weather.

Step Two: Take a Slow Drive

Purpose: To get a taste for the vehicle, its controls, and its responsiveness before attempting more difficult driving operations.

a. Sit in the driver's seat; adjust it for comfort and good visibility through the windshield. Make sure you and your "instructor" are buckled in using the seat belts. Set the side mirrors, and if a rearview mirror is of use, adjust it. (On some motorhomes you can see through the rear window.) Turn on the rear camera and monitor if the rig is so equipped.

b. Start the engine with the parking brake on and the transmission set in Park (or Neutral with a manual transmission). Let the rig warm up for a couple of minutes, especially if you're driving a diesel.

c. While the engine warms up, take a moment to study the controls. In a highline motorhome, with its numerous readouts and gauges, locate the important ones — the speed, tachometer, and oil pressure and temperature gauges — among the numerous dashboard displays.

d. Foot on the brake, release the parking brake and shift into drive. Then, with a deep breath, take your foot off the brake pedal and begin to drive slowly around the parking lot, avoiding obvious hazards. Keep your speed under 10 mph. The idea is to "feel" the rig and how it handles. Try the steering and the brakes. Keep an eye on the speedometer and tachometer to track your speed and how the engine is reacting. Then pull up to a spot and park. Should you be learning in a tow vehicle equipped with a manual transmission, you may want to spend more time learning to shift smoothly before moving on. Take your "instructor" on the ride for advice and explanations.

Step Three: Set Up the Cones

Purpose: To try out simple, precision maneuvers.

a. Look for a long parking lot stripe (assuming it isn't bisected by trees or streetlamps) and place four orange cones about one hundred feet apart. Your observer will watch this exercise from outside the rig, as occasionally a cone will get crunched and then pop upright as if nothing had happened. Without an observer, you wouldn't know if anything went wrong. Don't worry about running over a cone. This won't harm the cones, the rig, or its tires — that's why we recommend them.

b. Drive your rig in an "S" path around the cones as you've seen skiers and racing drivers do on TV. Make this a low-speed maneuver. You can accomplish it with a little practice.

c. Repeat the same experiment, but space the cones about fifty feet apart. This should also be a snap on a small rig. A large motorhome may require practice to avoid the cones. Repeat until you can drive this simple obstacle course five times in a row without incident. For owners of motorhomes shorter than twenty feet, set the cones twenty-five feet apart and practice this arrangement until you avoid killing a cone in two subsequent exercises.

Tip: Under/Over-Revving

Most RV engines should not "rev" under load — in gear — below 1,000 rpm, and they redline around 5,000 rpm. (Never exceed the redline point.) They produce the most power between 3,000 rpm and 5,000 rpm, but sustained operation in this range wears them out faster. Save the high rpms for climbing hills, not for average highway or city driving. Check with the maker for exact information.

Step Four: Rig Width Exercise

Purpose: To give you a feel for keeping a rig, especially motorhomes, centered in the lane. As you'll read below, the first time you drive an RV, especially a motorhome, you may stray too far to the right of the lane.

a. Set the cones up in two parallel rows, using the long parking lot stripe for one row. The rows should be about two hundred feet long, each made up of three cones, with 9.5 feet between the two rows. Your mission, should you choose to accept it, is to drive the path between the cones at least five times in a row without running over one. This is a 20-mph speed maneuver. You will treat the cones as the stripes of a lane on a road or highway. Your instructor should watch this exercise from outside the vehicle.

Tip: Motorhomes — Stay to the Left

The most common RV driving problem, especially for owners of extra-wide motorhomes, is a tendency to drive too far to the right, because when you pilot a car, you automatically center it in the lane. But many RVs are wider. So subconsciously spacing the left side of the RV from the lane stripes as you do your car puts the right side of the craft on the curb, in the adjacent lane, or scraping parked cars.

Step Five: The Slow In-Town Drive

Purpose: To experience an easy drive in light traffic. Try this only when roads are clear of ice and snow.

a. To the tune of "One Sunday Morning," not "Born to Be Wild," please, arise early, warm yourself with a cup of coffee, and warm up the rig while you're drinking it.

b. With the sleepy instructor in the copilot's seat, ease out of the driveway, storage area, or wherever and cautiously slip into the nearly nonexistent traffic. With your skills and confidence from the parking lot exercises, you can try your hand at negotiating the nearly empty streets with your instructor warning you to move left if you get too close to the right edge of the lane. Fifteen minutes and you'll have enough experience that you'll instinctively center your rig in the lane while not losing your ability to center a passenger car.

c. Take a few turns. Enjoy the morning. Tool through back streets as well as thoroughfares to learn how the ol' girl handles over bumps and accelerates from a stoplight.

Step Six: The Busy In-Town Drive

Purpose: To learn how to coexist with other vehicles. In theory, nothing changes once you master Step Five, but in practice, driving gets a little more complicated when cruising through traffic. Even the smallest micro (when provisioned and manned) has more inertia than most cars, although with good brakes, stopping may not require much additional distance. Swerving, however, may bring pressures to bear that your rig isn't designed for (especially if you overloaded it).

a. Take a rush-hour cruise through a busy downtown, using the skills you've acquired in the previous steps. It should go smoothly if you practice keeping adequate stopping distance between your RV and the vehicle in front. Experiment carefully with changing lanes and making turns. You should control the rig's progress rather than the traffic dictating the route because you're too timid to make a move.

b. Keep at it until darkness begins to descend so you can also try driving with headlights. This is your opportunity to test your true "feel" for your rig, since you can see and sense less around you. Uncomfortable? Have your instructor take you home and repeat Step Five a few times, then try again.

Step Seven: Your First Freeway/Highway Drive

Purpose: To try your new skills out at higher speed. This is an important exercise, as most RVers go the distance on the highway, freeway, or interstate.

a. Rig warmed up, head for the closest freeway access, preferably outside commute hours.

b. Merge with the traffic, after admission from a metering system if relevant, and practice changing lanes, using turn signals and careful judgment. Make sure that you are traveling at least 50 mph to avoid overly annoying the drivers behind you.

c. Once you are comfortable with "freeway basics," exit and enter the freeway or highway several times (not at rush hour) to hone your skills in judging and merging with traffic. If this exercise makes you uncomfortable, revisit Step Five.

Step Eight: Basic Parking

Purpose: To learn how to drop the rig into parking in the most basic situations. Basic parking is, well, basic. Sliding the rig alongside a curb doesn't take much practice, but you should try it to get a feel for getting a motorhome or tow vehicle with towed vehicle into the right place at the right time.

a. Set up the six orange cones to make an artificial curb. (Why use an artificial curb when there's plenty of the real thing around? When parking an RV you can't see the curb. You need experience in judging distances. Plus a concrete curb can damage your vehicle, but the cones won't.) Then, without disturbing the cones, "park" with the front of the rig six inches from the curb and the rear no more than twelve inches from it. Practice makes perfect.

b. You should try a curved curb too, by arranging the cones in a slightly curved pattern and attempting to dock your rig as close as possible. This is an extra-credit exercise.

Step Nine (As Appropriate to Your Rig): Backing and Parking a Motorhome

Purpose: To learn the basics of motorhome docking in a back-in situation (common).

a. Set up the orange cones to make two thirty-foot-deep rows with about sixteen feet between the rows.

b. Have your instructor use hand signals to guide your backing in and finally parking the coach. (Why no special hand signals? Because there are no standards, and you may need to rely on a stranger with his or her own system of arm movements to assist in docking your coach.)

c. Once you have successfully "docked" three times in a row, narrow the cones to twelve feet apart and try again. You may wonder why in an RV park's twenty-two-foot by forty-eight-foot space you need this degree of precision. It's because while you may have twenty-two feet of width, half may be concrete for picnicking and the other half gravel for parking. Even one wheel up on the concrete will mean a seriously unbalanced rig.

Step Ten (As Appropriate to Your Rig): Backing and Parking a Trailer or Fifth-Wheel

Purpose: To learn the basics of tow vehicle trailer/fifth-wheel docking in a back-in situation. The ideal situation for tow vehicle trailer/fifth-wheel arrangements is the pull-thru. You simply drive into the space, set the brake, and that's that. You're ready to set up. But pull-thru spaces are limited in number at campgrounds, and many parks don't offer them at all. For that reason, you must learn how to back a trailer or fifth-wheel into a parking space.

Safety Chains

You've seen the safety chains that hold your rig together should you incorrectly perform the hitching or something breaks or comes loose. These are vitally important to safety because without them catastrophe could strike with no awareness on your part.

We once saw a two-stage gravel truck cruising well in excess of the then 55-mph speed limit. What the driver didn't know was that the main hitch had snapped and the only thing holding the second trailer to his rig was those safety chains. We helped avoid disaster by honking our horn to get his attention and using hand signals to indicate that the trailer was about to go its own way on a busy freeway. Slowing gradually to maintain control, he made it successfully to the shoulder and finally a full stop. On the way back, a tow truck driver could be seen scratching his head, looking at the broken components. "How to tow something like that?" was likely his thought.

a. Practice this routine with the cones as in Step Nine, with your instructor using arms to guide you backward without jackknifing the rig. It will take some practice to become proficient, but anyone can do it. You need to keep in mind that your rig is like a hinge. When backing, turning the steering to the right moves the trailer off to the right. Turning to the left does the opposite. Minimally turning the steering wheel is the best way to learn how to dock. Rash movements may put your rig through a camp's electrical hookup or the neighbors' barbecue.

b. Headed in the wrong direction? Pull out and start again, until you can do it twice in a row with the trailer settling into the correct position on your "lot."

Step Eleven (As Appropriate to Your Rig): Leveling/Unhitching/Rehitching

Purpose: To familiarize yourself with setting up camp.

a. More free training: When you buy your RV or a new tow vehicle/hitch, trailer/fifth-wheel, or motorhome, have the seller, as part of the deal, teach you how to operate the equipment. Learn how to attach and detach the trailer or fifth-wheel and set the leveling equipment. If no leveling indicators are provided, head for the RV repair shop and have them add these so you can tell when the rig is set up correctly. Get a complete tour with explanation of hookup functions, system operation, and basic maintenance and a description of any mysterious controls. When buying from a private party, verify maintenance tips with a dealer's service department to prevent relying on questionable information.

Step Twelve: Uphill All the Way

Purpose: To learn the correct shifts required to climb a grade. With the advice of your instructor and a read-through of your motorhome's, chassis's, or tow vehicle's owner's manual, you should experiment climbing hills (grades).

a. Begin with minor grades and literally work your way up. The main task in climbing a hill with a heavy RV (in proportion to its chassis or tow vehicle) is to keep the engine and transmission from overheating, while the rpm stays in a range in which the engine supplies near maximum power without producing an awesome amount of heat or hitting the red line (running too fast). Watching the tachometer, you can learn when to shift to keep everything running as cool as possible. You will also learn if the drivetrain isn't up to the task before tackling a steep hill on a hundred-degree day. Regearing may be necessary with some arrangements but you can't pull a twenty-foot trailer with a three-cylinder Geo Metro, although somewhere, someone has probably attempted it.

Step Thirteen: Downhill Racer

Purpose: To learn control of your rig on downhill grades. (Warning: This procedure assumes that you know that your tow vehicle's/camper's brakes are in proper shape and adequate to handle the load. When in doubt, have them checked at an RV service center.) There are two or three components that dictate downhill reduction in velocity (braking): the brakes in a motorhome or tow vehicle and towed entity and the engine. You want to learn the right combination to effectively slow your rig without overheating the brakes and their fluid or overrevving the engine.

a. Practice braking on easy downhill grades and work up (down?) from there to learn how to balance factors. Additional adjustment and experimentation may be required to mate a trailer or fifth-wheel to the tow vehicle, as their brakes must work in tandem to gracefully stop your rig. You want an approximately equal amount of braking in both vehicles so that they respond identically to brake pedal pressure.

Ready to Roll

You've seen films of boats being launched, complete with breaking the champagne bottle over the bow. There's always that moment of breath-holding when she hits the water and everyone watches anxiously to see whether she actually floats. Launching a newly purchased RV evokes some similar emotions, but don't break the champagne over the front or you might knock out a headlight or bust the windshield. We do suggest that you celebrate, however — *after* you get to your first camping spot.

Put your rig through a careful postpurchase inspection (or post-rental inspection). The inspection should include review of all systems we've presented in the book and all the checklists we covered in Chapter 11. Then, as proud new owners of a home on wheels, you'll need to learn how to operate all functions, operate emergency fuel cutoffs, and test all major systems, and you should install fully charged fire extinguishers.

Tip: The Bridges of Madison County

You should know your rig's maximum height — tires fully inflated but antennae down. Include roof pods and satellite dishes, if any, in this measurement. RVs don't normally have the vertical clearance problems of large trucks, but you shouldn't approach a covered bridge in backwoods Vermont or a low overpass in Mexico without checking the clearance first. Otherwise, your rig might become a convertible of sorts.

Breaking It In

You're now ready to roll, but on a new rig, you want to follow the tow vehicle or motorhome chassis maker's break-in instructions, which may range from a strict regimen to nonexistence. Easy acceleration for the first ten minutes (no hills) is best, and if you're driving a diesel, a five-minute warm-up and then light acceleration for the first fifteen minutes in the cold months is an engine-wear-saving measure. Keep in mind that on a new vehicle, it takes about one hundred miles of use to get maximum traction from the tires and effectiveness from the braking system. You should allow extra stopping distance. A new tow vehicle, be it car, truck, or van, should be broken in without the RV connected.

The Wet Test and Taking a Trip

After finishing driving lessons and equipping the rig with minimal supplies, take the rig on a wet test on the road. (Remember, a wet test means that tanks are loaded with fuel and water.) The wet test goes like this: Load fuel, water, and propane, after having the attendant flush air from the propane system (with all pilot lights out). Pull out carefully, getting a feel for the wheel. Drive a few blocks, stop, and look underneath for fluid leaks or the distinctive odor of a propane leak. If everything looks shipshape, run the appliances, heater, and AC with generator if you have one, and test all the plumbing. With the tow vehicle's or motorhome's engine turned off, look briefly at the engine for leaks. No problems? You're ready for the road!

Drive, He Said

On the road your task is to keep your RV — be it travel trailer, fifth-wheel, or motorhome — in a parallel position in both horizontal and vertical planes in respect to the road. This is easy for the experienced driver handling a well-maintained rig, but you must be aware of weather conditions and untoward road conditions. In addition to the hazards that affect passenger cars, such as slick roadbeds, poor visibility, and police on motorcycles, RVs are affected by wind, severe cold that freezes the motorhome's lengthy fuel lines, and hot weather that overheats all but the sturdiest tow vehicle or motorhome engine and transmission. Even stop-and-go traffic can be taxing on an engine responsible for transporting such a heavy vehicle or vehicle combination.

Hey You — Don't Move!

Do you really need to traverse Colorado's twelve-thousand-foot Loveland Pass in a snowstorm? Can you really handle that overloaded trailer in a windstorm? Should you drive the rush hour in Phoenix, Arizona, when it's 118 degrees outside, your engine temperature gauge is approaching the red, and the radio confirms that traffic is stop and go for miles?

The answer is "no" for all of these scenarios, except in a life-and-death emergency. Driving in adverse conditions is especially risky for the inexperienced RV driver or those driving a newly purchased or recently rented rig with which they lack familiarity. Taking the risk of a life-threatening accident, an expensive breakdown, or simply a high-stress day is contrary to the concept of the otherwise soothing RV lifestyle.

By far, the best fix for all bad weather, and most mechanical or system problems, is to simply stay put — even if it means sleeping on board in the local Safeway parking lot. If travel is a must, you must weigh your options carefully. When we aren't comfortable driving for any reason, we spend another day at the beach, see a few more sights, or curl up with a good book. We simply move it out another day. (Don't forget to change any campground reservations that might need postponing as a result of your stayover.)

Put all road maps, calendars, and itineraries in a closed storage space for the duration of your extra stay. Out of sight is out of mind. Of course, should an early snow find you camped out in a remote burg in the frozen north, then it's time to look for winter accommodations unless, with careful planning, you can make it out of the mountains and into the Sunbelt. This is a potential emergency, if it finds you short of cash, a long way from town, broken down, or in an RV better suited to San Diego than to St. Paul.

Take Her Out of Orbit, Mr. Sulu

Before we leave driving behind, here are a smattering of additional tips to consider when you're in the captain's chair of your big rig. These are based on our personal experience, so consider them guidelines, not rules.

The Big Rig in the Big City

There are environs where large RVs of all sorts dare not tread. We would never try taking a thirty-six-foot motorhome through midtown Manhattan. It can be done, but it certainly isn't our idea of fun. We avoid Los Angeles for the same reasons. When we must pass through L.A., we take a leisurely cruise late at night when the traffic is minimal or avoid the city completely by choosing an inland route. Should we not have a tow or towed vehicle along to see the sights, we rent a car for a day. Even if you are comfortable crossing the Brooklyn Bridge (we hear it's for sale, by the way), there's no place to park a large rig in the core of New York City. When we go to New York, we park in a nice camp in New Jersey and take the train into the city. We stay a night in the Big Apple (in a hotel) and then return to the rig when we've had enough culture for one visit.

303

The Big Rig in the Misty Mountains

When heading for the hills, look for signs prohibiting trucks or limiting them to certain lengths. This usually indicates a route on which your RV is too long to navigate the curves. It's also possible that bridges that can handle an ordinary automobile can't take heavier vehicles, including motorhomes. You can also ask at a local gas station before attempting a questionable route. Study your road maps. They may indicate length limitations and seasonal closings.

We once ended up in Leadville, Colorado, instead of Aspen because we didn't notice the "road closed during winter" details on the map. We thought we had discovered a shortcut to Aspen. Instead we discovered a historical gem in Leadville, with nineteenth-century buildings, nice people, and even a small ski resort, but we lost our reservations in Aspen that winter. Oh, well. We had fun anyway. If you're not as easily amused as we are, we recommend paying attention to the details on the maps and guidebooks.

How Fast Is Too Fast?

The eternal juggling of fuel economy and speed is now more complicated since some states allow RVs (all vehicles, actually) to travel at 75 mph on the rural portions of the interstate. The best fuel economy in a heavy rig is guestimated at about 50 mph — far too slow on a busy freeway where huge trucks illegally travel the slow lanes at 80 mph in a 75-mph zone. You should measure your rig's fuel consumption by comparing mph to mpg in a notebook to discover its optimum fuel-economy-versus-speed ratio. Then, based on traffic and road conditions, keep your speed under 65 mph for small, carefully loaded rigs and under 60 mph for larger ones. Drive slower if you aren't comfortable with these numbers or are carefully minding your fuel economy budget.

Yes, you may irritate a few speeding truckers who don't mind risking their lives as well as those in the vehicles around them. But in a large RV, especially one with a mediocre suspension, at 75 mph, a sudden, strong crosswind could cause a momentary loss of control. And you don't want that to happen.

Freeway Etiquette

You'll notice that when you change lanes to pull around a slower truck, the driver may flash his headlights. This tells you that your vehicle is in the clear to pull in front of him. You should do the same for truckers and other RVers. When a truck or RV pulls out from behind you to pass, once the other vehicle is a safe distance ahead of you, flash your headlights or brights once to show that they have clearance to change back into your lane.

The basics of handling a big rig are easy enough. You'll learn the ropes best by starting out on short trips and gradually increasing your mileage and time away from home or hotel. This is what we call bear-pit training. They put you into a bear pit and you either learn to train bears or take the unpleasant alternative.

In the next chapter, we'll look at basic maintenance. Most of these operations can be handled by you and will help keep your RV shipshape and ready for the road. If doing it yourself sounds too technical, just remember to have these things done by a mechanic as required. At least the chapter will tell you the services you need to ask about.

Chapter 13

Basic Maintenance

All tow vehicles and motorhomes require regular and timely maintenance. And while you're at it, any towed vehicle or tow platform also requires adequate looking after. In this chapter, we aren't going to tell you how to get under an engine and yank the oil filter, but instead explain what needs to be done. (The manual that came with our long-sold Southwind motorhome — built on a Chevy chassis — barely touched on key issues. In fact, in its generous sixteen pages of information, there was embarrassingly little information provided on operation or taking care of the drivetrain.)

If you're comfortable working on automotive systems, you may choose to handle out-of-warranty service yourself. Otherwise, use this section as a guide for directing an RV service center and have its mechanics do the dirty work. Listen to their suggestions, as every brand or vehicle model is unique in its requirements. But if they suggest hemming the piston skirts or replacing the soles on the axle boots, it's time to look for another shop.

This chapter also discusses other aspects of systems unrelated to the drivetrain. For example, did you know that you need to periodically drain the water heater to purge it of mineral buildup?

RV: A Heavy Load

For all but the heavy-duty bus models, an RV is probably the heaviest load your vehicle can pull or motorhome chassis will handle. A coach is a weighty proposition that wears engines out prematurely. You can reduce the chance of premature failure by following basic maintenance procedures and sound operational principles that take into account your engine's extra-heavy load.

When you are crossing Death Valley and the engine temperature nears the red zone, stop, have a soda, and let the poor thing cool down before hitting the road again. Or plan trips to avoid drivetrain overheating and excess wear. You can avoid engine or transmission overheating by not heading through Los Angeles at rush hour on a hot day. Drive during evening hours after the sun has set and the traffic is lighter. Don't drive every mountain pass "because it's there." Proper maintenance and intelligent management and use of resources are key to keeping your rig in shape and enjoying the trip, rather than spending precious vacation days in a Motel 6 while the rig is repaired by inexperienced technicians at Al's Garage.

Regular Inspections and Maintenance

Before embarking on a trip or on a weekly basis, we make the following inspections. (When the rig is in storage, we still inspect it every thirty days or so.) This quick checkout takes about ten minutes. It's best done on a cool morning with a steaming cup of coffee in your hand. That way, the rising sun and the songs of the birds will make it that much more fun. Plus, you'll get a timely start, if your expedition is a long one, secure in the knowledge that your rig is in running shape.

Tip: Working on Your Rig?

When working on your RV, always block the wheels to eliminate the possibility that it will roll over you. We use four eight-inch-thick blocks cut into triangles for the job. Put one on each side of each rear wheel. Camping World sells a metal contraption for this purpose that only works on rigs with dual axles. It looks as if it will work, but we've never tried it.

Tip: Oil as Coolant

Engine oil and transmission fluid do more than lubricate. They also provide substantial cooling. That is another reason you should keep their levels full, especially in hot weather.

Fluid Drive

The first order of RV operation is maintaining the correct fluid levels. As part of our pre-hit-the-road routine, we check fluid levels and top up any that are even slightly low. You should too as this inspection takes only a minute, except in motorhomes, in which the designing engineers placed several fluid reservoirs under the padded hump in the driver's compartment.

Oil and Filter

Change the oil and filter more frequently than your manual suggests. We do ours at a shop every two thousand miles or four months, whichever comes first. In unusually dusty conditions, we do it even more frequently. The filter removes from the oil any impurities and metal worn from the engine. Without removal, the particles eventually grind engine innards down. And a blocked filter increases oil pressure by slowing its passage through the engine. This contributes to engine overheating and ineffective lubrication.

Change the filter in combination with an oil change and use quality oil and a name brand filter. We use only top-grade oil, and for the current turbodiesel truck, we insist that the shop use a diesel-compatible oil from a name brand supplier (Pennzoil, Valvoline, Castrol, and so forth). The filter should be replaced with a name brand unit too. There are less expensive ones on the market, but for all you know, they're packed with newspaper rather than quality filter membranes. We carry four extra cans of oil with us, to top up the engine oil, although since the truck is new, adding oil has been a rare occurrence. Avoid mixing brands and weights of oil if possible. Note that diesels require diesel-compatible lubricants.

Brake Fluid

You can see the level of the brake fluid in its translucent tank. Unless topping up is required, do not remove the top for inspection. Otherwise fluid contamination can occur. Never mix brake fluids with fresh ones of a different rating. We never mix brands either.

309

Tip: Big Bubbles, Some Troubles

Modern radiators are sealed. Instead of adding coolant directly to the radiator, you put it into a plastic tank (with the engine cold, please). Since the radiator is sealed, it's possible to get a bubble of air in the top that keeps the storage tank from adding coolant. This results in less coolant than the engine requires and is a hard-to-find problem for the novice mechanic. If you suspect such a problem, with a cold engine, force the top off the radiator and look inside. If coolant is not covering the internal fins, then you've found your problem. Add coolant directly to the opening in the radiator. If you damaged the cap when removing it, buy another before operating the vehicle.

Coolant

We use a mix of 75 percent coolant and up to 25 percent water as coolant level drops while we're on the road. It's worked well for us, but you should follow your maker's instructions as to coolant and carry extra for topping up. In an emergency, in which your rig's engine boils over, use tap water to get you to the next town. If the problem persists, rather than wrecking your engine by overheating it, shut down and investigate. You could have something as simple as a hose that leaks or a radiator thermostat that fails to open. Sudden and persistent overheating problems are usually cheap to fix, but may require a tow truck to get you to where it can be repaired. Coolant has a fixed life and may eventually cause rust, especially if mixed with water. Assuming you aren't driving an air-cooled VW van, have the cooling system drained, flushed, and replenished at least once a year.

Tip: Transmission Fluid and Power Steering Fluid — They're Not the Same

Years ago, you could buy transmission fluid and use it in your power steering. This is no longer true. Each system requires its own special operational fluid. Violators of this rule trying to save a buck may have to replace seals after breaking down in the endless desert scrub of Texas.

Transmission Fluid

In a new rig, change the fluid in transmission and rear end annually. On an old rig, ask the advice of a transmission shop. Sometimes changing the fluid in an old automatic transmission results in gear slippage or shifting problems. Better yet, if the old guy has hauled you around the country for one hundred thousand miles, have a new unit put in.

Power Steering Fluid

Power steering fluid is added to a reservoir as needed, which is not very often. Check that you are using exactly the fluid the manufacturer demands. We once had to spend $400 to rebuild a power steering system after the wrong fluid precipitated a serious leak. Power steering that groans when you turn the steering wheel hard over may be defective, or more likely a leak has dribbled the fluid out and you need to top it up regularly until you get the leak fixed.

Vehicle Respiration

Vital to performance, engine temperature, and power are the air intakes. All vehicles filter the air through paper cartridge filters. (Oil-based filters were once common, but it's unlikely you'll encounter one.) The cartridge filter is very simple — clean air passes through its paper membrane and particles are trapped while air flows into the engine. When enough particles accumulate, air flow to the engine is reduced and combustion in the cylinders weakens. For that reason, change the air filter every two thousand miles, or every five hundred miles in dusty or sandy environs. Filters cost less than $15 for most rigs and replacement takes about one minute for unsnapping the clasps, replacing the element, and snapping the unit back together. The time may be slightly longer for a front-mounted motorhome engine, since you have to revolve the interior cowling to reach the air cleaner. It's always on top or at the upper side of the engine and easy to reach. The only tool required is a rag for wiping your fingers should they become greasy.

Leaks

Always look under the coach for leaks or wiring hanging down. If a leak is discovered, move the rig and inspect it after noting its location in relationship to your rig. Here is what to look for:

- Evidence of a leak. First, take a deep breath with your head near the base of the tow vehicle or motorhome. Smell gasoline or diesel? (If you're new to diesel, one fill-up will etch its odor in your mind forever.) Shut down all pilot lights and get professional help. Warn the tow driver or mechanic of a possible fuel leak, as gasoline is highly volatile and evaporating gas produces explosive vapors. Fuel leaks are uncommon, but they can occur anywhere from the fuel tank to the fuel lines leading to the engine to the engine itself. Connections to the fuel pump may leak as well if it's not mounted inside the fuel tank as are those in modern rigs. If propane is leaking in its liquid form (incredibly unlikely), head for the hills after warning the neighbors!
- Clear water near the engine. Probably excess water from the engine air-conditioning if you have just driven to camp with the dash air on.
- Red liquid. Power steering fluid leak or transmission leak or boilover after too hot a climb into the mountains. Note the stain's location. Is it under the power steering pump or the transmission? If large amounts are present, do not drive the rig until it's repaired.
- Green liquid. Coolant leak or boilover on older rigs. Green liquid near the black water tank indicates a leak in the system or a sloppy job of dumping waste.
- Water of indeterminate color. Could be a leak in the fresh water, roof air water, or gray water systems. To find out, add a dye or substantial food coloring to the gray water tank and hope the leak repeats itself. Do this with the AC off. No color? It's the fresh water. No leak, crank on the air-conditioning and look for water drainage.

- Brown and oily liquid. Engine oil. Note: Diesel oil leaves extremely black stains, unlike all but the most tired gas engines. A large leak precludes driving the rig, and towing and repair is much less expensive than fully replacing an engine frozen through a lack of lubricant.
- Brown but not very oily liquid. Brake fluid. Big trouble if there's more than a drop or two. With the engine running have someone press the brake pedal to the max while you watch for leaks. If fluid is appearing near or on the wheels while the pedal is pumped, consider having your rig towed to a shop. You could lose fluid and your brakes suddenly as leaking seals give way under pressure.

Quarterly Inspections

Not all inspections must be made before every jaunt into town, but they should be made on a regular schedule. We've chosen a quarterly calendar schedule (January 1, March 1, July 1, and October 1) to make a thorough inspection in addition to the regular checks that we do before every trip and once a month while docked. We do most of this ourselves, assuming that while a professional RV mechanic could do it better, we either can't afford it or may be camping hundreds of miles from the nearest service provider.

Freon

The freon used in dash air differs chemically from the freon used to power roof air-conditioners. Your engine-driven AC unit may use freon or its environmentally more benign replacement. The days in which you could head to Target and get a freon kit for topping off the air-conditioner (if you didn't attach to the wrong side of the compressor and blow your hand off) are over. Now, only air-conditioning shops can handle this task.

The good news is that conversion from freon to its replacement is not that expensive, unless your vehicle is so old that it's on the endangered species list. You can use the same thermometer employed to check the roof AC units. With the AC on (choose the

Max setting to close external vents) and the fan set high, measure the unit's temperature while driving by inserting the thermometer into a duct on the dash. A reading of forty-five to fifty-five degrees is acceptable, with variation subject to the vehicle's interior temperature and the time you have driven with the AC on. Readings above fifty-five degrees indicate service is required.

Tip: The Rural Garage

There are some garages both in cities and in otherwise uninhabited nooks that will take advantage of you. After an initial diagnosis, you may be stunned with the repair charges. Just as for surgery, get a second opinion even if means an expensive tow into town. Kim — then a broke college student — once had his crummy Volkswagen Beetle's engine rebuilt when running became irregular. Six months later, with the problem continuing, another shop *with* an experienced VW mechanic diagnosed the problem as a faulty distributor. With its warped shaft, it broke set after set of the points used to control the spark. Nothing was wrong with the engine before or after the rebuild.

In the sticks, you may find this attitude more common. Stuck on a ridge 120 miles from the nearest town, a local garage may tow you and set to work fixing the problem. Get a written estimate of the charges, and since you won't have anything else to do, stay around and watch. Count the parts used and write a description of them in a notebook. Make this work obvious so that the mechanic knows that you want a quality job with each part you're charged for machined or replaced as appropriate. Most shops are honest, but some will take advantage of people they know are in a desperate situation. Assume that a personal check — even reasonably local — will not be honored, but you can always ask. We stash a few name brand travelers checks for such emergencies.

Tip: Undercoating

A favorite add-on to rig sales — especially new ones — is undercoating. The coating supposedly protects against rust and quiets the ride somewhat. Improperly applied, it may in fact encourage rust with pockets that hold salt against the steel bottom. If you plan on choosing undercoating, price it at other shops before making a commitment. You may find the dealer's charge for this service unreasonably high. You may also find that the maker provides it and paying to add a second coat will accomplish nothing.

The Fuel Filter

Most people don't change their engine's fuel filter often enough. In an RV, frequent changes are required because the large engines pull more fuel and block up the filter that much faster. We change ours every month or two. Depending on your rig, a filter costs about $5 to $10 and takes only a few minutes to swap out. Note: A transparent filter casing may show a membrane that looks clean, but lacquer and other see-through buildups have little color and a pressure test is the only way to check filter condition. But since filters are cheap and easy to change, why bother?

Tires and Wheels

Tires should be tested for correct air pressure before any trip, especially if the rig has been parked for a while. As part of our "preflight inspection," we also look for cracks, uneven wear, and objects such as nails that have invaded the tire but haven't yet produced a major leak. (If you find a nail and the tire is fully inflated, head for the closest gas station at slow speed or bring out the spare.) We also check that all lug nuts are securely tight. Campers with alloy wheels instead of basic steel ones should look for fine cracks in the alloy, which indicate a wheel that's about to fly apart on the freeway. Replace it with the spare and then replace the wheel. Always check the spare too!

Brakes

At the same time we have the oil changed, we have an RV mechanic check the brakes on all wheels of our tow vehicle and fifth-wheel. He looks for wear and tests that the braking pressure is evenly matched on the fifth-wheel and between the tow vehicle and the fifth-wheel. A cursory check of the axles and bearing should be part of this inspection.

Salt Buildup

Salt from ocean air can be hard on rigs and electrical systems. But if you drive your rig in slushy conditions, you quickly build up salt from the mix used to melt snow. The best solution is persistent rinsing with a garden hose, if the weather is warm enough. Otherwise, take the rig to a truck wash where personnel can rinse the bottom with power washers. Do this with the rig unhooked, inverter turned off, and generator shut down.

Cracking Up

Since few RVs, except micros and those owned by the wealthy, are garaged, they get a strong dose of weather on a daily basis. This ages everything from paint to rubber door and window seals, unless you have a handy shade tree, as we do. The most important element to protect from the sun is your tires. Otherwise sidewall cracking will occur and you'll be driving a unit with a possible crack turning into a major blowout. Remedy this in two ways:

1. Check tires frequently for cracks, nails, and debris stuck in them, and correct and even tire pressure.
2. Avoid the suntan. Shield the tires from the sun with plywood or, better still, a tire cover from a camping store. The covers are a superior solution because you can fold them up and they weigh far less than plywood. Sun protection will greatly

increase tire life expectancy (and possibly your life expectancy should a crack break through). We prefer shade trees that shelter the unit through the brightest/hottest times of the day.

Never change RV tires from their rims, even if you have some experience changing tires. A blowout of a large truck or RV tire has done in more than one professional.

A Nice Body

On a nice sunny day, as part of our inspection, we carefully go over the external body components and towing system components looking for cracks. With the rig's ladder or a standalone ladder, we also inspect the roof for panel separation and cracks in caulking around pipes, vents, and roof-mounted devices such as antennae. (If the rig is really old, you may not want to walk on its roof, especially if your body weight exceeds 150 pounds.)

Check the entire body of the vehicle for any kind of panel failure or separation. Also check the tow vehicle's side of the hitch for failure, loose bolts, and general wear. If you catch problems early, repairs tend to be less expensive, and such safety-related problems as hitch failure can be found before you find out the hard way.

This chapter has presented the basics of RV maintenance. It was designed for RVers who aren't professional mechanics. Any problems discovered during maintenance and inspections should be referred to an experienced RV mechanic or body shop that specializes in such rigs. If the problem is serious enough and renders the rig dangerous to drive, get it towed in, rather than risk your life.

Chapter 14

Storing the Rig in Winter

Many RVers live comfortably in their rigs throughout the year. Others store their rigs over the long winter months. The best winter storage arrangement is an RV-sized garage, but since few of us have or can afford one or have the room, you must prepare your rig for Jack Frost's frozen breath. When your rig is stored, you must protect it from:

- Damage from freezing water. Water expands when frozen and water-carrying components become more brittle.
- Creatures such as rodents moving in for the winter. All openings should be carefully inspected each spring. Droppings are a sure sign of intervention by birds or rodents.
- Damage from fuel, AC, and refrigeration chemicals.

Most manufacturers provide specific instructions for protecting RV components during storage. Some of their instructions may differ from our general recommendations. In all cases the manufacturer's recommendations take precedence.

Water: It Gets Bigger as It Freezes

It's impossible in most rigs to fully purge the water tanks and the associated plumbing. Because water expands when it becomes cold and freezes, pipes and fixtures can be seriously damaged. To avoid freezing, add a winterizing chemical, available from any RV supplier, to your fresh water tank before draining it. Choose a nontoxic chemical designed for everything from the black water system to the drinking water. Follow the manufacturer's directions exactly and don't skimp. In the spring, violators of this rule will get a basic lesson in hydromechanics when their tanks and pipes split. After adding the chemical, run all water system outlets, from the kitchen sink to the toilet, to ensure that treated water replaces untreated water in the pipes throughout the rig.

Unloading Fresh Water

Obviously, with the fresh water line disconnected from city pressure, let the system drain for several hours by opening all valves, both inside and outside the coach. Even if it's just dripping, let it drip until no more water is evacuated. *Make sure the water heater is turned off to avoid overheating or burning yourself!*

Remove any inline water filters and store them in a temperature-controlled environment. Drain the hot water heater by opening its inlet and its drain cock to the atmosphere. Do this only after it's been shut down for twelve hours to let the contents cool. This also helps clean accumulated gunk from the unit.

An Option

Kits are available that use compressed air to force system evacuation. If you're winterizing a highline coach with extensive water storage/heating/delivery options, this may be a good idea. Of course, if you can afford such a coach you can also afford a mechanic to handle the winterizing process for you.

Let Aunty Freeze?

If you are confident that tank lines are voided and tanks are drained, you're done. If not, consider using commercial antifreeze to protect the lines. *Do not use automobile antifreeze* — it's a deadly poison! Buy the chemicals at Camping World designed for winterizing RVs. Follow the instructions for mixing and adding them. They'll protect your rig, and flushing them come spring is safe and easy.

Tip: The Easy Way

Drive your rig up to a yard that specializes in winter storage of RVs (and probably boats) and let it take care of all tasks. As always, get recommendations before turning your rig over to Wally's Winterhaven Wonderland Storage, Inc., or some other storage house. You want intelligent attention paid to your rig in readying it for winter and keeping an eye on it through the colder months. Good winterizing service and storage aren't that expensive, but we would be careful about choosing a name from the *Yellow Pages* without some initial checking on the company's reputation. Ask fellow RVers. If your rig includes unusual equipment such as a massive satellite dish, ask what special procedures will be used to protect it. If the response is, "Oh, they seem to make it through all but the worst blizzards by themselves," keep looking.

Gray and Black Water

Drain the water tanks completely. If you don't use an antifreeze chemical in the system, leave the valves open and the caps off for the winter. This prevents pressure from building in the tanks. In environmentally sensitive regions (such as your garage), place a bucket under the outlet to catch any overflow. We open all drains from the kitchen sink to the waste water at the same time to provide as little vacuum as possible when emptying all sources of water storage and delivery. If you intend to use an antifreeze chemical designed for use in the water tanks, follow the manufacturer's directions.

Okay, Admit It . . .

Every RVer adds water to his or her antifreeze once in a while when the coolant gets low. If you're one of those people (shame on you!), drain the cooling system and fill it with a coolant compatible with January in Madison, Wisconsin.

Owners of Older or Simple Rigs

If your rig contains minimal plumbing and it's all easily accessible, consider draining tanks, pipes, and tubes and take your chances that you have successfully evacuated the water from the system. We do this by removing the hot water heater and the pump and connecting overflow hoses that lead to the parking lot in case we missed any. The water heater and pump winter in the garage where a large and efficient furnace keeps everything well above the thirty-two-degree mark.

Fuel Fixes

Add a winterizing fuel stabilizer to the tanks in your motorhome, fuel tank in a stored tow vehicle, generator in a fifth-wheel, and any vehicle used exclusively for towing and ignored until the groundhog sees or doesn't see his shadow. You should run all engines briefly to introduce the additive into the fuel lines and injectors.

For Diesels

For diesel owners, special winterizing fuel additives are available. Never use a winterizing chemical designed for a gas engine in a diesel engine and vice versa. Mixing in the additives is best done before the weather turns really cold. Otherwise, fuel may be already gummy in consistency, and the additive will have trouble breaking down the sludge.

Tip: An Older Rig?

We don't recommend the compressed air approach to clearing water lines in old rigs. Even in good conditions, the pressure may destroy the plumbing or precipitate a leak.

Tip: Polar Bear Habitat

If you store your rig in *really* cold temperatures, test your antifreeze solution. In a really cold climate, it may be inadequate. Alcohol never freezes, right? We once bought a sealed bottle of a famous Russian vodka as part of a wedding gift. Upon inspection, it was found to be frozen nearly solid. The owner of the store casually explained that he kept his coolers extra cold.

Powering Down

You should remove batteries from the coach and store them in a garage or other area in which the temperature is relatively stable. Before putting them away for the season, top up the fluid levels with distilled water. We wipe ours down with a slightly moist cloth and rub the terminals with a light coat of grease. Motor oil will do. This prevents corrosion. Check the batteries once a month and top up the liquid level if necessary. Never overfill them because the overflowing liquid is acid. As mentioned, never smoke while doing this or expose batteries to open flame because extremely explosive hydrogen gas is present. Never touch your eyes or mucous membranes when handling, filling, or wiping lead-acid batteries. Violators of this simple rule should flush their stinging eyes with water and call 911 for an ambulance. To avoid accidental trouble, put the hand you aren't using in your pocket as electricians do.

The Air Intake

A source of rust, especially if you live near salt water, is — you guessed it — salt air. We remove our air filter and store it indoors. (It looks real nice next to the Mr. Coffee.) Then, using a plastic dry-cleaning bag and masking tape, we wrap the engine's air intake after squeezing as much air as possible from the bag. Use the masking tape to compress the bag. Do not tape it to the engine, since it probably won't stick there anyway.

You can wrap the exhaust pipe too. Before sealing the intakes, run the engine for a few minutes, let the pipe cool so it won't melt the plastic bag, and seal it with the plastic and tape. If, however, your exhaust has holes in it, this effort is futile.

Vents and Pests

To limit encroachment by creatures, cover all vents — even the one on the roof that connects to your toilet. (Pierce this one with a pin to allow gases from the septic system to escape.) We used to use duct tape, but had problems removing not only the tape but the adhesive left behind. Today, we use inexpensive contact paper to make a great seal. (Choose a decorator color that matches your rig!) The residue left by the tape or contact paper can be removed with rubber cement thinner (available in any art supply store). Wipe the remaining glue using a paper towel or a cotton ball that has been soaked in solvent. Never smoke during this process and wash your hands before eating. You can also trap or poison pests, but we've had the best luck making coming aboard difficult.

Inside Out

Empty your rig of all foodstuffs and wipe down all cabinets and the refrigerator. We tape our reefer's door open to keep moisture from accruing. Large, plastic, self-sealing bags are employed to store all RV "china," place settings, and cookware. These bags cost little, keep everything dust-free, seal out the vague odor of food inside, and can be used for food storage next season.

For Long Winters

If you plan a long storage period, you should also protect your tires. The easiest way is to jack the rig up and drop tire pressure to about 20 psi. Do not use the levelers (should you have them). They are designed for a few days in camp, not a September to

June session. Besides, even extended, one or more may allow a tire to touch the ground if you're parking the rig in the backyard.

Time to Go

Winters do end, unless you live in the mountains of Colorado. (Well, they end there too, but they just seem to go on forever.) To ready your rig for your first venture out on the highway in spring, here are the steps:

- Unseal all vents and don't forget the ones on the roof.
- Look for evidence of birds' nests and rodent damage. Take appropriate steps to clear all openings and be nice to the birds by gently relocating them, following the advice of the local Humane Society.
- Flush all tanks. Use baking soda to clear out the unwholesome flavors the drinking water tank may have absorbed.
- Check for leaks and use the bubble bath test described in Chapter 8 to ensure that no leaks are present in the propane system.
- Take a short cruise around the block and use all onboard systems to check their operational status.
- Make notes of anything that needs repair and take care of the problems before heading off to Katmandu via the Arctic Circle.

In the next chapter we present some of the neat gadgets you'll want to check out for making RVing even more fun, regardless of the time of year or the temperature outside.

Chapter 15

Gadgets and Options

Yes, we admit it, we like technology so much that giving it all up for a week in the boondocks is difficult, especially when you miss *Gilligan's Island* reruns and *Ricki Lake* interviews. (Come to think about it, these are two good reasons for severing links with civilization and leaving town forever.) Of course, part of the underlying concept and enjoyment of the RV lifestyle is that you can hook into modern living when you want to and unhook when you've had your fill. For those who prefer going "native," this chapter is probably not necessary reading. But for most RVers, the gadgets and goodies are part of the fun of running a rig.

RV Technocracy — What Is It?

All the technical goodies that you don't really need but love to enjoy are part of RV technocracy. Technology provides the opportunity to live a lifestyle as automated as you can imagine — or not. *RV technocracy* is something like *democracy;* you get to choose how much nature and how much technology you want to incorporate in your lifestyle on the road.

Please keep in mind that the options presented in this chapter are only a portion of the morass of technology available for RVs. Every new Camping World catalog contains at least one item we hadn't heard of previously and don't know how we lived without. As you camp, you'll see all kinds of technology — for addressing all kinds of needs. How about a self-expanding sewer hose that requires only connection to the dump drainage and then snakes back into its lair at the back of your rig? Or a driver's seat insert that massages you while you're at the helm? (Not recommended for sleepy drivers at night.) While some of these devices bite into your pocketbook, for former urbanites who feel the call of the wild a little too alien, these products provide comfort and sometimes entertainment.

Technology to the Rescue and a Few Other Things You Should Know About

With RV batteries, inverter, or generator, you can operate almost anything. Many portable devices, such as cellular telephones and notebook computers, can be recharged while the rig's hooked up. Business travelers can assemble a sophisticated electronic setup that rivals the office. Complete audio/video systems are standard on many rigs, with everything from videodisc to surround sound available as options. (We've even seen a large-screen TV on a luxury bus.)

As with anything RV-related, however, we recommend you study your need for each device or system and whether it's appropriate for your rig, lifestyle, and pocketbook. Be aware that many devices fail to perform as expected. Almost all RVers have a tale or two to tell about goods or services that failed to live up to their promise or premise. We point out some of the turkeys we've purchased to show you what we mean. Fortunately, none of our missteps were expensive. Our favorite failures include:

- **A twelve-volt DC hair dryer.** We bought this thinking, "That's great, we can shower and dry our hair without hooking up or turning on the noisy generator!" This Taiwan-manufactured toy couldn't dry the fur of a damp mouse, although it certainly drained the coach batteries fast enough. Adding to its failings was the sonic effect, which made a jet engine seem quiet in comparison. All it needed was a sonic boom to complete its inadequacies. It was priced at $28, and we and a lot of other campers had plenty of laughs trying it out and showing it off. It became the quintessential rubber chicken of RV equipment jokes.

Communications: See Chapter 21

With the multitude of traditional and high-tech communication gear available to RVers (how about a telephone that allows you to call anywhere in the world from anywhere in the world?), we've created Chapter 21: Keeping in Touch. If you're looking for communication devices, turn to that chapter.

- **Space-saving three-legged folding chairs.** Copied, according to the literature, from a traditional Japanese design, these were less comfortable than sitting on a jagged rock. When folded, they did save space, but that was a byproduct of inadequate construction and minimal use of materials. In addition, unless set upon flat concrete or a similarly solid surface, the triangular arrangement of the legs would twist if the "sitter" moved and dump him or her to the ground. They were priced at $44 for two at better camping stores everywhere.

- **A transparent thermometer that attached to exterior RV windows.** The device used the vacuum adhesion capabilities common to certain plastics. It blew off on its first highway trip, although the maker claims that 100-mph winds would fail to dislodge it. Hah! Lost somewhere on Interstate 8. Call us if you happen to find it. We're offering this neat twelve-volt hair dryer as a reward.

While these items turned out to be duds, there are some neat toys available. Later in the chapter we present some ideas for your consideration. But before you install that satellite disk, transceiver, and Sony Trinitron, always keep in mind both the added weight and the possible imbalance of the vehicle. Many systems are made for RVers, since campers are prime users of technology. But special lightweight systems often cost more, and if you add enough of them, you'll still overload your rig. If you've followed our advice and performed the simple calculations required, you'll know whether that eighty-five-pound satellite system will overload the rig, when combined with full tanks, occupants, and food. Don't forget that installation kits required for many items add weight too.

Fortunately for technology buffs, market pressure from users to reduce prices has forced manufacturers to cut costs. Today's technology, gadgets, and systems have fewer parts than ever and robots assemble many electronic systems with almost no human intervention. (No, this isn't good for jobs, but it certainly cuts the price of a twenty-seven-inch TV from the era when actual people built them from one thousand parts.) This has also reduced weight.

Computers are a prime example of the evolution of portable technology. Our first portable computer was an early NEC laptop that made your knees sag if you used it on your lap. (As a laptop, it must have been meant for a prehaircut Samson.) Today, complete color notebook computers with built-in sound and a CD-ROM drive weigh less than six pounds, and cost under $2,000! The number of components has been reduced from thousands to hundreds, and makers have gotten better at building a more reliable product using lighter materials. New models also use less energy and shut down to save power when not in use. That's another plus for the on-the-road set. Now if we could just get a low-energy-consumption waffle iron — or better yet, a hair dryer.

Power Mad

Yes, we've already talked about it, but you need to know more: You must consider not only device weight, but also power consumption before you decide to use a piece of technology. Twelve-volt devices can empty coach batteries, and 115VAC appliances can overload not only campground electricity but that of your rig as well. Running multiple devices naturally increases the load.

You can work around this problem by relying on devices that employ rechargeable power and rechargeable batteries. Charge batteries when docked and then use them to power devices such as computers, communications systems, and shavers. Charging draws little shore power, so your RV and campground outlet are safe, and devices that work off batteries are usually built to conserve power. And that's exactly what you want in an RV's electrical environment.

Tip:
One Thousand Kilometers, and Closing, Sir

And you thought having a camera on the back of your rig was cool! Advanced RADAR Technologies offers a RADAR system that evaluates your distance from objects behind your rig. A readout shows the distance and beeps increase in frequency as you move closer to objects. Neat, huh! Call ART at 810-415-8780, if you can't live another minute without one of these gadgets.

Tip: A Refreshing Sleep

If you rely on battery-operated charging for high-tech equipment, consider charging while you're asleep. That way, surges in campground power are less frequent except for the switching on and off of "environmental appliances" (heating and AC).

All About Batteries

Going portable with battery-operated electronics? You should first know a little more about battery technology. The storage of electricity is a rapidly evolving field as engineers look for the perfect battery: one that provides unlimited energy, charges in minutes from any kind of power source, and is environmentally benign. Sadly, none of these goals have been met. The best news is today's batteries provide longer life, many are rechargeable, and recycling is finally removing their toxic chemicals from the landfill mix.

Lead-Acid

Your vehicle is powered by lead-acid batteries, discussed in Chapter 8. They were briefly used in handheld electronics, but the technology was abandoned.

Carbon-Zinc

The batteries of yesteryear. Forget them.

Nicad

The old standby rechargeable, the nicad can be repeatedly re-charged, but for it to take a full charge, it must be fully discharged first. You can either drain it dry or buy a "deep-cycle" charger for this purpose. Nicads have a shorter charge life (time between charges) and deliver less current than other battery technologies.

Alkaline

Now available in rechargeable formats (at last), these batteries produce more current than do nicads. The unrechargeable formats must be disposed of after use, unlike nicads, making them less environmentally friendly.

Lithium

Longer-lived than alkalines, these batteries are not rechargeable but seem to last forever when demands on their power are modest. We use them in battery-powered clocks and calculators — applications where we don't require battery changes often. Some elements, such as inexpensive programmable remote controls, forget their settings at each battery change, so lithium is the perfect technology for avoiding this occasional search for the control's missing manual. (When you have to worry about the remote control, you'll get the true feeling of the rough quality of life on the road.)

Nickel Hydride

Like nicads, nickel hydride technology allows these batteries to be recharged many times. Found in newer cellular phones, pagers, and computers, they provide current similar to that provided by alkaline batteries, offer a longer charge life, and don't require a complete discharge to fully recharge them.

Getting Your Batteries Recharged

Rechargeable batteries are best charged on shore power, because you may have trouble finding a compatible twelve-volt charger. It can also be argued that charging one battery from another is, to employ an ancient cliché, robbing Peter to pay Paul.

When recharging, employ only the charger designed for the battery you're using, otherwise an explosion may result. We run our twelve-volt computer equipment off an adapter that plugs into the cigarette lighter. (Adapters are available that tap the coach wiring in a fifth-wheel or trailer, since it's unlikely you'll want to plug into your truck's lighter and run wires in and out windows.) Have an RV shop install it, because you want to add the new load to a circuit with the capacity to handle it.

New Technologies

Right now there are probably half a hundred experimental battery technologies being tested. The pressure for building the ideal battery we described earlier is stronger than ever before. Everything from communications devices to electric vehicles demands immense improvements to existing battery capabilities. So far, no major breakthroughs, but any day now, as scientists have been assuring us since World War II.

★ This symbol means that we would recommend this option to any RVer as a useful and handy device.

? This may work for you, but before you buy, stop and think about its demands on your RV, its electrical system, and the price tag.

✖ We don't need to explain this one. Don't waste your money.

Some RV Technologies to Consider

With so many new products for RVs, it's hard to keep track of them. Many, but not all, fall into the electronics category, with the advent of simple computers-on-a-chip costing as little as 50 cents in quantity. For years a computer engineer friend who builds everything from simple control systems for machines to top-secret projects for the U.S. government's Scandia Labs joked about computerizing toasters. His contention: Why bother computerizing a toaster anyway? A few years ago, he had to eat his words when the first computer-controlled toasters hit the shelves. In this section, we present twenty options and offer our editorial opinion on their worth for the RVer.

★ Gas Sniffers

You *must* add (if they're not included) electronic sniffers for smoke and carbon monoxide, and we would recommend one for propane as well. These resemble the familiar smoke detectors you should have at home. Follow the New Year's tradition of replacing their batteries on December 31 whether they need it or not, even if it means trudging through the snow to an ice-covered RV kept in storage in the winter months. Buy two for long rigs and avoid putting a smoke detector over the cooking area, because it will trigger like yours at home when you burn the toast. Available at any camping store, detectors install in minutes with a screwdriver. Follow the maker's instructions for placement and buy only those designed for RV use. That's why you should get them at a camping store rather than Kmart.

Tip: A Mobile Washing Machine

For those less endowed with space or money, you can do the old camper's laundry trick. Put one sturdy trash bag inside another and the "dirties" inside, with an appropriate amount of water and soap, and tie it off tightly. Store it in a hold or the back of the tow vehicle and head for town. This generates agitation and (one hopes) cleans your clothes like one of those "washday miracle" products. Longer drives mean cleaner clothes. (Never use salt water, as this will make for sticky, greasy clothing.)

Rinse the clothes carefully to get the soap out of them and hang them out to dry. We've had good luck combining the drying process with our regular scrub brush–and–hose roof cleaning on a sunny day. After cleaning and allowing the roof to dry in the sun, we spread the clothes out on it. Weight them with clean rocks if there's a wind. You get not only fresh, clean clothes but an RV roof that looks to be in showroom shape! Great for bleaching jeans into a condition that New Yorkers pay hundreds of dollars for!

★ Water Pressure Regulators and Filtration

Explained earlier in the book, these two components are critical for preventing major structural damage through leaks and maintaining your health when traveling through Podunk City with its Depression-era water-cleansing system.

? Washer and Dryer

Hate laundromats as much as we do? Water-conserving washers and dryers are available for your RV for about $900 street price. No, they won't do the laundry for a family of six, at least not in one load, but they will keep you out of a dull spell in the "coin-op" or the campground's laundry room with its attendant spiderwebs. Note: Only those with RVs with the room required and capable of handling extra weight and water demands should consider such an option.

Before forking over extra money for an on-the-road mechanical laundromat, ensure that it meets your expectations. The least expensive models fail to clean clothes to our expectations, and dryer operation can be quite inefficient. Water and power use are involved and you might be better off taking the clothes over to a stream and beating them with a stick on a flat rock. It's been done.

? Trash Compactor

"Honey, will you take out the trash?" A call to action — hauling a tiny trash can full of, well, we won't get into it, to a distant trash receptacle. For highline coaches, a trash compactor is available. Instead of two trips to the disposal unit a day, one trip every few days is all that you need. These units usually come as a built-in option on a highline motorhome, so you can add one to your Class A, if it can handle the weight. The downside? Just because trash becomes more compact, it doesn't get lighter when you finally haul it off. You'll also need a supply of special trash bags, and for warm-weather travel a deodorizing spray helps too.

★ Catch the Wave

Can't sleep due to too many noises in camp? Want an afternoon nap but the next-door neighbors are dancing to the "Jailhouse Rock"? Consider a wave generator. It's a machine available at Radio Shack, The Sharper Image, and stores that handle electronic gadgets. About the size of a small clock radio, this device produces soothing background noise that effectively masks other sounds. Place it by your bed. You can choose sounds such as *Ocean Breakers*, *Wind in the Willows*, *Babbling Brook*, and usually several more. While the sound isn't high fidelity, it works. Running fans or air cleaners is another noise-masking technique.

★ Are You Full of Hot Air?

Concerned about your tire pressure, but don't want to wander around the rig every day getting your hands black with a manual pressure indicator? Have arthritis that makes such operations difficult or painful? Here's the solution, albeit an expensive one — Tiremate. Tiremate's sensors are wireless transmitters that replace each wheel valve cap. When pressure drops below a preset pressure, an alarm sounds on a dash-mounted readout. The offending tire is indicated by an LED readout. What a great way to monitor not only the rig's rolling stock, but the status of the all-too-often-neglected spare. Tiremate is available through Camping World's mail-order catalog.

★ Minibikes

No, we aren't talking about the noisy gas-powered minimotorcycles popular in the 1960s, but about the convertible foot-powered bicycles that fold up small for RV storage and expand into adult-sized frames while you're camped. Made by Dahon and others, when folded, they take up about as much room as a fat briefcase. There are a number of models on the market, and the larger ones are the easiest to assemble and power, but if you're in a small Class C, you may have to settle for one with sixteen-inch wheels. These require a little more pedal pressure when climbing hills, and they look odd with their tiny wheels and long stems to the handlebars and seat. But they are small when folded down. Always ride a bike before purchase, because some models may not suit your physique.

You can also carry motorscooters, motorcycles, or a complete Harley-Davidson on your RV if it can handle the weight and you can handle the bill for the bike. These naturally add weight, but camping stores sell a variety of carriers for almost any two-wheeled vehicle, and you should look at any external transportation just as you look at the storage compartments and pods in any RV. Lock or no lock, think twice before parking your classic Electroglide on your bus-style RV's exterior and heading off to bed.

? Avoid the Embarrassment of Dishpan Hands

Just as promised in those awful old commercials, you can avoid dishpan hands — not through special soaps or rubber gloves, but with a real RV-based dishwasher. Heating their own water, these units wash the dishes required for a camping-type meal for four. Using only three or four gallons of water, these units can be mounted permanently in a kitchen cupboard or in a nook. Operation requires a fifteen-amp circuit of shore or generator power, so don't run the AC and the microwave while washing the dishes at an elderly campground.

✖ Tire Inflation Valve Extenders

Provided or added to the inside tires on dual wheels or as a convenience for filling a hard-to-reach spare, these rubberized extensions eventually rot or may be damaged by pebbles kicked up by the road. Once affected, your tire deflates. And more than one RVer has gone for the spare to fix a flat, only to find the rubber extender has rotted and drained the tire of air.

? Startalk

It's always been difficult to watch television in an RV unless you're in a campground equipped with cable or located in the midst of a large city. However, for wealthy RVers this hasn't been a barrier to watching Miss Vanna every evening. They watch TV via the stars. Cranking up the satellite dish, they home in on a satellite carrying the programming of their choice. This is the Jetsons' idea of RVing. Larger dishes provide better picture quality, but they weigh more. You pay a monthly fee to watch many channels, as they are scrambled otherwise. There are an estimated five hundred channels out there, but many are repeats of others, and the foreign-language transmissions are valuable only for those boning up on Polish while camping. But *with* a "sat dish," and camped in a remote park, you'll make a lot of new friends very quickly.

How Did Western Civilization Go On Before This Invention?

Available at Camping World is Ball Cap Buddy. It's a can't-live-without affair that allows baseball caps to be washed in a washing machine without losing their shape. And here you are, scornfully asking whether space-age technology *has made a difference* to improving the lives of millions!

? Startalk with DSS

DSS is a new satellite service with a dish about the size of a large pepperoni pizza. Smaller, lighter, and easy to use, it is compatible with even the smallest rigs. You, however, must be prepared for a monthly bill and must have the means of receiving and paying it. With 150 channels, it sounds good, but many of these are sports and pay-per-view events. Many channels are purchased separately or as packages. For example, if anyone wants to watch it, MTV is currently running $2.95 a month with DirectTV. The more channels you subscribe to, the higher your bill.

? Even More Startalk

The GPS (Global Positioning System) was mentioned earlier. This system allows you to locate your position anywhere on Earth, within about fifty feet. (It's more precise for military users, but unless you're Boris and Natasha, your device will lack the codes required to get down to the square inch.) Handheld GPS units are available from sporting goods discounters for less than $200 (and prices continue to collapse). If, however, you spend your RVing time on the interstate, you probably don't need one of these cool gadgets.

A Computer Sextant

We haven't seen one yet, but Ultradata (314-997-2250) has announced a system that allows you to specify your starting point and destination on a personal computer. It then analyzes the best path for your trip and "dumps" it to a handheld device. As you drive, you simply follow the device's instructions. What a way to go.

? Even *More* Startalk

For those with a lot of money (about $3,000 at this writing), there's Sony's unique navigation system. A set of compact discs — actually CD-ROMs — allows you to look at maps of most of North America in color on a video monitor (on your notebook computer). It's a great system for getting out of the Bronx ASAP, but the high cost and the need to buy updated CDs as cities evolve make it costly indeed. Some people don't even spend this kind of money on a complete, used trailer.

Acura, Honda's highline automobile, already offers this system on its coupes. (It doesn't use CD-ROM, but a proprietary disk technology.) Our guess is that this technology will become standard in highline motorhomes in the near future. GPS is combined with CD-ROM data to pinpoint your exact location. It can even supply localized directions to the nearest ATM and other resources many RVers depend on.

Tip: Chemical Dehumidifiers

These are small units that soak up moisture from an RV without the use of outside power. We've never tried them. If you do, ensure all access ways are open for free air circulation and place several units at intervals throughout the coach. Change the elements as instructed, because once the unit's chemicals become saturated with water, they stop working.

★ Putting Yourself on the Map

If you are traveling with a personal computer, there are several packages available for mapping the best route from Point A to Point B. You tell the program where you are and where you plan to go, and it assembles a route and maybe even includes sightseeing opportunities along the way. Since there are a number of these programs on the market, we won't recommend one. Instead, head for a large computer store such as CompUSA and browse the offerings. Recommendations from computer-literate fellow RVers are of use as well.

✖ Coming In from the Cold

We talk about winterizing RVs and the associated issues in Chapter 14, but beware of "dehumidifiers" that cost as much as a small air-conditioner. These *are* air-conditioners, and while they do a good job of knocking the water out of the interior, they do a better job of raising your electricity bill. Skip these $300 units and follow our steps in preparing your coach for the cold. A carefully protected open window will work nearly as well and costs nothing to buy, install, or power. If, however, you live in Churchill, Manitoba (home primarily to thousand-pound polar bears), then one of these units may be mandatory, electric bill be damned.

✖ Fuel Savers

A variety of additives and subsystems exist that claim to save gas or diesel. Many of these systems are crudely designed to limit fuel consumption, which starves you of power, or simply don't do anything at all. Don't add them to your tow vehicle or motorhome without substantial recommendation from qualified experts or users. And *weird* additives (sorry for lack of a better word) may cause damage to your fuel lines or engine. Octane boosters may make the engine run hotter.

Who knows what's in them? They may contain something that actually does improve mileage at the cost of damaging fuel lines or injector apparatus. The "experts" or "users" you rely on should be people who have no financial interest in your buying and installing the system or buying sixteen cases of an additive.

★ Steady as She Goes, Mr. Sulu

There are quite a few stabilizers on the market that do everything from making a trailer easier to tow (the basics of which were discussed in Chapter 10) to making the aft areas of an inexpensive motorhome a comfortable walk-through while on the road. These are options that should be considered. We'll cover a few in this section, but again, don't overimprove your rig to the point that the money you put into it will never be seen again. And again, if a potential RV purchase exceeds this simple maxim with options, then you're looking at the wrong rig.

Tip: A Rough Road to Travel

Be careful that you match the strut (shock) to your rig. It takes an expert "suspension man" (or "suspension woman") to evaluate your rig and match new shocks to it. The wrong ones will provide a spongy ride and wobbly cornering or a hard ride that makes a rough road like a trip in a Jeep through Australia's Outback while the driver quenches a large Foster's to keep the dust "from the back o' me throat, mate."

Aftermarket Shocks

Many manufacturers build shock absorbers superior to what the chassis manufacturer or coach builder included, as many use stock shocks that wholesale at about $2.99 each. Do not be deluded by dealer claims that these add-ons will improve your vehicle's weight capabilities (GCWR and GVWR, discussed in Chapter 9). Instead, consider that the right match of shocks will add stability to your rig and improve the ride, especially over rough roads. Purchasers of used rigs may need to replace the shocks anyway, and the purchase price of quality shocks is much less than that of quality tires, although you may need to retrofit both systems.

There are two advantages to quality shock absorbers:

1. They do a better job of soaking up the bumps instead of passing them on to the passenger cabin. Not only is the ride more comfortable for the human passengers, but excessive vibration and frequent vector changes in inertia ("the shakes") damage the rig's structural members and loosen interior fittings and appliances. Unlike the factory or old shocks, quality shocks won't bottom out except under the most extreme circumstances, such as the mother of all potholes in New Jersey.

2. Upgraded shocks not only work better, but last longer. Built with better seals and sturdier overall construction, most will last seventy-five thousand to one hundred thousand miles or more between changes. During this same period, you may replace the "el cheapo" shocks two or three times. With replacement costs and labor factored in, the quality shocks are actually less expensive, assuming your tenure in the vehicle is long-term.

Which to Buy?

We've had good luck with Bilsteins. Gas-pressurized, they made a substantial improvement in our Southwind's handling and ride on rough roads. (To be fair, we replaced the factory shocks with the Bilsteins at 19,500 miles. The originals may have been already shot at that time.) But there are other manufacturers' models available, and we suggest you look at more than one brand before choosing. Assume that you will pay about $100 per wheel for quality shocks, but it's money well spent.

Tip: Riding on Air

Air bags are filled with — you guessed it — air! That means that as with a tire, you must verify the pressure and add air as required to maintain efficiency and coach balance. This means crawling under the coach with wheels blocked and measuring the air pressure, topping up with a gas station air hose where necessary. Pressure in the two bags on each axle should be identical or you'll experience an uneven and unsafe ride.

Air Bag Suspension

Not to be confused with in-dash air bags used for crash protection, inflated air bags are used in many motorhomes between the coach and the chassis and the body to make the ride smoother and (though we doubt this one) to increase the rig's GCWR and GVWR ratings.

Yes, the addition of air bags makes a big difference in a motorcoach's ride. The ol' Southwind came factory equipped with inexpensive front bags, which made for a pleasant ride from the cockpit. But heading to the back while in motion (not recommended or legal in some states) meant either crawling or grabbing anything available, as the vertical and horizontal shaking rendered controlled movement near impossible.

The addition of air bags to the rear axles changed all that. The rear became as smooth as the front. In fact, we've read an account of air bags installed in a motorhome that stabilized it to the point that a passenger could actually sleep comfortably in the rear queen bed while the rig trekked the highways!

Unique Towing Systems

We've discussed trailer hitches in Chapter 10, but made only a passing reference to the high-tech models. A basic trailer hitch costs only a couple of hundred dollars unless you plan to pull the RV equivalent of the Empire State Building around with you.

But for those pulling large, heavy rigs, a high-tech hitch may be in order. Otherwise the swift passing of a large truck is white-knuckle time, requiring a firm grasp on the steering wheel to keep the tail (the trailer) from wagging the dog (the tow car). The basic premise of high-tech hitches is that they increase the rigidity of the mating of two vehicles, providing help in fighting high crosswinds or, when that big truck zooms by, keeping the trailer from developing a mind of its own.

More to It

If you increase the rigidity of the coupling, the dog wags the tail, but the laws of physics have yet to be repealed. Consider what a loaded eight-thousand-pound trailer can do to the thirty-two-hundred-pound car towing it. Inertia is on the side of the trailer, not the car. Simply making a stronger link between vehicles does not fix the problem, as the trailer must still be able to turn corners after the car has straightened out. It must also be able to remain with all wheels on the ground at zero degrees while one side of the tow vehicle rotates ten degrees as the driver's side rotates up on a hillock. (To demonstrate this effect, think of your hand as the tow vehicle and your wrist and forearm as the trailer. Using the other hand, gently twist your "tow vehicle" hand. What happens to your wrist and arm?)

One Hitch to Consider

One hitch that longtime RV guru Bill Farlow experimented successfully with is the Pull-Rite (Pulliam Enterprise, 219-259-1520). The hitch, priced at about $700 plus installation, effectively damps the tail-wagging-the-dog syndrome. It's one of several on the market. Bill reports that even a passing tractor-trailer had no effect on the rig with the Pull-Rite.

Again, for the added safety and ease of use, this may be the unit for you, but look at everything available before purchase. Beware of miracle claims — all hitches are a compromise of one sort or another. For the more expensive ones, the dealer may arrange for you to drive a vehicle with one coupling towing your trailer. Even though the vehicles involved may not be the same size and weight as yours, you'll get at least some idea of the feel of a quality high-tech hitch.

★ Stop-and-Go Traffic

Other options improve trailer brake performance (well worth the money) for both the tow vehicle and that being towed. You should get expert advice before buying one of these, however, since there are a number of these systems on the market and not all of them will be compatible with your towing arrangement. We like the ones that are self-correcting, so a light touch on the brakes doesn't lock the trailer brakes. Some systems are seriously compromised by weather, and what works perfectly on a crystal-clear seventy-degree day may act differently in the snow at minus ten degrees. Test before buying.

★ Ensign Crusher, Slow to Impulse Engines

Overheated brakes are a common and potentially panic-inducing problem on any rig. Hot brakes may "fade" — a euphemism for heat-related failure. U.S. Gear's D-CELERATOR can be employed in diesel rigs to assist braking downhill on long grades. It uses the engine's exhaust pressure to slow the rig and avoid overheated brakes and related problems.

★ Automatic Levelers

We mention leveling in this chapter because motorhome users without levelers on their rigs will probably want to install a set, and all RVs should be level when parked. Not all camping sites are equally level or flat, unless you enjoy the all-concrete variety (we don't). Even some of those aren't perfect. For this reason, you need to understand the basics of RV leveling, or if you can afford it, buy an automatic leveling system that, with a touch of a switch, melds your rig in perfect symmetry with the shape of the earth. Leveling is important because it makes the RV more comfortable. We've been told by their manufacturers that leveling is vital to the performance of RV refrigerators, but have not heard anything from other RVers on this subject. But maybe luck was with them (and us), or this is a problem confined to older units.

Aside from the refrigerator, a level RV is important for other reasons. If you have a spouse and sleep in the same bed, in an unleveled arrangement, you may find him or her rolling with the coach and onto the floor. Cooking is more difficult too, as food-stuffs, bowls, and fruits head south off the counter. And you can't bake a layer cake in an oven at a twenty-degree angle.

Electrically powered leveling systems are reserved primarily for motorcoaches. When you consider that the same thing can be accomplished, although in a less suave manner, with pieces of wood, it may be hard to justify the $600 to $1,200 price of an automatic system. But for motorhome owners, this easy solution is hard to resist.

Depending on the system, either three or four levelers do the job. Older systems allow you to adjust each leveler separately while watching a gauge. In modern systems, a computer unfolds the levelers and then, upon contact with the ground, balances the rig by adjusting each leveler. Most are keyed to your ignition, so you can't start the engine without putting up the levelers. *Keep hands away from the levelers during setup!*

One last note: Levelers can only level a rig parked on terra firma. If you park in mud or shifting sand, the system will constantly attempt to level the coach as the soil under the "feet" shifts from the weight of the RV. If you frequently camp in rugged conditions, carry three or four (depending on the number of levelers you have) two-inch-by-one-foot square pieces of durable wood. Coat them with an epoxy sealant against moisture. Then, before initiating the leveling procedure, place one board in the place where each leveler will come down. This will help in all but the most temperamental conditions. Better yet, you should avoid these soil conditions al-together — your rig might get stuck.

In this chapter we've looked at a number of useful technologies that may or may not be appropriate for you. Even more goodies are discussed in Chapter 21: Keeping in Touch. The purpose of this chapter was to make you aware of the options, not to recommend that you buy them. Probably 50 percent of RVers own and use none of the devices we've described here, and they still have a great, safe time traveling and living in their rigs. In the next chapter, we'll look at ways to stay safe on the road. Yes, some of these also involve technology.

Chapter 16

Safe and Sound RVing

Throughout this book, we've mentioned safety-related issues. In this chapter, we feature the major safety concerns, with a focus on disaster prevention and your health. While RVing is generally a safe, relaxing, and get-away-from-it-all experience, occasional natural or manmade disasters may intervene. You, on the highway, are more vulnerable than families huddled around the TV set in a nice house in the city.

To be on the safe side, follow our safety advice throughout this book and this chapter, *and keep your insurance payments up to date.* Further, always keep people informed of your whereabouts. This is very important when traveling in isolated or storm-prone areas.

Tip: Underpassing

When driving in severe and sometimes sudden weather changes, the safest place is under a highway overpass — earthquakes excepted. While we don't recommend RV occupancy during severe storms of any kind, you're probably safest under the heavy concrete and bracing of the overpass. Stay put until the storm has passed, keeping in mind that a brief clearing of the skies may be the respite before the rest of the storm, or a waiting period until the next thunderstorm "cell," rather than the end of the affair.

Tip: Got a Dually?

Many units have four tires on one axle, called a "dually" in the tire biz. You'll need a special but inexpensive tire gauge to check the tire behind the one closest to the exterior of the RV. Get one at Camping World or a similar store. Tell them what you are looking for and they'll show you exactly what you need. Price? Less than $10.

Inclement Weather

Touched on in other places in this book, weather is a major factor in safe and easy handling of any kind of rig. We stay put when the sky darkens and the rain pours or the outside world whitens with the quiet sound of soft falling snow. If we're in camp, we stay there. If we're on the road, we find the closest rest stop, truck stop, roadside restaurant, grocery store, or just about anywhere where fellow human beings congregate and food is likely available. Gas stations even work in a pinch.

Radio Days

Monitoring a weather radio is very helpful. Get the forecast and then listen to the changes throughout the day while watching the skies. For use in the United States, Radio Shack offers models that produce an audible alarm if a major weather advisory comes through. You can also try to head for the nearest camp, but unless it's nearby and doesn't require driving remote side roads and mountains, it's best not to take the chance or you'll be skidding off the road before reaching it.

Tires

Keeping tires in good repair is key to safe driving. We've found quality radial tires superior to ordinary truck tires in handling, ride quality, and tire life span. They also seem to bond to the road better in adverse weather conditions, such as rain-slicked asphalt.

Study your rig's donuts (tires) regularly. When you need to replace them, avoid retreads at all costs. If you don't know what to get, drive the rig to the closest RV shop. There, some knowledgeable person with the name Gus, Jack, or Ray stitched into his shirt will take one look at them. He'll tell you what you're dealing with, appraise each tire's condition individually, and estimate replacement cost, if necessary. You get a free air pressure check thrown in, too.

Where to Buy "Them Big Black Donuts"

Tires are one of the least interesting purchases anyone can make (right up there with toothpaste and books about RVs), but since your life is literally riding on them, you want the right tire at the right price. Where to go? Good question, since it's a tradeoff. Head for an RV shop and get the best advice but usually a higher price. Head to Price/Costco or a regular tire shop for a better price, but little experience with fitting an RV with the right tire for the job. What do we do? We get on the phone after writing down the numbers (size) of our present tire and call about six shops to build consensus *and* get the best price.

Note that any serious wear on a tire demands immediate replacement. RVs, because of their weight, put the maximum stress on tires. If your tires' sidewalls are cracked, or if a tire makes a noise as it rotates (cupping), get it replaced ASAP. Don't risk driving that last 120 miles to the next city to save $5 per wheel. Okay?

Wheeling and Dealing

Tires are an expensive part of an RV, especially if you go radial, and we recommend that you do. Tires are one of the most frustrating things to buy because, in our experience, you'll get a high level of misinformation (known in the trade by the technical term "BS") and price variation from dealers as the spiders string their web to ensnare you without revealing the total charges. Some quote prices with complete installation including balancing and valve stems. Others run your charge card and have some flunky roll four, six, or eight tires out the door to your rig and walk away. The deal is done as far as they're concerned, like you can mount and balance a fifty-pound tire yourself . . .

All rigs have two tires up front (big surprise, that) and some have one or two axles in the rear, with one axle having four wheels (called dual or a "dually") on it to support the motorhome's enormous load. That means you may need four, six, or eight tires, depending on your rig. Inspect all tires carefully and ensure that all are inflated at pressure specified by a knowledgeable RV shop. For micros, maximum pressure is probably appropriate for the back with 5 to 10 percent less in the front. Big fifth-wheels, trailers, and motorhomes require the experienced eye of a professional RV mechanic or house that handles truck tires.

Equality

For safety reasons, never have a tire on one side of an axle inflated differently from the tire on the other side. This causes handling problems and may trash the tires. Never overinflate or underinflate either — this can cause premature tire failure, usually at the worst time when you're cruising down the freeway, fully loaded (and probably overweight).

No Exceptions!

There are some conditions you shouldn't drive in. Period. You may want to race your rig across the state for the jubilation of the birth of a close relative's child, or the sad affair of a funeral, but this does not justify putting your life and those of your passengers at risk. Instead, park your rig safely and stay put with telephoned apologies or wait the weather out. Twelve hours makes a big difference in meteorological terms but not, one hopes, to the emergency at hand. Avoid chartered planes as a replacement in bad weather. More than one person has taken to the air in weather too poor to drive a tank in, and, well, you may or may not know who Buddy Holly was . . .

352

Tip: The Spare

All RVs are equipped with a spare tire (or should be). When checking pressure on the tires — a regular procedure — check the pressure on the spare. Also, be sure that, if it's mounted on the rear, the sun hasn't heated it to the cracking point.

Windy Conditions

Depending on your rig's height and suspension, wind may present a minimal problem until crosswinds reach a certain level. Some RVs, such as tall motorhomes with basement storage and inadequate suspensions, may find a fourteen-mile-an-hour crosswind more than enough to push the rig sideways and make driving a chore. Know your rig and its limits. Don't assume because you can more or less hold it in one lane now that the weather won't worsen or that a big tractor-trailer won't add that extra degree of sway that pushes your rig one step too far.

Dust Storms

Pull off the highway as far as is safe. Turn off all exterior lights so a vehicle following your lights doesn't pull off with you and find out the hard way that you're stopped. We turn our lights off immediately after leaving the freeway in emergencies and pull to a prudent and fast stop.

Rain

Moderate rain is drivable, as long as it's not accompanied by heavy wind. Reduce your speed, allow plenty of stopping distance, and pull off if visibility or wind becomes a problem. Keep in mind, if it's the first rain of the season, roads will be exceptionally slick; oil from a summer's worth of leaky cars will cause roads to be like Teflon as oil rises from the road and combines with water.

Snow

Driving a rig on snow or ice is difficult. Yes, you can put chains on your tires, but it's a dirty, heavy job. Wait for the roads to be cleared and then drive as though on wet pavement, keeping speeds low and maintaining a significant distance between you and the vehicle in front for safe stopping. If the snow or water is freezing or frozen, stay off the road, especially when hauling a trailer.

Serious Weather Conditions

Tropical storms? Twisters? Listen intently to your weather radio! Initially, with a storm warning, seek shelter under an overpass as explained earlier in this chapter. Turn off propane and ensure that the refrigerator isn't running. Unhook from electrical power. If there's time, tie down your rig with multiple nylon ropes to trees or heavy pipes (see the movie *Twister* if you think inclement weather can be trifled with!) and evacuate for a human-style shelter, but only if there's time. *Never leave yourself in the path of a hurricane or tornado even if you risk losing your rig.* Storms move in unpredictable patterns. Even one miles away may change or reverse course in minutes.

A Washout

RVers either camp in permanent parks or choose a spot of their own where property ownership is not apparent. In many parts of the country, flooding is a problem. Fortunately, most flooding occurs with substantial warning and adequate time to move the rig to higher ground. But one kind of flood that can occur almost everywhere but is predominantly found in the pseudo-barren soil of the western deserts (parts of Arizona, California, Nevada, Oregon, New Mexico, Texas, Washington, Wyoming, British Columbia, and so forth) is the flash flood. In the desert, there exists a weather phenomenon called a pocket storm. This may be anything from a light sprinkle to a vicious thunderstorm that may soak forty square miles while the adjoining territories see nary a drop.

The hard soil of sunbaked landscapes tends to be very dry but unabsorbent, so the water from a storm follows the path to the low ground — a streambed or dry wash. A heavy downpour precipitates flash floods that you can't anticipate. You may see nothing, even though fifty miles away a full inch of rain falls in a five-minute period. And where did you camp? In a wash where the rain collects and washes you and your rig away.

The Solution

In flash flood areas, park on high ground. When looking at a sheltered canyon or arroyo, study (with flashlight if necessary) the sides. Look for high-water marks and evidence of water activity such as streaks, mud, and fine sand in the presence of surrounding sand that's much coarser. This indicates a wash and a flash flood path. Get out of it immediately! It's better to put up with colder air and wind than to embrace the calmness of an empty wash. An empty wash can suddenly become a full one. Better yet, avoid low-lying land and camp in the hills when choosing a spot for a free night's camping.

Fighting Fire with Fire!

This section is *alarming* and we don't mean that as a pun. An RV is unlikely to catch fire, and we don't want to panic you, but you should be prepared for an emergency. Your RV has a large amount of fuel and propane gas onboard, and most of the fabrics, wood, particle board, and other materials used in its manufacture are flammable. You must take special precautions to keep from burning down the house. Simple precautions, such as remembering to extinguish all flames and pilot lights, including that of the refrigerator, when loading gas, diesel, and propane, can save your life. You also need to carry appropriate fire extinguishers.

Tip: One in Ten

We have one extinguisher instantly available (on a quick-release mount) for every ten feet of RV. Round the footage number upward for safety. That gives an eighteen-foot Class C two extinguishers, and a forty-five-foot beluga whale of a motorhome five of the things. One should be located by the galley, because as far as we can tell, this is the most common source of RV fires. Motorhomes should also have one close to the engine (front or "pusher") in the rare event of an engine fire.

Know How to Get Out

All people in the RVing party should have multiple escape routes prepared in advance. Long motorhomes, fifth-wheels, and trailers should have more than a single exit door. In fact, the purchase of a vehicle without a second door or emergency escape would be a questionable decision.

Your best action, unless the fire is truly controllable, such as a small kitchen fire, is to *get out*. Grab kids (we would grab the cats) *and leave!* Get away from the vehicle, because propane or, in a motorhome, gasoline or diesel may explode. You should also get the neighbors out if other rigs are parked close to yours, as they have flammables just like yours. RV fires are rare considering the fuels aboard, but the possibility is a good reason to keep your insurance up to date.

Silver Blaze

We spoke with the deputy fire marshal for San Diego, California, when we were moving (yes again) from apartment to RV. David Francis of the SDFD told us that RVers should purchase a fire extinguisher rated 20 BC, as it can best put out the kind of fires RVs experience. "What about Halon?" we asked. Mr. Francis explained that Halon is the ideal chemical for fighting computer room fires because it leaves no significant residue, but the 20-BC units are more versatile and make shorter work of a blaze than Halon.

This seems important when you consider that a less efficient extinguishing system may not leave residue but may allow your RV to burn to the chassis because it can't kill the flames fast enough. Saving the rig is more important than the difficulty of cleaning up the mess later, so an extingusher that works faster than Halon but leaves a mess makes perfect sense.

Fires are one of the biggest causes of disasters in RVing. Yes, fire may be the key to civilization as we know it, but in an RV, it's deadly. The best fire management system is prevention. You've probably heard this before. It's obvious that you should keep the kids away from matches and lighters at home or on the road, and it's also mandatory to carry fire extinguishers in the rig. Here are some other safety measures to follow:

- Ventilation saves lives. Crack the windows open a bit when heating the RV with propane or solid fuel or preparing meals.
- Evaluate your parking spot for vegetation that could fuel flames. If there's enough to really burn and it's dry, change spots (move the RV), trim the overgrowth with the owner's permission or, better still, payment for eliminating weeds, or drive off into the sunset and camp elsewhere.
- Never burn any kind of barbecue, whether it is gas fired or uses briquettes under an RV awning or trees. Follow camp-ground instructions for disposing of ashes. Fires of any kind are prohibited in most national parks during the summer and a "no-burn" warning may be declared for entire counties, although this won't preclude you from using indoor cooking facilities.
- Always smoke outside the unit. Ensure that all ashes go into an ashtray with a sealed top. (You push the button to open and use this device.) Such ashtrays can be found at drugstores and tobacco specialty shops. Better still, give up smoking. It's a healthier, safer alternative.
- Immediately evacuate an RV in which flames have taken hold on furniture, walls, curtains, ceiling, or carpets. At this point, you want to get away from the vehicle with all family members and pets, because such a fire may breach the fuel lines and

tanks and the vehicle can explode. Forget attempting to fight such a fire. Your only reward may be an extended stay in a hospital burn ward. If you're parked in an area serviced by a fire department, time wasted fighting the fire might be better spent running to a phone and calling the professionals.

Forest Fire — Get Out of There!

If you see smoke in the distance, stay away. Forest fires are serious, be they a brush fire fueled by scrub or massive, ancient conifers exploding into flames. At the first word of a forest fire within fifty miles of your camp, pack up and head for a major road and preferably a town or city. As with airliner crashes, emergencies are nearly unheard of, but when they do occur, you want to be *gone*. Even if a fire is miles from your camp, leave!

Forest fires spread rapidly, especially in increasingly drought-ridden North America. Unlike a campfire that sparks and crackles as a log is added, a forest fire can engulf several acres faster than you can run from the firestorm. For that reason, leave the area posthaste. But there's more to escaping a fire than finding the entrance ramp to the freeway for many campers. Get directions out of the camp and to safety. Backwoods roads may lead directly into it!

If fire danger is imminent, leave your "camp" behind, barbecue grill and all. Hit the fastest route out and don't look back until you're clear of the area. That may be twenty or one hundred miles depending on the blaze and the fuel that's feeding it. Follow instructions from firefighters and peace officers. They know the fire's position, wind direction, and the intensity of the blaze. Do not attempt to predict the fire's path — you won't know the effects of wind direction and rain or thunderstorms, or the condition of the forest. Some areas may be moist and wet, while others are explosively dry. Your goal is to get out of there as quickly as possible. Don't stop to hose down your rig (it won't help anyway). Don't take time to salvage goods outside the rig. Nothing material is worth the risk required to protect it.

Tip: Breaking Out

This may sound dumb, especially if you kick one of these when heading for the bathroom at night, but we keep a basic red brick in cabins not adjacent to a door. You should do the same. In a fast-moving fire, you can smash the closest window with the brick and escape. The tempered glass used in modern RVs is difficult to break. The bricks reside on the floor and on making camp we make sure that they are exactly where we want them in case smoke or the dark of night makes them difficult to see. Alternatively, you can position an ax for just such an emergency, but personally, we'd rather kick a brick than an ax blade while half asleep in the dark.

Sleepy Bear

Everyone has seen the Sleepy Bear logo and as an RV driver, you don't want to be one. As the driver of several tons of vehicle and passengers, it's your responsibility to ensure that you don't precipitate an accident as you slump over the wheel from exhaustion. There's little question that sleep deprivation is a major source of RV accidents. Add to that a glass of wine at dinner and you have the recipe for *major disaster*. Not surprisingly, many RV accidents involve a single vehicle — the RV. Drivers fall asleep, miss turns in the dark because of fatigue, and on a snowy road mistakenly think they can handle a fifteen-thousand-pound vehicle as if it were an Oldsmobile Cutlass. Accidents occur when sleepy drivers can't react fast enough when the idiot in the opposite lane passes twenty cars and crashes head-on with the RV.

Too tired to drive? Pull over and rest at the first safe spot. After all, you do have your bed in the back ready to fall into. We often pull off at the next service station and ask to camp at the back for a few hours. Get a quick nap and then get out of the clerk's hair, since he or she may allow it but the station owner or manager may be less than pleased. Offering a $20 bill reportedly works wonders if you're desperate, but when we've asked (three times) we've never been refused a spot to rest, nor has anyone accepted any bribes for accommodating us.

The best way to avoid driving while overtired is to pace your trip. The wrong way to pace a trip is to drive from San Francisco to New York and back in two weeks. The right way to enjoy your RV trip and keep it safe is to drive less than 300 miles per day. An ideal plan would be to drive only 100 to 150 miles per day. That way you have time to stop and enjoy yourself. RVs are best used for recreation, not as vehicles. Also, try to keep it comfortable. Too many people crowded into an RV can result in frayed nerves and tired drivers.

Despite all the different sizes, lengths, and types of RVs available, they all accommodate about the same number of people. Don't stuff more than six people into your RV if you intend to get any rest. Even a forty-foot Class A motorhome has only three beds (sometimes four, if the people are small). Unlike a passenger bus, which grows in capacity with its length, RVs grow only in features and comfort as they get larger.

Tip: The Creeps

This hasn't happened to us in years, but if you feel uncomfortable in a campground for any reason, leave, even if it means losing the $19 you already paid to stay. If the neighbors are a problem, ask for a different spot or negotiate for at least part of your money back. Trouble is almost unheard of, but if you're not there, you won't be a part of it.

So far, we've left only one campground. It had heavy smog and a million ants, and our awning, if fully opened, would have hit the trailer of the oddballs next door. Our neighbors, living in a pint-sized trailer, were nursing an eleven-year-old girl with a broken leg. "Hubby" was of the paranoid type, and sadly, yelling was the evening's entertainment. What to do? Since no other berths were available in the park, at 12:45 A.M., a disgruntled manager refunded our money, apologized, and then steamed off to take matters up with the people next door. There was nothing in the paper the next morning about the confrontation.

Rig Security

In some RV parks, longtime residents may keep track of you and your movements and activities as if your life paralleled *Days of Our Lives* episodes. You'll find such gossip hounds with nothing else to do in parks that are best described as "semiresidential." The locals in these parks have lived there for months or even years. This gives neighbors time to meet, befriend each other, and form a tight network of informal relationships. While the nosiness may initially annoy you, it has an upside. If your rig is approached by strangers while you're away, the campground manager or police may be immediately summoned as the would-be crooks try to steal the pair of plastic pink flamingos you placed decoratively near your rig's door.

But nosy and protective neighbors may not reside in parks in which the majority of residents are transient. Some parks feature security guards. Still, we know of one RVer who had a towed car, parked only feet from his rig, completely stripped of its interior, even though security guards were supposedly on the premises. For that reason, rather than relying on the gossip network or a sleepy guard snoozing under a tree, you should take responsibility for basic security yourself.

Alarm Systems

If your rig is not furnished with a quality alarm at the factory, you might consider adding one. As with cars, your main concern is damage or removal of parts or personal possessions or complete removal of the vehicle. No alarm will deter an experienced thief from his or her agenda, but enough noise will discourage the bungling amateur or the opportunist, assuming you routinely arm the alarm and lock your rig up tight.

Sounding the Alarm

An RV security system is slightly different from that of a car. Your main concern is the opening of doors, windows, storage compartments, and subsystem access panels, such as the one that houses the generator. Such alarm systems are comparatively simple. A tiny switch mounted on the inside of the door to the rig and similar window switches activate the alarm. An alarm designed for car use provides you with (yet another) wireless transmitter that fits your keyring for the same purpose. You arm the unit via the control when you leave and disarm it when you return. If the rig has been "violated," the audible answer-back code will indicate a break-in. More sophisticated units also display green or red LEDs to show no entry or a break-in.

The choice of an alarm system isn't difficult, but learning to use it effectively takes some thinking. You may forget it's armed, enter the rig, and sound the alarm at 1:05 A.M., to the disgust of your neighbors. Test the system and practice using it. It should become second nature to follow these steps:

When Leaving Your Rig

- Ensure all windows and doors are locked with a deadbolt. (Pet owners will have to make different provisions in warm weather. If you're traveling with an animal, either take it with you on a leash, leave the windows fully open if it's hot, or start the generator and run the air-conditioner[s] in southern summers.)
- Depending on your alarm setup, arm it before leaving the vehicle but within the time allowed. Or leave the secured vehicle and arm it with the remote.

When Reentering Your Rig

- Stop and think. Is the alarm armed?
- If it is, look for warning LEDs of entry or use your remote to confirm through the audible signal that no one has entered the rig. If the alarm indicates entry do not enter without armed law enforcement officers preceding you.
- Look around you, especially at night, to ensure that no one is waiting for you to return and unlock the door.
- Disarm the alarm upon entry, and rearm it once the door is

362

secured, especially in uncomfortable, urban areas. Most RVers only use their rig's security system when in urban parks or remote settings located far from help. If a camp is that uncomfortable, we leave the system armed while in or near our rig. Then, ASAP, we pack it in (after a quick nap if necessary) and move on.

One Option to Avoid

Sophisticated car alarms incorporate one or more sensors that detect vibration, such as someone breaking a window or bumping the rig with a car. These are not appropriate for most RVs. Doubtless your alarm seller will insist on this option, but you should avoid it because with a large vehicle, a slow wind that gently rocks your rig is enough to tell the sensor to sound the alarm. Avoid this kind of sensor as well as ultrasonic motion detectors. They don't work well in any RVs because of the compartmental nature of most rigs. You can't sleep with one either, since rolling over in bed is movement — a motion detector will detect it and fire up the alarm system.

Protect The Keys

You've just traded in your old motorhome and have the keys to that shiny new rig. As you force them onto your keyring, you notice the front door and storage keys look like the ones you turned in, but shinier because they're new. What's happening here?

On inexpensive rigs, many parts added by the manufacturer are generic. Once the basic drivetrain and chassis are purchased from its maker, framing and carpentry added, most of the fixtures, including locks, are bought from a third company, which may equip 70 percent of the rigs with the same lock. With that in mind, your best option is to change the locks if you can find a locksmith who will handle the chore for a reasonable price. Or leave the generic locks on the storage compartments, but at the very least ensure that your rig's front door is rekeyed for a proprietary key. Keep anything more precious than a garden hose inside the rig

363

instead of in the compartments underneath. Otherwise, you'll find yourself waking up in the night and listening for the scratchy sound of a burglar's key entering the lock. For crude security, storage compartments can be locked with a simple hasp-padlock arrangement. This is less than attractive, especially on sleek motorhomes in which the new hardware is apparent.

Don't Forget the Roof Pods

Everything secure? Don't forget to padlock the roof pods if you use them. Burglars of all sorts from the junior-high-school juvenile delinquent to those with forty years' experience (twenty in the slammer) will seek access to anything they can. Roof pods may be a prime target. Big padlocks are the best insurance against invasion unless the thief is willing to risk the noise and attention of breaking their heavy plastic casings.

Be Cautious

A certain amount of caution is always called for in an RV, just as it is anywhere. Be careful of managing all aspects of the RV lifestyle, but don't become obsessed with worries over break-ins or other mishaps. If you're a full-timer and begin feeling this way, it may be time to see the doc about something taken daily. Of course, if you only feel that way about where you're currently camped or at 3:00 A.M. when the rig is suddenly surrounded by bikers, then it's not you that's the problem.

Tip: For Urban RVers

A new electronic system, not available in all cities, allows the police to directly trace your rig and recover it for you. Local car stereo stores can install the system and set you up with service. This system works only in cities at this writing, and the city's finest must have their patrol cars equipped with a transponder that can find your vehicle.

Firearms?

Arm yourself? We don't carry firearms in our rig. We don't recommend them either — but the choice is yours. We rely on pepper sprays as protection against large predators — both animal and human. Should you choose to carry a firearm in your rig, keep in mind the prohibitions against weapons in Canada and Mexico and register your weapon so you don't violate state ordinances, especially the severe ones in the state of New York. Your proof of registration should accompany you in your rig. If you are pulled over, and the peace officer chooses to search your vehicle, declare the presence of the weapon and its permit immediately, before the search begins.

What weapon should you choose? For the confines of an RV and limited storage a pistol is probably best. You can turn and fire in far less time than with a rifle. While a small-caliber pistol lacks the stopping power (in movie cliché terms) of a rifle or shotgun, its in-your-hand presence is enough to scare the hell out of even the most hardened criminals, and it is compact to handle, store, and carry. The weapon must also be easy to reach in an emergency, but out of the reach of children. Many states will hold you criminally responsible if the kids do themselves or others in with your too-easy-to-get-to gun. Everyone in the family should take a class on the use and management of firearms. More people damage themselves with their weapons than damage criminals. Don't let this happen to you.

Shopping in Strange Parts of Town

If you're low on provisions or fuel, you may innocently get off a highway and find yourself in an unappealing part of town. If you're really uncomfortable and affairs haven't reached the desperation point, such as the fuel indicator below the "E" mark, get back on the road and try another exit. During such a stop, you may feel vulnerable, but generally no one will bother you, as they have more important crimes to commit.

To be on the safe side, keep all openings, such as windows, sealed and go in pairs and accompany children to restrooms in gas stations. Lock all doors when you leave the rig or when parked with occupants inside. Look for well-lighted gas or food stops and stock up at the first place you find, regardless of price. Then blow town. Avoid nighttime gassing up in such areas, and plan your schedule to avoid that must-have Whopper at 2:00 A.M. in downtown Detroit. The best way to avoid such adventures is planning. Check out the map and anticipate your fueling needs before you get stuck somewhere you'd rather not see.

Avoid Carrying Cash

It's risky carrying cash on any trip, as you may lose it, be robbed, or have your rig ransacked while you're off shopping. This is also true of Mediterranean cruises or an expedition to the Antarctic. The obvious alternative is not to carry anything negotiable, such as greenbacks with portraits of presidents or Canadian bills with the Queen's image. Some rigs offer a floor safe as an option. (We've been told this is the first place thieves break into — so we don't consider the safe that safe.) If you must carry cash as opposed to travelers checks, consider a money belt or have a hidden pocket somewhere and use it to keep large-denomination bills, so it doesn't bulge. Carry a few small bills in regular pockets or a wallet so you can pay for supplies without displaying a large bankroll. Handing over a wallet with less than $100 may satisfy a thief, while the bulk of your money remains covertly stashed.

These same bills can be presented should you be robbed, although we and the police recommend full cooperation if you are confronted by a burglar. Turn over everything, even if it means cash, wallet or purse, jewelry, and that pair of gas-inflated Reeboks. Nothing physical is worth your life or the life of a family member or friend. If the criminal element is stupid enough to steal your rig, tow vehicle, or a vehicle you were towing, a call to the police beats trying to protect it yourself.

There is also a new technology for finding stolen vehicles via radio. See page 364 for information in case you missed it. In our years of life in land-based homes and camping, the only major criminal incident occurred in a "secure" house in the suburbs. We've never been burglarized, robbed, or even harassed while on the road or in camp — but we are also careful where we stop, keep our rig locked when appropriate, and dress like campers, not society patriarchs. If you're smart and safe, you'll probably never need to worry about the seedier elements of society.

Tip: Odd as It May Seem

Don't advertise your membership in the NRA (National Rifle Association) with window or bumper stickers. According to a burglar alarm expert we know, this attracts a criminal element interested in swiping your arsenal.

Noah's Ark Revisited:
Keeping the Creatures out of the Rig

Bugs and animals share the habitat you are invading with your camper. In fact, they were there first. Actually, with any luck, you won't meet any creatures great or small, but you should be aware of their existence to avoid them or keep them at bay. The most annoying creatures are of the insect variety. One morning we woke, stretched, and headed for the pint-sized galley to make a pot of "filter" coffee only to find that ants had taken over the galley, en masse. (And there are worse bugs than ants.)

As a result we've finally come up with a procedure that so far (fingers crossed) has worked 100 percent of the time. When camped, we spray all elements that touch the ground with a small dose of household pesticide — tires, stair steps, and so forth. For hoses attached to the hookup, a cardboard disk with a hole in it is freshly sprayed and attached to each hose. They look like miniature versions of the disks ships use to prevent uninvited rodents from coming aboard from lines tied to docks.

For invasions by creatures other than ants (common), here's another cheap fix to try. Should you have invasion of bugs or rodents, park your rig for a week (after following our winterizing steps) in a cold, snowy location. (This is assuming you can live with someone else in a house or hotel for this time.) Winterize the rig to protect the water tanks and then let the cold freeze the little devils' buns off. You may still have a problem next spring when their eggs hatch, depending on the time of year and length of infestation involved. A longer, colder exposure may zap the eggs as well as their hatched brethren.

Controlling Pests with Professional Pest Control

Last ditch. Call a professional pest control firm. Depending on what part of the country you're in, for $25 to $75, they will come in to do away with critters of all kinds. Note that food should be stowed. Leave the rig's windows and doors closed as prescribed by the pest control personnel, then open them and let the rig air out for an hour or two before reentering. Follow any instructions about wiping counters and don't walk about the rig barefoot for a few days.

Pets should not occupy the vehicle during this process and pregnant women should avoid occupancy for at least forty-eight hours, depending on what was used for vermin control. This works best when you can stay for a month and call the firm back if the problem reappears, as they usually offer a thirty- to ninety-day guarantee that you won't be, er, bugged again.

This Is Not a Complete List

There are many creatures to avoid, but they are easily avoided for the most part. Ticks are probably the nastiest, and you have to check everywhere on your body for them. (And we do mean everywhere — this can be fun with someone you love.) There are also fun beasts such as snakes, kissing bugs — we don't even want to talk about them — gila monsters, and spiders whose bite destroys skin. Chances are, you won't encounter any of these creatures, so don't worry about them. For the especially paranoid reader, studying up on bugs will provide comfort, in that you'll never meet any untoward creatures unless you go out looking for them.

A Three-Point Pest Control Program

This three-part program is simple and designed to keep your rig insect free. For an overnight stay, you can probably skip steps 2 and 3 because there's little chance of an invasion during a short stay. If you object to pesticide use, look for alternatives in books on organic gardening.

#1 Have an RV garage put your rig on a lift and caulk around openings where lines and wires penetrate the interior. These openings are how most insects such as ants reach your galley. A gook caulk job should last about five years since sun will rarely affect it as it does the sealer on the roof.

#2

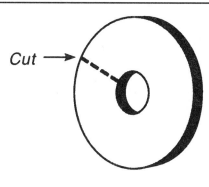

Cut →

Assemble cardboard disks with a hole in the center for each of your shore lines (water, electricity, etc.). Each line should fit snugly in its interior hole. Cut the disk so that it can be affixed to the line. Seal the disk with Thompson's Water Seal or a similar product so that rain doesn't make it soggy.

To use: Place the disks about halfway between your rig and the hookup point. Make sure they don't touch the ground. Give them a light coating of bug spray.

#3 Lightly spray bug spray around the tires and your porch step if it rests on the ground. If you remain hooked up during your stay, spray the hitch as well to keep ants from using the "overland approach." Bugs *can* get onto your rig if they fall from overhanging trees, but there's not much you can do about that. Most of the problem originates from the ground up, unless an overhanging tree branch physically touches the RV.

You can make these disks out of cardboard or any kind of lightweight, flexible material. (Avoid metal, as it may eventually cut into your lines.) They keep bugs away from your rig and discourage rodents as well. Spray them with any color lacquer-based spray paint to keep the rain from melting or rotting them. Then spray them with insecticide or strong repellent to keep the more gallant varieties out of your rig. This is not a "must do" precaution, but you'll find it helpful in areas below thirty-five degrees in latitude and in most of North America in the spring and summer.

Tip:
Feeling Bad About Insect and Rodent Control?

Yes, the word "control" is a euphemism for killing vermin. But look at it this way: Wiping out one hundred ants that have taken up residence in your pantry is superior to eventually having to do in ten thousand of their descendants.

The Real Pests

In addition to insects, the most pesky animals you'll likely encounter are more annoying than harmful. Smart camping and food management discourages visits from the animal kingdom.

- Birds. Yes, they're among nature's most wonderful creatures with their plumage and bright songs. But when one builds a nest in your rig's roof-mounted sewage vent, it can become dangerous. (Methane gas can build up in the black water tank and explode should someone light a cigarette while using the facilities.) Avoid this problem by regular inspection of all openings for animal activity.

- Raccoons: Smart little devils, they come late at night and raid whatever they can get their paws on. Afraid of you, sudden light, and noise, they depart quickly when detected, but with their stealth, they can clean out an outside ice chest used for food storage in minutes. Smart stocking of food avoids this problem. Banging pots and pans and turning on lights spooks them, as it does most bears. Coons can grow to be quite large and are horribly strong. Don't corner one. Allow it to run away, even if it has a Gallo salami in its mouth.

- Rodents. Ranging from cute squirrels who secrete seeds in your rig's furnace exhaust (it must cook them nicely), to mice and their larger relatives, rodents can cause problems. Mice and their relatives move in when a cold snap occurs. This is usually more a problem for RVers camping long-term in the same spot than for those migrating across the continent. A light coat of creosote on your tires will discourage these newcomers unless a tree branch touches your rig, providing an additional access way. Few campers need worry about such vermin or take preventive measures. Just check for droppings in your RV's secluded compartments or bring a pet cat along for dedicated sentry duty. We do.

Bigger Trouble

We aren't experts in this area, although we read enough guidebooks on the subject, some with conflicting information. See the local campground owner or, better still, forestry officials for better and more detailed information. Even the local police department in a rural area will have information on dealing with the local wildlife should you have to.

Though this is usually only a problem if you camp really remote and alone (one RV in one thousand acres of scrub or woods), the scent of your food may attract a bear or a cougar. Both are readily scared off with noise, such as loud banging of pots and pans, and turning on exterior lighting, including porch lights, headlights, and spotlights. Take refuge in your camper should you feel threatened. Few bears, other than polar bears, will attack such a vehicle, and with your noise and lights, you'll scare off all but the hungriest. Have the pepper spray or even a fire extinguisher where you can grab it. Note that a handgun may do little to slow a large bear. (We discuss firearm and pepper spray restrictions north and south of the border later in this chapter.).

Putting It out to Lunch

Take normal camping precautions and stow all food carefully. Food waste should be disposed of in bear-proof waste containers or buried away from the rig. Normally, these animals won't come near you anyway, so they aren't a big worry. When your rig is parked away from other campers, barbecuing is not a good idea in bear-intensive territory because bears *love* barbecued food. (It must be the A-1 Sauce.) At night, hours after supper, they may quietly show up and take your barbecue grill and trash bags apart in search of a late-night snack.

Tip:
Pepper Spray and Firearms over the Border

When crossing the frontier into Canada and Mexico, you are subject to scrutiny. You and your vehicle can legally be taken apart down to the chassis level if contraband is suspected or the so-called customs officers want to harass you, as is standard procedure for rock 'n' roll bands. You can also be searched when returning to the United States. Removing tires from rims and tearing open the gas tank are not unheard-of procedures. U.S. Customs even operates a massive X-ray machine that can inspect a vehicle as large as a truck at the Mexican border.

You cannot bring firearms into Mexico or Canada without a nearly impossible to get permit. Should you attempt it, you may be subject to a fine and irreversible confiscation of your weapons. Jail time is also possible, although unlikely unless you try to smuggle quantities across the border or are carrying fully automatic assault weapons (also illegal in the United States). Canada does not allow the possession or importation of pepper sprays or mace either. Since these don't cost much, replace them upon your return to the States.

Bearsville

Should you be confronted by a large carnivore and unable to back away quietly, waving your arms and yelling loudly won't hurt. This makes your opponent nervous, in that you may turn out to be more of a threat than it is to you. If you're carrying firearms, try to avoid shooting the poor beast unless an attack is imminent (incredibly rare). Then back away slowly. Tree climbing is an alternative if confronted with a brown, grizzly, or polar bear, but black bears and big cats can climb trees faster than you can. Fortunately, black bears tend to be the least aggressive of North America's bear family, and all but the most starved cougars are easily spooked.

If you climb a tree, don't leave it until help arrives or you're sure (if that's possible) that your would-be friend has gone off chasing ground squirrels. If possible, drive off, even if it means leaving your trailer and outdoor setup behind. Your life and those of your family members are worth more than a trailer. Besides, the forestry people will help you retrieve things later.

Pepper Spray

We take hikes (in city centers and woods) with pepper spray canisters that can be grabbed quickly from belt or backpack. Found in backpacking stores and many drugstores, these small aerosol wonders can disable man and beast. We are thankful that we've never had need to use the spray. And the only bears or cougars we've ever seen while RVing were safely isolated in city zoos. (Note that in some states a permit is required to possess pepper spray, but in years of camping, spray plainly in view, no one has said a word to us, including forest rangers trained in local law enforcement.)

Should one attack you (a large carnivore, not a forest ranger), hit it full in the face with a big blast of pepper spray, and that will be the last you see of it. These sprays also work wonders against human interlopers. Aim for the eyes. This will disable the most determined attacker.

Leapin' Lizards, Annie!

When camping in alligator and "croc" country, keep children and pets away from swamps and bodies of water. Stay out of swamps, lakes, rivers, and streams, and keep the kids focused on organized activities. Or, if they want water, an RV park swimming pool does a good and safe job of providing it. We *have* seen small alligators in Florida streams, but at the time, they were too busy in courting exercises to bother with us. Since these creatures are about as bright as a tomato, their attacks are unlike those of other predators mentioned. If it moves, they will grab it with lightning speed and head for the bottom to drown it. They're stupid enough to snag a bowling ball if they see one rolling on a riverbank or lakeshore.

Snakes are another, albeit rare, problem. Avoid lifting rocks in the desert and swimming in bayous in the South. Keep your dog from running unleashed through grass and wild country. Explain these procedures to the kids. Snake-training books are available for teaching dogs, although we have not experimented with these methods due to our current lack of a canine.

Backpacking Safety

Get specific information should you plan to leave your home-on-wheels and backpack through the back country. According to an account we read several years ago, a group of black bears learned to charge backpackers so they would take the pack off, leave it, and run, as is conventional camping wisdom. (The bears are after the food, not the people, and all bears are *extremely* bright when it comes to learned behavior.)

The bears then go through packs and eat everything from foodstuffs to sunblock (yum). If you plan to backpack, get current and specific advice from local officials working the area you plan to tackle. Leave word where you're heading and when you will be back so emergency teams can find you should you get lost or invited in for dinner by a bear, so to speak. Menstruating women should stay out of bear country, since this attracts the locals, according to a bear book we studied based on a Forest Service report.

A White Christmas

Avoid backpacking in the back country when heavy snow is on the ground, unless you're highly experienced. Even then, go in pairs, not solo. Carry emergency communication equipment workable in the area as a safety precaution. Leave a map of your route and notes and dates of your plans with such officials as the park ranger. That way if you don't turn up, someone will start looking for you and have at least some idea where to look. Consider the purchase of an emergency transponder that communicates a radio-based alarm and helps rescuers find you.

If you are alarmed by this section — don't be. The number of bear and big cat attacks in the United States is close to nil, although you should take precautions and not tempt fate. Avoid hiking in the dark and hang all food in plastic bags or backpacks from the (high) branches of a tree. That way, in the unlikely event that predators come around, they'll head for the gratuitous treats and ignore you. Keep your fire bright, and for the particularly paranoid, camp with large numbers of other campers, as few predators will risk approaching a group of humans listening to Elvis CDs at high volume.

Health Care on the Road

All RVs should be equipped with a quality first-aid kit, in good condition (meaning you should open it up at least once a year and check the status of the contents). You also need to take your required prescription medications with you on your trip. For RVers who travel in the backwoods, far from civilization and health-care workers, we recommend taking a basic course in first aid from the local community college, YMCA, or Red Cross. For peace of mind, we also recommend that all RVers, and especially those with disabilities and health conditions, take the following on all trips:

- Copies of all relevant current medical records. Your doctor can provide these for you.
- A list of any and all medications taken. (Actually, all RVers should probably follow this advice, especially if they tend to be on the road for more than a few weeks at a time.) Be sure to include dosages taken on the list.
- The name, address, and phone number of your regular physician(s).
- Health insurance information and telephone numbers, as appropriate.

If you have a particular health condition or allergy to medication, we recommend registering with Medic Alert Foundation. Wear your registration tag or wristband at all times. This registration will allow health professionals to provide you the best care if an emergency should arise. To register, contact:

Medic Alert Foundation
P.O. Box 1009
Turlock, CA 95318
800-344-3226

Always keep the information and medications in an easy-to-reach area of the RV. Traveling partners should always be aware of the location of these items. With these simple precautions and some planning, the RVing life can be enjoyed by almost anyone.

When medical attention is required on the road, if time and circumstances permit, always contact your family doctor before getting treatment. If the situation is an emergency, waste no time. Phone for an ambulance or rush to the emergency room or urgent care facility.

If you intend to stay in remote locations, away from specialized treatment centers, you may want to invest in insurance for helicopter or airplane transportation to an emergency room. If you are not already covered for air evacuation by your regular health insurance provider, contact:

Sky-Med
Tower Group International
P.O. Box 2387
Brentwood, TN 37024
615-370-8802

Dealing with Disabilities on the Road

Airlines, with their narrow seating and insistence on checking wheelchairs as baggage, can frustrate the most agile paraplegic. For someone severely impaired, the complications can be downright dangerous. It is difficult to get wheelchairs in cars. Hotels and motels, despite federal regulations, generally supply poor accommodations for the disabled traveler. Simply getting into and out of bed can be an acrobat's trick, and you can forget about using the shower in most rooms. Imagine driving for hours without finding an accessible toilet. Such all-too-common situations are not uncomfortable, they are unhealthy for disabled travelers. However, a properly selected RV with a few modifications is a "home on the road" for the wheelchair user. RVs provide convenience, comfort, dignity, and privacy unsurpassed by other means of travel.

Many people with disabilities, some in wheelchairs and others infirm, enjoy the RVing lifestyle. Those we've met on the road with disabilities include people confined to wheelchairs and people living with diabetes. We've encountered RVers who manage their cancer, heart disease, multiple sclerosis, kidney disease, and other serious ailments on the road. Many of these people claim the travel, sights, and fresh air help soothe their ailments as well as their souls. Being free to travel is only one of the benefits of RVs for persons with health restrictions. Perhaps more important is the sense of independence that RVing provides.

Equipment for the Physically Challenged

Most RVs can be set up to accommodate a variety of physical problems. Everything — from lifts (rather than steps) that provide access to the craft to supplemental oxygen systems — can be added to a new or used RV. This may require investigation to find a system compatible to both you and the rig, and the best place to start is the ads in such magazines as *Motorhome* and *Trailer Life*. Shop price too, as different systems with similar benefits may vary widely in cost. Some systems may be tax deductible, as an RV is a second home and you must have access to medical equipment. Don't make any assumptions, however — contact the IRS for information.

Modifications can be made to most rigs by the manufacturer or a competent RV shop to accommodate disabilities. We have seen the following modifications made to accommodate various disabilities: Motorhomes and trailers can be equipped with wheelchair lifts and full motorized hospital beds. Hallways can be made wide enough for wheelchairs to maneuver comfortably. Many newer RVs already offer slide-outs and wide-body designs that make such modifications almost unnecessary.

For those who require walkers or canes, steps can be made wider and rails added for secure entry to and exit from the rig. Bathrooms can be equipped with safety bars around toilets and in showers and bathtubs. (Some manufacturers offer such bars as a standard option.) Hospital-style commode chairs can be found to fit over RV toilets if needed. A standard toilet chair can be put in some rigs. We even know of people who have had dialysis machines placed in motorhomes. Such RVers travel to the nearest hospital for regular treatments, but can do the dialysis themselves in between home bases.

A little thought and ingenuity can make anyone comfortable in an RV. For instance, if you need medication daily, make sure you either carry enough for the whole trip or can obtain it without delay as needed. If you need special equipment, see if you can carry it with you. Oxygen and dialysis machines require routine maintenance on the road, and you need to be able to obtain the necessary supplies on a regular basis. Looking into medical centers and hospitals in a city as you arrive can help you get the services and supplies you need.

The rig itself is not the biggest issue for most people who travel with disabilities or health restrictions. When traveling with any type of disability or illness, the most important requirement involves assuring that proper care is available in the areas to which you travel. The nature of local medical facilities should be established in advance. When you enter a new camping area, ask other RVers or a local pharmacist for recommendations on medical providers in the area. Make sure you contact health providers in advance of arrival if your need for care is acute. If you want more information about traveling with disabilities, contact:

Handicapped Travel Club
667 J Ave.
Coronado, CA 92118
619-435-5213

This chapter has presented RVing safety tips and ways to avoid problems. Some of this may seem like the dark side of RVing, but when you weigh the problems against traditional living in a house bolted to a concrete foundation or a simple drive to the 7-Eleven, the risks aren't really that large or that threatening if you plan for safety. While you can't move that house of yours away from the crime in the city, you can move your RV and make choices about where to park and camp. In the next chapter, we'll look at some of the wonderful options for camping and parking your RV. And always remember, as an RVer, there's always an open road to freedom awaiting you.

Part III

RV Lifestyles
and Activities

Chapter 17

Parks and Campgrounds

There are many kinds of parks and campgrounds to visit in an RV, ranging from primitive to luxurious. The prices range from free to exorbitant. Each type of campground and park provides advantages and disadvantages. When we want unlimited hot water and lots of movies to watch, we stay in full-service parks with all their amenities (and expenses). When we're into scenery, we go to a national park. In this chapter we talk about fee-based parks and campgrounds. In the next chapter we present options for camping free across the continent.

Five Kinds of Campgrounds

There are five broad categories of campgrounds for RVers. There's no firm line of demarcation between one kind and another. Even within a category, campgrounds are like people — no two are exactly alike. We've already mentioned our low-risk policy of paying for only one night instead of committing to a month or more. Learning the nuances of a campground is like shopping for a land-based home. It takes time to fully explore the "neighborhood" and make sure it's right for you.

In addition, campgrounds change with the seasons. At peak time, you may be surrounded with forty rigs, the laughing and chatter of a big barbecue, and special events sponsored by the camp. Off-season may find you sharing twenty acres of scrub with no one but the camp's owner/manager and a handful of diehards who plan to winter in the snow or bake in the summer heat of the Southwest.

Tip: The One-Night Rule

We pulled into a campground late one night. Half-asleep and with encouragement from an ad in one of the campground directories, we paid the proprietor $144 for a one-week stay. (She looked as sleepy as we were.) Once we had docked, the power kept going on and off as a powerful electrical storm must have repeatedly hit transmission cables, killing our air-conditioning for as much as an hour (in the desert in July). The next morning, lacking sleep, we surveyed our prepaid "home." What a dump.

It was at that point that we made a rule: *Never pay in advance for an extended stay until you stay in the camp one night first, even if it means paying full price and risking that you'll have to move on if the camp becomes fully booked during your one-day "test."* We live by this rule and it has saved us annoyance and money and made RVing a lot more fun.

Our Bias

Before we discuss camps, let us briefly explain our biases. First, the word *campground* is somewhat of a misnomer, as some RV parks resemble a campground as much as a convenience store resembles an urban supermall. We prefer semirural camps with plenty of local flora (plants, cactus, trees — whatever) and substantial space between RVs or camping spaces. We do appreciate plentiful clean water, and when we are paying to camp, we expect enough electricity to run at least one air-conditioner without causing a brown-out in the warmer months. Our favorite kind of park is located amidst the trees, mountains, deserts, beaches, or small towns — away from civilization, but not so far from civilization that a grocery run takes two hours in each direction.

Low on our list are parks that consist solely of asphalt and concrete, although we know many RVers who prefer this kind of "sanitized" camping. We also dislike camps composed largely of mobile homes (not because of the residents — we've met lots of interesting people in such facilities), because most mobile home parks aren't properly equipped for RVs and RVers. Connecting to the electric power may require an oddball adapter, and rates may be unrealistically high. In one park, "for just $5" in addition to the overnight fee, the owner would "lend" us an adapter for the duration of the stay.

If left with no alternative because the parks are full, undesirable, or unavailable, we find a quiet, rural side road (no housing tracts and outside the city limits so we aren't violating any ordinances) with a shoulder strong enough to support our camper and "live wild" for a day or two. While we've been visited by a local farmer, worried that we were there to heist her veggies, once we shared a cup of tea with her, she asked us to pull onto the dirt road leading to her family's farm and stay as long as we liked!

The Private Rural Park

Often located near a major attraction such as the Grand Canyon, these parks are usually tranquil and offer hookups superior to those in the destination park, although they typically have less charming rates. Other private parks are found on older highways and at junctions that were bypassed by the interstates. (You can tell a private park from a public one because private parks have names and advertising; public parks usually have "rangers" or other public officials at the booth. Many private, rural parks are perfect for those looking for a destination to "get away from it all" or escape the blizzards back home on the cheap.

Regular campers — often retired — visit these inexpensive parks in groups, with several RVers having met in the same camp every year for a decade or more. Key to such a park is that it be well maintained, but not to the point that the facilities compromise the natural setting. Clear air and quiet are important ingredients, and there shouldn't be a railroad line or freeway hidden by a copse of trees to spoil the effect.

Some of these camps may be significantly difficult to reach and you should inquire whether your forty-five-foot monster can make the climbs and the turns. Ahh . . . but what a feeling to breathe fresh air and listen to nothing but the birds!

Tip: Read the Rules

Ask to see the written rules of a prospective campground before paying. If they don't have any, then don't worry about it. That means the rule is there are no rules.

The Public Rural Park

A huge number of parks are run by city, county, state, or federal governments. Some, the nation's foremost tourist attractions, require reservations made months in advance (Yosemite, for example). There's usually a limit to the number of days you can stay at such a park, because others want to enjoy the site too. Often, the overnight fees are low, especially in city-run campgrounds, and a well-planned itinerary of public parks makes for a wonderful and inexpensive vacation. The downside is that you can't inspect the park before you rent, because the best ones are full of revelers with reservations made long before you arrive.

We mentioned that owners of large, power-hungry rigs should ensure that their unit can be accommodated in the park's berths as well as its hookups. Some large rigs simply don't fare well in rural camps. Rural camps vary considerably. Some may have little more than a potholed gravel road leading to a grassy berth. Others may be fully improved with chain-link fences for security, concrete pads, a store, and unavoidable tour guides explaining how to avoid meeting the local fauna. We're being overbearing here, because most rangers, docents, and volunteers are friendly and helpful and work for almost nothing to make your stay pleasant. They even teach kids safety lessons and tell stories. But there was this one guy who . . . well, we'll skip that for now.

Parks, whether maintained by federal, state, or county officials, vary in format and facilities. You won't know what to expect until you arrive. At one attractive park located in a hot agricultural valley (above one hundred degrees in June) the grass was watered for two hours early every morning, creating a steam bath after the sun had hovered for about two hours. Our second night, dual air-conditioners running full blast and wasting precious electricity, we packed it in and obtained a partial refund. At least the grass looked healthy.

The Concrete Resort

Found outside such trendy watering holes as Palm Springs in the West and the Hamptons in the East, these full-service campgrounds offer everything from elaborate golf courses to pottery lessons. RV berths are concrete with full hookups for maximum AC, cable TV, and even land-based telephone service. You get a regulation picnic table, one tree, and maybe even a row of carefully arranged rocks added for decorative purposes.

While this isn't our idea of camping, the activities provided can be fun. The most expensive parks tax the pocketbook with overnight fees of $35 and up. Before signing up, check that the amenities and services you wish to enjoy are included in the campground fee. (One odd campground, albeit an inexpensive one, charged $2 more for a key to the pool.)

Prissy Campgrounds for Old-Timers

Some parks may be noncommittal about availability and price until they've glanced at both you and your rig. When in doubt, park your rig out of sight, then register at the office. If pressured for a description of your camper, be vague and just mention how wonderful it is and how much you enjoy camping in it. Otherwise, owners of run-down, older, but still viable rigs may be handed the classic line, "There's no room at the inn."

Our Best-Case Park

We found a beautiful park in the redwoods with rates next to nothing for weekly or monthly stays. The only extra charge was for electricity. And, since the park was located in the mountains, AC consisted of open windows and a fresh mountain breeze. The rich smell of pine was intoxicating. Where is it? It's our secret.

Tip: Reverse Discrimination

In our thirties (many moons ago now) when we began our RV odyssey, we were occasionally turned away by parks even though we dressed nicely and drove a new and clean motorhome. Apparently some parks only rent to seniors, although this little detail doesn't appear in campground guides, as it's technically illegal in most states. The hatchet-faced manager of a park in the Rockies explained that the park was fully booked. Odd, as her forty-two-space park contained only eleven ancient trailers and one RV and it was near nightfall.

Two Parks from Hell

When considering a city park, check out the neighborhood, because noise is a potential problem. We found ourselves with a week's booking (before instigating our one-night rule) in a park located next to a boxy building that looked as anonymous as a crooked telemarketing company. No signage. No demarcated parked stalls even in the large asphalt lot. Odd, but innocuous.

When we arrived, early on a Saturday morning, silence reigned. But the business turned out to be a noisy salsa-style nightclub. The din began around noon and increased in volume until 2:00 A.M. When the crowd started smashing beer bottles on the cars in the parking lot, a gaggle of police cars finally sent the partygoers home or, for all we know, to jail.

A second unhappy park was located next to a railroad track with frequent commuter trains. (The tracks were neatly disguised with massive oleander bushes.) Beginning at 4:00 A.M., not only did trains shake our rig, but warning bells from a nearby intersection went off loudly upon each transgression of the crossing. Very relaxing. Happily gone to bed early, we were out of there as fast as a quick brush of the hair and teeth (with different brushes, of course) and on our way to peace and quiet.

Tip: Noise Keeping You Up?

If you find yourself unable to sleep because of noise but don't need cooling, run your air-conditioner's fan, even if the weather is cold. Running only the fan uses little power and effectively masks outside noise. You can also purchase machines from Radio Shack, The Sharper Image, and others that produce soothing background noises such as ocean waves breaking as surf.

The Urban Camp

Every city has multiple RV parks and towns of any size have at least one. Some are located in blighted sections of town, and many of the residents live there permanently, some to take advantage of the minimal monthly rents, some because their rigs would disintegrate even if they could afford to move them. We use these parks as way stations between destinations although we avoid them when possible for fear of criminal activity. In-city parks are usually of the concrete wonder variety with shriveled trees and residents who appeared as extras in the movie *Return of the Living Dead.* (If you missed this flick, this comment is not a compliment. If you did miss it, keep it that way.)

They Aren't All Bad

Not all urban parks are located in less-than-enjoyable sections of a city. Some are bright, engaging, located near important landmarks or shopping, and make you want to expand your planned week's stay into a month or more. Campers employ the well-located ones as a jump-off point to explore the city or locality. Some in-city parks are a lot of fun with activities and easy access to cultural sites such as museums or historic locations.

Perform the one-night test before a long-term commitment to a busy park. Or get the recommendation of a reliable RVer who has stayed there recently before plunking down your $24 to $45 for one night's stay. Urban parks in desirable areas cost more than rural parks because the land, services, and protection money paid to Big Ted, who represents the local "insurance" scheme, don't come cheap.

Mobile Home Parks

Mobile home parks are a dilemma to the RVer unfamiliar with a park, but in need of a break from the road. You may be allowed to stay overnight or for an indefinite length of time at a park, depending on the park's regulations and your age. (Some parks allow only seniors for permanent stays, but younger people are allowed for overnight stays. No one knows why.)

If you do stay for one night, you'll be categorized as an "over-nighter" — at a charge similar to that of an RV campground. Mobile home parks vary significantly in the "respectability" (for lack of a better word) of the residents. Most consist of seniors who may not live there year round (snowbirds). Others are a mix of the urban poor and oddballs of all kinds. We could tell you about a couple . . .

The Next-Door Neighbors

You can get a good idea of the park from its residents. What quality of rigs are parked there — clean, relatively new ones or a mix of converted schoolbuses and trailers that look as if they've sat parked since the Nixon administration? Cars on blocks, sagging mobile homes, and trailers with plastic sheeting on their roof to seal leaks are not signs of a good park — even for a one-nighter.

Campground Pricing

Campground pricing ranges from $0 to more than $35 per night (the latter may include greens fees for golf at a really fancy camp). Average is $12 to $20 for a full hookup (water, power, and so forth). National parks tend to be slightly less expensive and those located in state, county, and city parks are also less costly, depending on their location and what they provide. For public parks, prices range from $5 (growing rarer these days) to $17 per night.

As of this writing, the average parking space is about $10 to $20 a night, although you should expect to pay more for coastal sites and popular attractions, such as the Grand Canyon. Note that you'll likely pay as much to stay in a national park with fewer amenities and limited hookups because the park systems try to keep the site looking natural rather than running a fifty-amp service conduit under a pristine redwood tree. Otherwise, park rates typically reflect the camp's proximity to attractions, hookup quality, and amenities offered. In general, but not always, public parks are the cheapest, most basic (and the prettiest).

Tip: Nosy Staff and Mysterious Rules and Regulations

Cranky staff, "landlords," or owners are also reasons to pass on a campground. Our least favorite is the nosy landlord. We caught one looking in our lighted windows after dark. When we approached her across a darkened field during an after-dinner walk, she was enormously embarrassed. Her explanation? She wanted to ensure that we had only two cats with us, and not three as we do now. Hah!

We've also encountered a few parks in which the rules mitigate the fun. Strange-but-true regulations are found in strange-but-true campgrounds: "No barbecuing after 9:00 P.M." was one of the most bizarre campground regulations we've encountered (so far anyway). Whether they were worried about noisy chefs or about hitting a camper with barbecue lighter fluid instead of the briquettes in the dark is unclear.

Or, "Are you two having fun? If you aren't having fun, then I must ask you to leave tomorrow." Fortunately, we were having fun and became friends with the eccentric campground owner (and his pleasant wife) who issued this dictum.

A Longer Stay?

At private campgrounds and some public ones, weekly and monthly stays significantly reduce campground charges. A camp with a daily rate of $22 might cost only $85 for a seven-day stay. That works out to about $12.15 per day. Monthly rates may be even lower, especially in off-season when few campers visit. Electricity is often charged separately for campers on longer stays, so you must factor its cost into the bill, although in camps where air-conditioning is rarely run, the power used is nominal. Besides, you don't have to hook up the power unless you want to.

The No Hookup Hookup

Rural parks are often located on land that costs next to nothing per acre. Rather than build two hundred hookups when chances are slim that more than sixty will be used even in peak season, owners leave the rest of the land fallow. You can rent a "space" on this land for next to nothing — typically $2 to $8 per night — since other than the security and conveniences of the campground, you're really just renting a parking spot. This saves money, although you may be charged separate fees for loading fresh water or using the dumping facility. You won't be able to get *Gilligan's Island* reruns on the cable stations, but most handle this breach in the structure of Western civilization with aplomb. Avoid grassy knolls and soft ground in the rainy season or what you save on the spot may be negated by the cost of a tow truck to winch your rig from the muck.

Be a Good Sam Member and Save Money

Every RVer should join the Good Sam Club or other RVing clubs (see General Resources for RVers, in the back of the book), the AARP, and automobile associations that offer camping and services discounts to RVers. Membership in the Good Sam Club typically knocks 10 percent off the nightly rate (call 800-234-3450 for info) at campgrounds, and it may get you discounts on propane, food sold at RV parks, and RV-related services and supplies. Membership, at this writing, costs $12 per year for first-timers and $23 for repeat members. Note: The Good Sam discount infrequently is applicable to weekly and monthly rates, especially in the western half of the United States.

Good Sam is a great deal for RVers of all kinds. This club now has more than one million members, so they must be doing something right!

Buy a New Membership or Assume Someone Else's?

The classified ads in newspapers and RV magazines will have listings for club memberships for sale. Priced substantially less than a new membership, they may be a good deal. But, before buying one, verify in writing that any transfer fees (common) or other charges or restrictions will be paid or negated by the seller. Also verify transfer restrictions and costs with a senior manager of the organization you plan to buy into. Then follow the other advice in these pages for checking out the campgrounds and the financial stability of the membership organization.

Membership Campgrounds

Membership campgrounds have received some bad press over the years because many companies have gone bankrupt or failed to build the parks they promised in their literature. Not all membership campgrounds are a bad deal, however. There are a number of membership arrangements available. Choose one carefully, because while the Good Sam Club costs next to nothing and saves you a few bucks on a nightly rental or an oil change, the "buy-in" fees at membership camping clubs can be pricey even though you get little more than reduced camping fees at camps that may or may not have any space available.

Some membership campgrounds are similar to a condo

timeshare arrangement (but less expensive). You pay a one-time fee, a yearly membership charge, and a small daily charge for use of the campgrounds that are owned by or affiliated with the club. Most parks are also members of reciprocal-use conglomerates such as Camp Coast to Coast (CCC) or Resort Parks International (RPI). CCC, for example, has over five hundred parks in its directory, in all fifty states and a few in Canada and Mexico. For an additional fee, members of home parks may become members of the reciprocal-use club and have use of all parks in the system for a small fee (less than $4) per night. In these parks you are limited in the length of time you can stay in a park and the number of times you can visit.

As you can see, membership plans are many and varied. Some companies have several parks, some only have one park, and some are only a front to get you into a conglomerate camping program. Prices vary from around $500 (for single-home parks) to several thousand dollars for multipark systems. Yearly maintenance fees range from under a hundred dollars to several hundred dollars. The additional CCC and RPI dues and their nightly camping rates vary, depending on the program. Remember, you aren't buying real estate or the right to park in a specific location. You are buying a membership, similar to that in a country club.

CCC offers a good way to try out membership camping. It will sell you coupons for six to twenty-four nights for use of membership parks and their facilities. Six coupons were about $60 at press time. If you buy more, the price per coupon goes down. No salespeople will bother you while you are camping. Contact them for more information at:

Camp Coast to Coast
64 Inverness Dr. E.
Englewood, CO 80112
800-368-5721

RPI offers centralized reservations for its parks. The company, owned by Southmark Company, has about three hundred affiliated park resorts. Some RPI resorts are also CCC parks. For more information on the RPI programs, contact:

394

Resort Parks International
3711 Long Beach Boulevard
P.O. Box 7738
Long Beach, CA 90807
800-635-8498

Extra activities, standard at some campgrounds, may or may not be included in the membership rates, so it is important to read the fine print of the agreement before you join. When you buy a membership in a home park, you are allowed to use that park within the terms of the agreement (which vary). Most of the time you'll also pay a yearly maintenance fee. A typical restriction is that once you have spent two straight weeks in the park, you must be out of the park for at least a week before you can return. This is to prevent the use of the park as a home.

Buying a membership is not really free camping. You'll pay thousands of dollars for a good club, but the cost per night goes down each time you use the membership. If you compare the cost of a KOA (Kampers of America) or similar private campgrounds in the area, you'll find that it won't take too long to recover your costs.

Your home park can be very critical to the value of your membership. With some plans you can't stay in any affiliated park that is within 150 miles of your home park. In this case you might want your home park to be a small, debt-free park, far from where you live or travel. That way your home park dues are small and you can stay almost anywhere. The debt level of your home parks is very important. Check it out. More than one RVer has lost a home park with more debts than assets. Alternatively, you might want your home park to be the best place to stay in your area, so you don't have to stay anywhere else. Of course both of these suggestions assume that you're not a member in a multiple home park plan. Multiple home park plans tend to be more expensive but also more flexible.

Unlike the rosy picture painted by the club's salesperson, membership clubs can work out to be less convenient or more expensive than you're led to believe. Plus, if the club goes belly-up, your membership goes with it. We suggest you steer clear of these organizations unless you've thoroughly examined the offering, what you receive for your money, and the firm's reputation and stability, and you like their options for campgrounds. Make sure you actually want to stay in the camps that are available. (Most plans offer free nights to try out their camps, but during a test run, you'll see more salespeople around your camper than flies.)

There are different membership options in some programs that let you decide how you want to camp. You can camp with full hookups or park in the woods and live like a bear. Some of the plans allow full-time camping in their parks. Their literature discloses all pricing and restrictions without a personal visit by a salesperson. Full-timers on the right program may pay as little as $2 per day (not including electricity). The flexibility of this arrangement intrigues us, but you must still check it out to ensure it's right for you, since rates may change or your lifestyle may require a wider range of camping venues.

What Does a Campground Look Like?

Campgrounds are like people — they range in personality from the awe-inspiring Daniel Boone to the oddball Andy Warhol to the jaded . . . we'll drop this clumsy metaphor at this point. You get the picture. One park, lodged in a forest in Flagstaff, Arizona, features an elegant restaurant with singing waiters (and full hookups). Another, down the road, features ancient trailers and cabins that look as if the paint holds them together. On Friday night there's what we'll politely describe as an "escort service" dressed primarily in Spandex garb. Some parks are little more than asphalt parking spaces with water and power hookups. Others sport a few trees and nothing else.

What's on Offer?

Do campground amenities match your needs as well as the hookup capabilities? Are these facilities provided at no extra charge? One park with a massive ad in a campground guide (which should have checked the listing before running the ad or the listing) touted a movie theater, three restaurants, and an RV service facility. We thought, "Hummm . . . time for an oil change, tune-up, dinner, and a movie — let's go!" Upon arrival and *after paying,* we found that none of these amenities had been built. That's why, before we pay, we check things out, even walking the pools and recreational facilities if we plan to stay long enough to use them and don't want to be disappointed.

But what facilities there are! You may have a choice of everything from ceramics classes in a well-equipped lab to scuba-diving expeditions to riding all-terrain vehicles (ATVs) on campground-owned sand dunes. There are theatrical events, costume parties for the residents, and regular get-togethers to meet the neighbors. Even the Friday fish fry or wiener roast puts you in contact with many fascinating people.

You can brush up on your reading too, since most large campgrounds have a library of some sort. We stayed in one rural park that had converted an ancient trailer into a lending library — the only one for forty miles, with about four thousand volumes. Best of all, the park library welcomed not only campers but also local residents to check out books at no charge.

Are You Tired of It All?

We compromise on parks if, after a long day, sleepiness threatens our driving safety. Holing up for a night in a dumpy park is better than risking a traffic accident. You may also happen upon a beautiful park with little to do and no activities in the surrounding area. After a few days in the fresh air, you find yourself twiddling your thumbs or working through that Michener novel you've been putting off for years. At this point it's time to make that big decision, "Is this a transition from a normally hectic lifestyle or am I simply bored out of my gourd?" If you settle on the latter point of view and haven't paid six months' camping fees up front, pack it in and move on or head for a new spot to live.

Full-Timing All the Time

Can you settle into a job and career while staying put in an RV? Settling into an RV as an alternative to a land-based home is tough on some people, easy for others, and impossible for a few.

Before you blow into town for a new job and life in a trailer park, test your resilience camping in the same rig for an extended period of time. You may be fully compatible with a compact lifestyle and comfortable with life in the slow lane after work. Or you may want to expand your space with a house and a lease. We usually rent a comfortable condo or apartment and sell the rig during these periods. There are also specific houses designed to combine the RV with a partial house. We would advise you to study such an arrangement before you buy.

A weakness of this scheme is that should you want to unload the hybrid house/RV living quarters, it may be tough to find a buyer, especially if you're competing price-wise with the builder of the settlement. The developers may be able to offer a new "house" for less than you can afford to sell yours for. That makes for a tough negotiation.

Tip: A Condensing Environment

Sounding more like an ecological problem than one that directly affects you, a condensing environment is one that's so humid that condensation appears everywhere. Found in the southern United States, Puerto Rico, and, obviously, Hawaii, it causes rust and corrosion very quickly. This ruins sensitive electronics such as the notebook computers many RVers now carry. What to do about it? While you can't hamper its effect on the RV's exterior, you can run the air-conditioner. The AC will dry the cabin air quickly and efficiently. If you're dealing with delicate electronics in such a situation, keep them in the main cabin or open the drawers or cupboards they're stored in, so that the air is released and replaced with dry air from the air-conditioner. Keep doors and windows closed, for obvious reasons.

Campground Guidebooks and Electronic Guides

The *Trailer Life Campground/RV Park and Services Directory* and *Woodall's Campground Directory* are standards for locating campgrounds. Be aware, however, that some of the most fun rural parks we've stayed in are not listed in either of these books or any of the competitive volumes. We stumble upon these secret parks by driving back routes and old highways bypassed by the interstates. Some we find on recommendation from fellow RVers. Still, you should have one of the guides in your rig at all times to help plot your trips.

Where to Go for Guides

Most bookstores carry these phonebook-sized camp guides. You'll find them at the bottom of the travel section in stores whose regular shelves can't handle books more than nine or ten inches tall. As you would expect, Camping World and other RV stores handle them as well. Many public libraries have campground guides, but since you can't take them with you on a long trip, we suggest buying one instead of borrowing.

Try to get the latest issue. Rates, dates, and amenities are subject to change. Buy two guides (*Trailer Life* and *Woodall's*), because they are different in listing quality and attitude. A cozy campground that appears in one may not show up in the other. Our only complaint is the weight they add to our craft.

These books also provide directions for getting around, hookup information, and lists of facilities and activities. Other information may include details on rig clearance (not all parks can accommodate big or tall rigs), altitudes, weather, and maps. The guides carry an increasing number of listings for "what to do and what to see." RV service listings are also included as well as basic state and provincial maps, coupons, ads, and a calendar of major public events, categorized by state. *Trailer Life*'s book also rates campgrounds by facilities, cleanliness of restroom facilities, and attractiveness, although we're a little unclear on the standards employed (as our experience and *Trailer Life*'s are often at odds).

How to Use a Camping Guide

If you plan a trip using a campground guidebook, study your options with a map in hand. We limit our driving to no more than four to six hours a day, regardless of miles. We also take it easy in the mountains and break for lunch as the engine temperature begins to climb.

You can map your whole trip out before leaving with a guidebook, but sometimes what looks promising in the book is unacceptable once you get there. Camping/parking in busy areas (Disneyland/Walt Disney World in July, for example) may also require reservations far in advance of your travels. Weather may cause camps to close without notice. Some mountain campgrounds aren't open year-round due to the five feet of that cold white stuff blocking access to would-be winter visitors. Opening and closing dates are usually noted in the campground guide listings, but if you're camping close to these dates, you might be in for a surprise when you get there. It's best to call ahead. In the desert, some camps close in the summer, as few RVers choose to vacation in 118-degree heat combined with violent thunderstorms. (Even without heaters, swimming pool temperatures reach the mid-nineties! Hardly refreshing.)

Spaciousness

Most campground guides list the space of the sites on offer. Take these with a grain of salt. While they are generally accurate, you may not get the full flavor of the berth's spaciousness or lack thereof. Are these spaces jammed together like a miniature suburb or are they separated by trees and the lay of the land? Really small spaces are difficult in warm weather. By leaving your windows open to save money on electricity or to enjoy the clean air, you may get an all-night sonata of your neighbors' snoring or the drone of their air-conditioner. You must come, see, and conquer for yourself. If it's late when you arrive, stay one night and head for greener grass on the other side of the hill the next day.

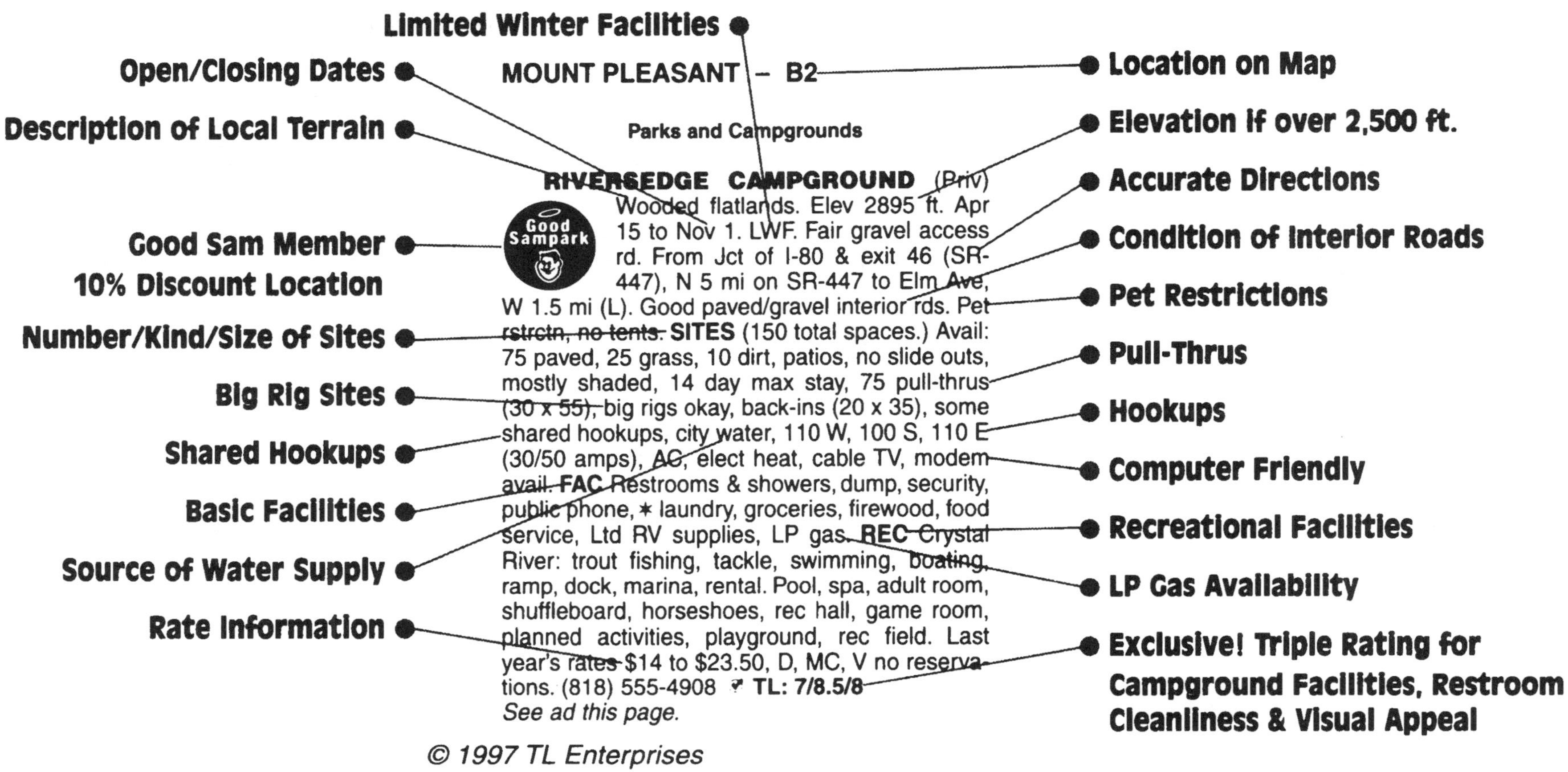
Limited Winter Facilities
Open/Closing Dates
Description of Local Terrain
Good Sam Member
10% Discount Location
Number/Kind/Size of Sites
Big Rig Sites
Shared Hookups
Basic Facilities
Source of Water Supply
Rate Information
MOUNT PLEASANT – B2
Parks and Campgrounds
Good Sampark
RIVERSEDGE CAMPGROUND (Priv) Wooded flatlands. Elev 2895 ft. Apr 15 to Nov 1. LWF. Fair gravel access rd. From Jct of I-80 & exit 46 (SR-447), N 5 mi on SR-447 to Elm Ave, W 1.5 mi (L). Good paved/gravel interior rds. Pet rstrctn, no tents. SITES (150 total spaces.) Avail: 75 paved, 25 grass, 10 dirt, patios, no slide outs, mostly shaded, 14 day max stay, 75 pull-thrus (30 x 55), big rigs okay, back-ins (20 x 35), some shared hookups, city water, 110 W, 100 S, 110 E (30/50 amps), AC, elect heat, cable TV, modem avail. FAC Restrooms & showers, dump, security, public phone, * laundry, groceries, firewood, food service, Ltd RV supplies, LP gas. REC Crystal River: trout fishing, tackle, swimming, boating, ramp, dock, marina, rental. Pool, spa, adult room, shuffleboard, horseshoes, rec hall, game room, planned activities, playground, rec field. Last year's rates $14 to $23.50, D, MC, V no reservations. (818) 555-4908 TL: 7/8.5/8
See ad this page.
© 1997 TL Enterprises
Location on Map
Elevation if over 2,500 ft.
Accurate Directions
Condition of Interior Roads
Pet Restrictions
Pull-Thrus
Hookups
Computer Friendly
Recreational Facilities
LP Gas Availability
Exclusive! Triple Rating for Campground Facilities, Restroom Cleanliness & Visual Appeal

A campground listing gives name, directions, number of spaces and what size rigs they accommodate, hookup information, facilities and activities (most of the time), and rates (Copyright 1997 TL Enterprises).

And Now for Something Completely Different

The Ultradata people, makers of the RoadWhiz — a pocket-calculator-like object that directs you to hotels, gas, stations, restaurants, shopping, and routes, now offer one for campers, called the RV Navigator. It does much of what the RoadWhiz does, but also electronically directs you to listings of more than ten thousand campgrounds. RV Navigator even lists camp amenities and activities. Just punch in your location in the computer and look at the camping spots available. The unit then provides road directions to the one you choose. It helps you find diesel fuel, malls, restaurants, hospitals, rest stops, and more. Another Ultradata product locates golf greens, provides directions for reaching each one, and describes the green. Neat, huh? Call 314-997-2250 for more information. The device weighs a lot less than a guidebook and doesn't suffer from coffee stains and torn pages.

Campground Guidebook Terminology

In the campground guides you'll run into phrases you may not be familiar with. Here's a (very) brief glossary of terms to know:

- Pull-thru. A pull-thru is a spot in a campground that lets you drive your tow-rig straight through and keep driving to get out. It saves backing in, which is a little difficult for towed rigs. The opposite of a pull-thru, if you haven't guessed, is a "back-in." This is difficult enough for motorhomes, but trailer and fifth-wheel operators will need an assistant to park evenly. Maybe Camping World should sell those lighted torches used by ground personnel to guide a 747 to its parking spot.
- Grassy flatland. Intended to describe the park's environment, "grassy flatlands" could be anything from an Irish meadow with sweet clover to a desert spread of jumping cholla, a cactus named for its habit of sticking its spines into anything that brushes it. You won't know what some of the descriptions mean until you get there, unless you know someone who actually stayed there within the last couple of years.
- Urban park. Another meaningless description. Such a park

could be anything from a park with an unobscured view of the World Trade Center to a parking lot in the middle of a small town. Since RV parks take up a lot of land, an inner-city location with a low daily rate may turn out to be in a neighborhood you wouldn't want to visit.

- City water. The campground is directly hooked to water provided by a town or city. Many campgrounds use well water, which can be wonderful or brown and foul. That's why we use a water filter, and you should too. In really miserable camps or in Mexico, we bring our own containers and buy purified water.

- No slide-outs. Slide-out rooms can make your rig spacious, but if you can't slide out the room, you may be more cramped than you would be without the slide-out. A park with prohibitions against slide-outs probably has narrow spaces without enough room to slide out the extensions. Treat this as a warning, because you'll be given a spot with no more than a few feet between rigs on both sides. Translation: sardine city. In reality, many parks don't allow or have room for slide-outs — so, before you pay extra for a slide-out rig, you might want to consider how often you'll really be able to use that extra room in the places you plan to travel.

Visiting the National Parks and Recreation Areas

There are hundreds of parks, recreation areas, and monuments administered by the National Park Service. Whether you visit Mount Rainier, the Grand Canyon, Acadia, or the Statue of Liberty, national parks offer diverse activities such as living history programs, environmental education and nature walks, Junior Ranger activities, interpretive walks, and seasonal festivals. Many of the parks offer camping spaces suitable for RVs, although some have length limitations that preclude the larger rigs from camping inside the park facilities. Many parks are crowded during peak season, so planning will make your visits more enjoyable. For information on the parks and specific park requirements, go to the World Wide Web at http://www.nps.gov or call the park directly.

Always check the status of parks before you drive. Some parks may be closed, even if you have camping reservations, by fire hazard, weather, or other unpredictable circumstances. Be aware that there are limitations on the length of rigs at every park, some as short as twelve feet, and length of stays. For specific park information contact the parks in advance about reservations, permits, regulations, activities, access status, RV camping limitations, and general services.

By the way, not all national parks are crowded. If you want peace and quiet, check out the lesser-known areas. Send a check or money order for $1.50 (check the current price) to the address below for a copy of a brochure that describes these gems in the wilderness:

Lesser Known Areas of the National Park System
Superintendent of Documents
Consumer Information Center
Department 134B
Pueblo, CO 81009

If you want to learn even more about national parks, check out these publications:

National Parks Visitor Facilities & Services
The National Park Hospitality Association
1331 Pennsylvania Ave. NW, Suite 724
Washington, DC 20004-1703
202-682-9507

The Complete Guide to America's National Parks
National Park Foundation
1101 17th St. NW, Suite 1102
Washington, DC 20036
202-785-4500

The above publication is also available in many bookstores. The price is under $20 as of this writing.

National Parks Passports

If you intend to frequent the national parks, then you should get one of the passports that allow people to enter fee areas without additional charges. The government has established the Golden Eagle, Golden Age, and Golden Access Passports for frequent park visitors. The passports will save you money if you travel to several areas that charge entrance fees. The passports are non-transferable and cannot be lent to someone else. Check current information about passports on the NPS World Wide Web site (www.nps.gov).

The Golden Eagle Passport is an entrance pass to those national parks, monuments, historic sites, recreation areas, and national wildlife refuges that charge an entrance fee. The Golden Eagle Passport costs $25 (at this writing) and is valid for one year from date of purchase. Purchase a Golden Eagle Passport at any NPS entrance fee area. The Golden Eagle Passport admits the pass holder and any accompanying passengers in a private vehicle. The Golden Eagle Passport does not cover or reduce use fees, such as fees for camping, swimming, parking, boat launching, or cave tours. Thus, you'll still need to pay for your camping space if you intend to stay over in your rig.

The Golden Age Passport is a lifetime entrance pass for those sixty-two years of age or older. The Golden Age Passport has a one-time processing charge of $10 (at this writing). You must purchase a Golden Age Passport in person (it is not available by mail or telephone). This can be done at any NPS entrance fee area. At time of purchase you must show proof of age (be sixty-two years old or older) and be a citizen or permanent resident of the United States. The Golden Age Passport admits the pass holder and any accompanying passengers in a private vehicle. The Golden Age Passport also provides a 50 percent discount on use fees charged for facilities and services such as camping, swimming, parking, boat launching, or cave tours. (This discount can save a bundle for seniors who live in their RVs.) The Golden Age Passport does not cover or reduce special recreation permit fees or fees charged by concessionaires.

The Golden Access Passport is a lifetime entrance pass for persons who are blind or permanently disabled. It is available to citizens or permanent residents of the United States, regardless of age, who have been determined to be blind or permanently disabled. You may obtain a Golden Access Passport at any entrance fee area by showing proof of medically determined disability and eligibility for receiving benefits under federal law. The Golden Access Passport admits the pass holder and any accompanying passengers in a private vehicle. Where entry is not by private vehicle, the passport admits the pass holder, spouse, children, and parents. As with the Golden Age Passport, the Golden Access Passport also provides a 50 percent discount on fees charged for facilities and services but does not reduce special recreation permit fees or fees charged by concessionaires.

Reservations at National Parks

Reservations for individual and family campsites are accepted at national park sites that are very popular. These include:

Acadia National Park
Assateague Island National Seashore
Cape Hatteras National Seashore
Death Valley National Park
Grand Canyon National Park
Great Smoky Mountains National Park
Joshua Tree National Park
Rocky Mountain National Park
Sequoia and Kings Canyon National Parks
Shenandoah National Park
Whiskeytown National Recreation Area
Yellowstone National Park
Yosemite National Park

Reservations for some national parks are provided by the DESTINET Corporation (discussed below), but most national parks are first come, first served. As of this writing, reservations for family campsites may be made no sooner than eight weeks in advance and up to the day before your planned arrival. Reservations for group campsites may be made no sooner than twelve weeks in advance. Reservation volume is heavy and time is needed to process the reservation. Plan ahead and make your reservation for popular sites as early as possible. RV reservations may be handled by third-party companies, such as Amfac. Contact the park because vendors and regulations change frequently.

State and Local Parks

There are many more state and public parks than we can list in this chapter. For a free list of state travel directors who can provide more information on some of these camping options, send a self-addressed, business-size envelope to:

The Travel Industry Association of America
1100 New York Ave. NW, Suite 450
Washington, DC 20005

Making Reservations at National, State, and Local Parks

Even with contacts and guides, making reservations for campsites can be time-consuming. DESTINET provides an alternative. DESTINET is a leading supplier of information and reservations for RVers and campers. The service provides camping reservations for most major public parks in North America, as well as many private campgrounds. DESTINET is the reservation service for up-to-date information on pricing, inventory, and reservation/cancellation procedures for over forty thousand camping locations across North America (but only a few national parks).

Reservations through DESTINET may be made by calling 1-800-365-2267 within the United States, or call 619-452-8787 if you're calling from outside the United States. You may also fax reservation requests to 619-546-1709. Be sure to include a credit card number and expiration date in order to secure the reservation. DESTINET accepts Visa, MasterCard, and Discover for reservation deposits.

In this chapter, we covered a lot of ground, but then you literally do cover a lot of ground in RV parks. In the next two chapters we consider places you can go for free and other things you can do from your RV.

Chapter 18

RVing for Free Around the Country

The dream of all (okay, most) RVers is the pristine, full-service, no-charge RV camp. You drive into a parking space with a gorgeous ocean view. You run self-contained for a week at a time and spend nary a penny except for food and a little gas and propane. These opportunities exist. Each summer scenic roads are filled with RVers parked on the shoulders and it's one continuous party, with cook-outs, swimming, and even live music when some people get together with guitar, horns, drum, or a synthesizer or two. Staying for weeks, the party goes on and on . . .

A free week on the beach near Santa Barbara was one of our favorite experiences. Spending only $29.13 for food, a little fuel, a little beer, and two trips to dump our tanks, we lived on the beach for a week! Where else can you attend a continuous party, meet new friends, swim in the ocean, and have a magnificent view for less than thirty clams?

When winter comes, many of the free campers, mostly full-timers, head for Quartzite, Arizona, near Lake Havasu, or even coastal Mexico. Others head for the famous, free camping spots in "Slab City," the abandoned Camp Gilmore army base near the Salton Sea in California. Here RVers live for next to nothing, enjoying free sunshine and fresh air. There are numerous sites like these across the United States that allow essentially free camping. The best way to find these sites is to ask fellow campers and get careful directions, because not all spots are easy to find.

Bureau of Land Management Facilities

On Bureau of Land Management (BLM) land, you can camp free for a couple of weeks or buy an inexpensive permit for longer stays ($50 at this writing). There are nearly 272 million acres of wild land administered by the Bureau of Land Management just waiting to be explored. The land includes soaring mountain peaks, roaring whitewater canyons, colorful cactus deserts, sage brush prairies, and hillside meadows. Whether you seek a solitary fishing respite, a white-knuckled mountain bike ride, rip-roaring rapids, or serene wildlife exploration, there are recreation areas in California, Arizona, Alaska, Oregon, Utah, Montana, Wyoming, Colorado, Idaho, New Mexico, and Nevada to choose among. If you want to learn more about the 1,730 miles of national historic trails, 9,000 miles of floatable rivers, 248 campgrounds, 574 hiking and cycling trails, and 150,000 miles of fishable streams, not to mention hundreds of caves, recreation sites, lakes, and reservoirs, we recommend *America's Secret Recreation Areas*, by Michael Hodgson (Foghorn Press Edition, ISBN Number 0935701613; price, $17.95).

The book contains descriptions of each recreation and natural area and recommends activities within each region, including mountain biking, horseback riding, hiking, backpacking, camping, whitewater rafting, kayaking, canoeing, spelunking, wildlife observation, fishing, and climbing.

You can also call the local BLM office. Look them up under U.S. Government listings in the phone book or call the Washington, D.C., office at 202-208-3100. Local offices can issue camping permits and may have a list of available "parks" with no charges and no hookups. Ask for *Recreation Guide to BLM Public Lands*.

Other federal agencies and Native American organizations provide free and inexpensive camping on sites in their domain. Here are some sources that can provide more information on these inexpensive camping alternatives:

U.S. Army Corps of Engineers Projects
20 Massachusetts Ave.
Washington, DC 20314

National Forest Service
U.S. Department of Agriculture
201 14th St. SW
Washington, DC 20013
202-205-1523

National Wildlife Refuges, A Visitor's Guide
U.S. Fish & Wildlife Service
Publications Department
4401 N. Fairfax Dr., Room 130 WEBB
Arlington, VA 22203

Visitor's Guide and Campground List
Navajo Nation Parks and Recreation Department
P.O. Box 308
Window Rock, AZ 86515

Free or not, avoid desert camping in the summer as you would winter camping near Hudson's Bay, Canada. Well, we would, anyway. It's simply too hot in the desert and you'll either melt from the heat or cook your generator trying to run the air-conditioning. Fall through spring is wonderful in the desert with sixty-five-degree days in December. Spring brings a massive bloom of flowers with even the normally staid cactus sprouting blossoms. Camping outside a park is safest with other campers parked nearby. You need to establish your comfort level with camping alone. If the idea makes you nervous, camp around other RVers or head for a conventional (fee-based) campground.

A Guide to Free Camping

Camping free is easiest when you have a guidebook and know what to expect before you get to camp. Don Wright's *Guide to Free Campgrounds* was in its ninth edition last time we picked up a copy. If you can't find it at Camping World, order it from Cottage Publications at 800-272-5518. Most of the camps listed, at least the ones we've tried, are located in beautiful settings, although power, water, and dump stations aren't located around the corner. Still, you can't beat the price or the fun. Wright also wrote a two-volume guide on campgrounds priced under $10 per night and a volume on Army Corps of Engineers sites — also available from Cottage Publications. These are highly recommended for the camper on a budget, like us.

More Places to Camp for Free

Beyond federal lands, parks, and Indian reservations, there are less traditional places you can park around the country. We describe some of our experiences with these options in the next pages.

At the Local Mall

Big malls used to provide a great place to camp for the night, but recent security concerns may result in the staff's asking you to move your rig once the shops close. We've found that if we ask politely, some guards will let you stay overnight, as long as you promise to be gone before the mall opens. Asking pleasantly is key to getting permission to stay. And please don't spoil it for other RVers by dumping your black water in the parking lot. We've tipped more than one security officer with a six-pack of beer. That not only provided camp space but free security for us and our rig.

Strip Malls

Many small strip malls, especially those with twenty-four-hour grocery stores, work well as overnight stops. Park. Do some grocery shopping and hope there's no overzealous security guard. (If there is, being surrounded with shopping bags from the mall shows that you are a customer, not a freeloader.)

Tip: Wind and Sea

If you plan on extended camping near the ocean, you'll definitely want to consider the effect of salt air on electronics. It will also affect exterior surfaces, especially chrome and brushed metals. While any humid environment (central Florida or July in Arizona) is hard on electronics, the air off the ocean is especially hard on electronics during any time of year. When we travel to "freebie" jamborees along the coast of central California, we put any electronics not in use into sealable plastic bags and remove as much air as possible from them before sealing. Seal the bag with the AC running so that the air sealed inside will be as dry as possible.

Truck Stops

Safer for parking than a rural road or a rest stop, a truck stop offers a place to sleep, albeit a noisy one. A few truck stops offer basic hookups for RVers (for a charge, of course). If parking is free, gas up and chow down in the diner. If there's a charge for parking, choose your prospective berth carefully, as some trucks run freezer engines all night that may keep you awake. Around dawn about twenty trucks may simultaneously start their engines and let them idle for twenty minutes. To mask the noise, we use a wave-sound generator placed near our bed (see Chapter 15) to allow us to sleep. It's not a perfect solution, but it reduces the bothersome clunka-clunka-clunka of aging diesel trucks roaring off at all hours of the night.

Tip: For a Few Dollars More . . .

In Mexico, a tip of a few dollars/pesos works wonders for parking almost anywhere. Just make sure you pay the person who actually controls the parking spot.

Rest Stops

Camping at rest stops is generally a security risk. We cook meals and take breaks at rest stops, but sleep at them only if we're so tired that an accident from lack of rest is a risk. We never stop for long if we're the only big rig on the site. Park between other RVers and the big trucks. If their drivers are awake, introduce yourself and offer something to drink or a snack, so they know you're there. (We barbecue dinner and share it, if it's not too late.) Then take a short siesta and hit the road again as soon as you can. Camp at rest stops with windows and doors closed and locked, and leave as soon as you're rested — set your alarm, even if it's for 4:00 A.M. By this time, your protective trucker friends will likely have moved on as well.

City Parks and Beaches

Most cities have specific prohibitions against camping of any kind on the street or in a park not designed for it. (This is perhaps a somewhat cruel trick against the homeless, as most parks and beaches now "close" at sundown or before midnight.) Forget such venues and find a Safeway and park away from the store but where the center's lights keep your rig in plain view.

At Sandie's House

If you can stuff your rig into a driveway (watch out for the roof's protruding rafters), you can probably camp at a friend's house for several days. It helps to know the city's law, and more important, whether anyone bothers to enforce it. Long stays may be resented by the neighbors, especially if your rig is unusually large or looks as if it's ready for the boneyard. Use discretion and you can have power and water hooked up as well.

In the Boonies

Park off a rural road? That's a tough one. The answer is determined by your comfort in doing so, where you park, and whether you're blocking the road to Farmer Brown's house. You might find a four-hundred-pound cow or a flock of chickens in your living quarters after opening the door for some "fresh country air." For those willing to forgo the amenities of national parks or commercial campgrounds, there are hundreds of free campgrounds all over North America. The National Forest Service and Bureau of Land Management (discussed earlier) administer most of these sights. For long stays, you may need a permit. Utility companies and lumber corporations offer free camping on some of their properties as well. Obviously, in such camping places you'll be living without hookups. You'll need to learn the tricks of the trade for conserving water and power that we discuss later in this chapter.

Unoccupied Buildings

We've camped behind empty office buildings a number of times without problems. Generally, the police ignore them (and us), and since they're not near populated areas, no one bothers with an RV parked for a day or two. But, again, this practice will depend on your degree of comfort with the area, and we wouldn't even consider it behind a building in downtown Detroit. We prefer new glass and metal office buildings with no occupants and large "For Lease" signs out front.

This sounds silly — in fact it is silly — but to tell whether a building with no lights or company signs is occupied, head around the back and see if there's a Dumpster in use. If there's no Dumpster, or one that's empty, chances are either the building is unoccupied or the trash company came around just before you got there.

Tip: High Stakes

Watch out for the deals in parks tied to gambling establishments or offers to "experience" a membership campground as a prelude to signing up. Both can be very expensive considering they're "free." Just a few nights in one of Las Vegas's "bargain" parks can put you out of business for good if you gamble.

During "free" nights testing a membership arrangement you'll be bombarded every waking hour with sales pressure to sign a membership contract.

The Invisible Man

When camping free outside a park it helps to be pseudo-invisible. Check out your prospective camping location before setting up a forty-foot motorhome and cranking up the satellite dish, rolling out the bright-pink awning, and popping a can of beer while readying the barbecue for the steaks with noticeably fragrant mesquite chips. If you must camp discreetly, a smaller RV works best, and it helps if the rig looks as unused as a motorcycle on a rainy day. Hide bigger rigs out of sight on land with lots of brush for cover. Heed the "No Trespassing" signs and grazing bulls with long, sharp horns. Never park on open land without inspecting its suitability first. If you get stuck, you're in for trouble.

Life Without Hookups

At its most primitive, living in an RV — be it tent with Coleman stove and lantern or thirty-four-foot Newell — is a minor adventure in survival. You must maintain adequate foodstuffs, water, and minimal creature comforts even if low water supplies preclude bathing and leave you smelling like a goat. Likewise, a dead battery, empty fuel or propane tanks, and a larder containing little more than spoiled milk and moldy green "tuna surprise" won't help much.

In some ways, it's much like life in the movie *Apollo 13*, except that in an RV you won't have to worry about running out of oxygen or burning up upon reentry. Of course, the crew on Apollo 13 didn't have to worry about snakes or grizzly bears! As in a space mission, careful planning and sometimes radical improvisation are central to successful boondock camping. In fact, many RVers become experienced in living among the birds and the bees (and the bears) and wouldn't have it any other way. For the "wild camper" the rules are slightly different in that you don't have a nice safe concrete pad to park on nor uninterrupted thirty-amp electricity to run the rooftop air-conditioners, water pump, and microwave.

Wilderness Camping Hints

Some of the most useful conservation tips are mostly common sense: Switch the lights off when not in use. Learn to "quick flush" the toilet rather than letting the water run. Stock the pantry with healthy, long-lived provisions. Install multiple batteries. Use awnings and fans to keep cool, instead of the air-conditioner. Carry extra drinking water in collapsible jugs. To learn more tricks of camping without shore power, ask and watch fellow RVers.

Here are some basic tips we've discovered that can help extend your stay without hookups:

Conserve Water

You need to conserve water when you're not hooked up to a water supply. You can load enough water to last a week or more if you take sponge baths and recycle the dishwater to flush the toilet. If you are sloppy you will simultaneously run out of water and fill up the holding tanks. Don't let the water run while washing dishes. When taking a shower, wet your body, then turn the water off. Then soap yourself down and rinse. This will save gallons of water to allow you to extend your wilderness stay.

Tip: The Coast Guard Rule

The United States Coast Guard has sound advice for boaters, which you can adjust slightly for RVing in the middle of no-where. Called the "two-thirds rule," it states that when heading round-trip (by boat), you should plan on using one-third of your fuel getting there and one-third getting back. Why the extra one-third? Because should you run into a severe storm, you'll have this extra fuel to use in the emergency, which may involve strong winds and unexpected currents.

Follow this rule with RV fuel *and* food *and* water, and what might constitute an emergency for other RVers will mean little more for you than a few extra hands of poker while you wait for the rain to subside.

Keep the Refrigerator Level

The refrigerator runs off propane or 115VAC, so you must select the power source from time to time and start the operation on that source. The unit must be level or in motion to stay cool. This is very important when camping in the wilderness. Try to find the most level campsite possible.

Understand Your Power Systems

When in the wild, you are your own electric company. Monitor battery power regularly and keep the batteries in good condition. Learn how to operate and maintain the generator. Install an inverter to operate accessories from the battery power if you don't already have one. Use a portable generator if you don't have a built-in model to recharge your batteries. Use solar power (this will require minor modifications to your rig's electrical system, but they're well worth the effort in extended off-road capacity). Install low-wattage lights.

Tip: Power Shortage

To conserve battery power, just changing the standard incandescent bulbs used in most RV fixtures to fluorescent bulbs can add substantial battery life. For highline motorcoaches, temporarily take the bulbs out of the floor lighting, since you don't absolutely have to have it.

You can live any way you want in an "unhooked" RV. Choose between power-on living with all amenities carefully rationed but fully available, or a "no-power" world with battery power, propane, and fuel saved for a rainy day. Again, we choose the middle ground: a site that's not too hot or cold to save heating and AC power and has access to drinkable water, and food and a dump station less than an hour's drive away. Why? Because it's safe and easy and fun too. We usually hit the sticks with another couple. That way, we can entertain each other and have more resources at our disposal, should an emergency occur. All four of us are experienced RV drivers and in camping we explore the surroundings, play chess, and listen to music on battery-operated equipment.

Monitor the Holding Tanks

You should not empty the holding tank onto the ground — it is illegal in most places and awesomely inconsiderate of the environment, other RVers, and landowners. In a full-size rig, two people should be able to make a seven-day trip without emptying the tanks if they are careful with water use. Don't forget that the holding tank needs some chemical to keep the odor down. Get some before you leave. In a pinch dishwashing liquid (Joy or Dawn) works fine. Squirt about one-quarter to one-half cup in the toilet and flush every twelve hours.

If you are on the road but not renting campground space, you can still dump your holding tanks in parks for a small fee. Public campgrounds and rest stops often have free dump sites. Ask other RVers about the "honey wagons" that come around to coyote camps and RV rallies and other places that RVers park without hookups. These entrepreneurs offer water and dumping services.

Tip: Bad Water Gulch

Camping in Mexico or some other place where fresh water is at a premium, fill a couple of gallon plastic milk bottles of even dubious water and let them stand in a warm place, or better still the sun. Then use them for your shower as described above. For an added touch, find a plastic shower fitting that mounts firmly to the bottles! You can use this same technique to fill most RV toilets too (keeping it out of your fresh water system), if you can get access to enough water to fully empty the black water tanks. On a two-valve toilet, press the pedal that opens the valve, then add water and dump into an appropriate sewage disposal unit.

Increase the Propane Capacity

If you ration the use of the furnace and other propane-driven devices, your propane fuel can last a very long time. If you find you run low on fuel during your trips, consider getting larger-capacity tanks to replace the standard tanks on your rig.

Start Out Slowly

Step One

There's more to the wild life than just ensuring that you have enough charcoal briquettes for the hibachi. Before you plan that seventeen-week expedition on the Pan-American Highway, camp in no-hookup campgrounds for a few days. Deliberately deprive yourself of outside fuel, water, sewage extraction, and trips into town for supplies. Assume that the TV and radio don't work because you're too far from a city to receive anything. Then ask yourself, how do you feel? Relaxed? Bored? Happy as a clam? And how did your management of limited resources work? Are you out of water on day three because of daily showers by each member of your camp? Are the coach batteries deader than a doornail? Are you out of propane gas or diesel? If you need to get out, simply pack up and roll. You don't have to unhook, since nothing's hooked up.

Step Two

If you enjoyed your life in the boondocks and were successful living for a few days without hookups, then try a stretch in the wild, although you should travel with another RVer in case you run into problems. Just chatting to each other on a CB radio is fun and you have the security that companionship brings.

Step Three

Now evaluate your success in hookup-free camping. Did you and your cocampers get along and enjoy one another's company? Did this style of camping represent the easy life for you, or were you bored or worried about running out of battery power every time someone switched on a light? In addition to your personal take on camping, how did your rig hold up? Were the water and fuel tanks' capacities adequate? Did you drain the coach batteries through sloppy power management? Can you add capacity to your rig — taking weight into consideration — that will overcome these shortcomings? Did the rig's layout lend itself to long-term camping? If the answer to this last question is negative, then there's no reason to own an RV, since a tent will do almost as well and they're a lot less expensive. If you passed these tests and still had a smile on your face, you're fully capable of free camping. Congratulations!

Now you may want to hit the library for books on camping to pick up advice and tips we can't fit here. Or, if you disliked or essentially failed the tests of basic self-reliance, try again, or plan on campground camping. Most of the time we prefer hookups, so don't feel bad if you do too. The nice thing about RVing is the ability to choose to camp in the way that suits you.

Tip: Tiring Problems

When camping in the boondocks, you may drive rough roads and pull off into a camping site so designated because it's a semilevel clearing among the trees or cactus and lacks a surplus of one of our major natural resources — mud. With such crude roads and camps, you might want to install innertubes in your rig's tires. These protect against a stray saguaro needle or weekend camper's broken beer bottle flattening a tire. Do this only after consulting an expert or two. In heavy rigs, the tubes may add to tire heat at freeway speeds. But, if they're compatible, for about an extra $15 to $20 a wheel you can buy peace of mind when traveling that rough road.

Energy Conservation

If you go native with no hookups, you must ration energy, be it lights-out at sundown (actually lights never on) or careful use of propane (make sun tea instead of boiling water for the regular stuff). Use a solar panel to keep a charge on the coach batteries and always ensure that the electrical "block" between the coach and engine batteries works. Otherwise you may be unable to start your tow vehicle or motorhome. You can run the generator to recharge the batteries if you have one, assuming that that leaves you enough fuel to reach town.

Once started, the engine can complete the charging process, although it may take an hour of driving to charge the batteries to the point where they will successfully crank the engine. Keep in mind that battery efficiency is compromised in cold weather. (Aging batteries that provide ten-minute cranking in seventy-five-degree Florida may provide less than ninety seconds of starter activity in a minus-thirty-degree night in Maine.)

Tip: Where Am I?!

With a GPS receiver (thanks to military satellites that ring the Earth) you can locate your position within about twenty yards of accuracy anywhere on Earth. Neat, huh? Just make sure your maps are Mercator projections (showing the curve of the globe) and list latitude and longitude. Government-issued topographical maps are best, with their precision information. But you may need a glovebox full to cover a couple of large counties. (Note: At this writing, you can buy GPS technology at sporting goods stores, but you may need to ask your friends with a sailboat for good advice on which unit to buy. The clerks we queried seemed lost when we mentioned GPS or handheld receivers for this powerful replacement for the star Polaris.)

Saving Gas or Diesel

Not driving or operating a generator is the easiest way to save fuel (a hot tip that, huh?). But there are several useful if seemingly uninventive ideas for saving fuel when freeloading, er, free camping. They are:

- If camping with other RVers, take turns going into town. Except in a marginally powered rig, five hundred pounds of groceries won't use more fuel or power to drag up a hill than a loaf of French bread. This saves time, fuel, and effort as you share the costs of the trip.
- Live slower. Avoid powering the air-conditioner(s) or microwave with the generator if you have one. Except in the desert when it's one hundred degrees in the shade, a cool drink under a tree or the awning isn't a bad alternative to dual air-conditioners howling and the generator growling while you sit inside, windows and doors buttoned up.

Tip: Blowing It

Never, never, NEVER (you got that?) STORE PROPANE TANKS IN A SEALED COMPARTMENT OR INSIDE A RIG! These tanks are designed to bleed off excess pressure, and propane leaks from them and builds up in enclosed spaces. Once camped, we place extra tanks away from camp since propane stoves, refrigerators running on propane, and the barbecue grills can ignite the propane. (Read the etched warning on the tanks and/or owner's manual.)

Getting There Is Half the Fun

When approaching a real wilderness, you want to do as little as possible to disturb it. Naturally a multiton rig isn't very good at this. We avoid the rainy/muddy times and then depend on whatever public roads are available to carefully maneuver heavy rigs into place. A camping spot is selected when the road peters out or becomes too rough for our rigs. Large thickets of trees not only stop our progress, but provide ideal shade in summer months. If a parking spot is difficult to reach due to potholes, plants, or uneven ground, progress slowly with someone walking in front of the rig, looking for sand or mud traps, potential danger to burrowing wildlife, or hard-to-see hazards such as twenty-foot drops. Try to park where a sudden rainstorm or unexpected blizzard won't make it impossible to rereach a serviceable road. Never park in a gully in the Southwest or close to an innocent-looking streambed anywhere. A torrential rain can change these into rivers in seconds.

If you get bored with all the free camping possibilities, maybe you need more things to do. In the next chapter, we present some options you may have forgotten to consider.

Chapter 19

More Things
to Do

You'll never run out of things to do while RVing. Some cost money. Others require only the fuel to get there. The beauty of America (and Canada) is available for free. All you have to do is drive and look. No charge! Kim uses pastels to render landscapes. Sunny keeps a journal of the events. At every corner, there is something new to draw or write about.

If visiting standard tourist venues tops your list of travel priorities, the joy of RVing is the ability to drive your home to the attractions. Almost every major tourist site, from Walt Disney World to the national parks, offers camping options for RVers. Getting tired? Head for the rig and take a siesta. No hotel charges. No rush to the airport for a late flight. Eat homemade food instead of greasy fast-food fare. Put your feet up, have a soda, and peruse the maps and brochures to decide on the next day's itinerary.

Besides the standard tourist destinations, there are hundreds of things to do in RVs that don't require long lines or exorbitant admission fees. In this chapter we present only a few of the many options for entertaining yourself from your RV.

Caravans, Clubs, and Jamborees

Many RVers travel in groups. There are special RV caravans and clubs for everyone from seniors from Milwaukee to artists and craftspeople interested in exploring Indian pictographs in the Southwest. Look in RV club newsletters, the Internet, and ads in the RV magazines for organized RVing events.

Some caravans are impromptu, in which a group of RVers

Creative World Rallies and Caravans provides organized RV caravans that are unique and fun. With an organizer handling the details, all you have to do is follow the leader to fascinating places, go on cookouts, or, as in this photo, cross the Mississippi with your RV on a barge. Call them at 1-800-732-8337 for a free catalog of organized RV activities. They offer international RV tours as well.

befriend one another and head off into the sunset in search of the perfect camping spot. Others are like an organized tour with tour director, a planned itinerary, and, of course, a fee. If you want to travel to Mexico, for example, there are many caravan companies that will guide RVers through the scenic and cultural wonders of the country. Check out the ads for commercial caravan vacations in the RVing magazines.

Jamborees are opportunities for hundreds of RVers with similar interests to play and party. Arranged either formally or informally, a (usually large) group of RVers meet at a predetermined spot on a specific day, week, or month. Activities may be structured or impromptu, depending on the jamboree. Many times RVers also offer crafts, food, or advice for sale at these affairs.

Naturally, not everyone arrives at the same instant. Once camp is established, jamboree participants head off on hikes, swim together, or prepare delicious dinners with cooperative use of hands and provisions. After dark, the sing-along commences and, yes, a few people may have a bit too much to drink.

Arrangements may be made with reservations at public or private campgrounds, but more typically jamborees are held on "freebie" property, which may include anything from the road beside a rural beach to a grassy knoll in Dallas. There's usually no charge for attendance. There are no hookups either, so living primitive is the word of the day. For that reason, RVers make new friends as they rely on each other for a couple of extra eggs, help with minor mechanical problems, and security. Jamborees, like caravans, are announced in the standard RVing magazines and club newsletters. (Refer to the General Resources section for lists of these.)

Consider the Activities at the Camp

If caravans or jamborees sound like too many people around, just choose a camp of your own. When selecting your camping sites, consider the activities you want to pursue. The camp should accommodate as many preferences as possible. Ask whether the nightly rate includes the activities before you stay. You may be able to participate in the same activity — fishing, for example —

for free, just a few yards down the river from the park. So check out the free activities in the area before you pay extra.

If you want to play tourist by visiting all the museums, monuments, or historical sites in an area, get some maps from the chamber of commerce as you drive into town. Use pushpins or colored markers to mark your agenda. You can also use the pushpins-in-the-map approach to document your stops along the way. Many RVers display maps outside their rigs that show how many states they've visited. It's a fun way to communicate your love of the road to others you meet along the way. You can buy magnetic and plasticized maps for this purpose from Camping World and other RV supply stores.

More Activities to Consider

Beyond the hiking, golfing, movies, swimming, dancing, and standard attractions of well-endowed RV parks, there are far more activities available to RVers than you can imagine or than we can fit into this book — even if we doubled or tripled its length. Activities range from those provided at a campground for toddlers to opportunities to explore North American history by visiting the actual sites where important events took place.

Of course, you can always go to the pricey attractions in an area, like Walt Disney World and Universal Studios. Most of the time we prefer the free attractions along the way. The options for inexpensive entertainment are diverse. As signs pop up along the road, simply check out the sights. Check out local newspapers for current happenings and sports events. For lists of fairs and festivals around the continent, check out the RVing magazines, bulletin boards, and guides to annual events available in most bookstores. Always visit the chamber of commerce sites on entering a new city and the welcome centers at the borders of most states. Most states and the Canadian provinces have an 800 number for requesting information on attractions. Here are the Canadian numbers:

Alberta Travel
800-661-8888

Tourism British Columbia
800-663-6000

Travel Manitoba
800-665-0040

Tourism New Brunswick
800-561-0123

Newfoundland and Labrador Tourism
800-563-6353

Northwest Territories Tourism
800-661-0788

Nova Scotia Department of Tourism and Culture
800-565-0000

Ontario Travel
800-668-2746

Prince Edward Island Department of Tourism and Parks
800-565-0267

Tourism Quebec
800-363-7777

Tourism Saskatchewan
800-667-7191

Tourism Yukon
403-667-5340

For state tourism offices, call the 800 information operator and ask for the state office, division, or department of tourism for the state you're interested in visiting. Most of these offices provide free brochures about the activities in the state as well as calendars of events. All states that we know of provide these numbers, but you may have to guess how the number is listed. Is it California Department of Tourism or the Visitor's Bureau? Directory assistance personnel tend to be very literal and won't help much in your search because their very jobs depend on getting you off the line as quickly as possible. Desperation time? Visit a bookstore and get the number from a guidebook to the state you're visiting. Better still — buy the book and skip the free travel info.

Check Out the Free Sites Across the Continent

Some of the most rewarding activities are free or almost free. We always take time to savor the local culture, learn about the heritage of an area, and try new foods. Here are some additional suggestions to consider for your RV outings:

- Try local wineries for wine tasting and tours. There are also cheese factories, breweries, and farms that offer tasting tours.
- Visit historical museums and landmarks.
- Take the free tours of state capitals, military bases, and factories.
- Attend all the fairs, festivals, and parades you can find. The tourism offices and RV magazines offer calendars of these events.
- Stroll through the college campuses along your route. Most large campuses offer free tours. Almost all campuses have a visitors' center or information office that will provide brochures on the campus and calendars of current events you can enjoy for free or at very little cost. We've enjoyed lectures and seminars, plays, musical performances, dances, and athletic events at campuses around the country. Sometimes we actually learn something in the process.
- Check out the fisheries and game reserves around the continent. Many offer educational tours and fishing opportunities.
- Visit churches, cathedrals, and architectural sites.
- Follow the trails of the pioneer settlers, such as the Oregon or Santa Fe trail. Check out the travel section of bookstores

for guidebooks on these historical adventures.

- Travel all of the remaining Route 66 while reading *On the Road* (by Jack Kerouac). We've done it. Leave the interstates and take the parallel routes to really get a flavor for the towns along the way.
- Set a goal to camp, golf, fish, or swim in every state — and do it.
- Explore the public gardens around the continent. This is a great way to learn about local flora.
- Take pictures (or paint them) of sunsets and sunrises from every camp.
- Go to the birthplaces of famous people or to sites of important historical events.
- Visit the mansions of the rich, famous, and not-so-famous. Some of these sites charge admission, but the fee is usually low.
- Track down old family members and friends, or visit ancestral homes and birthplaces.
- Take up bird watching. Get a guide at a bookstore for the areas you intend to visit.

Back to Nature

If none of these ideas sounds good, try harvesting some mushrooms or other wild edibles for dinner. Wild mushrooms, especially morels, and fresh wild berries are among the most prized of wild edibles, commanding wildly high prices at gourmet markets. As with any wild food, you must be absolutely certain that the mushrooms or other flora are indeed edible before you ingest them. If you're inexperienced, consult a local mycological society or a savvy friend. Before you go mushroom harvesting, get a good book on mushrooms for hints on finding, drying, storing, and preparing the wild fungi.

Take walks or hikes. If you don't feel like experiencing the great outdoors, consider expanding your intellect. Go to a local library and read a book. It's free, entertaining, and the possibilities are endless.

Of course, you can always do nothing in particular. As an RVer, you can always choose to think, relax, and just enjoy the environment around the rig. Just head for the hills and put the stress of urban life behind you for a few weeks. Always take a pack of playing cards along to pass the time with fellow travelers and people you meet in camp.

If you really want to get away from it all, do it. Pick a nice flat spot that you won't get bogged down in if it rains and simply camp. Wake to the calls of birds instead of the drone of the city. We could go on and on — but we think you get the idea. If you want to do it, you can do it in an RV.

Chapter 20

Crossing Borders

Mexico and Canada are popular destinations for RVers. Both offer adventure, but for different reasons. Most of the time, crossing the border is uneventful, although delays can be annoying. With knowledge of customs laws and some preparation, you can usually breeze through even into Mexico. However, an RV often gets a thorough search at the borders. After all, it's a large vehicle with space to store enough contraband to supply all the addicts in New York City for a year. In this chapter we'll briefly address the most common customs and travel issues for RVers crossing the borders to the north and south, but we recommend that you get up-to-the-minute advice from the appropriate authority before crossing any border, because the regulations are constantly in flux.

State to State

You may be stopped and searched simply when crossing a state line. The inoffensive officials at these stops are looking for fruit and vegetables they want to keep out of their state for pest control reasons. Since you live in your rig, you may be carrying *contraband* carrots! Eat or dispose of all fresh produce *before* entering states such as California where an inspector will confiscate your fresh goodies.

You'll also encounter border patrol stops in states bordering Mexico. The officers may wave you by or they may have you pull into a secondary inspection area and go through your rig for illegal immigrants hiding in the black water. All vehicle occupants who are not U.S. citizens or vacationing Canadians must show proof of their legal right to be in the United States. Undocumented foreigners will be hauled off the rig and possibly deported. Those forgetting their green card are subject to a felony charge and huge fine. People with Mexican genotypes seem unfairly targeted more than blue-eyed blonds.

United States to Canada

Most crossings into Canada are trouble-free if you look organized. No passport is required, although you should have some identification that indicates your citizenship. Therefore, we recommend taking a passport. You should bring your vehicle registration and a policy or letter which indicates that your vehicle insurance is valid in Canada. On occasion vehicles are searched at the border. Don't be dismayed if your vehicle is singled out. If you don't have anything illegal, you'll quickly be on your way.

You are limited in the amount of liquor (forty ounces of liquor or wine or twenty-four twelve-ounce cans or bottles of beer per person) and cigarettes (fifty cigars, two hundred cigarettes, or 2.2 pounds of tobacco) that can be imported without duty, so reduce any such stocks beforehand. Up to twenty-two pounds of meat and $30 worth of dairy products can be brought in (it's unlikely you'll have more than this in a fully stocked RV, so don't worry about it).

Pistols and revolvers are prohibited in Canada. Canadian Customs will hold any gun for you until you return to the border. Don't try to hide a gun. You may forfeit it, or if they don't like your lack of a forthright declaration, arrest you if you fail to declare the weapon. If you plan to cross a different border on return, the gun can be shipped from a gun shop on the United States side to your home. Smuggling a handgun is a serious offense.

Tip: And Who Told You That, Sir?

When making inquiries of customs and immigration officials, always get the name, first and last, of the agent providing the information. In five calls to Canadian customs several years ago, we got four different answers. If you don't have the name of the person who provided the information, you'll be completely at the mercy of the agent you're currently dealing with.

Tip: Prescription Drugs

Should you travel with prescription drugs, leave them in their original packages with your name on the label. Vitamins should likewise be stored in their bottles to avoid confusion should you be searched at the border. Note that many drugs that can be bought over the counter in Mexico and Canada require a prescription in the United States. Customs may ask you about them and search your rig if they become suspicious. Amusingly (depending on how you look at it), collections of herb teas stored in unmarked Baggies really set them off.

Hunters should join a Canadian hunting club before leaving for Canada and inquire how to acquire a hunting rifle legally for use in Canada rather than bringing their own. (Get addresses of such clubs from the ads in the backs of hunting magazines.)

If you bring a current rabies certificate, you can bring your dog or cat into Canada. Up to two pet birds can be brought in as long as they haven't been in contact with other birds for at least ninety days. Other pets require special permits. To determine what is required, contact:

Chief of Imports
Animal Health Division
Food Production and Inspection Branch
Agriculture Canada
Ottawa, Ontario, Canada K1A 0Y9

Expensive goods should be inspected and documented by U.S. Customs before leaving the country so that duty is not assessed on your return. U.S. Customs authorities can be like Canadian officials — pleasant and professional or short, rude, and nosy. The better you're prepared to cross the border, the more likely you'll get the former rather than the latter.

For the most current information on import restrictions, duties, and travel restrictions, as well as camping possibilities in Canada, contact any Canadian consulate in major American cities, or call one of the tourism offices for the Canadian provinces listed in Chapter 19.

Tip: Demonstrate Your Wealth

You may be asked to show money if an official is worried that you may be entering a foreign country to live on the public dole. We recommend taking travelers checks to show the officials. Don't feel embarrassed about being made to prove your material ability to sustain yourself in Mexico or Canada. It's done every day to those who visit the United States from Mexico and Canada as well.

Canada to the United States (Canadians)

Canadians can spend up to six months each year in the United States (very convenient for snowbirds). After that, they can't return to the United States for six months. No paperwork is required, although you should carry identification.

Canada to the United States (Americans)

You'll need the same paperwork to get back into the country that you needed to get out. Again, you'll be limited in the amount of purchases from the other country you can bring into the United States and the amount of alcohol and tobacco you can bring in without paying duties. Since both are generally cheaper in the United States, skip bringing them altogether.

If your papers are in order, you'll normally be processed quickly. Coming back to the States can be difficult, as they may use X-ray equipment to search your rig. Grooming helps — don't look like beach bums arriving to tap the country's welfare system, and chances are you'll sail through customs procedures with a wave of the hand. Note: If you are searched, don't take it personally unless you *are* a smuggler. As before, searches are often random, although a nervous attitude on your part or a very heavy person with a skinny individual's wardrobe will shift inspectors into high gear.

Tip: Forget the $4 Bottles of Premium Tequila

Mexican liquor prices are a major temptation to stock up. Don't bother, because you're allowed only one liter per adult on return. Extras will be unceremoniously dumped down a drain at the entry port. (You can ask for the empty bottles back, but who would want them?) Never cross the border while intoxicated. A sobriety checkpoint may be located just inside the United States. This shouldn't be a problem since no one would drive an RV after "having a few" anyway.

United States to Mexico

Crossing the border to Mexico is easy. The *libre* (free) zone extends into about sixty miles south of the border. Beyond that, you must have a tourist visa. You can get the applications for the visa at any American travel agency. It's best to get tourist papers before entering the country, as in our experience the length of stays permitted were longer when tourist cards were issued at the Mexican consulate rather than at the border. You can apply for a maximum six months' stay in Mexico.

Make sure you have the same identity, ownership, and insurance papers discussed for crossing into Canada. Mexican insurance, as mentioned in Chapter 4, is a must for all but the most foolhardy. If you don't own your rig, you must also have notarized permission by the owner to take it south.

The real Mexican checkpoint for tourist papers and vehicle documents is about sixty to ninety miles south of the border. Even though you crossed the border without a problem, at the inland checkpoint the officials may go through you and your rig with a fine-toothed comb. Remember, as in Canada, it is strictly forbidden to bring guns into the country. Hunters should leave their expensive rifles at home and join a hunting club, as was suggested for Canada.

For the most current information on RVing in Mexico and travel requirements, contact a Mexican consulate or one of these tourism offices:

Mexican Government Tourism Office
70 East Lake St., Suite 1413
Chicago, IL 60610
312-606-9252

Mexican Government Tourism Office
10100 Santa Monica Boulevard, Suite 224
Los Angeles, CA 90067
310-203-8191

Mexican Government Tourism Office
405 Park Ave., Suite 1002
New York, NY 10022
212-755-7261

We suggest that first-time RVing visitors to Mexico get hooked up with a tour guide and caravan. Many Mexican caravan trips are advertised in the standard RVing magazines. Make sure your tour company has extensive references before you go. Before traveling extensively in Mexico on your own, we recommend a thorough reading of *Carl Franz's People's Guide to Mexico* (published by Ten Speed Press) to get a flavor of the culture and adventure you can expect to find.

On returning from Mexico, tourist cards should be turned in at the border, but few people bother. All non-Americans must show visas or green cards that allow them into the country or be turned away. When crossing into the United States, your vehicle may be waved through or "hit" for a complete search. The Americans may even use high-tech devices to X-ray your tires and gas tank for contraband. They can legally disassemble the entire rig, should it strike their fancy. We cross in Tijuana. Traffic is heavy and extraordinary searches are saved for the most suspicious people and vehicles. We have yet to be searched when crossing back into the States from a Mexican sojourn.

RVing Around the World

The restrictions and bureaucratic hassles of importing your own rig are simply too extensive to make a short intercontinental trip worth the effort. Still, RVing in other countries can be the adventure of a lifetime and provides an opportunity to experience the culture of an area that rarely happens in other forms of travel. If you are considering RVing in other continents or countries, contact the official tourist offices or consulates before making plans. The visa, paperwork, camping, and import requirements are different for every country.

To avoid the surprises of doing it on your own, tour companies lead RVing caravans to Australia, New Zealand, Europe, and even Africa. A good travel agent can help you find caravan trips in RVs if you want to go with a group of other people. If you already know the country and want to travel without a guide, you can rent RVs on most continents. The major RVing clubs offer information on international rentals.

Beware that all the rental tips we suggested in Chapter 5 apply to international RV rentals — especially the need to read the fine print before you sign the contract. You may also need an international driver's license and special insurance. As in all aspects of international travel, check out the requirements *before* you get to the destination country.

Chapter 21

Keeping in Touch

Keeping in touch while on the road has never been easier. New communications technologies make it possible to call almost anyone from anywhere on the continent. If you choose full-timing or long vacations, you can even manage mail and finances from the comfort of your rig. RVing businesspeople can send and receive faxes, read and respond to e-mail, and produce full-color reports and proposals while seated at a picnic table under an eight-hundred-year-old redwood tree or wherever the RV happens to be parked. The key to staying in touch with family, friends, and business associates is a little planning and ingenuity on your part, coupled with careful employment of modern technologies and knowledge of services offered by the post office and wireless communications providers.

The growing network of ATMs (automatic teller machines) and the banking industry's move toward a paperless, cashless economy assists RVers in managing even the most complex finances. Financial technology empowers you to handle everything from making automatic payment of monthly bills to acquiring cash on the road to handling investment transactions.

Talk Is (or Isn't) Cheap

Keeping in touch with the gang back home or at the office is easy. So far, there's no Dick Tracy–style wrist phone, but wristwatch-based pagers are already common. Of course, sending and receiving ordinary mail may be all the communication you need. One of the best ways to get away from it all is to hop into the rig without telling anyone where you're headed, and even if you have a cellular phone for emergencies, if they don't know where on the continent you're located, no one can call you. If they do know, leave the thing turned off, except when you need to make an outgoing call. You can even elect to receive calls should you need or want to. This section will give you the lowdown on the upside of on-the-road communications.

Mail Bonding

The United States Post Office is one of the best mail services in the world. (Believe us. We've lived in other countries in which a letter mailed to the house next door might take a week or more to arrive.) But for keeping up with on-the-roaders, standard postal service leaves something to be desired. Obviously, you can mail a letter from almost anywhere, even if it means sending your mail with someone going into town for the day, while you enjoy a siesta in a hammock. But receiving physical mail (in comparison to electronic mail) is more complicated.

Your Gettysburg Address

The main trouble with mail services as a full-timer with an ever-changing address is getting the mail forwarded to you. The post office allows you to file change-of-address cards ten working days in advance of your "move." (Note: After you file the card, there is typically a two-week delay before you see the first piece of forwarded mail. After that, it tends to arrive in bunches.) In theory, bulk mail and magazines are not forwarded, but we've regularly received at least 50 percent of such material. Forwarding is in place for one year and the American post office does a good job of it. Canadians and Mexicans may not be so lucky with mail forwarded within their countries because fees may be incurred or the system may fail in readdressing your letters. Foreign mail is *rarely* forwarded from one country to another, although it may be ungraciously returned to the sender months later.

If you plan on an extended stay, you may be allowed to receive forwarded mail at your rig. This is most common in mobile home parks where the mail carrier will overlook your tentative status in the park and assume that even though you live in a motorhome or dinky trailer and can leave on a moment's notice, you're as permanent as the other residents living in moldering mobile homes that date from the 1950s.

If you can't receive mail at the park, simply rent a private post office box at one of the many mail service outlets around the country, such as Mailboxes, Etc., and have the mail forwarded there as discussed below.

Now, if you plan to stay put in one place for a year, this forwarding service may work out. Most RVers choose other options, however. While this is not strictly kosher in post office terms, you can try sending a second change of address for your next location. It's worked for us when changing recipient addresses from the one used on the original form to a new one. However, if you move frequently, you can take advantage of two other options for getting mail that are more flexible than forwarding from your original home-based address. These include general delivery service and mail forwarding services.

General delivery service is free but not always reliable as you move from town to town. Mail forwarding services involve charges but offer significant advantages for full-timers in terms of actually getting all of your mail. The program you choose depends on the volume of mail you receive, how important mail is to you, your budget, and the amount of time you spend on the road.

General Delivery

To use general delivery services, have your mail addressed to your name c/o General Delivery. Include the name of the junction, town, or city with the post office you plan to use and the ZIP code as part of your address. It helps to briefly introduce yourself to the postal employees and leave a slip of paper with your name on it so they recognize your name and hang on to your mail when it arrives. Then make a daily or regular expedition to get your mail by asking for it at the post office. Bring a photo ID until the postal workers recognize you. Let them know when you move on and file a change of address slip, assuming you have a new long-term destination or permanent mail base.

443

The P.O. Box and Mail Forwarding

If you intend to move a lot, we recommend that you rent a permanent post office box either at a post office or from a private shop such as the Mailboxes, Etc., chain rather than depend on general delivery service. Many people use the rented post office box to establish their permanent state of residence for purposes of voter registration, driver's license renewal, and legal documents, as well. Choose the state and locality carefully — because there are tax advantages and registration fee differences in various states. Remember, as a full-timer, you can choose to travel wherever you want. You can also choose to be an "official" resident of any state by setting up a permanent address there.

To get a post office box, you'll need to fill out paperwork and proffer proof of identification. Boxes are available in various sizes and pricing is based on the size as well as your length of tenancy. Shop price. Most private shops offer discounts on longer-term rentals. The post office will lock you out of your box should you be so much as a day late in your payment. Late payment policies vary among the private companies. If you use a private postal service, make sure the company is financially stable. Choose a national chain and a location that's been in business for a while.

The post office often has the best rates, but should you plan on receiving correspondence or packages shipped via UPS, Federal Express, or other private carriers, none of these services can deliver to a post office box run by the federal post office. However, private carriers will deliver packages to most private mail box companies. Many of the private mail services will forward mail to you at your current location for postage charges and a small fee.

There are also private mail forwarding services. Choose a vendor who offers reasonable fees and prompt service. Good Sam Club, for example, offers a mail forwarding service that works well and is experienced with the shifting needs of RVers. It's a good place to start.

The Mail Drop

We rarely employ mail services when we travel as part-timers. Instead, dear old Mom receives our mail and dumps it in an insulated envelope with enough postage to ship a brick of gold. Of course, we supply twenty-four of these envelopes (with postage) annually. All she has to do is place two weeks of our correspondence in an envelope and mail it. This nets us twenty-four giant packages each year. We ask her to leave out the weekly "Have You Seen Me" mailers and the junk solicitations to save weight. You can use this technique too if you have friends or family who don't mind the minor hassle involved and the use of their address.

Cellular Phones

Of all the communications technologies that have made RVing an even greater pleasure, cellular telephones are probably the most important. RVers can now call and be called from almost anywhere near a major city. Cellular telephone service really has a lot more in common with two-way radio than a standard telephone. As you move across a city, town, or rural area with cellular service, your telephone call is routed to the nearest transmitter with a circuit available for your call. Then as you move away from the cellular station currently handling your call, it is automatically "handed off" to the cellular station that you are approaching (usually) without your knowledge, although the system fumbles occasionally.

There typically is more than one *cellular service* in each city and you subscribe to only one of them. Once you leave the cellular system that you subscribe to, and enter a new one, you go into *roam mode,* in which the local system lets you use its service for an additional fee. But once you are connected into the cellular network, you can chat with almost anyone in the world who has a conventional telephone. Unfortunately, roaming gets expensive, with charges for the air time (talk time) added to long-distance fees and any taxes that may be applicable.

Tip: Strange but True

It's common that calls get switched with analog cellular systems. You'll find yourself talking to another party. The other party's caller will then end up talking to the person you called. This makes regular cellular an unlikely vehicle for emergency communication. Odd. The digital system's promise (and premise) is that it will erase this problem for good.

The Upside of Cellular Communications

- Works much like a conventional home telephone. There's no learning curve involved.
- You can be reached in the United States with an access number provided by the cellular with "Follow Me" technology. With this service activated, callers dial your back-home area code and cellular phone number and the system tries to find you.
- Can be used to communicate with remote computers for use of the Internet, online services, or a company back home. "Cell" phones can even send faxes with a computer or a special cellular fax modem.
- With direct-dialing capabilities, you can get immediate emergency assistance. Some cellular service providers give you directions, inform you what movie is playing where, or even make restaurant reservations. Dial 1411, *411, or 411 — the same number you use for directory assistance. If you just need a phone number, the service will give it to you and then dial it too.
- Hands-free mode allows you to carry on a conversation without taking your hands off the wheel. Passengers close to the mic can join the conversation at the same time.
- Some cell phones will let you dial by voice commands. This sounds better than it actually works in the phones we've tested.
- A service now lets you receive calls anywhere in the United States. Using satellites as cellular transmission sites, this ser-

vice is expensive. But for the mobile businessperson, it might be a viable and necessary option.

■ Prices are dropping due to heavy competition, so check with cellular providers for current rates. Already free service on weekends and evenings is becoming commonplace in some cities. These charges do not include long-distance charges or additional services such as a message center — an answering system for when you aren't available.

The Downside of Cellular Communications

✖ Expensive (meaning small and portable) phones are "free" with a one-year contract at many outlets, although mounting a vehicle phone requires installation and associated charges. Basic service runs from $20 per month, in which you pay by the minute, to more than $60 a month, in which you receive several hours "free." If you're an RVer who travels extensively in one region, check out the coverage area. You may find one cellular service has much wider coverage than another.

✖ Service is not available in many remote locations or small towns. Your phone will show No Service in its readout at such times. When barely in contact, you may lose a call in the middle as you move into and out of range or experience significant noise making communication impossible.

✖ New digital phones may cost more than today's models. For now, this transition appears to have slipped into the late 1990s on most systems.

Kinds of Cellular Phones

As with most technology, there are several kinds of cellular phone models, with the most compact being the most expensive. The prices of phones are plummeting from the four figures to 1 cent with you signing a one-year service contract. There are several phone options, including:

• Vehicle-based telephones. The most powerful phone is

447

mounted in your tow vehicle, trailer, fifth-wheel, or motor-home. Providing three watts of radio output, these provide the best reception in fringe areas. Keep in mind that mounting may be important. In a motorhome, you can always reach the phone, but in a tow vehicle or trailer-based arrangement, should you mount the phone in a truck cab, if your "co-camper" heads off to town with it, you'll have no access in an emergency or if you get a simple whim to talk to someone.

- Handheld phones. The most convenient phones are hand held. Use them anywhere that you aren't inside a steel and concrete building or RV. These phones vary in size from units with weight measured in ounces to larger phones that weigh several pounds. Naturally, you want the most compact unit possible, but beware of small units with limited battery life. Handheld telephones are much more limited in power output, because placing a high-powered radio transmitter next to your braincase while using the phone is probably not a good idea.

- Dockable phones. These consist of a car-mounted unit offering full transmission power and a handheld phone that acts as the handset while the phone is docked in the car mount. To go fully mobile, you detach just the handset portion of the phone and walk away. Naturally, the smaller handheld portion of the system has less transmission power than the full system. For reasons unknown, since their installation is identical to that of most car phones, dockable systems are expensive.

Pagers and Paging

Before cellular phones became popular and affordable, the only way to reach someone on the road was either via pager, through painfully expensive car telephones, or via crackling mobile radio. Today, cellular phones have supplanted the original car phone systems and two-way radios, except for use by taxis and emergency response teams. But for some mobile professionals, pagers are still a less expensive and viable option.

Tip: Get the Best Antenna

While few purveyors of cellular systems will bother to talk about antenna systems, just as on a portable radio, the antenna is a key link in limiting the range of a cellular phone. The most common antennae are ones that mount on the inside and outside of a window. These jump the radio signal across the glass, which is sandwiched between the antennae and the wire that carries the signal to the transmitter, and sacrifice some of the signal. A better alternative is an antenna that is directly wired to the transmitter. Some dealers may not want to sell you such a unit because they are more work to install than the ones that simply stick to the glass.

Essentially there are two kinds of pagers — fairly basic and "intelligent" models. Basic pagers work something like the units of yesteryear. They beep, buzz, or silently vibrate to inform the wearer of a page. The tiny readout at the top shows the number to call, or a disembodied-sounding voice transmits the message, and that's pretty much the extent of their services.

More sophisticated pagers have large readouts that not only provide the phone number but also display a complete message. These units also allow users to scroll through the pages received throughout the day, allowing you to make an immediate response to important calls and look up numbers for less important calls later in the day. To send messages to these units, a keyboard must be purchased in addition to the pager. As you would expect, this combination is more expensive than a basic pager, and you must have someone — a service or receptionist — to "beam" you the message.

SkyTel

Need to be available anytime or anywhere? Consider SkyTel's expensive paging service (800-456-3333). With it, anyone can reach you almost anywhere in the Western Hemisphere. Using satellite transmission rather than ground-based paging antennas,

SkyTel can keep you in touch. Service, at this writing, is about $30 per month for the United States, including the pager and voicemail where callers can leave you a detailed message for you to follow up on once you're paged. Want to get away from it all? Then avoid this system.

The Upside of Pagers

■ Generally less expensive to operate than a cellular phone.
■ Compact. Most models offer a vibrator to silently alert you to a page.
■ With SkyTel you can be reached almost anywhere — even in remote wilderness areas, providing you aren't down in a narrow valley or cave.

The Downside of Pagers

✖ No two-way voice capabilities — that means a trip to a pay phone to establish communications unless you have a cell phone or other wireless communication system at hand. Between the telephone charges for long-distance calls made from a pay phone and pager charges, a cellular phone may be almost as economical, and you can skip the trip to a phone.
✖ Until you call those who paged you, they have no idea whether you received their message or not.

Tip: The Great Outdoors

What do you do if you are using a handheld or portable "cell" phone and the signal indicator indicates a weak signal or the No Service indicator is on or lit? Get out of your rig and move twenty feet away from it. Then look to see if signal strength has improved and make your call. Inside an RV, cell phones with integrated antennae lose transmission power in the rig's steel frame and exterior. Still no luck? Try playing King of the Hill. With fewer man-made and geological formations to intercede in your transmission, perhaps you can make radio contact.

Tip: Getting Credit Where Credit Is Due

When arranging cellular or pager service, the service provider will check your credit and make sure that you pay your bills on time. This isn't because they are unusually paranoid, but because some users have run up huge phone bills in the thousands of dollars and then gone south. By checking your credit, the company ensures that you are likely to pay for the service in a timely manner. If your credit is thin or bad, or if you don't have steady income, a substantial deposit may be required.

Citizen's Band (CB) Radio

Citizen's Band radio has been with us for decades. It grew in popularity so fast in the late 1970s and early 1980s that the FCC (Federal Communications Commission) added more channels to the system at the expense of HAM radio operators by taking part of their radio frequency spectrum away for CB use. CB radio is a vibrant source of communication in which anything can be and is blurted out to the world. Some operators use illegal transmitters to give them a range of a state or half a continent.

For RVers, CB is cheap to purchase — under $100 — and provides a medium for communication with other RVers and with the big rigs, which almost always have a CB radio in their cab. With changes in Mexican law, you can now use CB in Mexico, with channels assigned as follows:

- Channel 11 for emergencies.
- Channel 12 for RV caravans of all sorts.
- Channel 14 for general use and chat (best if you speak fluent Spanish).

Squelch It

One additional point: We leave our CB on most of the time to pick up travel information and accident warnings from other RVers and truckers. But if you're sensitive to foul language or traveling with kids — especially in the city with its numerous teenage CBers — you may want to keep the volume down and use the squelch control to zap conversations that are inappropriate or that contain sexually explicit dialogue. At one time, the FCC prosecuted this kind of illegal on-air behavior, but it gave up in the 1970s when hordes of new users joined the CB bands because of the enormous popularity (for reasons unknown) of the movie *Smokey and the Bandit.*

Rig to Rig

In a caravan of RVs or traveling with friends following each other rig to rig? How to contact each other? Cellular technology will not be available in the wilds and is expensive per call. CB will work, but as you reach a city, even with constant channel switching, you may not get a "break" long enough to give warning of a low tire on the rig in front of you.

If you plan to maintain close proximity while on the road, explore other radio options at the local Radio Shack or communications store. Found in the *Yellow Pages* under Radio Communications & Equipment Systems, most of these low (radio) power devices require no FCC licensing as long as you use them within the guidelines provided in the owner's manual, and you'll have a "clear channel" most of the time, especially in rural areas.

Tip: Policing the Airwaves

In the United States, all radio communication is regulated by the FCC. *If* it can find you, violations include the use of obscene language, failure to get off the air when it's required for an emergency, use of illegal high-powered equipment, and many more points. Breaking FCC rules can be costly, with jail time and fines of $10,000 per day for illegal operation. Be good or you may find yourself in irons and Santa will deliver a lump of coal at Christmas instead of that new set of electronic levelers you asked for. (See Chapter 15 for leveler info.)

Ham Radio

Ham radio is often known as "amateur radio" even though old-time Ham operators often have more knowledge of radio and electronics than the engineers who run broadcast stations. Ham is a worldwide medium. With distance restrictions limited to equipment power and antenna location, Hams have helped out in national emergencies of all kinds. When regular telephone connections are broken, be it from natural disasters or internal political strife, Hams stay on the air and provide news and information not available elsewhere.

Ham radio is fun to listen to on shortwave radio. Becoming a Ham in the United States requires a license. The test for a novice license no longer requires a working knowledge of Morse code, making it easier to get started. Old-timers still use their "sticks" (Morse code keys) more than the microphone and you'll hear them frequently on shortwave bands frequented by Hams. Contact your local Ham/amateur radio club for information on tests and licensing. Most clubs provide free training, and Hams stick together and offer free advice. To find a Ham club in your area, call one of the dealers listed in the *Yellow Pages* under Radio Communications & Equipment Systems. Chances are, in a communications store other than Radio Shack, the person who answers the phone will be a Ham.

A Ham in a Trailer Park

If you're new to radio but not RVing, you may have noticed a No Ham Radio Operation Permitted clause when checking into a camp. This is because mobile Hams tend to disrupt neighbors' radio and TV reception. A Ham (or even CBer) with a powerful "linear" — an amplifier that boosts radio power — can actually cause the fuel-injected engine of the rig next door to stall when the operator keys (turns on) the microphone. What a great way to keep your neighbors from moving on. Get a Ham set and a license and kill their engines every time they try to drive away. They'll be there forever, or at least until the FCC catches up with you.

Faxing Systems on the Road

A full-sized office fax machine is not a practical item for toting around, but alternatives are available. There are two ways to send and receive faxes while on the road — via a fax modem built into a notebook computer (explained later in this chapter) or organizer such as the OZ series from Sharp, or using a cellular telephone faxing system. The first option is convenient because a fax modem typically weighs only a couple of ounces and is completely contained inside your computer, but you can't fax paper documents. A cellular faxing system is easier to use, but these machines are expensive and slow enough to run up your cellular bill. Unless your fax requirements are limited to a page or two, or if you don't mind large bills for airtime and the wait, you may want to convert to a hybrid phone that can work on both analog and digital systems, so that you can send faxes in high-speed digital mode.

Computer Communications

We've mentioned computers several times in this book. On the modern RVs, computerized controls monitor everything from engine fuel injection to converter operations. You can ignore these pseudo-intelligent devices because they work quietly and only make their presence known if and when they fail. But a personal computer is different. A growing number of RVers use notebook computers with rechargeable batteries for everything from writing letters to keeping the checkbook in check to plotting the fastest route from Roswell, New Mexico, to Henryetta, Oklahoma. Those who use RVs to travel on business rely on computers to keep in touch with the office, track sales leads, and track customer contacts and billing as they traverse the state or continent.

All Computers Great and Small

There are literally hundreds of portable computers on the market — these range from tiny "palmtops" with keyboards that bring new meaning to the words "cramped fingers" to clunky "lugables" that are portable in name only because they require an AC outlet to function. Larger computers are simply too big for an RV, require 115-volt power, and are impossible to store in all but the largest closets — room that may be required for other items. The ideal computer for the RVer is the notebook. Running on internal batteries, coach power, or 115 volts when plugged in, these machines fit in your lap or on the smallest table. Once very expensive, the notebook is now the standard in mobile computing.

What Can You Do with a Computer on the Road?

With a computer in your rig, you can do all the usual computer tasks from managing finances to communication to entertainment and keeping a log of daily adventures. Anything that can be done on a personal computer in a home or business can also be handled on the road.

New to Computers?

Choose one with a fast microprocessor (IBM PC-compatible Pentium 100 — or better — or Apple PowerPC). Units with color screens larger than ten inches are the easiest to read, and an active color matrix screen is substantially crisper than the less expensive standard color or dual-scan color screen. The Macintosh is the easiest to learn, but the newest version of the software that makes IBM-style machines run (Windows 95 or NT) has reduced the learning curve, which was once formidable.

If your head reels after a day of computer shopping, get a computer-knowledgeable friend to assist you in the selection process. Insist (gently, if your friend is trying to help) that you see both the IBM and Macintosh platforms. Most novices gravitate to one or the other, although having taught computer science for years, we've seen that students find Macs easier to learn and use, but the current line of Macintosh notebooks hasn't impressed us much with their small screens. (We hear this is changing.)

Tip: Avoid Computers Made in Taiwan

Taiwan is making great strides toward democracy (at last), but they generally build goods inexpensively and too often with flaws after corners are cut. We tested six Taiwanese-built notebooks in the past four years: One performed admirably, but the other five failed within twenty-four hours of purchase for one reason or another. Products from Malaysia and Singapore are also suspect. Should you buy one, also buy the extended warranty after carefully inspecting the document for any "gotcha" clauses.

A Portable Printer

Today's portable printers are about the size of a rolled Sunday newspaper and are unlikely to leak ink as did their predecessors. They print using microfine sprays of ink. Like small computers, a number of rechargeable battery-based printers are on the market with several offering full color from a palette of nearly 17 million colors. Test these printers in-store. With power on, most will print a test page for you, so you can compare print quality. This comparison assumes that each has been properly set up by store personnel, which is not always the case.

A Personal Choice

The choice of a computer seems to be only a half step in complexity and importance below choosing a spouse. You want a machine that you can relate to, that you feel comfortable using, that meets your needs, and that has a nice touch to its keyboard and a mouse or mouse-equivalent that works for you. As an RVer, you also want a computer and printer that lends itself to RV use, is rugged, and stores compactly.

Stowing Them

Computers should be stored firmly wrapped in blankets, because you don't want them sliding around or absorbing too much vibration. Computer printers must be stored so they cannot roll over. Otherwise you may experience ink seepage and a real mess. Pay special attention to ink seepage as you ascend altitudes in excess of five thousand feet. The reduced air pressure may precipitate postnasal drip in the ink cartridge. Check it once at high altitude. No leak at eight thousand feet? Then forget about it — but stow it upright at all times, just in case.

Modems and Cellular Modems on the Road

If you are new to computers, a modem is an electronic device that sends and receives computer files over ordinary telephone lines. Cellular modems can handle the same task via transmission over the cellular phone system. Modems are useful because they allow you to exchange files and information with your office and hook into electronic mail systems where you can perform online research or use the service's electronic mail services.

Fax Modems

Fax modems are devices that allow you to send and receive computer data and faxes on a computer. To receive a fax with such a system, the tiny fax modem masquerades as a real fax machine, so that it can effectively communicate with standard office model machines. For small portable computers, the fax modem for the system is usually made by the computer's manufacturer and may be so small that it measures about the size of four quarters placed side by side. While a fax modem is a great convenience on the road, some units are easier to use than others. A well-designed fax modem automatically sends a cover sheet page for you, makes sending and receiving faxes easy and relatively automatic, and doubles as an effective modem as well.

Tip: Picture Phone — Year 2000

It's already possible to have voice communication through the Internet with the right software and equipment. Soon, real picture phone technology will also be available to those with a $90 color computer camera and software. This breakthrough appears headed initially to the Internet. Aside from the "cam" and software, it may turn out to be otherwise free of charge! For some reason, the phone company is less than happy about this development.

Online Services

Many RVers enjoy traveling the information superhighway through cyberspace as much as they enjoy traveling paved roads through real space. All you need is a phone jack in a camp or a computer and modem that are compatible with your fax machine. You can travel through the Internet, America Online, CompuServe, Microsoft Network (MSN), Prodigy, and a host of specialized online computer services. You can use these services to exchange electronic mail with anyone in the world if you have their electronic address. The visual, multimedia portion of the Internet, known as the World Wide Web, provides access to everyone and everything from shopping centers to schools to RV clubs to restaurants.

America Online, a commercial information service, provides access to the Internet and World Wide Web, as well as to its own information services for shopping, travel, investment, and reference. America Online is easy to learn and use, and you can send e-mail between any of the major information networks through its facilities.

If you don't subscribe to a commercial service such as America Online or CompuServe, to reach the Internet you'll need a private service provider. To locate the best national Internet service providers, look in the *Yellow Pages* under Computers-On-Line Services & Internet or get a copy of the magazine *Internet World* at any major bookstore. Then shop features and price. (Avoid hourly charges.) You want a "graphic access account," sometimes called a PPP or SLIP account, and a Web browser — preferably a current version of Netscape.

Check out all the fees before you sign up for any service. Many services will send you free startup kits that allow you to try the service for free for one month. You'll need a valid credit card for the free trial, but the service won't charge the card unless you forget to cancel the service before the trial ends.

New to Online?

We recommend trying America Online first. The company provides local (toll-free) access numbers for most of the United States and Canada. To get a copy of the free software to start the service, head for the computer magazines at any supermarket or bookstore. Chances are one of the magazines will include the disk or CD-ROM for a free trial. Follow the instructions for loading the software and you're online!

What's on America Online and other online services? More than we can write about here. But here are several samples:

- *The New York Times*, *The Chicago Tribune*, and several other major newspapers. You can read the *Times* about the same time as early morning New Yorkers do. There's also a Reuters feed and more magazines than we can count.
- Chat rooms for general interests and specialized ones for hobbies.
- Kids' activities.
- Stock quotations and business news.
- Games of all sorts.
- Free software.
- Internet and World Wide Web access.
- Online shopping.
- Online travel reservations and ticketing.

Using the Internet on the Road

The first thing to remember is that using the Internet or other online services from an RV is not going to be as cheap or as easy as a home connection. You can continue to get service from your current provider, but the problem is in finding compatible connections on the road. Most of the large national providers have local numbers in most urban areas, but only a few rural areas are covered. This certainly means a long-distance call to your "national" provider when you are staying in the woods. You could also call your current provider long-distance via a number of plans. The major long-distance companies (AT&T, Sprint, MCI) offer long-distance discount plans, in which all calls to a particular town (say where you live and your service provider is) are made at a discount. If there is no cellular service, and the park doesn't offer plug-compatible phone lines, you won't be able to visit cyberspace at all.

Personal 800 numbers can save you money on long-distance charges to online providers in remote areas. These can be set up to call any number you choose, like your providers. You certainly want one where a PIN or password is required. You could sign up with a provider that offers 800 access, or you could go with one of the providers that offer "free" access. These providers get their money via profit sharing with the long-distance provider, and some restrict which provider can be used.

Finding a Phone Jack at the RV Park

What the rapidly growing segment of cyber-literate RVers want and need when they are traveling is the ability to plug their portable computers into a regular telephone outlet and, using a local credit card or 800 number, connect their computer to their online service provider. One very important fact: Portable computers generally cannot tap into an ordinary pay phone, although new pay phones offer this option. The phone must be data compatible and offer connection through a regular modular phone jack. You'll find such phones in airports, but not in most campgrounds.

The online RVer should bring the equipment he or she needs:

the computer, the modem, and even a length of telephone cable to link the computer to the telephone jack. All the RV park need supply is access to a phone jack. Ideally, the phone jack would be located in at least a semiprivate area near a desk (or table) and chair, and also close to a standard electrical outlet. Most of the portable (laptop or notebook) computers RVers have will operate directly from their own power source. But the computer's modem can run a battery down fairly quickly, so a standard electrical outlet is helpful. We have seen RV parks with small work areas set up inside laundry rooms, in small semiprivate offices, in libraries, in ballrooms, and even within the park's business office area. In some cases the RV park manager has not yet been able to set aside a dedicated space and simply invites the RVer to use a desk and chair usually used as part of the park's office setup. While this is an entirely suitable way to "get going," it can be a bit inconvenient for both the park management and the RVer trying to get a bit of online business accomplished.

Most parks that provide access for online RVers offer a telephone outlet that is restricted to local calls, credit card calls, and toll-free (800 number) calls. As a responsible RVer you should know how to program your computer to connect to online services using one of these three options. By using a restricted line, the park ensures that there is no possibility that it would incur long-distance phone charges, whether inadvertent or otherwise.

Naturally, the most convenient setup for RVers is to have a phone connection available at the site, along with other utility connections. This is the only viable way for RVers who travel with "full-size" computer systems. Some parks have phone lines available to individual sites that cannot be used unless they are first "connected" by the local telephone company. Both the lead time and the service charges associated with this sort of hookup make this option virtually useless for the short-term RV guest. For the full-timer, this option works out fine.

An increasing number of parks are offering in-park "instant phone" connections, for an additional daily charge in the range of $2 to $4. So long as these added charges are reasonable, they certainly would qualify a park as "modem friendly." Parks that do not have the underground wiring to support phone hookups at individual sites may still offer in-park phone services using new

461

wireless products being developed by AT&T and others. As more wireless options become available, these should provide new, low-cost options for improved park phone systems.

The primary determinant of whether an RV park is "modem friendly" is whether the park's owners and managers are willing to provide short-term guests with the type of telephone access required to get online. However, any reasonable option for permitting the RVer to gain access to online services should, at least at this point in time, be sufficient to qualify the park as "modem friendly." And while an in-park phone system is, of course, the best ultimate solution, for now it should not be a requirement for a park's qualification as "modem friendly."

It's true that easy-to-access phone jacks are not yet available at most RV parks — but we expect this to change quickly. RVing advocates have been lobbying RV park owners to make data-compatible connections and phone lines available in parks. As a result, a growing number of parks understand cyberspace travel as well as they understand RV travel. Among these, to name a few, are Fidalgo Bay RV Resort, located in Anacortes, Washington; Queen Valley RV Resort in Queen Valley, Arizona; Voyagers RV Resort located about ten miles east of Tucson, Arizona; Junipers Reservoir RV Resort, on an eight-thousand-acre working cattle ranch about ten miles west of Lakeview, Oregon; and Red Bluff RV Park, near Red Bluff, California. These park owners really understand computers. (These are also on our list of favorite RV parks. Contact information is provided in the standard RV campground guides.) They have actually set up separate spaces and phone lines so RVers can use online computer services.

Some parks are using e-mail and setting up Web pages to take reservations and provide information on facilities and activities to online RVers. We hope and expect to see more parks like these in the future. RVers who frequent cyberspace will find many more recommendations on online-friendly parks on the chat channels and Web pages dedicated to RVers.

For Love or Money

Forget the love part, we're here to talk about on-the-road money management. With increased (and necessary) improvements to account security in a world that can transfer half a trillion dollars around the world in seconds and the improved efficiency of modern forgers in building fake IDs and assembling false documents, everyone is more careful about electronic transactions. Us too. For that reason, when on the road, you may meet with anything from a casual approach to accepting credit cards to careful scrutiny of your photo ID and a clerk comparing the signature on the back of your credit card to the one you scribble on the sales slip.

Personal checks are another matter. We've had no problem cashing them in the same state as our driver's license, but otherwise forget it. (Forget New York City no matter how much ID you present.) Sometimes even money orders, cashier's checks, and unfamiliar (other than American Express) travelers checks may be politely refused, especially in Mexico. Sometimes the same clerk who accepts a $20 travelers check will refuse a $100 check because the risk is that much greater. And if you're passing Bank of the Red Tide or Joe's Saving and Loan travelers checks, be prepared for thorough scrutiny.

A Cash Economy

While "camping" in the big city, you have multiple options available for almost any kind of cash or credit transaction, but once you are out in the sticks, options dwindle rapidly. Generally, in small towns, while the gas station may accept credit cards, local supermarkets probably won't. Be prepared for all possibilities by carrying a mix of cash, credit cards, and travelers checks. Plan on cashing large travelers checks in advance of leaving the Big City. Local vendors may not trust your checks, or at a Mom and Pop breakfast eatery, they may have just opened with $40 in small bills and coins for the day's change. Plan on showing a passport, driver's license, or one other credible ID if you're trying to pass a check for $100 or more, even at a bank and especially in Mexico and Canada.

Banks

For RVers who plan to remain in the United States, the best bank is one that has branches in many states. At this writing, banks are crossing state and regional boundaries, but so far, no national entity has emerged. (Expect this to change.) The slow move to national banking is in part due to banking regulations, the reluctance of banks to take major steps that may prove financially disastrous, as did the deregulation of American savings and loans in the 1980s, and the massive amount of capital required. For now, if you travel regionally, look for a bank that spans the states you are most likely to visit.

Bookkeeping Services

You can have an accountant or bookkeeping service handle your bill paying and taxes. For most of us, unless your last name is Getty or Hearst, it's probably too expensive. Plus, unless you run a company with a bookkeeper who handles (and is trusted with) this kind of money and your power of attorney — not to be given lightly — you'll still have to go through accounts each month and determine who to pay and how much to send them. That means receiving reports or mail directly and then sending notated information to your CPA — a lot of work with little gain for most RVers.

The No-Bill Approach

The best way to manage monthly bills if you're a full-timer is to have no recurring bills or the possibility that one may suddenly be imposed on you, such as a renter who fails to pay rent on a mortgaged property. You can't escape every bill, but do you really need that Neiman Marcus charge for expensive underwear incurred a year ago?

Tip: Your Secret Code

Your personal identification number is what secures your account. Even if someone steals your card, without that number he or she can't use it. You already know about keeping this number a secret: Don't write it on the card or on your possessions and don't use obvious numbers, such as your birthday or five fives, but what you may not know is this: While American banks allow up to twelve digits, foreign banks may not. For that reason, should your travel plans include destinations in Mexico or further south, limit your PIN to four digits or you may not be able to use your card.

Take It to the Limit

To avoid serious misuse of a stolen card or an unscrupulous account holder, most banks limit ATM transactions to $150 to $600 per day. While this sounds adequate unless you're planning on breaking the bank in Vegas, there's a catch to it that you, an RVer, should be aware of. Otherwise you may find yourself without access to funds during a long weekend or after depositing money on a Friday night.

The rule is this: Any withdrawal made after banking hours on Friday (usually 3:00 P.M. in the United States, even if the bank is open until 6:00 P.M.) accrues until the following Monday at midnight. So, if you have a typical $300 daily limit, have a $50 dinner Friday night, purchase $150 in fuel on Saturday, and blow $100 on souvenirs on Sunday, your card won't work even if you have $12,000 in your checking account. Effectively, you'll be locked out from card use until 12:01 A.M. (early Tuesday) as the bank catches up on its transactions and refreshes your "daily" limit. If Monday is a holiday, then the refreshing won't happen until Wednesday at 12:01 A.M.

Credit Cards

Most of you are probably all too familiar with credit cards. Accepted almost everywhere in the modern world, they are convenient. But for the RVer they are a source of problems, as bills get paid late if you don't have a reliable mail-forwarding service, automatic payment, an accountant to handle your bills, or Mom to write checks on your behalf. There are two kinds of credit cards: those that you pay off each month in full (American Express) and those that allow you to accrue a bill and pay monthly interest on the payments (Visa, MasterCard, etc.). Credit cards are convenient on the road for making payments, but paying the bills in a timely manner when in the woods is not so convenient.

The Bottom Line

"Enclosed: Just sign this application for a 6 percent MasterCard with no annual fee!" Read the fine print. After the first year or if you're five minutes late with a payment, the interest rate reverts to 17 percent to 22 percent. Keep your credit cards to a minimum and read the fine print on these one-time special offers. You may be surprised at what you find hidden in the boilerplate agreement on the back of the form you sign. Besides, with each new card, be it for Lane Bryant or American Express, that is one more bill that you will need to make sure you receive and pay each month. Ugh!

Debit Cards

Many banks provide a new kind of card called a "debit card." Looking like a standard Visa card, this piece of plastic provides ATM access, guarantees checks to a certain limit, and works like cash at the grocery store and with a growing number of merchants. At those stores that don't take debit cards, the card works like an ordinary Visa, except that the money comes out of your checking account instead of your line of credit. To use the card as a debit card, you need a PIN (personal identification number). Be aware

Tip: What About Your Paycheck While on the Road?

The easiest arrangement for the mobile professional who spends a lot of time on the road is to have your paycheck automatically deposited in your bank. This allows you to access the funds while on the road and any automatic payments can be satisfied. If your employer doesn't offer such a program, its bank probably does. Open a checking account at the same bank that issues your paycheck and arrange for it to automatically deposit your check in the new account.

Making Deposits

The ATM is a marvelous machine for handling withdrawals and transfers, and, as mentioned, for selling you postage stamps, but for deposits, you're out of luck. To make a deposit, you must use your bank's machines. Other banks' ATMs simply won't allow it, probably because if the transaction goes astray, they'll have to look for it and find it, fix it, or get sued.

With that in mind: How do you make deposits? While there are plenty of ways to get cash while traveling, your paycheck or customer payments made to you are more difficult to process because, while ATMs dole out cash, generally only those run directly by your own bank accept deposits. Banks with branches in more than one state are becoming more common as banking rules are being relaxed. Instead of banking with Cucamonga Savings and Loan, consider opening at least a checking account with Wells Fargo or another interstate bank that has branches in many states.

A second option is to use overnight services to ship checks to your company or your bank for processing. Shipping a bunch of checks via second-day air to your home bank costs a mere $9 to $14 depending on the distance involved and the carrier you choose. There are many convenient points in every city for dropping off overnight parcels ranging from FedEx kiosks in shopping center parking lots to Mailboxes, Etc., stores that exist almost everywhere. Shipping the checks is statistically probably safer than carrying them around for the duration of your trip, plus you or your company gets faster access to the cash.

Not Insured, But . . .

While banks wrestle with the interstate problems, you can use nationwide brokerage houses to handle your cash. Stock brokerages such as Dean Witter Reynolds and Charles Schwab have offices all over the country. Opening an account — which may or may not require a substantial stock or mutual fund buy — provides you with checking services and a debit Visa or MasterCard. You can then make deposits at any of their hundreds of nationwide outlets or, as with a bank, mail them the checks. The two disadvantages are that, unlike money in your bank, money with a brokerage house is not federally insured, and most brokerages won't accept cash. You can get around the latter by taking your cash to any bank or savings and loan and having it magically transformed into a cashier's check. There might be a small fee for the service.

As you've learned in this chapter, with some planning and common sense, from the road you can do any of the communicating or investing that you can do from a stationary home. If you don't have any money to play with, then you have other needs. That's why we wrote the next chapter, which explains how you can make and save money while living in your RV.

onade. *Clark's Flea Market USA* and similar publications, available in many bookstores and libraries, provide listings of flea markets, crafts fairs, and swap meets around the country.

If you have serious handiwork or art you want to exhibit and sell, then consider joining one of the caravans of RVers who make the rounds of arts and crafts festivals around the nation. You can also sell crafts on consignment through shops and malls. You can also sell crafts made by other people. Many savvy RVers pick up bargains in one city and sell them for a profit in other parts of the country. Many skilled RVing craftspeople set up a network of shops to distribute their crafts around the country. Lightweight, portable crafts are best suited to RVing. And, obviously, you'll want to choose a craft that can be accomplished within the confines of your rig.

Jobs on the Road

Crafts and hobbies are not the only source of income on the road. Growing legions of RVers augment their incomes and even support themselves through traditional jobs they find in cities as they travel. Many teachers, nurses, college professors, musicians, and even marketing consultants make their careers on the road. If you have special credentials or consulting skills, then you likely know how to find work on the road. If you plan to stay in one place for a while, finding a job while living in an RV is not different from finding a job from any other residence. If you are a nurse, register with the nursing registry. If you're a college professor, contact the local colleges. If you're a carpenter, register with the local union office.

If you're interested in short or seasonal work assignments, many opportunities offer themselves in parks and tourist locations. RVers often staff private campgrounds in return for free campsites and a small stipend. Others enjoy seasonal work as store clerks, wait staff, handypeople, and fee collectors in-season at resorts and parks. Although the pay rarely exceeds minimum wage, the surroundings and stress-free working conditions compensate working RVers in other ways. If you are interested in finding employment at parks, campgrounds, and private concessions in tourist areas, the best source of information for national opportunities is *Workamper News*. At this writing, a one-year subscription is only $23 from:

Workamper News
201 Hiram Rd.
Heber Springs, AR 72543
501-362-2637

Park concessions are another lucrative source of work for campers. Most park concessions, such as hotels, restaurants, and tours, are under private operation. Hiring for concessions is handled locally by the concessionaires in the parks. *The National Parks Trade Journal* provides information on the needs of many larger parks. You can order a copy from the National Parks Service's Web site, www.nps.gov.

You should definitely check out the experience-rich book by Craig Chilton, *How to Get Paid $30,000 a Year to Travel*, if you want to turn your wanderlust into profit. Craig explains, in detail, how you can deliver RVs and trucks from factories to dealers for hefty profits. At this writing the book is available for $29.95, including shipping, from:

Xanadu Enterprises
P.O. Box 3147
Evansdale, IA 50707-0147
319-234-0676

A Lighter Approach to Management of Natural Resources

We are resourceful and you can enjoy this lifestyle by being that way too. At one park that we stayed in, the locals apparently camped year-round for free, doing odd jobs and recycling aluminum soda and beer cans for a few extra dollars. In addition, a small garden had been planted and tended on a stretch of vacant but apparently fertile soil next to the RV park. Taking turns, the

to volunteer work may be tax deductible.

As a volunteer, you may work a few hours a week or month, seasonally, or full-time. You may work weekdays, weekends, during the day, or at night. The amount of time to be volunteered will be agreed on by you and your supervisor before you start.

Although as a volunteer you are not considered a federal employee, you are eligible for compensation for medical expenses if you are injured while performing your official volunteer duties. Also, if you should be sued for property damage or for personal injury that occurs while carrying out these duties, the federal government will defend you (under the Federal Tort Claims Act).

As a volunteer, you may be asked to wear a special uniform. Whether you wear a uniform or not, as a VIP you will be a representative of the National Park Service and will be required to act accordingly.

Applying for a VIP Position

You can request an application to become a volunteer from any National Park facility. Telephone numbers are provided in the General Resources section of this book. You can also request an application on the World Wide Web at http://www.nps.gov if you are hooked up to the Internet. The Web site has the latest information on volunteer applications, which may have changed since this book was written.

Complete the application and return it to the parks where you would like to volunteer. (You may apply to more than one park.) Be specific in describing your talents, skills, and job interests. Each park has its own needs and is looking for volunteers with the skills and talents to accomplish certain tasks. The more specific you are, the better chance you'll get a position matched to your abilities. Obviously, parks want people who are personable, reliable, and flexible.

If you feel the application does not permit you to provide enough information about yourself, or if you have questions about the park's VIP program, send a letter with the application. If you can live in your motorhome or trailer, but would require certain utility hookups in the park, say so. If you can live without hookups, state that as well.

After receiving your completed application, a VIP coordinator for the park will review your application and contact you, usually by mail. (Thus, if you're a full-timer, you'll need a P.O. box or other permanent mailing address to get the responses.) If your talents and skills appear to be ones that the park needs, you will be contacted to discuss further details. Not all people who apply as volunteers are accepted. Sometimes a park finds that there is no match between an applicant's abilities and the park's needs at that time. Volunteer applicants will be notified if this is the case.

If you are selected to become a volunteer, you and the National Park Service employee who will supervise you will sign an agreement. This agreement will describe your duties and responsibilities, outline a tentative work schedule, and detail other conditions of the working arrangement. And then, after appropriate training and orientation, you will begin work as a volunteer.

Ultimately, whether traditional worker or volunteer, if you need to make money to maintain your RV lifestyle, opportunities abound. If you're flexible, patient, and inventive, whether a full-timer or long-term vacationer, you should be able to prosper from your RV.

Saving Money on the Road

RVing can be expensive if you don't know the tricks of the road. If you have unlimited funds, staying in luxurious campgrounds with exorbitant fees may be fine. For most of us, however, money is a limiting factor in our RVing lifestyle. Since almost everyone needs more money, the following section provides fifteen proven strategies for saving money on the road gleaned from our own experience and that of the hundreds of RVers we've encountered in our sojourns around the country.

1. **Extend your stays in primitive parks.** Parks with hookups obviously cost more than parks without them. If you learn to conserve your power, water, and propane, staying in primitive parks without power can provide a less expensive way to live in your RV.

Access to sites may also be difficult. The General Resources section of this book provides a list of free and inexpensive camping sources. We cover many of the options in Chapter 18.

14. **Plan.** Although this may sound obvious, a simple plan for getting to the next park can save not only money, but nerves. Look in your campground guide for discount parks on the road. Call ahead for rates and availability. Make reservations when you can. Choose regions of the country, like the Midwest, that offer lower rates. If you don't like planning your adventures, at least stop driving early in the day so you have enough time to find a camp at a reasonable rate.

15. **Limit your driving.** Fuel is a major expense in RVing. If keeping expenses at bay is important to your lifestyle, learn to conserve fuel. Make your stays longer. Use a bike for short trips to stores. Travel the shortest routes between camps to save money on fuel, even though you might sacrifice experiencing some of the scenery. Avoid roads under construction and stop-and-go city driving that eat up gallons of gas and diesel.

The Bottom Line

Beyond volunteering in exchange for free rent, most money-saving secrets for operating your rig are really common sense. For example, when you see fuel at reduced rates, fill the rig's tanks even though you really don't need to stop. If you find an inexpensive campground with free power and water, stay longer than originally planned to take advantage of the bargain. When produce is cheap and fresh, indulge in the bounty. Far and away the most important money-saving advice encompasses the regular maintenance of your rig. Yes, oil changes are expensive and cleaning takes time, but a well-maintained rig will save you money in the long run by keeping you RVing longer without extended trips to the mechanic — and those are trips that all RVers want to avoid.

Chapter 23

Kids and Pets on the Road

Togetherness — the word is almost synonymous with RVing. If you plan for kids' and pets' comfort, RVing can be a fantastic opportunity for togetherness. However, if you expect the kids to love ten-hour days driving in the back of the rig, forget it. And don't expect the pets to stay put all day in the rig without exercise or a special treat after dinner. RVing is fun when you let people and pets have fun. Even teenagers will enjoy RVing if you take time to find parks with activities and sites that hold their interest.

Keep Them Happy

Entertainment is the key to success when traveling with kids — be it a set of brightly colored plastic keys for an infant to games, electronic or otherwise, for older siblings. Microwave popcorn is a must-have, even if greasy, diversion. Most family-oriented camps have plenty of kids' activities in the form of swimming, organized hiking, contests, and more. An increasing number of camps also offer video arcades guaranteed to vacuum quarters from your pockets like a Hoover with a turbocharger.

You will find that some parks cater to families better than others. Some separate families from those adults who want total quiet. Campground listings often suggest their attitude toward children. They may have organized activities for the little ones, or a No-Children-Under-Eighteen policy. Campgrounds that don't mention it probably accept kids, but may lack specific child-oriented entertainment. If the weather is warm and the park offers a swimming pool, they'll have loads of fun anyway. Don't forget to smother them in sunblock for a day of activities and swimming.

buy and use recreational vehicles.

Buying and using a recreational vehicle is a personal choice. It means that some of the vacation time will involve food preparation, washing dishes, trudging across the campground to the bathhouse (although most travel trailers and some fold-down campers have built-in showers and potties), possible bad weather, and some planning. Some families look at vacation as a time to get away from preparing meals and doing dishes and want to eat out every meal on their trip. Thus, RVing is not for everyone or everyone would be doing it. However, camping brings the family together in a shared experience that creates memories that you will cherish forever — and unlike other vacations, RVing becomes increasingly cost effective each additional time you go, and the larger your family grows (and the more your family eats!).

Make the Trip Memorable

Making the RVing experience a memorable one for all family members takes some effort on the parents' part. At home, after a long day of work/motherhood we tend to plop down in front of the television. When camping, we cuddle up under the stars in front of a campfire toasting marshmallows and remember how much we love each other. In the morning, the kids wake up and put on their clothes so they can go outside to the playground (usually within sight of the camper) while parents enjoy a cup of coffee before preparing breakfast. Contrast this experience to the marathon of trying to get everyone organized in a motel room so you can get ready to find an affordable restaurant that everyone will like.

You will forever treasure the memories of family closeness when you take a well-planned RV trip. There is nothing more fun for children than singing, watching TV, reading books, and playing games as they travel down the road. Children and parents alike love roasting marshmallows and hot dogs over an open fire in the evening. You get to be a part of the nature that surrounds you without giving up the comforts of home. You are also free to visit the places you are interested in on your schedule. Spend as much or as little time as you want at each place. You are free to travel at your own pace, and you don't have to stick with an itinerary.

When taking kids along, most of the fun is in the going, and no matter what happens there is something entertaining to do in an RV. If you forget some very important item (a favorite toy or a food item), you may be able to purchase a substitute. But make this part of the adventure.

Planning and travel pacing are two components of successful RVing with children. Kids can get bored with too much driving or if they have to stay inside the rig because of bad weather. Anticipate children's need to roam around and explore. Enjoy the trip, not just the destinations. Here are some more tips for assuring that RVing is fun for the entire family:

- *Let the kids help with planning, navigation, and camp selection.* Write down what you plan to take with you (clothing, food, and supplies). If kids help select the places to stay and the food to eat, they will enjoy the trip. In the process they'll also learn about geography, map reading, and nutrition.

- *Create a scrapbook of the trip as you go.* Get a bound book with large blank pages. Bring pens, pencils, and crayons for drawing in the book. Don't forget the tape or paste for incorporating brochures, pictures, and other memorabilia into the scrapbook. Encourage the kids to draw pictures of the campground, people they meet, and daily activities. Include maps, telephone numbers, and directions. Make this a fun family project. Even the youngest can tape the items in the book.

- *Make the trip an adventure, not a chore.* Don't plan the fun out of the vacation. Suppose you get one hundred miles down the road and the engine dies while you are in a gas station and the tow truck can't get there until the next day. Don't fret. You have a bed to sleep in, food to eat, games to play, and great people (the family) to keep you company.

- *Give each child a storage box for toys and personal items.* Many discount stores sell large plastic containers in bright colors that are perfect for this purpose. Put each child's name on his or her box. About one week before the trip give the box to the child. Allow your kids to take as many toys, books, or other personal items as they want, as long as the things fit into the box with the lid shut. Parents should take their own box as well to fill with reading materials, family games, playing

Extra Charges

As with extra passengers and kids, some campgrounds accept pets but charge a per-diem fee for each. This is ridiculous in the case of a well-trained dog and an owner who cleans up for his or her pet. It's especially ludicrous for a cat that never leaves the RV and uses a litter box.

Your Pet Rhino

Unusual pets such as ferrets, potbellied pigs, and Tyrannosaurus rex are not tolerated in most parks. At this writing it's illegal in some states to own these pets. Campgrounds have considerable latitude in refusing you space should you be traveling with a Bengal tiger, walrus, or horned ungulate regardless of how tame and friendly it appears. We don't recommend exotic pets of any kind be taken in RVs unless you test their adaptability to the environment and check that parks will allow the creatures to camp with you.

At this point, we've covered all the family members and their entertainment on the road. In the next chapter, we present some of our tricks for cooking gourmet meals from a small galley. Finally, it's time to eat.

Tip: If You Love Your Pet . . .

Since RVers often follow the warm weather, they may park in a shopping center to buy groceries. Pets don't sweat for cooling. Instead, they pant. If the air they're inhaling is already hot, their body temperature becomes dangerous or fatally elevated. Either bring your pet with you (if possible) or run the generator and an air-conditioner. If the weather is sunny but less than ninety degrees and your windows are screened, you may be able to leave them all open, but check the rig's interior temperature every half-hour until you are sure that the interior isn't reaching more than eighty degrees Fahrenheit. (Measure it with a reliable thermometer, not waving a wet thumb in guestimation.) Parking in the shade helps. Note: Open windows present a security risk.

Chapter 24

The RV Chef: Cooking on the Road

Hi-ho, hi-ho, it's off to lunch we go — in a Winnebago!
— COLUMNIST JONATHAN SUSKIND

Even the most well-equipped RV kitchen has its limits when it comes to food preparation and equipment. But with a little practice almost anything that can be made at home can be made in an RV. The secret is managing the space and ingredients to suit the galley. RV cooking is a whole new approach to food preparation and ingredient management that lets RVers enjoy a full range of tasty delights from limited supplies and restricted utensils.

Millions of hungry RVers muse about pungent coffee sipped in scented air and lingering aromas of steaming stews. In their imaginations, the food warms the soul as well as the body. These piquant images augment our fantasies of life away from the stresses and complexities of everyday living. But in the limited galleys of motorhomes or on small campstoves, meal preparation can be a constant frustration to those who lack the skills to realize the flavors. Visions of ample meals savored beneath canopies of stars soon degrade into a monotonous reality of bologna sandwiches and barbecued beast. Repeat repasts of Kraft Macaroni & Cheese and extended encounters with Chef Boyardee can weaken our appetites for traveling. Outdoor meals too soon forfeit the aspirations of the tastebuds for the limitations of the galley.

But it doesn't need to be that way. The fantasy of savory cuisine and ample meals in open air can be realized — if you know how to put a small galley to maximum use. As an RVer you can easily and regularly prepare healthy meals that also taste good — if you know the methods of small galley cooking.

or uninteresting diets make for stressful, unhappy, fatigued, or even ill travelers. But food on the road needs to accomplish more than tasting good — it needs to give you the nutrition you need to stay healthy and active.

You need to eat more than hot dogs and toasted marshmallows. Bring a wide range of foods — and incorporate plenty of fresh ones. Meal plans on the road are the most fun (and healthy) when you creatively incorporate local ingredients with a mix of cached perishable and nonperishable supplies. We enjoy choosing fresh produce at local pick-your-own farms and orchards. When we see signs along the road, we almost always stop and try the local fare. Fresh food won't keep in an RV refrigerator as it does in a twenty-seven-cubic-foot side-by-side. However, if you keep your rig properly leveled so the refrigerator works to its maximum potential, you can keep vegetables and other perishables fresh for many days.

Stock your galley with a healthy combination of foods that are low in fat but high in taste and variety. Use red meat sparingly. Grains, vegetables, fish, and chicken are preferred for regular consumption. Bring plenty of dried foods and spices. Staples such as rice, pasta, and beans can be made into diverse meals. These staples also keep for long periods if properly stored in an airtight plastic container.

Stocking a galley requires planning and forethought because incorrect storage wastes space and incorrect loading can dangerously destabilize a vehicle. Stocking is important for other reasons too. Depending on the outing, proper stocking can mean the difference between eating well and going hungry. Storage must take into account special requirements such as environmental temperature, humidity, and the possibility of damage to foodstuffs by pests and vermin. Always protect foods (and leftovers) in airtight containers. To keep the bugs away, always refrigerate fruits when ripe.

Saving Money on the Food Supplies

Full-timers and part-timers will probably be more concerned with budget on the road than vacationing RVers. To save money on food, try shopping in membership stores and large supermarkets. Avoid convenience foods such as packaged dinners, premixed salad dressing, boxed mixes, and spaghetti sauces. These items are easy to make up on your own, even from an RV galley. For example, you can make up muffin and biscuit mixes from your favorite recipes and store them in labeled plastic containers. You can even mix up your own granola from rolled oats, raisins, and nuts. Your own mixes will likely taste better — and you'll save a bundle in food costs.

The key to successful, frugal RV shopping is making a list of required items and sticking to it. Avoid impulse buying — unless you're on vacation. Planning meals is also a way to reduce the temptation to buy junk food at the convenience stores along the way.

Don't expect to freeze much of your food. Yes, new, expensive rigs offer respectable freezer storage, but most RVs are limited to freezing a few ice cubes, some OJ for breakfast, and the occasional ice cream for dessert. You might get a couple of steaks in there, if you work at it.

Cookbooks for RVers

Most of our favorite memories of eating in the RV are of dishes prepared with intuition about the ingredients rather than a recipe. We tend to look for recipe combinations that are simple, reliable, nourishing, cheap, and not too exotic. For example, scrambled eggs can be made more interesting by adding a bit of grated cheese or chopped green onions or even a bit of dried parsley.

Even though lots of tasty dishes can be prepared without recipes, many people prefer recipes to guide their meal plans. Unfortunately, the standard *Better Homes and Gardens Cookbook* and other similar reference cookbooks are great for home-based cooking, but the methods, equipment, and ingredients don't work in the galley of an RV. Most cookbook recipes demand too many bowls, im-

The Best RVing Recipes

We look for some key factors when reviewing recipes for RV fare. Beyond being tasty, easy to prepare, and geared toward small galley preparation, we look for recipes with these features:

- The recipe yields servings for two to four people (the typical number of people in an RV at one time) or is easy to adapt to serve this number.
- Cooking instructions are provided for the microwave.
- Little or no cooking is required with a stove or in an oven.
- There is a limited number of steps.
- The ingredients in the recipes are easy to find and stock in an RV — including commonly available items such as onions, carrots, bottled lemon juice, grains, canned milk, pasta, and beans.

Sunny has included some of our own favorite RV recipes that minimize cooking but maximize flavor in her cookbooks *Lemon Tree Very Healthy* and *The Pasta Gourmet* (written with Michelle Sbraga and published by Avery Publishing).

You can get a copy of Sunny's cookbooks at a local bookstore. We're sure you have great recipes for the road as well. Write to us through e-mail (kimbaker@aol.com) with your favorites and maybe we can include them in our next edition of the book or in one of our cookbooks. We love to try new food ideas on the road.

Now that you're fed, we've covered just about everything you need to get started in your RVing life, whether as a vacationer, a part-timer, or a full-timer. Wherever the road takes you, we hope your RV adventures are whatever you want them to be, and always safe and satisfying.

General Resources for RVers

We've included information on specific suppliers and references throughout the book. For quick reference, the following lists include the most frequently requested sources of information for RVers.

General Information on RV Manufacturers and Dealers

These groups and associations can provide general information on RVing standards and lists of dealers and manufacturers that meet (or don't meet) their standards.

Family Motor Coach Association
8291 Clough Pike
Cincinnati, OH 45244
800-543-3622

RV Consumer Group
P.O. Box 520
Quilcene, WA 98376
360-765-3846
Fax: 360-765-3233

Recreation Vehicle Industry Association
1896 Preston White Dr.
Reston, VA 22090
703-620-6003

RV Rental Association and RV Dealers Association
3251 Old Lee Highway, Suite 500
Fairfax, VA 22030
703-591-7130

RV Clubs

In addition to the general RV clubs listed here, almost every RV manufacturer boasts a club for those who own one of its vehicles. Contact the manufacturer or an RV dealer for information on manufacturer-specific clubs.

Good Sam Club
P.O. Box 11097
Des Moines, IA 50381-1097
Headquarters: 805-667-4100
Information: 800-234-3450

International Family Recreation Association
P.O. Box 6279
Pensacola, FL 32503
904-477-2123

National RV Owners Club
P.O. Drawer 17148
Pensacola, FL 32522-7148
904-477-2123

RV Magazines

These magazines are useful resources for all kinds of RVing information. As an RVer, you should subscribe to two or three of them to keep informed of the latest developments in the RVing world.

Camping Canada
2585 Skymark Avenue #306
Missassuaga, Ontario, Canada L4W 4L5
416-624-8218

Escapees
Escapees Club
Route 5, Box 310
Livingston, TX 77351
409-327-8873

Family Motor Coaching
Family Motor Coach Association
8291 Clough Pike
Cincinnati, OH 45244
800-543-3622

Highways
A Good Sam Club Publication
29901 Agoura Road
Agoura, CA 91301
800-234-3450

Motorhome, Trailer Life
TL Enterprises
29901 Agoura Road
Agoura, CA 91301
800-234-3450

Major RV Suppliers

The following are information numbers for major national chains and mail-order houses that specialize in RV supplies and services. There are also many local suppliers around the country that are not listed here. Look for these companies in the *Yellow Pages* of the local telephone book under Recreation Vehicles — Equipment, Parts and Supplies.

Camper's Choice
P.O. Box 1546
502 4th St. NW
Red Bay, AL 35582
Free Catalog
800-833-6713

RV Direct
P.O. Box 1499
Burnsville, MN 55337
800-438-5480

Camping World, Inc.
Three Springs Rd.
P.O. Box 90017
Bowling Green, KY 42102-9017
24-Hour Corporate Information Number: 800-626-5944
Free Catalog: 800-845-7875
Mail Order: 800-353-0850

RV Campground Directories

The following directories are updated regularly. They are available in most major RV supply stores or can be ordered from bookstores:

Camping Canada Directory
Trailer Life Campground/RV Park & Services Directory
Wheelers RV Resort and Campground Guide
Woodall's Campground Directory

For KOA campground information write to:

Kampgrounds of America (KOA) Directory
Box 30558
Billings, MT 59114-0558

RV Buyer's Guides

Trailer Life RV Buyer's Guide
800-234-3450

Woodall's RV Buyer's Guide
847-362-6700

RV Search Network (800-746-7478) provides a national registry for used and new RVs. For local dealers who handle used RVs, check out the *Yellow Pages*.

Federal Campgrounds and Reservations

Bureau of Land Management
U.S. Department of the Interior
1849 C St. NW
Washington, DC 20240
202-208-3100

National Parks
Contact individual parks for current information.

General Information: Visit the World Wide Web at
http://www.nps.gov.
Camping Reservations: 800-365-2267
Customer Service: 800-388-2733

U.S.D.A. Forest Service
U.S. Department of Agriculture
201 14th St. SW
Washington, DC 20250
202-205-1248

RV Park and Camping Reservation Service

DESTINET
800-365-2267 (for calls from within the United States)
619-452-8787 (for calls from outside the United States)
619-546-1709 (fax number for reservation requests)

INDEX

The employees of G.K. Hall hope you have enjoyed this Large Print book. All our Large Print titles are designed for easy reading, and all our books are made to last. Other G.K. Hall books are available at your library, through selected bookstores, or directly from us.

For information about titles, please call:

(800) 257-5157

To share your comments, please write:

Publisher
G.K. Hall & Co.
P.O. Box 159
Thorndike, ME 04986